JOHN BIRCHENSHA: WRITINGS ON MUSIC

Music Theory in Britain, 1500–1700: Critical Editions

SERIES EDITOR

Jessie Ann Owens, University of California, Davis, USA

This series represents the first systematic attempt to present the entire range of theoretical writing about music by English, Scottish, Welsh and Irish writers from 1500 to 1700 in modern critical editions. These editions, which use original spelling and follow currently accepted practices for the publication of early modern texts, aim to situate the work in the larger historical context and provide a view of musical practices

Also published in this series:

A New Way of Making Fowre Parts in Counterpoint by Thomas Campion
and *Rules how to Compose* by Giovanni Coprario
Edited by Christopher R. Wilson

Synopsis of Vocal Musick by A.B. Philo-Mus.
Edited by Rebecca Herissone

A Briefe and Short Instruction of the Art of Musicke by Elway Bevin
Edited by Denis Collins

A Briefe Introduction to the Skill of Song by William Bathe
Edited by Kevin C. Karnes

John Birchensha: Writings on Music

Edited by

CHRISTOPHER D.S. FIELD
University of Edinburgh, UK

BENJAMIN WARDHAUGH
University of Oxford, UK

ASHGATE

Published by
Ashgate Publishing Limited
Wey Court East
Union Road
Farnham
Surrey, GU9 7PT
England

Ashgate Publishing Company
Suite 420
101 Cherry Street
Burlington
VT 05401-4405
USA

www.ashgate.com

British Library Cataloguing in Publication Data
Birchensha, John, fl. 1664–1672
    John Birchensha: Writings on Music. – (Music Theory in Britain, 1500–1700:
    Critical Editions)
    1. Birchensha, John, fl. 1664–1672. 2. Music theory – Early works to 1800
    I. Title. II. Field, Christopher. III. Wardhaugh, Benjamin, 1979– .
    781'.092

Library of Congress Cataloging-in-Publication Data
Library of Congress Control Number: 2008937959

ISBN 978-0-7546-6213-6

Bach musicological font developed by © Yo Tomita.

Mixed Sources
Product group from well-managed
forests and other controlled sources
www.fsc.org Cert no. SA-COC-1565
© 1996 Forest Stewardship Council

Printed and bound in Great Britain by
MPG Books Ltd, Bodmin, Cornwall.

Contents

List of Figures

Acknowledgements

The editors wish to thank the following for permission to publish from manuscripts and printed books in their collections, and for the help given by their staffs:

Bibliothèque Royale de Belgique
The British Library Board
The Governing Body of Christ Church, Oxford
The Royal Society.

They are indebted to All Souls College, Oxford, for hosting a seminar on Birchensha's writings on music in May 2006 as part of an interdisciplinary series, 'Music and Culture in Seventeenth-Century England'; to the conveners of that seminar, Dr Margaret Bent and Professor Jessie Ann Owens; and to all who contributed to the subsequent discussion. Professor Owens, the Series Editor, was responsible for introducing the editors to one another, and has provided much wise and expert advice. They would also like to express their thanks to the Bodleian Library, Edinburgh University Library, the National Library of Scotland and St Andrews University Library; to Dr Barra Boydell, Dr David Cram, Dr Penelope Gouk, Professor Peter Holman, Dr Noel Malcolm, Dr John Milsom, Dr Jacqueline Stedall and Dr Robert Thompson for help and encouragement; and to the staff of Ashgate Publishing, in particular their commissioning editor, Heidi Bishop.

Some material in the Introduction is partially based on a paper by Christopher Field, 'Birchensha's "Mathematical Way of Composure"', which was read at a colloquium at the National University of Ireland, Maynooth, on 2 April 2005 and is published in *Music, Ireland and the Seventeenth Century*, ed. Barra Boydell and Kerry Houston (Irish Musical Studies, 10; Dublin: Four Courts Press, 2009).

Introduction

Birchensha's Reputation as a Music Theorist

As a music theorist John Birchensha (*c*.1605–81?) has always been something of an enigma. To Henry Oldenburg, the first secretary of the Royal Society, he was 'the judicious and extraordinarily skilful Musitian Mr. *John Birchensha*; who, it is still hoped, if he be competently encourag'd and assisted, will in due time publish to the world a Compleat System of Musick'.[1] John Evelyn knew him as the inventor of 'a mathematical way of composure very extraordinary: True as to the exact rules of art, but without much harmonie', while Matthew Locke once accused him of representing 'the Platform of insignificant Innovation'.[2] If anything, later writers have tended to be less flattering. Charles Burney saw him as 'a kind of musical adventurer' who promised more than he or anybody could perform; François-Joseph Fétis, the director of the Brussels Conservatory, bought an autograph manuscript of his 'Rules of Composition' in 1851 but concluded that their scientific value was nil; and in the late 1970s Professor Rosamond McGuinness found herself forced to declare that 'compared with [Christopher] Simpson, one cannot escape the suspicion of charlatanism in dealing with John Birchensha'.[3]

If Birchensha is remembered nowadays, it is usually either through the eyes of Samuel Pepys, who took composition lessons from him in 1662, or on account of the interest that his ideas aroused within the newly-founded Royal Society. He was the only professional musician to appear at a meeting of the Society in the seventeenth century, though he was never elected a fellow: perhaps the nature of his profession would have been an obstacle to that, despite his apparent avoidance of any kind of musical employment

---

[1]   [Henry Oldenburg,] 'An Account of two Books. I. Musica Speculativa del Mengoli […] in Bologna 1670', *Philosophical Transactions*, 8/100 (9 February 1673/4): 6194–7000 [*recte* 6194–6200], at 7000.

[2]   *The Diary of John Evelyn*, ed. E.S. de Beer (6 vols, Oxford, 1955), vol. 3, p. 377 (entry for 3 August 1664); Matthew Locke, *Observations upon A Late Book, Entituled, An Essay to the Advancement of Musick, &c, Written by Thomas Salmon, M.A. of Trinity Colledge in Oxford* (London, 1672), pp. 7–8.

[3]   Charles Burney, *A General History of Music, from the Earliest Ages to the Present Period* (4 vols, London, 1776–89), vol. 3, p. 472; François-Joseph Fétis, *Biographie universelle des musiciens*, 2nd edn (8 vols, Paris, 1860–65), vol. 1, pp. 422–3; Rosamond McGuinness, 'Writings about Music', in *The Blackwell History of Music in Britain: The Seventeenth Century*, ed. Ian Spink (Oxford, 1992), p. 413.

that could be thought of as menial.[4] He aimed to publish a comprehensive treatise on the philosophical, mathematical and practical aspects of music, to be entitled *Syntagma musicæ*. Among much else, he envisaged that this book would make known to the world in definitive form two inventions of which he was especially proud: his 'Compleat Scale of Musick', and his system of 'Rules' designed to enable beginners 'to compose artificially and skilfully in a few weeks'. The Royal Society, some of whose members may have wanted to see in Birchensha a British Mersenne or Kircher in the making, gave the project its encouragement. In a tantalizing advertisement, subscribers were even promised that they would receive their bound copies of the book by 24 March 1674/5. With hindsight one can see that publication would probably only have thrown into sharper relief the incongruity at the heart of his musical philosophy: his commitment to Pythagorean principles of tuning. In this respect Birchensha appears to represent an extreme case of a musical theorist developing his ideas in dissociation both from the realities of musical practice and from the mainstream of contemporary scientific thought.[5] The fact that he was acknowledged to have been 'a profess'd *Violist*',[6] and so must have known at first hand of the problems of tuning an instrument with movable frets, makes this all the more baffling.

------

[4]   It has been suggested that Birchensha's 'low social status precluded him from membership': see Penelope Gouk, 'Music and the Sciences', in *The Cambridge History of Seventeenth-Century Music*, ed. Tim Carter and John Butt (Cambridge, 2005), pp. 132–57, at pp. 151–2. It should however be noted that in more than one source he is described as a gentleman.

[5]   Evidence of Birchensha's commitment to Pythagorean principles is to be found, first, in his commendatory references to Pythagoras, starting with his letter to the Royal Society of 26 April 1664 (see Chapter II: 'For [...] there are no certain rules given by any, whose workes I have seene (Pythagoras excepted) for the finding out the proper places of those simple intervals [...] without which the practicall part of Musick cannot well consist and be perfect'); and secondly, in his mathematical tables and discussion of ratios in the 'Compendious Discourse' (see Chapter III, especially, pp. 132–3 where the ratios given for such intervals as the comma, semitone, apotome, tone, minor third, major third, diminished fifth, tritone, minor sixth and major sixth all conform to Pythagorean doctrine). D.P. Walker relevantly observed that to all intents and purposes 'the Pythagorean scale became obsolete after Zarlino began publishing in the 1550s, except for a few extreme humanists, such as Girolamo Mei and, following him, Vincenzo Galilei in his *Dialogo* (but only in this work), and for archaic, ill-informed authors, such as Robert Fludd'. Walker's omission of any mention of Birchensha's name may be explained by the fact that little about his views on tuning had been published by 1977. See D.P. Walker, 'Seventeenth-Century Scientists' Views on Intonation and the Nature of Consonance', *Archives internationales d'histoire des sciences*, 27 (1977): 263–73, at 263; reprinted in his *Studies in Musical Science in the Late Renaissance* (London and Leiden, 1978), pp. 111–22, at p. 111.

[6]   Locke, *Observations upon a Late Book*, p. 34.

In the event, *Syntagma musicæ* never appeared, and the extensive manuscript drafts that Birchensha apparently made for it disappeared or were destroyed. His ambitious design was never entirely forgotten, thanks to the Royal Society's *Philosophical Transactions* (which reprinted his advertisement) and to Sir John Hawkins and Dr Burney, the historians.[7] But for 300 years after his death what remained visible of his legacy as a theorist and teacher – even the much-vaunted 'Rules of Composition' – seemed meagre and scrappy. Hawkins presented a manuscript containing a version of the rules to the British Museum in 1778, but those scholars who examined it often found it difficult to disentangle what was Birchensha's from what was not, or were puzzled to find that while the title mentioned '6 Rules' only five appeared to be given.[8] Notes on Birchensha's 'Grand Scale' were among the papers of the mathematician John Pell which were given to the British Museum in 1766, but they too were not easy to interpret.[9] Two publications that had appeared in Birchensha's lifetime – his translation of the chapters on music from Alsted's *Encyclopædia* and his preface to Thomas Salmon's *Essay to the Advancement of Musick* – both depended on the work of others.[10] By rendering Alsted into what passed for the vernacular, *Templum musicum* admittedly introduced new strands of theoretical thought into English musical literature, but the book's propensity to bemuse readers even as intelligent as Locke and Pepys hampered its usefulness.

In recent years, however, further texts from Birchensha's hand have come to light, largely as a result of research among the archives of the Royal Society by Penelope Gouk, Leta Miller and Albert Cohen.[11] The most substantial and important of these, his 'Compendious Discourse of the Principles of the

---

[7]   *Philosophical Transactions*, 7/90 (20 January 1672/3): 5153–4; Sir John Hawkins, *A General History of the Science and Practice of Music* (5 vols, London, 1776), vol. 4, pp. 447–9; Burney, *A General History of Music*, vol. 3, pp. 472–3.

[8]   Captain Silas Taylor's 'Collection of Rules in Musicke': London, British Library, Add. MS 4910, fols 39–61.

[9]   British Library, Add. MS 4388, fols 14–44, 67–8.

[10]   *Templum musicum: or the Musical Synopsis, of the Learned and Famous Johannes-Henricus-Alstedius, being a Compendium of the Rudiments both of the Mathematical and Practical Part of Musick* [...] *Faithfully translated out of Latin by John Birchensha* (London, 1664; facsimile edn, Monuments of Music and Music Literature in Facsimile, 2nd series, 35, New York, [1968]); Thomas Salmon, *An Essay to the Advancement of Musick, by Casting away the Perplexity of Different Cliffs. And Uniting all sorts of Musick {Lute, Viol, Violin, Organ, Harpsecord, Voice, &c.} in one Universal Character* (London, 1672; facsimile edn, Monuments of Music and Music Literature in Facsimile, 2nd series, 11, New York, 1966).

[11]   Penelope M. Gouk, 'Music in the Natural Philosophy of the Early Royal Society' (PhD dissertation, University of London, 1982); Leta Miller and Albert Cohen, *Music in the Royal Society of London 1660–1806* (Detroit Studies in Music Bibliography, 56; Detroit, MI, 1987).

Practicall and Mathematicall Partes of Musick', is contained in a manuscript which the author wrote for Robert Boyle. Other significant discoveries are a letter from him which was read at a meeting of the Royal Society on 27 April 1664, and a detailed synopsis of the unfinished *Syntagma musicæ*. Fétis's manuscript of the 'Rules' turned out to be still in the Royal Library in Brussels, where it had lain largely undisturbed from 1872 until Christopher Field obtained a microfilm of it in 1998. Meanwhile in 1991 Robert Thompson had drawn attention to yet a third version of the 'Rules', tucked away in Francis Withey's commonplace book in Christ Church Library, Oxford.[12] Between them these two sources add substantially to our understanding of Birchensha's 'mathematical way of composure'.

Now that all of his writings on music are collected in a critical edition – omitting only the Alsted translation and the preface to Salmon's *Essay*, the former because it would need a volume to itself (though Birchensha's dedicatory epistle and preface are included on account of their relevance to other items), and the latter because its natural place is with the *Essay* and the ensuing Salmon–Locke controversy – it is hoped that scholars will be better equipped to understand Birchensha's contribution to music theory, however slight it may have been, and to judge for themselves his competence, individuality and historical significance.

Birchensha's Life

Wood's Memoir

Biographical information about John Birchensha is frustratingly scant. His dates of birth and death, the identities of his parents and where he received his education and musical training all remain matters of speculation rather than of fact. In his writings he reveals little about himself or his background. We have no portrait of him, and despite the stir that his theories caused in the 1660s and 1670s his death appears to have gone largely unremarked.

It is fortunate, therefore, that when compiling his manuscript notes on musicians Anthony Wood, the Oxford antiquarian, penned the following brief memoir:

> Birchensaw (John)
> descended of a good family, lived when young with the Earl of Kildare in the citie of Dublin, drove thence when the Rebellion broke out in 1641, setled in London, instructed gentlemen on the viol & composed thinges of several parts. He was a gentile man and lived several yeares after K. Ch. 2

---

[12]   Robert Thompson, '"Francis Withie of Oxon" and his Commonplace Book, Christ Church, Oxford, MS 337', *Chelys*, 20 (1991): 3–27.

was restored to his Kingdomes. He hath publish'd <u>plaine Rules & Directions for composing in parts</u> – in one sheet.[13]

Wood probably never met Birchensha, but so far as it goes this note – written just a few years after the musician's death – has a ring of truth. One of Wood's informants on such matters was Dr Benjamin Rogers, the organist of Magdalen College, Oxford, who had spent three years in Ireland – part of that time as organist of Christ Church Cathedral, Dublin – before returning to England at the time of the 1641 uprising, and he may well have supplied Wood with first-hand intelligence.[14] No copy of the *Rules & Directions* mentioned by Wood is known to survive, but it was advertised for sale by John Playford in 1682, so it did exist.[15]

Early Years in Ireland, c.1605–1642

In his memoir Wood described Birchensha as 'a gentile man' and 'descended of a good family'. Others convey a similar impression, including Matthew Locke, who referred to him as 'a Gentleman (I fear) strugling under an obligation beneath either his Birth, Education, or Knowledge'.[16] Grattan Flood, the Irish music historian, asserted that he was a 'son of Sir Ralph Birkenshaw, Comptroller of the Musters and Cheques', but did not specify the source of his information, for which documentary confirmation has yet to be found. Nonetheless it is plausible that John's parents were Sir Ralph and his wife Elizabeth.[17] Ralph Birchensha was sent to Dublin by the English government

---

[13] Oxford, Bodleian Library, MS Wood D 19 (4), fol. 19. This was evidently the source for a similar note in Hawkins, *A General History*, vol. 4, p. 447. In Wood's manuscript *plaine* follows *A sheet of* deleted.

[14] H. Watkins Shaw, 'Extracts from Anthony à Wood's "Notes on the Lives of Musicians", Hitherto Unpublished', *Music & Letters*, 15 (1934): 157–62, at 158; H. Watkins Shaw, *The Succession of Organists of the Chapel Royal and the Cathedrals of England and Wales from c.1538; Also of … the Cathedrals of Armagh and Dublin* (Oxford, 1991), p. 410.

[15] 'A Sheet of plain Rules and Directions for Composing Musick in parts, by Mr. *John Birchenshaw*; the price 6d.' John Playford, *Musick's Recreation on The Viol, Lyra-way*, 2nd edn (London, 1682), sig. A4ᵛ.

[16] Locke, *Observations upon a Late Book*, p. 8.

[17] W.H. Grattan Flood, *A History of Irish Music*, 3rd edn (Dublin, 1913), p. 214. Many variant spellings of the name occur in documents, but Ralph seems to have preferred the spelling 'Byrchensha' or 'Birchensha', and John consistently signed as 'Birchensha'. By 1592 Ralph and Elizabeth already had five small children. For the suggestion that they were the Raphe Byrkenshaw and Elizabeth Morall who were married at Barnsley, Yorkshire, on 15 September 1586, see Christopher D.S. Field, 'Birchensha, John', in *Oxford Dictionary of National Biography*, ed. H.C.G. Matthew and Brian Harrison (60 vols, Oxford, 2004), vol. 5, pp. 806–7.

in 1598 as Controller General of the Musters, an important post involving frequent communication with the Secretary of State, Sir Robert Cecil, as well as with the Lord Deputy of Ireland. He appears to have received his knighthood between February 1616 and August 1618, and died on 8 December 1622.[18] If Sir Ralph and Elizabeth were his parents it is unlikely that John was born after about the first decade of the seventeenth century (if Elizabeth were 18 at her marriage, probably in 1586, she would have been 42 in 1610); and since John survived until at least 1676 – possibly 1681 – it is not probable that he was born before about 1600. A tentative date of birth of *c*.1605 can therefore be assigned to him, with 1600 and 1610 representing reasonably probable outer limits. (His employment at the Kildare household does not enable this range to be narrowed.) John would therefore have been one of the youngest children of Ralph and Elizabeth. It is tempting to conjecture that he may have gone on to study at Trinity College, Dublin, where he would have acquired a good grounding in Latin and mathematics. No entrance register for the college exists for the period 1593–1637, but it is known that another of Sir Ralph's sons was admitted to the privileged rank of Fellow Commoner in 1605, and presented the college with a goblet.[19]

Wood's statement that Birchensha 'lived when young with the Earl of Kildare in the citie of Dublin' until being 'drove thence when the Rebellion broke out in 1641' is our main evidence for believing that the inheritor of Ireland's premier earldom, George Fitzgerald, sixteenth Earl of Kildare (1612–60), took Birchensha into his service in some capacity. Birchensha's exact role in the household remains unclear. Although the phrase 'when young' might suggest apprenticeship as a boy musician, he is unlikely to have been engaged before 1630 at the earliest, and it is therefore more probable that he joined the household as a music master to the earl and countess, or as a tutor to their children. In 1629, at the wish of Charles I, the 17-year-old earl was sent as an undergraduate to Christ Church, Oxford, and his wardship was transferred to Richard Boyle, first Earl of Cork. The following summer he married Joan Boyle, Cork's 19-year-old daughter, in Dublin. Arrangements were made for

---

[18]   Information on Ralph Birchensha is mainly derived from volumes of the *Calendar of the State Papers relating to Ireland* covering the years 1598–1625 (London, 1872–1905); also, for the period 1592–93, from *List and Analysis of the State Papers, Foreign Series: Elizabeth I*, vol. 4 (London, 1984). For further details, see Christopher D.S. Field, 'Birchensha's "Mathematical Way of Composure"', in Barra Boydell and Kerry Houston (eds), *Music, Ireland and the Seventeenth Century* (Irish Musical Studies, 10; Dublin, 2009). After Sir Ralph's death his widow, Elizabeth, received an annuity of £100 from the king; Adam Birchensha (presumably their eldest son) received one of £50.

[19]   *Alumni Dublinenses: A Register of the Students, Graduates, Professors, and Provosts of Trinity College, in the University of Dublin*, ed. G.D. Burtchaell and T.U. Sadleir (London, 1924), p. 67.

the Fitzgeralds' castle at Maynooth, a 15-mile ride from Dublin, to be rebuilt and richly furnished as their home. By November 1632 Cork's chaplain was able to preach 'the first sermon made by a Protestant minister in any man's memory' in the restored chapel, and by September 1634 the house itself was ready for occupation. Above the gateway the carved and painted arms of Fitzgerald and Boyle symbolized the union of the two families.[20] Joan, the countess, had been brought up surrounded by music-making – including consort music for viols – at her father's homes in Lismore and Dublin, so there must have been music in her new house.[21] While it is unlikely that Kildare ever attempted to emulate Cork's lavish musical patronage, Birchensha's ability on the viol would no doubt have been considered a desirable and welcome accomplishment.

This period of relative peace and calm was brought to an end by the Irish rebellion of 1641. In January 1642 the castle at Maynooth was ransacked by insurgents. Birchensha fled to England, as Wood relates, perhaps accompanying Lady Kildare and her five children, who arrived in London early in February.[22] Whether any communication continued after 1642 between him and his former patrons is unknown, but it was to Lady Kildare's youngest brother Robert Boyle, the natural philosopher, that he was later to present the manuscript of his 'Compendious Discourse'.[23]

Civil War and Commonwealth, 1642–1660

After leaving Ireland, Wood's note tells us, Birchensha 'setled in London, instructed gentlemen on the viol & composed thinges of several parts'. This

---

[20] Information is drawn mainly from the papers, diaries and letters of Richard Boyle, 1st Earl of Cork, published as *The Lismore Papers (First Series): Autobiographical Notes, Remembrances and Diaries of Sir Richard Boyle*, ed. Alexander B. Grosart (5 vols, 1886), especially vols 3 and 4, and *The Lismore Papers (Second Series): Selections from the Private and Public (or State) Correspondence of Sir Richard Boyle*, ed. Alexander B. Grosart (5 vols, 1887–88). See also Jane Ohlmeyer, 'Fitzgerald, George, sixteenth Earl of Kildare', in *Oxford Dictionary of National Biography*, vol. 19, pp. 793–4. Searches through the Earl of Kildare's letter-book for 1628–37 (Belfast, Public Record Office of Northern Ireland, MS D. 3078/3/1/5; transcript in the library of the National University of Ireland, Maynooth) and the published diary and letters of the Earl of Cork have failed to uncover any references to Birchensha.

[21] Barra Boydell, 'The Earl of Cork's Musicians: A Study in the Patronage of Music in Early Seventeenth-Century Anglo-Irish Society', *Records of Early English Drama*, 18/2 (1993): 1–15; reprinted with minor revisions in Boydell and Houston, *Music, Ireland and the Seventeenth Century*, pp. 81–94.

[22] *The Lismore Papers (Second Series)*, vol. 4, pp. 267–9.

[23] Lady Kildare died in 1656; her husband, who was twice imprisoned for debt in the 1650s despite a pension from the government, died in 1660, and was succeeded by their second son Wentworth (1634–64) as seventeenth Earl of Kildare.

is partially confirmed by John Playford, who in 1651 included 'Mr. *John Birtenshaw*' in a list of teachers 'For the Voyce or Viole' with whom the city was 'at present furnished', alongside such other 'excellent and able Masters' as Charles Coleman, Henry Cooke and Henry Lawes, and ('For the Organ or Virginall') Christopher Gibbons, John Hingeston and Benjamin Rogers.[24] At some point he settled in Southwark, just across the Thames from the city of London, where he was living in February 1661/2.[25] It is possible that he was married, but we have no firm evidence of this.[26]

Besides giving tuition on the viol, it is likely that Birchensha taught pupils elementary composition, and that his 'Rules of Composition' had their origin in efforts to rationalize that teaching. By the late 1650s, it seems, the 'Rules' had begun to take shape. An early enthusiast for 'Mr Birchensha's way' was Matthew Locke's friend Captain Silas Taylor, already an amateur composer who had had pieces published by Playford. Taylor probably got to know Birchensha soon after moving to London as commissioner for the Westminster militia in August 1659, and he appears to have remained on good terms with both him and Locke. It is suggested below that the earliest layer of Taylor's manuscript 'Collection of Rules in Musicke', which consists of Rules 1–3 written out for Taylor by Birchensha himself, may date from as early as 1659–60.[27]

In 1655 and 1656 two millenarian tracts were published in London by a writer named John Birchensha. The question naturally arises whether these may represent another aspect of the musician Birchensha's activities during the Commonwealth. That the musician was drawn to the encyclopædic writings of Johann Heinrich Alsted, who was well known for his chiliastic beliefs, cannot be denied. The author of the tracts, too, commended Alsted's work; but he also expressed a degree of hostility to the use of music in Christian worship that is nowhere matched in the writings of Birchensha the musician. For this reason it seems improbable, unless further evidence should come to light, that they were the same man.[28]

---

[24]   John Playford, *A Musicall Banquet, Set forth in three choice Varieties of Musick* (London, 1651), sig. A4. Birchensha appears among the teachers 'For the Voyce or Viole', rather than 'For the Organ or Virginall'.

[25]   *The Diary of Samuel Pepys*, ed. Robert Latham and William Matthews (11 vols, London, 1970–83), vol. 3, p. 35 ('And thence over the water to Southwarke to Mr. Berchenshaws house').

[26]   The microfiche edition of the International Genealogical Index contains evidence of other Birchenshas in Southwark, however, including an Ann Burchingshawe who might possibly have been a daughter. She married James Tuching at St Olave's, Southwark on 7 February 1654/5; their daughters Mary and Hanna were baptized in the same church on 30 October 1659 and 22 December 1661.

[27]   See Chapter VIII.

[28]   *The History of Divine Verities. Written by John Birchensha* (London, 1655), reissued with cancel title-page as *The History of the Scripture:* […] *By J.B. a lover of peace*

In his letter to the Royal Society of 26 April 1664 Birchensha claimed to have devoted 'more then 20 yeares labour and study' – to say nothing of 'the expence of many 100.*ll.*' – to research into 'the Mathematicall and practicall part of Musick'.[29] From this it may be deduced that his speculative work commenced in earnest soon after his move to England in 1642. There is reason to suspect that he may have been largely self-taught in this field, but that does not explain why his costs should have run into hundreds of pounds. Some money must have been spent on forming a library of books on the theory of music, to be sure; yet it is by no means obvious that Birchensha was exceptionally widely read. One authority on whose works he undoubtedly placed considerable reliance was the Italian humanist Franchinus Gaffurius, particularly his *Theorica musice* (Milan, 1492). On the other hand Zarlino and Mersenne are never mentioned. He must have owned a copy of Alsted's *Encyclopædia*, from which he made his English translation in *Templum musicum*. He knew John Dowland's translation of *Andreas Ornithoparcus his Micrologus* (London, 1609) and Marcus Meibom's *Antiquæ musicæ auctores septem* (Amsterdam, 1652), as the dedicatory epistle to *Templum musicum* reveals, and there are clues that suggest he was familiar with parts of Kircher's *Musurgia universalis* (Rome, 1650). But even a rare and weighty tome could usually be got for no more than two or three pounds.[30]

---

and truth in Christ Jesus (London, 1660); *The Eagle Prophesie. Or, an Explanation of the Eleventh and Twelfth Chapters of the Second Booke of Esdras* [...] *By John Birchensha a servant of Jesus Christ* (London, 1656). The latter is listed in Wing's *Short-Title Catalogue* (reference: B2942), but the British Library's apparently unique copy (shelfmark E.902(5)) was described as 'missing' on a visit to the library in 2004 and is also so described in the *Thomason Tracts* microfilm series. 'Alstedius's Chronologie' is mentioned in *The History of the Scripture*, sig. A5^r. The latter work contains a list of 'Heresies and Romane Superstitions' between the years 381 and 1641 which includes such items as '*Psalmes* began to be sung (by turnes) by *Flavian* and *Diodore*', '*Anthemes* were brought into the Church by *Ambrose*', and 'The first use of *Organs* in the Westerne Church'; the author looks forward to the fall of Babylon (*sc.* the Roman Catholic Church) when 'The Voice of *Harpers*, *Musitians*, and *Pipers,* and *Trumpeters* shal no more be heard in her' (part 2, pp. 265–71; part 4, p. 91). John Birchensha the musician, in contrast, composed psalm settings, was content to follow Alsted in his praise of '*Orlandus*' [Lassus] who 'in his *Mottets*, [...] hath brought *Melopoesie* to his highest pitch' (*Templum musicum*, p. 72), and proposed to include in the Practical Part of *Syntagma musicæ* a section on 'Choral Musick, both *Roman*, and *English*'. He deliberately omitted from the final paragraph of *Templum musicum* Alsted's chiliastic reference to 'this evening of the world, when *Kyrieleison* and *Hallelujah* truly lie subjected beneath our feet'.

[29]   London, Royal Society, Letter Book Original, vol. 1, p. 143.

[30]   Pepys bought the 1630 edition of Alsted's *Encyclopædia* in October 1660 for £1, 18s; his copy of Kircher's *Musurgia universalis* cost £1, 15s unbound in February 1668; and his copy of Mersenne's *Harmonie universelle*, which had to be ordered from France, cost £3, 2s the following May, 'but is a very fine book'.

'Mr Birchensha's way' and the Royal Society of London, 1660–1665

From 1660 onwards, as the Restoration gave rise to sweeping changes in London's musical, social and intellectual life, the main thrust of Birchensha's professional activity appears to have shifted away from teaching the viol and towards teaching his 'Rules of Composition'. Because these rules were unpublished and could usually only be obtained by undertaking a course of lessons from him, he may have shrewdly calculated that the ability to compose by 'Mr Birchensha's way' had the potential to become a fashionable accomplishment. If enough people could be persuaded of the ease and effectiveness of this method of composition, he would be able to attract more pupils and command higher fees.

By a happy chance, one early composition pupil was the 28-year-old Samuel Pepys, whose diary gives a gripping account of his lessons in January and February 1662. After decades as an unchronicled and elusive figure, Birchensha dramatically enters the stage as a real person. His first appearance in the diary is on Monday, 13 January 1661/2, when he called on Pepys at home. Clearly the two men had met before – they may have been introduced to one another by Silas Taylor, with whom Pepys had become acquainted probably in 1659 when he was a clerk at the Exchequer – and the impression is given that the visit may not have been unplanned. Pepys writes:

> Mr. Berchenshaw (whom I have not seen a great while) came to see me, who stayed with me a great while talking of Musique; and I am resolved to begin to learne of him to compose and to begin tomorrow, he giving of me so great hopes that I shall soon do it.[31]

There were lessons on the next two days, and on the second Pepys gives a vivid picture of himself and his teacher working and relaxing together:

> This morning Mr. Berchenshaw came again; and after he had examined me and taught me something in my work, he and I went to breakfast in my chamber, upon a Coller of brawne. And after we had eaten, he asked me whether we have not committed a fault in eating today, telling me that it is a fast-day, ordered by the parliament to pray for more seasonable weather – it having hitherto been some summer weather, that it is, both as to warmth and every other thing, just as if it were the middle of May or June.[32]

The tuition continued for a further six weeks, with Birchensha visiting once or twice a week (it is not always possible to be sure when 'musique practice'

---

[31] *The Diary of Samuel Pepys*, vol. 3, pp. 8–9. (The punctuation of the passage has been slightly modified here.)

[32] Ibid., pp. 9–10.

means a lesson) and Pepys – who, despite being a keen and versatile amateur musician, had little previous grounding in harmony – spending as much spare time as possible on mastering the rules. Within a month or so he had achieved sufficient ability in two-part writing to compose a song, and to mark this achievement he was invited to Birchensha's home on 24 February to be shown his 'great Card of the body of Musique' – probably a chart of consonant and dissonant intervals in all practicable keys, similar to those found in Birchensha's 'Compendious Discourse' and in William Corbett's manuscript of the 'Rules of Composition'.[33] But Pepys was becoming concerned about the cost of his lessons. He writes:

> Long with Mr. Berchenshaw in the morning at my Musique practice, finishing my song of 'Gaze not on Swans' in two parts, which pleases me well. And I did give him 5*l* for this month or five weeks that he hath taught me, which is a great deal of money and troubled me to part with it. Thence [...] over the water to Southwarke to Mr. Berchenshaws house and there sat with him all the afternoon, he showing me his great Card of the body of Musique, which he cries up for a rare thing; and I do believe it cost much pains, but is not so usefull as he would have it. Then we sat down and set 'Nulla nulla sit formido', and he hath set it very finely.[34]

On 26 February Pepys worked with Birchensha on another song, 'This cursed Jealousie', to a text from Sir William Davenant's *The Siege of Rhodes*. Next day, however, a falling out between master and pupil brought the lessons to an abrupt end:

> This morning came Mr. Berchensha to me; and in our discourse, I finding that he cries up his rules for the most perfect (though I do grant them to be very good, and the best I believe that ever yet were made) and that I could not persuade him to grant wherein they were somewhat lame, we fell to angry words, so that in a pet he flung out of my chamber and I never stopped him, being entended to have put him off today whether this had happened or no, because I think I have all the rules that he hath to give, and so there remains nothing but practice now to do me good – and it is not for me to continue with him at 5*l*. per mensem.
>
> So I settled to put his rules all in fair order in a book, which was my work all the morning till dinner.[35]

---

[33] See Figures 3.3 and 9.1.
[34] *The Diary of Samuel Pepys*, vol. 3, pp. 34–5.
[35] Ibid, pp. 36–7.

Sadly, neither the fair copy of the rules mentioned here, nor the exercises that Pepys worked on during his course of instruction, appear to have survived.[36]

The year of Pepys's lessons, 1662, also saw Birchensha submitting papers to the Royal Society in an effort to capture its attention. It is possible that there were several of these, but the first that can be confidently linked to him was read by the Gresham Professor of Geometry, Lawrence Rooke, at a meeting on 16 April 1662, having been 'brought in' by a recently admitted member, John Brooke. A week later a committee of nine was formed, including the president, Viscount Brouncker, 'to examine the synopsis of Mr Berchensha', presumably meaning the paper of the previous week or an annex to it.[37] No copy of paper or synopsis survives, however, nor any indication of what conclusions (if any) the committee reached. Then on 12 November another paper of 'Mr Berchenshaw's' was brought before the Society. It was presented by Dr Walter Charleton, the translator of the first English edition of Descartes's *Compendium musicæ*; and Brouncker, who had written the 'Animadversions' that accompanied Charleton's translation, was 'desired to examine it'. Brouncker duly reported back the following week, 'objecting that he [Birchensha] made a half Note bigger then a whole Note, and every half Note of a differing Quantity, &c'.[38] As minuted, Brouncker's comments do not bear detailed interpretation, but they do indicate that Birchensha was promoting some specific theory of tuning at this stage.

It may have been in the following year, 1663, that Birchensha acquired his highest-ranking pupil: George Villiers, second Duke of Buckingham (1628–87), who was a fellow of the Royal Society as well as a gentleman of the bedchamber to Charles II. The evidence that the witty and versatile Buckingham learnt to compose in 'Mr Birchensha's way' is a letter from Robert Hooke, the Royal Society's curator of experiments, to Robert Boyle in Oxford, written at the beginning of July 1664. Hooke wrote:

---

[36]   There is no trace of the rule book in the *Catalogue of the Pepys Library at Magdalene College, Cambridge*, vol. 4, part 1: 'Music', ed. John Stevens (Cambridge, 1989). The version of 'Nulla nulla sit formido' for voice and guitar in MS Pepys 2591 is in the hand of Cesare Morelli, Pepys's domestic musician between 1675 and 1682, and should not be regarded as the same as the setting made in 1662.

[37]   Thomas Birch, *The History of the Royal Society of London* (4 vols, London, 1756–57), vol. 1, pp. 80–81; Miller and Cohen, *Music in the Royal Society of London*, p. 191. The other members of the committee were William Ball, Thomas Baines (Gresham professor of Music), William (later 3rd Baron) Brereton, John Brooke, Abraham Hill, Peter Pett, Sir William Petty, and Lawrence Rooke.

[38]   London, Royal Society, Journal Book Original, vol. 1, p. 87; cf. Birch, *The History of the Royal Society*, vol. 1, pp. 125–6. On the identification of Charleton as translator of *Renatus Des-Cartes Excellent Compendium of Musick* (London, 1653), and Brouncker as the 'Person of Honour' who wrote the 'Necessary and Judicious Animadversions Thereupon', see Chapter I, note 8 (p. 83).

> There is a gentleman here in town, that has a better way of teaching musick than what *Kircher* causelessly enough vaunted his *Ars Combinatoria* to be, whereby he has presently taught the duke of *Buckingham* to compose very well, though he knows nothing of the practick part of musick.[39]

That the duke dabbled in composition in 1663–64 is borne out by the Comte de Gramont's account of his experiences at the English court. Gramont describes how Buckingham used his charms on Frances Stuart, one of Queen Catherine's maids of honour, who was known as 'La Belle Stuart'. He tells of her passion for music, and of how the duke, a pleasant singer, composed *vaudevilles* for her delight.[40] Buckingham may have been thinking partly of Birchensha when he made Bayes, the playwright in his burlesque *The Rehearsal*, aver that nobody could properly write a play 'except it were by the help of these my Rules'.[41]

For Birchensha, 1663 was presumably also partly spent completing his translation of Book 20 of Johann Heinrich Alsted's *Encyclopædia* – the book 'In quo explicatur Musica'[42] – and preparing it for the press. Alsted's *Encyclopædia* was a widely influential work, especially in Protestant lands, and one of the features that no doubt commended it to Birchensha was its systematic organization. Every chapter, no matter what the subject, was divided into a series of 'Præcepta' (precepts), followed by a number of 'Regulæ' (rules). Nevertheless Birchensha's decision to nail his colours as a theorist to this particular mast was perhaps a little naïve. In the preface to *Templum musicum* he explains that he undertook the translation for the

---

[39]   Hooke's letter is printed in R.T. Gunther, *Early Science in Oxford, VI: The Life and Work of Robert Hooke, Part I* (Oxford, 1930), pp. 183–5; and in *The Correspondence of Robert Boyle*, ed. Michael Hunter, Antonio Clericuzio and Lawrence M. Principe (6 vols, London, 2001), vol. 2, pp. 291–3. It is undated, but internal evidence implies that it was written between the Royal Society's meetings on 29 June and 6 July 1664. For identification of the unnamed 'gentleman' as Birchensha, see J.C. Kassler and D.R. Oldroyd, 'Robert Hooke's Trinity College "Musick Scripts", his Music Theory and the Role of Music in his Cosmology', *Annals of Science*, 40 (1983): 559–95, at p. 594; Penelope Gouk, *Music, Science and Natural Magic in Seventeenth-Century England* (New Haven and London, 1999), p. 61.

[40]   The French text runs: 'Elle ne laissoit pas de se plaire à la Musique, & d'avoir quelque goût pour le chant. Le Duc de Buckingham [...] chantoit agréablement [...]: il faisoit des Vaudevilles'. *Mémoires du Comte de Grammont, par Monsieur le Comte Antoine Hamilton*, ed. Horace Walpole (Twickenham, 1772), p. 112.

[41]   George Villiers, second Duke of Buckingham, *The Rehearsal*, ed. Montague Summers (Stratford-upon-Avon, 1914), pp. 4–5. In particular, the name given to the first of Bayes's three rules, 'the Rule of Transversion', seems to be a humorous echo of Birchensha's 'Third Rule, called the Transverse Rule'. *The Rehearsal* was written in 1663–65 and first staged (after further revision) at the Theatre Royal, Drury Lane in December 1671.

[42]   'In which Music is explained'.

benefit of gentlemen who wished to 'understand the Rudiments and Principles both of the Mathematical and Practical Parts' of music, since he knew of no writer who had 'more fully discovered the Precepts, Rules, and Axioms of this Science' than Alsted.[43] The content was neither very up-to-date nor particularly well suited to English needs, however, and it is difficult to avoid the conclusion that by the time his translation appeared in print Birchensha's own theoretical views had moved on. His source, the edition of 1649, was virtually identical with the edition of 1630, which in turn was an enlarged version of the *Cursus philosophici encyclopædia* of 1620.[44] Moreover Alsted's material was almost all second-hand, gleaned from such writers as David Mostart, Erycius Puteanus and Johannes Lippius. So the 'ingenious Lover of Musick' who was hoping for a straightforward and lucid introduction to the subject would have found himself confronted with the 'bocedization' system of Mostart as well as the seven-syllable solmization system of Puteanus, and with Lippius's syntonic diatonic tuning of the scale as well as the 'old diatonic' tuning of the Pythagoreans. A few misreadings apart, Birchensha's translation and transcription at least have the merit of being faithful and literal. He even occasionally corrects errors in his source. On the other hand he makes no attempt to reconcile the contradictions inherent in the text, or to explain terms and concepts that a typical reader would have found difficult. His preface contains hardly any discussion of mathematical questions, being largely a manifesto and advertisement for his 'Rules of Composition', to whose efficacy (he asserts) 'many persons of Worth and Quality are able experimentally to testifie' – a hint that his practice as a teacher of composition was already extensive. One can therefore feel some sympathy with Pepys, one of those former pupils, who took a copy of *Templum musicum* with him to read when travelling by barge to Deptford and Woolwich on 4 March 1666/7, but declared that he 'understood not three lines together, from one end of the book to the other'. Even Locke found it difficult.[45] *Templum musicum* was dedicated to

---

[43]   See Chapter I.

[44]   That Birchensha worked mainly from the Lyons edition of 1649 can be deduced from the way errors peculiar to that edition were taken over into the English version: see *Templum musicum*, pp. 19–20, where Birchensha emends faulty music examples without realizing that they were correct in the 1620 and 1630 editions; p. 30, first example, where the ♭ sign is absent from the earlier editions; p. 63, first example, where the clef should be *c*'1.

[45]   Eighteen days later Pepys took Playford's *Brief Introduction to the Skill of Musick* with him on a similar boat journey, and found it much more congenial. See *The Diary of Samuel Pepys*, vol. 8, pp. 96, 124; Locke, *Observations upon A Late Book*, p. 38. One writer who was evidently influenced by *Templum musicum*, however, was the author of *Synopsis of Vocal Musick* (London, 1680), as Rebecca Herissone has shown: see *Synopsis of Vocal Musick by A.B. Philo-Mus.*, ed. Rebecca Herissone (Music Theory in Britain, 1500–1700: Critical Editions; Aldershot and Burlington, VT: Ashgate, 2006), especially pp. 11–22, 154–5, 158–65.

Pepys's cousin and patron Edward Montagu, first Earl of Sandwich, who was a fellow of the Royal Society and an amateur musician, and it was entered at Stationers' Hall on 5 February 1663/4.[46] On the title-page the author styled himself grandly, 'John Birchensha. Philomath.', though whether he meant 'lover of learning' or 'lover of mathematics' is not quite clear.[47]

In 1664, a few months after the granting to the Royal Society of its second charter, Birchensha again tried to interest the Society in his theories. This time he made a greater impression, thanks initially to the good offices of Silas Taylor, and to Sir Robert Moray, the man whom Gilbert Burnet called 'the life and soul' of the Society.[48] At the meeting on 20 April 1664,

> S[r]. Robert Moray suggested, that Capt. Taylor had mentioned to him, a Gentleman, who did pretend to discover some Musical Errors, generally committed, by all moderne Masters of Musick, touching the Scales, and the proportions of Notes, and desired to be heard by some Members of this Society, versed in Musick.

A new music committee was appointed to look into Birchensha's work, with the specific instruction to meet at William Brouncker's lodgings the following Saturday.[49] The committee was a weighty one, whose eminent members included Brouncker himself, Moray, the Earl of Sandwich, Robert Boyle and the mathematician John Pell. Moray was corresponding during this period with Christiaan Huygens about a range of topics, including music; Sandwich was the dedicatee of *Templum musicum*; Boyle was the recipient of Birchensha's 'Compendious Discourse', probably written during this or the following year; and Pell would later be the author of extensive calculations in response to Birchensha's ideas about tuning. At the committee's request Birchensha wrote a letter to the Society, dated 26 April 1664, which was read at the Society's

---

[46]   *A Transcript of the Registers of the Worshipful Company of Stationers; from 1640–1708 A.D.*, [compiled by G.E. Briscoe Eyre and Charles Robert Rivington] (3 vols, London, 1913–14), vol. 2, p. 337.

[47]   The Stationers' Hall register describes the work as 'Translated out of Lattin by John Birchensha, Philomathmaticus'.

[48]   *The Letters of Sir Robert Moray to the Earl of Kincardine, 1657–73*, ed. David Stevenson (Aldershot and Burlington, VT, 2007), p. 40, quoting from Burnet's *History of his Own Time*.

[49]   London, Royal Society, Journal Book Original, vol. 2, pp. 71–2; Birch, *The History of the Royal Society*, vol. 1, p. 416. In addition to those named above, the committee included Sir Paul Neile, William Ball, Thomas Henshaw, William Croone, Philip Packer and Dr Peter Balle. The Journal Book does not mention the previous appearance of papers by Birchensha before the Society, or the existence of an earlier music committee which overlapped in only two members (Lord Brouncker and William Ball) with this one.

meeting the next day.[50] Dr John Wilkins took the chair (in Brouncker's absence), and those present included Moray, Boyle, Pell, Charleton, Evelyn, Hooke and Oldenburg.[51] Two matters in particular stand out in Birchensha's letter. So far as the 'Mathematicall part of Musick' is concerned, he makes clear his commitment to Pythagorean principles of tuning, which he envisages being applied in a wide range of keys; while on the 'Practicall' side he enthusiastically cries up his Rules of Composition, by means of which 'not onely those, who skillfully can sing or play on some Instrument, may learne to compose, but also those who can neither sing nor play'. In support of these claims he again offers the testimony and work of pupils 'whose compositions shall be produced, and be exposed to the judgements of any, who desire to hear them'. After the letter had been read, Birchensha was called in to the meeting, 'thanked for his respect to the Society' and given an assurance that the committee would consider 'wayes to encourage and promote his designe and study'.[52]

A week later Henry Oldenburg, the Society's secretary, wrote to Dr John Wallis, the Savilian Professor of Geometry at Oxford, with a summary of Birchensha's letter. As a result, Oldenburg was able to bring to the meeting on 18 May 'two Letters, written to him from Oxford by D[r]. Wallis; one of May 7, the other of May 14, containing the Authors thoughts about the Musical proposalls of M[r]. Birchensha'.[53] In his first letter, Wallis commented:

> I suppose it very reasonable that the Gentleman be incouraged in his design; especially if such a person as your letter represents him. His censure of the Condition wherein Musick stands at present; I concur with: His Propositions are good.

But Oldenburg had not explained Birchensha's proposals in much detail, as is clear from the long letter of 14 May in which Wallis argued in favour of just intonation (in other words, the syntonic diatonic tuning of the scale):

> How far this may agree with Mr Birchinsha's Thoughts or Notions concerning the same subject; I cannot tell. For your Letter intimating onely

---

[50] See Chapter II.

[51] Birch, *The History of the Royal Society*, vol. 1, pp. 416–19.

[52] London, Royal Society, Journal Book Original, vol. 2, pp. 73–4.

[53] Ibid., p. 81. At this meeting Edward Cotton was added to the music committee. Oldenburg's letter of 4 May does not survive, but for Wallis's replies of 14 and 21 May see *The Correspondence of Henry Oldenburg*, ed. A. Rupert Hall and Marie Boas Hall (13 vols: vols 1–9, Madison, Milwaukee and London, 1965–73; vols 10–11, London, 1975–77; vols 12–13, London and Philadelphia, 1986), vol. 2, pp. 179–82, 190–201. A further letter from Wallis to Oldenburg on the theory of music followed on 25 May (ibid., pp. 202–3).

the Generall, both as to the Defects in Musick; & as to the Proposalls hee
makes of Supplying those Defects: it doth not at all appear from the rest what
his particular thoughts are, & by what methods he intends a restitution.

Apart from Wallis's letters, Birchensha's appearance in April 1664 before
the Royal Society and its newly formed music committee seems to have
given rise to two important texts. One was an exposition of his 'Rules of
Composition' which Birchensha prepared for Lord Brouncker; the other was
the autograph manuscript of his 'Compendious Discourse' which he wrote
for Robert Boyle. Neither text can be dated precisely, but it is probably no
coincidence that Brouncker and Boyle were both prominent members of the
music committee. 'My Lord Brounckers booke' – as Silas Taylor referred to
the former – is lost, but we know quite a lot about its contents because it was
the chief source for the second layer of Taylor's manuscript of the Rules.[54] The
Boyle manuscript is entitled 'A Compendious Discourse of the Principles of
the Practicall and Mathematicall Partes of Musick', and is the largest single
surviving source for Birchensha's ideas.[55] Its title page is inscribed, 'Written
by John Birchensha, for the use of the Honorable Robert Boyle, Esquire',
but nothing in Boyle's correspondence or published writings bears on the
manuscript or the circumstances in which it was produced and presented.
Forming a kind of appendix, but still an integral part of the manuscript, are
four pages of 'Directions how to make any kind of Tune, or Ayre, without
the helpe of the Voice, or any other Musicall Instrument'. The first mention
we have from Birchensha of rules for 'the making of excellent and good Aire'
in a single melodic line is in his letter of 26 April 1664 to the Royal Society.
The fact that 1664 was the period of Birchensha's most sustained contact
with the Royal Society argues that the Boyle manuscript should be assigned
to approximately that year. Its mathematical contents seem to fit in with the
chronological development of Birchensha's ideas in other datable sources in a
way which is consistent with this general date. Much the same seems to be true
of the stage that 'My Lord Brounckers Booke' represents in the evolution of
the 'Rules of Composition'. Though it is possible that the evidence is deceptive,
the likelihood is that both Brouncker's and Boyle's manuscripts were written
by Birchensha in 1664 or thereabouts.

Pepys's diary provides an incidental illustration of the interest that
Birchensha's ideas aroused among fellows and friends of the Royal Society
during summer 1664. On 10 June he relates how, after a committee meeting
in Whitehall, he went into St James's Park 'and met and walked with Captain
Sylas Taylor, my old acquaintance while I was of the Exchequer, and Dr.
Whore – talking of music and perticulary of Mr. Berchenshaw's way, which
Taylor magnifies mightily, and perhaps but what it deserves – but not so easily

---

[54] See Chapter VIII.
[55] See Chapter III.

to be understood as he and others make of it'.[56] The third member of this trio, 'Dr. Whore', was the physician and amateur composer William Hoare, who had been a fellow of the Royal Society since 1662.

At each of its weekly meetings from 6 July to 10 August 1664 the Royal Society performed experiments with vibrating strings.[57] The work partly duplicated that of Mersenne in Paris in the 1630s on the relationship between their frequency and their length, tension and density,[58] but the immediate stimulus for the Society's interest in the matter seems to have been Birchensha's appearance earlier in the year. On 3 August Silas Taylor was asked to invite Birchensha to the next meeting. Birchensha duly presented himself on 10 August, but when his aural ability to analyse small variations in the tuning of intervals was put to the test the results were disappointing.

> M[r] Birchensha being called in, tuned the string by his ears, to find how near the practise of Musick did agree with the Theory of Proportions: The effect was, that he could not by his Ear distinguish any difference of Sounds (upon the moving of the bridge) above half an inch, especially in 4[ths]. 3[ds]. and Tones: whereupon it was resolved, that a Virginal should be as exactly tuned as could be done, by the Ear, and then the Monochord be examined by it.[59]

The apparatus used, though referred to as a monochord, seems in fact to have been a dichord, consisting of a soundbox four feet long with two strings of brass wire, one of which was stopped using a movable bridge. The following week Taylor relayed to the Society Birchensha's offer of 'the fitting of a double Base-viol with gut-strings in such a manner, that, being divided, they shall serve better to discerne the Musical Notes by the Ear, than the wire-strings doe'. The offer 'was accepted, and M[r]. Birchensha desired by Capt. Taylor, to be Curator of the Experiment'. But it is not clear whether such an experiment was actually carried out, or what its outcome was.[60]

At least two of these meetings that featured experiments with vibrating strings were followed by concerts in which Birchensha took a leading role. The Royal Society's Journal Book makes no mention of these events, so they were probably not regarded as an official part of the Society's experimental

---

[56]   *The Diary of Samuel Pepys*, vol. 5, pp. 174–5.

[57]   Birch, *The History of the Royal Society*, vol. 1, pp. 446, 449, 451, 455, 456.

[58]   e.g. Marin Mersenne, *Harmonicorum libri in quibus agitur de sonorum natura, causis, et effectibus* (Paris, 1635–36), book 2, p. 14 (prop. 18).

[59]   London, Royal Society, Journal Book Original, vol. 2, pp. 118–19.

[60]   Ibid., p. 121. For a description of the 'monochord' provided for the experiments, see Birch, *The History of the Royal Society*, vol. 1, p. 451. The Society's decision to allow Birchensha to take charge of the experiment, rather than Robert Hooke, the Curator of Experiments, is noteworthy; but the absence of any report on the matter suggests that enthusiasm for the programme of musical experiments was waning.

programme, and if Evelyn and Pepys had not written about them in their diaries nothing at all would be known about them. Nevertheless the intention in holding them on Wednesdays in the early evening a short distance from Gresham College is likely to have been that members of the Royal Society could go on to them after their meetings.[61] The fact that Birchensha was involved suggests that part of the purpose behind the concerts may have been to let fellows of the Society hear music composed by pupils using his rules – thus providing the experimental demonstration of their efficacy which he had offered in his letter of 26 April – as well as to bring him and his own music to wider public notice. Perhaps the two events we know about, on 3 and 10 August, were part of a longer series. Evelyn, who attended the first of these concerts, had been present at the Society's meetings on 27 April, when Birchensha's letter was read, and 6 July, for the first of the series of musical experiments, and he was probably there again on the day of the concert, though his diary gives no details of any of those meetings.[62] His report of the concert is brief, but cautiously favourable:

> to Lond[on]: This day was a Consort of Excellent *Musitians* espe[c]ialy one Mr. *Berkenshaw* that rare artist, who invented a mathematical way of composure very extraordinary: True as to the exact rules of art, but without much harmonie.[63]

The concert that Pepys attended, on 10 August, took place at 'the Post Office', which prior to the Great Fire was situated at the junction of Threadneedle Street and Cornhill; possibly a 'banquetting house' in the garden behind the letter office was used.[64] Two of the Society's leading figures, Brouncker and Moray, were present, having been at the meeting beforehand and witnessed Birchensha's encounter with the monochord; others who had been at the meeting, and may or may not have gone on to the concert, included John Wilkins, Walter Charleton, Henry Oldenburg and Robert Hooke.[65] Pepys, not yet a fellow of the Society, went along to the concert at the prompting of Silas Taylor, who may have been partly responsible for organizing the event, but his diary entry shows that he did not enjoy it:

> Thence [...] by agreement with Captain Sylas Taylor (my old acquaintance at the Exchequer) to the post-office to hear some Instrument Musique of

---

[61]   See Gouk, *Music, Science and Natural Magic*, pp. 61–2. Meetings of the Royal Society were held in the afternoon between three and six o'clock.

[62]   Birch, *The History of the Royal Society*, vol. 1, pp. 416–19, 446–9, 457–9.

[63]   *The Diary of John Evelyn*, ed. E.S. de Beer (6 vols, Oxford, 1955), vol. 3, p. 377.

[64]   *The Diary of Samuel Pepys*, vol. 5, p. 238; vol. 10, p. 344.

[65]   Birch, *The History of the Royal Society*, vol. 1, pp. 457–9.

Mr Berchenshaws before my Lord Brunkard and Sir Rob. Murrey. I must confess, whether it be that I hear it but seldom, or that really voices is better, but so it is, that I found no pleasure at all in it, and methought two voyces were worth twenty of it.[66]

After August 1664 Birchensha did not appear again at a meeting of the Royal Society for more than ten years. We do know that on 9 June 1665 he gave a talk to some sort of learned audience on his 'Grand Scale', an outline of which survives among John Pell's papers, but there is nothing to show where this took place.[67] By the end of June the Great Plague was causing such alarm in London that meetings of the Royal Society were suspended, and were not resumed for more than eight months.

Later Years, 1665–1681

From 1665 onwards Birchensha's visibility in the surviving sources declines markedly, and little of a strictly biographical nature can be recorded with any confidence apart from his final appearance at the Royal Society in 1676. If the conjecture is correct that he was born in about 1605, he was now entering upon his seventh decade. Thomas Salmon confirms the impression that by 1672 Birchensha was a venerable enough figure to deserve Matthew Locke's respect – one 'whom he may justly reverence, both for his years and knowledg'. 'We may assure ourselves, that a Master of so long experience would never have commended impossibilities to the world', Salmon declared, referring to Birchensha's support for his own scheme to reform musical notation.[68]

Nevertheless his 'Rules of Composition' continued to arouse interest. Pepys describes in his diary a Sunday evening spent in Greenwich in October 1665 with his wife and his friend Thomas Hill, the merchant. After 'supper and discourse of Musique', the two men went on 'talking till midnight about Berchenshaws music rules, which I did to his great satisfaction inform him in'.[69] Just over a month later Pepys composed the song of which he was most proud, and which he can be seen holding in John Hayls's portrait of him, 'Beauty, retire'.[70] Despite his advancing years, Birchensha continued to give

---

[66] *The Diary of Samuel Pepys*, vol. 5, p. 238.

[67] See Chapter IV.

[68] Thomas Salmon, *A Vindication of An Essay to the Advancement of Musick, from Mr. Matthew Locke's Observations* (London, 1672), p. 64.

[69] *The Diary of Samuel Pepys*, vol. 6, pp. 282–3. Thomas Hill worked as an agent in Lisbon. It was there in 1673 that he came across the musician Cesare Morelli in the service of a Portuguese nobleman. On Hill's recommendation Pepys took Morelli into his household in 1675.

[70] Pepys composed this setting of lines from Davenant's *The Siege of Rhodes* on 6 December 1665, and sang it to Thomas Hill three days later; it was sung again at

instruction in his rules. Salmon became a pupil of his in about 1669, when he was 21, on the recommendation of Locke. He had entered Trinity College, Oxford, in 1664 and graduated as a Bachelor of Arts early in 1668. Even as a young man he had a good knowledge of the history and theory of music, and extolled the virtues of singing and playing the viol. Locke, writing in 1672, explains that 'about three years' previously Salmon had

> made his address to me for instruction in *Composition*; but I, never having contriv'd any method that way, referr'd him to Mr. *Simpson's Compendium of Practical Musick* for the first Rudiments, and to Mr. *Birchensha* (his now Publisher) for his further advance; assuring him I knew no man fitter for that purpose; it being in a manner his whole business. This advice was civilly and kindly taken, and after a short time put in execution.[71]

Before publishing his first treatise, *An Essay to the Advancement of Musick* (1672), one imagines that Salmon must have discussed at some length with Birchensha the imaginative and radical proposals for simplifying musical notation contained therein. Birchensha lent his pupil generous support by writing a preface for the book in which he commended the 'Ingenious Author'; Salmon, in turn, praised his teacher's 'knowledg and industry in Musick'.[72] The *Essay* sparked off a furious controversy with Locke, but there was encouragement for Salmon from members of the Royal Society. John Wallis sent him a letter of approbation, and the *Philosophical Transactions* carried a favourable review of the book which cited Birchensha's preface as representing 'the judgment of an able Master in this Art'.[73]

---

his home on 3 January 1665/6, this time by Catherine Coleman (the original Ianthe in *The Siege of Rhodes*) in the presence of Nicholas Lanier and Edward Coleman. Hayls's portrait (now in the National Portrait Gallery, London) was painted in March–April 1666. There is a version of the song in Morelli's hand in Cambridge, Magdalene College, MS Pepys 2803 (fols 111^v–112^v), but this, though related to the incipit in the portrait, is clearly a later adaptation. See *The Diary of Samuel Pepys*, vol. 6, pp. 320, 324; vol. 7, pp. 2, 53, 96, 257, 362.

[71]   Locke, *Observations upon A Late Book*, p. 3.

[72]   Salmon, *An Essay to the Advancement of Musick*, sig. A3^r–A5^r ('The Publisher to the Reader', signed 'John Birchensha'); Salmon, *A Vindication*, p. 32. Birchensha's preface was written no later than summer 1671, according to Locke, *Observations upon A Late Book*, p. 4.

[73]   Salmon's *Essay* (with Birchensha's preface) had been published by 7 February 1671/2. It was followed by Locke's *Observations upon A Late Book*, dated 11 April 1672; Salmon's *A Vindication of An Essay*, which took the form of an open letter to John Wallis, dated 1 June; and Locke's *The Present Practice of Musick Vindicated*, dated 24 July, but not published until 1673 (along with John Phillips's 'Duellum musicum' and an open letter to Salmon from John Playford, dated 26 August 1672). In *A Vindication*, p. 1, Salmon refers both to Wallis's letter of 7 February 1671/2 and to the review in

One autograph manuscript of the 'Rules of Composition' – the one that belonged to Fétis – seems to date from this period. Birchensha clearly took some pains over the writing of it. In the 1690s it was acquired by the violinist and composer William Corbett, but unfortunately there are no clues to the identity of the student for whom it was originally intended.[74] Birchensha liked to think of his pupils as 'persons of worth and quality' and, so far as we can tell, most of them were gentlemen or noblemen with an interest in natural philosophy and a love of music, such as Silas Taylor, Samuel Pepys, the Duke of Buckingham and Thomas Salmon. This may have been partly because only the relatively well-off could afford a course of instruction from Birchensha. By the standards of the day the £5 that Pepys paid for his six weeks of lessons was indeed 'a great deal of money', even if it bought private tuition at home, a rule book drawn up by the master himself and a small legacy of pieces one could claim as one's own. Pepys's salary in 1662 was £250 a year, but some of the king's musicians had to subsist on barely a fifth of that.[75]

Little is known about Birchensha's relationship with the musical profession, apart from the few hints dropped by Matthew Locke. But the fact that some of his compositions appear in a manuscript dating from the 1670s alongside work by such Restoration court composers as Locke, John Banister, Robert Smith and Nicholas Staggins may betoken closer links than are now apparent.[76] Towards the end of his life there are a few scattered signs that professional musicians such as Philip Becket, James Hart, John Lenton and Francis Withey had begun to take an interest in his ideas. Becket, who appears in the press in the early 1680s offering to teach gentlemen or ladies to compose by means of an 'enlarg'd' version of 'Mr Birchinshaw's Method', may have been the Philip Becket or Beckett who from 1660 to 1678 was a violinist, cornett player and

---

Philosophical Transactions, 6/80 (19 February 1671/2), p. 3095. For an account of the controversy, see Olive Baldwin and Thelma Wilson, 'Musick Advanced and Vindicated', *The Musical Times*, 111 (February 1970): 148–50. Wallis later contributed 'Remarks' on Salmon's *A Proposal to Perform Musick, in Perfect and Mathematical Proportions* (London, 1688), which were published as an appendix to that treatise (pp. 29–41). From 1673 until his death in 1706 Salmon was rector of Meppershall in Bedfordshire. Though never elected a fellow of the Royal Society, he took part in two meetings of the Society in 1705, demonstrating (with the assistance of the viol players Frederick and Christian Steffkin) his newly designed viol fingerboard; a letter from him in the *Philosophical Transactions,* 24/302 (August 1705), describes this. He also communicated with Sir Hans Sloane and Newton on the subject of enharmonic music.

[74]   See Chapter IX.

[75]   *The Diary of Samuel Pepys*, vol. 10, p. 131; Andrew Ashbee, *Records of English Court Music* (9 vols, Snodland, 1986–91; Aldershot, 1991–6), vol. 1, pp. 227–8.

[76]   New York Public Library, Drexel MS 3849. See Peter Holman, *Four and Twenty Fiddlers: The Violin at the English Court 1540–1690* (Oxford, 1993), pp. 313–15, 323, 325–6.

occasional composer at Charles II's court.[77] John Lenton, a younger recruit to the king's band, was appointed as a violinist in 1681 and became a successful composer for court and theatre.[78] If it is correct to surmise that he was the source (or one of the sources) for Francis Withey's copy of the 'Rules', he, like Becket, may have been schooled in Birchensha's method. Withey's professional work was based in Oxford, where from the late 1660s he worked as a cathedral singer, string player, music copyist and teacher, and there is no reason to think he knew Birchensha personally; but he was sufficiently interested in the 'Rules' to devote 16 pages of his commonplace book to them.[79] James Hart (1647–1718) provides another interesting case study. Described as a 'base from York', he was admitted as a gentleman of the Chapel Royal in 1670, and in 1692 was listed as one of the 'Priests of the Chapel'. He sang solo roles in *The Tempest* (1674) and *Calisto* (1675), composed numerous songs, and in 1676 was running a 'New Boarding-School for Young Ladies and Gentlewomen' in Chelsea with Jeffrey Banister, another of Charles II's violinists.[80] There can be little doubt that he was the teacher whose adherence to Birchensha's 'notions' is mentioned by Archdeacon John Baynard in a letter of 20 March 1693/4 to Dr William Holder.[81] Holder, the natural philosopher, clergyman, composer and fellow of the Royal Society, was sub-dean of the Chapel Royal from 1674 to 1689, so he would have known James Hart well. At the time of the letter Baynard was assisting Holder by checking proofs of his book *A Treatise of the Natural Grounds, and Principles of Harmony* (London, 1694), and arranging for copies of it to be sent as presents to deserving persons, of whom Hart was clearly one.[82] Baynard assured Holder that

> your Present will be ready for M[r] Hart; [...] I was formerly pretty well acquainted with him; and learnt a while of him: But I found him Wedded to M[r] Birchenshaw's Notions; viz That all Musical whole-notes are Equall; and no difference of Half notes from one another; and that the Diversitie of Keyes is no more then the Musical Pitch higher or lower; or will pass for

---

[77] *A Biographical Dictionary of English Court Musicians 1485–1714*, compiled by Andrew Ashbee and David Lasocki assisted by Peter Holman and Fiona Kisby (2 vols, Aldershot, Brookfield, VT, Singapore and Sydney, 1998), vol. 1, pp. 136–8; Holman, *Four and Twenty Fiddlers*, pp. 320–21.

[78] *A Biographical Dictionary of English Court Musicians*, vol. 2, pp. 717–18.

[79] See Chapter X.

[80] *A Biographical Dictionary of English Court Musicians*, vol. 1, pp. 550–51.

[81] London, British Library, Sloane MS 1388, fols 167–8.

[82] Baynard was also a friend of Pepys. See Poole, H. Edmund, 'The Printing of William Holder's "Principles of Harmony"', *Proceedings of the Royal Musical Association*, 101 (1974–75): 31–43; *Private Correspondence and Miscellaneous Papers of Samuel Pepys 1679–1703*, ed. J.R. Tanner (2 vols, London, 1926), vol. 2, pp. 285, 317.

> that, without any great Inconvenience: Your book may doe him a kindness,
> and rectify those mistakes in him.

This letter is valuable for the light it throws on Hart, but it has unfortunately also
fostered a mistaken view of Birchensha as an advocate of equal temperament.[83]
Either Baynard expressed himself badly, or his grasp of Birchensha's scale
theory was unsound; but it should not be assumed that Hart shared his error,
still less that Holder would have been misled by it.[84] Hart, if he was indeed
'Wedded to Mr Birchenshaw's Notions', would almost certainly have been
aware of the distinction between the diatonic semitone or 'lesser half note'
and the apotome or 'greater half note'. As a schoolteacher, moreover, he
would have been in an influential position to disseminate Birchensha's ideas.

One sign of Birchensha's wider recognition as an authority on musical
matters was the inclusion of his name by Edward Phillips, nephew of the poet
Milton, in the 1671 and 1678 editions of his English dictionary *The New World
of Words*. There, in a list of 30 or so 'learned Persons of this Age' eminent
in various arts and sciences, two are cited as representing music: 'Mr. *John
Birkenshaw*' and 'Mr. *Matthew Lock*'. It seems unlikely, however, that either
of them contributed to the lexicographic content of the work.[85]

---

[83]   This was largely because of its citation by William Barclay Squire in his article
on Birchensha in *The Dictionary of National Biography*, ed. Leslie Stephen and Sidney
Lee (63 vols, London and Oxford, 1885–1900), vol. 5, pp. 70–71.

[84]   No reply from Holder to Baynard survives, nor does he mention Birchensha
in his *Treatise*. But he had been a fellow of the Royal Society since 1661, and was a
member of its council when Birchensha exhibited his 'Compleat Scale of Musick' on
10 February 1675/6, so it is scarcely conceivable that he was unaware of the scale's
Pythagorean structure.

[85]   E[dward] P[hillips], *The New World of Words*, 3rd edn (London: for Nathaniel
Brook, 1671), unsigned recto preceding sig. A[1]; 4th edn (London: for Obadiah
Blagrave, 1678), sig. b[1]ᵛ. In the editions of 1658 and 1662 (entitled *The New World
of English Words*) the only musical name listed had been that of Dr Charles Coleman,
who died in 1664. For the fifth edition (1696) Birchensha's name was omitted and
Locke's was coupled with that of Henry Purcell, although by that time all three men
were dead. See Graham Strahle, *An Early Music Dictionary: Musical Terms from
British Sources, 1500–1740* (Cambridge, New York and Melbourne, 1995), pp. xvii,
xxxiv n.6. Other notable figures listed in the 1671 and 1678 editions include the Hon.
Robert Boyle (for 'Chymistry'), Robert Hooke ('Mechanicks'), Sir Jonas Moore
('Arithmetick', 'Surveying'), Elias Ashmole and Sir William Dugdale ('Antiquities'),
John Evelyn ('Architecture', 'Agriculture'), and Sir Peter Lely ('Painting'). Edward
Phillips's younger brother John was the author of 'Duellum musicum', a riposte to
Salmon's *A Vindication* (see note 73 above), in which Phillips alleged that Birchensha
had 'disclaim'd and deserted' Salmon's cause 'as altogether unwort[h]y of his Patronage':
Locke, *The Present Practice of Musick Vindicated*, p. 46.

Given the spirit of the time, it was perhaps inevitable that the claims made for Birchensha's rules – that they could turn a musical novice like the Duke of Buckingham into a capable composer in a matter of weeks, that everything was worked out mentally without reliance on voice or instrument – should attract the attention of satirists. In Thomas Shadwell's comedy *The Humorists*, first performed at Lincoln's Inn Fields by the Duke's Company on 10 December 1670, one of the characters is an 'ayery, fantastick, singing, dancing Coxcomb' named Mr Brisk, who 'sets up for a well-bred Man and a Man of honour, but mistakes in every thing, and values himself only upon the vanity and foppery of Gentlemen'. The play is set in London in 1670. Brisk goes around singing a 'Corant of *Berkenshawes* in D sol re', which his friend Drybob agrees is 'an excellent Corant', 'a very merry and luscious Corant'. A little later the tune comes to his lips again, as he walks about combing his peruke:

[Sings:] Fa, la, la, la,
that's an excellent Corant; really I must confess *Grabu* is a very pretty hopeful Man, but *Berkenshaw* is a rare fellow, give him his due,
[Sings:] fa, la, la,
for he can teach men to compose, that are deaf, dumb, and blind.

The whole passage is contrived to make the coxcomb seem pretentious and ridiculous, but it proves that allusions to Birchensha as a composer and teacher were capable of resonating with a London theatre audience in the early 1670s.[86]

---

[86] *The Complete Works of Thomas Shadwell*, ed. Montague Summers (5 vols, London, 1927), vol. 1, pp. 191, 217–18, 221; *The London Stage 1660–1800. A Calendar of Plays, Entertainments and Afterpieces Together with Casts, Box-Receipts and Contemporary Comment. Part 1: 1660–1700*, ed. William Van Lennep (Carbondale, IL, 1965), pp. 177–9. One corant 'in D sol re' (D minor) in the French style survives by Birchensha (New York Public Library, Drexel MS 3849/i–iii, pp. 101–2), and this may have been the piece that was used in the play. To describe any corant as 'luscious' would have seemed faintly absurd, of course, and particularly so if the composer was known for inventing a 'mathematical way of composure'. The juxtaposition of the elderly Birchensha's name with that of the upstart Louis Grabu, the most powerful figure in the 'private musick' of the English court, would have added to the overall comic effect. Born in Catalonia and trained in Paris, Grabu was sworn in as master of Charles II's 'private musick' in 1666 and (to the outrage of the displaced John Banister) as director of the Select Band of Violins in 1667. When Pepys entertained Pelham Humfrey to dinner on 15 November 1667, he found him outspoken in his disparagement of 'Grebus the Frenchman, the King's Master of the Musique, how he understands nothing nor can play on any instrument and so cannot compose'. The conceit of teaching composition to someone who was deaf and dumb would no doubt also have called to mind the current dispute between John Wallis and William Holder over the teaching of deaf mutes to speak. Both men – Holder in his *Elements of Speech*

Meanwhile Birchensha's book, *Syntagma musicæ*, was presumably progressing. In February 1665/6 John Pell spent some time calculating whole-number ratios for the microtones in Birchensha's 33-note scale. Pell may have carried out this task at Birchensha's request, for on one sheet he wrote, 'I gave Mr Birchens[ha] a coppy of this'.[87] By December 1672, the 'Hypothetical Discourse of Musical Sounds and Harmony' was far enough advanced for Birchensha to produce a printed 'Animadversion' outlining the book's contents and soliciting subscriptions.[88] It was estimated that the cost of engraved diagrams alone would come to more than £500. The subscription price was fixed at 20 shillings for a 'fairly bound up' copy, and it was promised that the book would appear by 24 March 1674/5. This allowed the author three and a quarter years to complete its writing and see it through the press. The work was intended for the 'Publick Benefit of all ingenious Practitioners and Lovers of this Science and Art' of music, but readers of the *Philosophical Transactions* seem to have been specially targeted as potential purchasers: an edited text of the 'Animadversion' appeared in the *Transactions* in January 1672/3. The only extant copy of the original printed sheet, signed and sealed by Birchensha, is associated with the papers of John Pell, who was a fellow of the Royal Society. Henry Oldenburg appears to have given Birchensha as much help as he could. Apart from editing the advertisement for the *Philosophical Transactions*, he wrote a letter on 7 June 1673 to Marcello Malpighi in Bologna, one of the Royal Society's foreign members, in which he requested a copy of Pietro Mengoli's recently published treatise *Speculationi di musica* (Bologna, 1670) on Birchensha's behalf:

> We have heard that the very renowned Mengoli has produced a treatise on hearing, sound and music. [...] There is a certain Englishman here, very well versed in both theoretical and practical music, whose name is Mr Birchenshaw. Since his plan is to publish a complete systematic study of music, he now desires to equip himself with Mengoli's work, my friend, and I really do not see how I can fulfil his desire.[89]

(London, 1669), Wallis by publishing a letter he had written to Boyle eight years earlier (*Philosophical Transactions*, 5/61 (18 July 1670): 1087–99) – set out their respective claims. Although Birchensha had nothing to do with any of this, there was in principle no reason why a deaf person could not be taught to compose music by using his rules.

[87]   See below ('Birchensha's "Grand Scale" and John Pell') and Chapter IV.

[88]   See Chapter V.

[89]   *The Correspondence of Henry Oldenburg*, vol. 10, pp. 6–9: 'Accepimus, Celeberrimum Mengolum tractatum edidisse de auditu, sono et musica. [...] Est hic Anglus quidam, in Musica tum theoretica tum practica apprime versatus, qui Dominus Birchenshaw appellatur; Cum ipsi consilium sit, integrum syntagma musicum in lucem emittere, amice in votis jam habet, operis Mengoliani copiam sibi fiere, quae quidem ipsius vota qua possit ratione expleri a me queant, equidem non video.'

In a lengthy review of Mengoli's *Speculationi* the following February Oldenburg (writing anonymously) again heaped praise on Birchensha, to whose expert assessment of those parts of the work which dealt with mathematical harmonics he was content to defer:

> Now, whether this Author [Mengoli] have by all these his Speculations and pains given a perfect *Scale of Musick* according to the true Proportions of Sounds, (which is the great *desideratum* in Musick,) we must leave to the judgement of the great Masters of Musick, especially to the judicious and extraordinarily skilful Musitian Mr. *John Birchensha*; who, it is still hoped, if he be competently encourag'd and assisted, will in due time publish to the world a Compleat System of Musick, after the method formerly taken notice of in these *Tracts*.[90]

Nevertheless a note of doubt can be detected in this reference to Birchensha's *magnum opus*. Does the conditional clause, 'if he be competently encourag'd and assisted', imply a realisation that Birchensha's powers were failing? that an assistant was needed to help sort out a decade's worth of drafts and revisions and prepare copy for the printer? that there had been difficulty in raising the necessary money for publication? Whatever the nature of the problem, Wednesday, 24 March 1674/5 was to come and go without *Syntagma musicæ* appearing.

On 10 February 1675/6 Birchensha appeared for the last time at a meeting of the Royal Society, still promising ('as he should be inabled thereunto') a forthcoming treatise. On this occasion he was given the privilege of addressing the Society in person, rather than having his paper read by a fellow, and he devoted the opportunity to showing and explaining his 'Scale of Musick'.[91] It is not clear exactly how this complex scale was displayed. One possibility is that by this time it had been engraved on copper, which would have allowed copies to be printed off and distributed to those present – although no such copy is known to have survived. At the end of his presentation Birchensha 'had the thanks of the Society given him for this respect and kindness', presumably by Viscount Brouncker, the president, and was 'exhorted to finish his Work, or at least, to publish this Systeme with an Explanation thereof'. In other words, the Society was still encouraging him to complete *Syntagma musicæ* or, failing that, to publish his 'Scale of Musick' separately – something that would have been easier to accomplish if the engraving had already been done. Oldenburg, in his conscientious way, sent accounts of the meeting to some of the fellows who had been unable to be present, and described how 'that famous and extraordinary Musician, Mr Birschinshaw, presented to the Society his new Scale of Musick'. One such letter went to the Lucasian

---

[90] [Oldenburg,] 'An Account of two Books', p. 7000.
[91] See Chapter VII.

Professor of Mathematics at Cambridge, Isaac Newton, the third and final instalment of whose important 'Observations' on light and colours had been read immediately after Birchensha's paper; another went to the physician and naturalist Martin Lister in York. Newton, in his reply (dated 15 February 1675/6), thanked the secretary for his 'account of Mr Berchhenshaw's scale of Musick', adding that he had 'not so much skill in that science as to understand it well'.[92] In addition, a detailed synopsis of all three parts of *Syntagma musicæ* was 'registered' in Oldenburg's own hand for deposit in the Society's archives. Presumably the transcript was made from an up-to-date plan supplied by Birchensha, since it is headed: 'An Account Of divers particulars remarkable in my Book; In which I will write of Musick philosophically, mathematically, and practically'.[93] It bears the annotation 'read Feb: 10: [16]75', although Birchensha's presentation to the Society that day, as we have seen, dealt with only a small (if central) section of the book. Just over three weeks later, Robert Hooke recorded in his diary that Birchensha's name came up during conversation at Sir Christopher Wren's house: 'Much discourse [...] of Meibomius, of Musick, and of Berchenshaw'.[94] Despite his failure to deliver on his promises, this 'extraordinary Musician' clearly still had the ability to provoke learned discussion.

After 1676 nothing more is heard of *Syntagma musicæ*. Birchensha probably died no later than 1681. On 14 May of that year a 'John Birchenshaw' was buried in the cloisters of Westminster Abbey, though it is not certain that this was the musician.[95]

Birchensha's passing roughly coincided with publication of the 'Rules of Composition' broadsheet which Anthony Wood mentions in his memoir. In the second edition of *Musick's Recreation on the Viol, Lyra-way* (1682) it was included in a list of 'Musick Books Printed for John Playford, at his

---

[92]   *The Correspondence of Henry Oldenburg*, vol. 12, pp. 332–5; *The Correspondence of Isaac Newton*, ed. H.W. Turnbull and others (7 vols, Cambridge, London, New York and Melbourne, 1959–77), vol. 1, pp. 417–21. Oldenburg's letter to Newton, which is lost, was written on or about 12 February; his letter to Lister is dated 10 June 1676.

[93]   See Chapter VI.

[94]   *The Diary of Robert Hooke M.A., M.D., F.R.S. 1672–1680*, ed. Henry W. Robinson and Walter Adams (London, 1935), p. 218. The conversation took place on 4 March 1675/6. Also present, apart from Wren and Hooke, was Thomas Henshaw, a member of the music committee set up by the Royal Society on 20 April 1664 to look into Birchensha's proposals. Meibomius was the Danish scholar Marcus Meibom, translator and editor of *Antiquæ musicæ auctores septem* (Amsterdam, 1652), who visited England in 1674–77.

[95]   Joseph Lemuel Chester (ed.), *The Marriage, Baptismal, and Burial Registers of the Collegiate Church or Abbey of St Peter, Westminster* (Harleian Society, 10; London, 1876), p. 202. In a footnote Chester suggested two possible identifications of the John Birchenshaw who was buried at Westminster: the author of the tract *The History of Divine Verities*, and the musician.

Shop near the Temple-Church', as 'A Sheet of plain Rules and Directions for Composing Musick in parts, by Mr. *John Birchenshaw*; the price 6*d.*'[96] It is not clear whether Birchensha authorized its printing; if he did, it is all the more regrettable that no copy can now be traced. Though there cannot have been a lot of room in it for music examples, it would have been interesting to compare a definitive formulation of the rules with their manuscript versions.[97]

On 1 December 1681 *The Loyal Protestant, and True Domestick Intelligence* carried the first of the advertisements in which Philip Becket offered himself as a successor to Birchensha:

> If any Gentlemen or Ladies are desirous to Learn Composition in Musick in Mr Birchinshaw's Method, having enlarg'd it, giving more liberty; or the Through Basse upon the Organ or Harpsicon; May in a short time attain unto it at a very Reasonable Rate, by Philip Becket. Those that desire to be his schollars, may leave a Note (with the Time, and Place where they dwell) at Mr Freeman's next Dore to the Bull Head Tavern in Cheapside, and he will wait upon them.

---

[96] Playford, *Musick's Recreation on The Viol* (1682), sig. A4ᵛ. Birchensha's *Rules* are the last item in the list, which would be consistent with a publication date in 1681–82. Items immediately preceding it include 'Musicks Hand-maid, Containing choice lessons for the *Virginals* and *Harpsechord*, newly Re-printed with Additions of plain and easie Rules for Beginners' (probably the edition of 1678); 'The *Pleasant Companion* [by Thomas Greeting], Containing New and Pleasant *Ayres* and *Tunes* for the *Flagelet*, with plain Instructions for Learners' (probably the edition of 1680); and 'The *Delightful Companion* [by Robert Carr], a New Book of Lessons and Instructions for the *Recorder* or *Flute*' (probably first published in 1681–82, but known only from the second edition of 1686). Hawkins's information about Birchensha's *Rules and Directions* in *A General History* (1776 edn, vol. 4, p. 447) appears to have been taken from Wood's memoir; the publication date given there, 1664, was almost certainly intended to refer only to *Templum musicum*.

[97] Playford's publication was probably similar in general appearance to item C5609a in Wing's *Short-Title Catalogue*, a broadsheet of 1673 entitled 'A COMPENDIUM, / *containing* / Exact RULES to be Observed in the COMPOSING of Two or more Parts, / Either for VOCAL or INSTRUMENTAL *MUSICK*.' This had been printed for the London bookseller William Gilbert, whose shop was in St Paul's Churchyard, and according to the 'Term Catalogue' for Michaelmas 1673 cost sixpence, the same as the Playford sheet. Five rules are given on '*how the* Concords *are to be taken*', followed by four rules on the taking of '*Discords* [...] by way of Pass, or Binding'; these are illustrated by music examples printed from movable type, mainly in two parts (using treble and bass clefs). Though it is very unlikely that Birchensha had anything to do with the publication, Gilbert and his anonymous author may have known something about Birchensha's teaching of his rules and decided to offer the public an inexpensive substitute. See Edward Arber, *The Term Catalogues, 1668–1709 A.D.* (3 vols, London, 1903–6), vol. 1, p. 151. The only known surviving copy of the *Compendium* is in Harvard University Library.

Another similar announcement followed on 12 October 1682.[98] We do not know whether Becket's improved version of the 'Rules of Composition' proved a success with pupils, but his advertisements are unlikely to have appeared while Birchensha was still alive.

The Practical Part of Music

Principles and Elements

The opening section of Birchensha's 'Compendious Discourse', despite being only seven pages long, provides an instructive introduction to his views on the 'Principles and Elements of the Practicall part of Musick'. If it appears less approachable in certain respects than the first part of Christopher Simpson's *Compendium of Practical Musick*, which was written at about the same time and was similarly concerned with rudiments and first principles,[99] it should be remembered that Birchensha conceived it as a preamble to the 'Mathematicall Part' of his treatise, that it is predicated on a Pythagorean system of tuning and that it was not intended for publication in the form in which we have it. Birchensha's purpose was not so much pedagogic as scientific.

Since Birchensha probably began writing the 'Compendious Discourse' shortly after completing his translation of Alsted, it is not surprising to find that Alsted's influence is initially apparent, both in the manner of organization – precepts first, followed by rules – and in the actual content. He begins by setting out eight 'principles', 'axioms' or 'theorems' relating to such fundamental matters as the musical scale and musical notation. He goes on to deal with the 'Elements of Practicall Musick' in 13 short chapters. (The division into chapters, both here and in the 'Mathematicall Part', was only introduced at a late stage, probably when Birchensha drew up his table of contents.) He evidently strove to use terms precisely and to express ideas simply and lucidly, though he sometimes achieved only partial success. On the very first page, for example, he lays down a gnomic axiom which is likely to have taxed the understanding even of Robert Boyle: 'The Progression of musicall Keyes, is either continued or Discontinued'. Behind it may be recognized one

---

[98]   Michael Tilmouth, 'A Calendar of References to Music in Newspapers Published in London and the Provinces (1660–1719)', *R.M.A. Research Chronicle*, 1 (1961): 1–107, at p. 5.

[99]   The first part of Simpson's *Compendium* originally appeared separately as *The Principles of Practical Musick Delivered in a Compendious, Easie, and New Method* (London, 1665). Simpson dedicated it to his young pupil Sir John St Barbe, Bt (1655–1723), with the comment that part of it had been 'framed for your particular Instruction; and (indeed) the whole for the Benefit of such as be of the same Form with you'.

of the precepts in Alsted's chapter 'De Signis soni Musici', but Birchensha never really explains what it means.[100]

Fortunately such opaqueness is fairly infrequent. From time to time Birchensha shows himself capable of coming out with a vivid, down-to-earth phrase, such as his remark that a ten-line stave tends to 'Dazel the Sight'. His discussion of staves or 'systems', and the way in which several five-line staves may be conjoined in 'an Abacus, melopoetick chart, or Compositary', draws again on Alsted, and hence (indirectly if not directly) on a more original source, Johannes Lippius's *Synopsis musicæ novæ* (Strasbourg, 1612). Neither man is mentioned by name, however. In chapter 3, Birchensha does refer to a greater scholar, Heinrich Glarean, but without revealing much knowledge of his work. The list of modes that he gives owes more to Gaffurius.

Some of Birchensha's musical terminology is undeniably striking. Few readers in 1664 would have been familiar with 'pentagram' (meaning a five-line stave) or 'leiger line' (which as 'ledger line' was to become standard usage). One term much used by him, but liable to be misunderstood by the modern reader, is 'key'. Birchensha basically uses 'key' in the sense in which the Latin word '*clavis*' was traditionally used, that is to signify the letter-name of a note (A, B, C, D, E, F or G). 'Signed keys' are the clefs which show the position on the stave of F, C or G. By a 'fict key' he means any note which, by applying a sharp or flat sign, is raised or lowered by the interval that he terms an 'apotome' or 'greater half note'. Another possible source of confusion is Birchensha's description of the keys B and E as naturally 'sharp' (because each lies only a semitone or 'lesser Halfe note' below C and F), and C and F as 'flat' (because each lies only a semitone above B and E); other keys he dubs 'perfect'. Clearly 'sharp key' and 'flat key' do not here signify 'major key' and 'minor key', as they sometimes may do in this period.[101] Nevertheless 'key' could refer to the key-note on which a scale was built; consequently musicians might speak of an entire composition being 'in a key'. In his 'Directions how to make any kind of Tune, or Ayre' Birchensha uses the term in precisely this modern sense, when he teaches that when composing a tune one of the first things to be decided is 'In what Key you will make it'.

Another problematic term is 'voice'. Sometimes it is used as the Latin word '*vox*' was traditionally used, that is to refer to a note by its solmization

---

[100]   Johann Heinrich Alsted, *Encyclopædia septem tomis distincta* (Herborn, 1630), p. 1198; *Templum musicum*, p. 26. Alsted is here concerned with the naming of notes, which is done by means of seven letters or 'keys' (A, B, C, D, E, F, G) and six solmization syllables or 'voices' (*ut, re, mi, fa, sol, la*). Where the latter occur 'continuously' in a scale of music, no 'mutation' is involved; where 'discontinuously', there is mutation. Birchensha may have sought a principle on which to found his 'Table of the Mutation of musical Voices' in chapter 5, in which remote transpositions occur.

[101]   Christopher Simpson, *The Division-Violist: or An Introduction to the Playing upon a Ground* (London, 1659), p. 11.

syllable. In chapter 4 of the 'Practicall Part' Birchensha gives what at first sight looks like a fairly conventional diagram of the gamut, showing in parallel the letter-names of the scale from G to aa, their 'voices' or 'denominations' in the Guidonian scale and their names in the 'Greek scale according to Pythagoras'. On closer examination, however, it turns out to be anything but conventional. Six-syllable solmization is replaced by the four-syllable system favoured in seventeenth-century England, but at the same time new columns are introduced which take the gamut far into the realm of 'fict keys' and mental mutation, with scales starting on B♭, E♭, A♭ and D♭. In the ingenious 'Table of the Mutation of musicall Voices' that follows (see p. 104) Birchensha demonstrates how to transform a natural (or 'Mixolydian') scale of G into scales of C, F, B♭, E♭, A♭, D♭ and G♭, without changing either the positions of the notes on the stave or their denominations: this is done by using different clefs at the same time as prefixing signatures of one, two, three, four, five, six and seven flats. No comparable table of sharpward transpositions is given, perhaps because of the curious but prevalent rule that whereas the addition of a ♭ sign to a note altered both its pitch and its denomination, the addition of a ♯ sign altered only its pitch.[102]

Birchensha's list of note-values in chapter 7 contains a surprise by showing not only the demisemiquaver (which he terms 'demiquaver'), but also the hemidemisemiquaver (which he terms 'semidemiquaver'). Another up-to-date feature, shared with Simpson's *Principles of Practical Musick* (1665), is the appearance in chapter 10 of the sign for the *petite reprise* or small repeat. Chapter 11, which deals with time-signatures or 'Signes of the Moode', breaks new ground by including such relatively unfamiliar signatures as **2** and **⁶4**, as well as signatures appropriate to such fashionable dances as the 'Bransle' and 'Gavot'.

Finally Birchensha turns to the subject of intervals which are 'of use in harmony'. Here may perhaps be seen the first stages in the development of his 'Grand Scale'. In chapters 12 and 13 he takes a chromatic scale of G, converts it into a scale of fourteen notes by including the diminished fifth (D♭) as well as the augmented fourth (C♯) and the diminished octave (G♭) as well as the major seventh (F♯), and shows what interval each of the fourteen notes makes with the 'Unison' or root (G). These fourteen intervals he classifies under three categories: consonant, concinnous, and dissonant. Consonant are the octave and perfect fifth; concinnous are the minor third, major third, diminished fifth, minor sixth and major sixth; dissonant are the minor second, major second, perfect fourth, augmented fourth, minor seventh, diminished octave and major seventh. As if to emphasize the continuity with Pythagorean theory, Greek as well as Latin and English names for each interval are listed. Birchensha then goes on to demonstrate how any note of his fourteen-note scale may

---

[102]   Rebecca Herissone, *Music Theory in Seventeenth-Century England* (Oxford, 2000), pp. 99–100.

serve as the 'assumed Unison' and generate its own scale, using double flat and double sharp signs where necessary so as to preserve the integrity of the scale's interval structure. The resultant table of consonant and dissonant intervals 'in All Keys practicable by our Instruments' is significant, not least because it served as a point of contact between Birchensha's scale theory and his teaching of composition. We know this because it also appears at the front of an autograph manuscript of the 'Rules of Composition' (see Figures 3.3 and 9.1). The 'great Card of the body of Musique' which Birchensha showed to Pepys on 24 February 1661/2 may have been something similar. What takes the breath away, however, is the nonchalant use here of the phrase 'in All Keys practicable by our Instruments'. Birchensha, the 'profess'd *Violist*', is content to end the 'Practicall Part' of his discourse with a vision of voices, violins, viols, theorbos, harpsichords and organs performing together in Pythagorean harmony, it seems, in keys as extreme as A♭ and C♯.

The 'Animadversion' of 1672 and the synopsis of 1676 show that much of the foregoing material relating to the 'Elements of Practicall Musick' would have been taken over into the Practical Part of *Syntagma musicæ*, as would the 'Directions' for melody writing and the six 'Rules of Composition'. In addition, Birchensha planned to broaden the scope of the book by introducing further 'practical' topics. One chapter was to have been devoted to the 'Rhetorical part' of music, and would have shown with the aid of examples that 'in Music there are the like Elegancies that are found in Rhetoric, and do answer the figures thereof', while another would have considered 'the Idiom of Singing, proper to divers Nations'. He even proposed to include instructions on how to play from a 'Bass continual' on the theorbo or harpsichord, in spite of the appearance of Locke's *Melothesia* in 1673.

'How to make any Kind of Tune, Ayre, or Song'

It may have been Alsted, or more properly Lippius as transmitted through the medium of Alsted's *Encyclopædia*, who provided the original stimulus for Birchensha to draw up his 'Directions how to make any kind of Tune, or Ayre'. Under the rule 'More Simple Melody, which is called Monadie, is first to be composed', Alsted declared: 'A young Composer should first compose the most simple Melodies, which arise not from Musical *Dyads* and *Tryads*, but from *Monads*.'[103] Neither Lippius nor Alsted offered much in the way of

---

[103]   Alsted, *Encyclopædia* (1630), p. 1203, Regula II ('Melodia simplicior, quæ dicitur monodia'), as translated by Birchensha in *Templum musicum*, pp. 62–3. In this section Alsted drew on Johannes Lippius, *Synopsis musicæ novæ* (Herborn, 1612), sig. G1ʳ–G2ʳ, including a music example of Lippius's which is correctly shown in the 1630 edition of the *Encyclopædia* but printed with the wrong clef (*c*'3 instead of *c*'1) in the 1649 edition and in *Templum musicum* (p. 63). On Alsted's indebtedness to Lippius, see Benito V. Rivera, *German Music Theory in the Early 17th Century: The Treatises*

guidance on melodic construction, however. The first we hear of Birchensha's intention to formulate directions for melody-writing is from his letter to the Royal Society of 26 April 1664, where he promises rules 'which shall contain all things, that appertaine to the making of excellent and good Aire in any part or kind of musick: and all thinges, which belong to the consecution of sounds in a single part'.[104] His decision to write out his 'Directions' for Boyle on two spare leaves at the end of the 'Compendious Discourse' may have been an afterthought, but it was a fortunate afterthought, for this is the only copy of them that survives.[105]

The 'Directions' are divided into three categories: first, 'Things to be Preconsidered, and Resolved on'; secondly, 'What you are to observe in makeing a Tune'; and thirdly, 'Negative Precepts'. Among the first things to be decided are what type of tune one wishes to compose (such as 'Corant: Gavott &c'), and what key it will be in. Here, Birchensha appears surprisingly progressive. In the mid-1660s the gavotte was only just beginning to come into vogue in England, while the range of key-notes he says to be 'in common use' is unusually wide, including as it does E♭ and F♯ at a time when compositions in E♭ major or F♯ minor were still very rare. Keys are not classified as 'major' or 'minor'; instead, you need to decide 'whether your song shall be flatt or sharp, in the 3ᵈ. 6ᵗʰ. and 7ᵗʰ', bearing in mind that some keys are naturally flat in these degrees while others are sharp, but that by means of ♯ and ♭ signs you can force them 'to be otherwise Accidentaly'.

In the second category, Birchensha lists twelve points to be observed in 'makeing a Tune'. Some of these seem too vague or too basic to be of much help to a beginner – for example, that you are to 'observe the proper movement of such a Tune', that 'your Tune must be formal' and that 'you must observe the Stopps and closes' appropriate to it – but the explanation for this may be that the pupil would have been provided with a 'Coppy', or pattern, whose rhythmic character and phrase structure were intended to be imitated. Under the heading 'Negative precepts' Birchensha warns of 'rocks' to be avoided in melody-writing. These include leaping a diminished fifth or a tritone (something which Calvisius and Butler also cautioned against),[106] and coming 'too often to a note; especially after the same manner'.

In some respects the 'Directions', as they have come down to us, seem tentative and underdeveloped. The advice to place 'passing closes' and

---

of Johannes Lippius (Studies in Musicology, 17; Ann Arbor, MI, 1980), pp. 55, 146–7, 173–4.

[104]   London, Royal Society, Letter Book Original, vol. 1, p. 147.

[105]   See Chapter III. For a discussion of the 'Directions', see Leta Miller, 'John Birchensha and the Early Royal Society: Grand Scales and Scientific Composition', *Journal of the Royal Musical Association*, 115 (1990): 63–79 at pp. 68–70.

[106]   See Charles Butler, *The Principles of Musik, In Singing and Setting* (London, 1636), pp. 45–6, where Calvisius's *Melopoiia* (Erfurt, 1592) is also cited.

'formal closes' in 'som mediation or Intermediation of your key' lacks clarity, partly because there is confusion between arithmetical and harmonical 'intermediation' of the fifth, and partly because the student is chiefly dealing with a treble line, not a bass. Some of the terminology in the third section appears unsound, such as the use of 'defective 3^d' or 'false 3^d' for a diminished fourth. These flaws suggest that the 'Directions' were still at a formative stage when Birchensha made the copy for Boyle.

Birchensha cannot have been unaware of the difficulty of distilling the technique of melody-writing, 'making Airy Tunes', into a few concise and easy guidelines. He admitted that this was a task 'which most Men think impossible'.[107] Yet he remained convinced that it could be done, and that pupils could learn to work mentally 'without the help of the voice, or any other Instrument'. As late as 1676 it was still his resolve to publish 'a Definition, and discovery of the Parts, of which Melodious Tunes, call'd Aires, are constituted: with Directions and Rules, by which good Aires or Tunes (of any sort or Mood) may be made: Which skill and art is, by most Musitians, thought impossible to be attained unto'.[108]

The Six 'Rules of Composition'

Birchensha's preface to *Templum musicum*, published in February 1663/4, is virtually a manifesto for his 'Rules of Composition'.[109] 'If Musick be an Art', he claims, 'then it may be contracted and collected into certain Rules which may discover all those Mysteries that are contained in that Science, by which a

---

[107] Others had of course attempted to describe good melody. Butler referred to 'the *Cantus* or Tune; such as may delight a Musical ear, thowgh it bee sung alone by it self', and observed: 'The melodi of which Parte consisteth much in reporte: soomtime of fewer, soomtime of more Notes; soomtime of half a Strain, soomtime of a whole Strain, in the same vers [...]. Modulations in Melodi ar more smoothe, facil, and fluent, by Degrees, than by Skips: [...] and Skips ar better to Consonant than to Dissonant Intervalls: as to a Third, a Fowrth, a Fift, and Eight, and soomtime a Sixt: but seldom to a Sevnth, or Ninth; (and that not without soom special cauz) and to a *Tritonus* or *Semidiapente* never' (*The Principles of Musik*, pp. 45–6). Almost a century later, however, Chambers's *Cyclopædia* still maintained that melody-writing could not really be taught by rule: 'Melody being chiefly the Business of the Imagination, the Rules of its *Composition* serve only to prescribe certain Limits to it; beyond which, the Imagination, in searching out the Variety and Beauty of Airs, ought not to go [...]. In the Variety and Elegancy of the Melody, the Invention labours a great deal more than the Judgment; so that Method has but little place'. Ephraim Chambers, *Cyclopædia: Or, An Universal Dictionary of Arts and Sciences* (London, 1728), s.v. 'Composition'; quoted in Strahle, *An Early Music Dictionary*, p. 80.

[108] See Chapter VI (Practical Part, §19).

[109] See Chapter I.

man may become an excellent Musician, and expert, both in the Theorical and Practical Parts thereof'. In particular, he informs readers of rules that

> may be yet further, and are already, in part, contrived (drawn from the Mathematical Principles of Musick[)], by which, musical Consonants and Dissonants (artificially applied and disposed, according to the nature of their Proportions, and by the forementioned Canons) may afford, in 2, 3, 4, 5, 6, 7, or more parts, as good Musick, that is, as agreeable, artificial, and formal, as can be composed by the help of any Instrument.

It is clear from this passage that his 'Rules of Composition' were not yet fully 'contrived', and were still undergoing development and refinement. On the other hand they were by no means completely untested. Pepys, for one, had been taught them two years previously, and we are told that a number of other pupils had already benefitted from them:

> To the Completeing of such forcible Rules I have contributed my Mite, whose Certainty and Reality has been Experienced by divers, and may likewise be further known unto others, if they please or desire to understand them. [...] And that this way is found out and effected in a great measure, I say, many persons of Worth and Quality are able experimentally to testifie.

In his letter to the Royal Society of 26 April 1664 Birchensha elaborated further on the thinking behind his rules.[110] He argued that

> as for the Practicall part of Musick, which hath respect to Composition, it is so obscure, that few do understand it, but doe grope at their worke, as men in the darke [...]. It is so difficult, that many after the expence of most of their lifetime in laborious practise, do not attain to such a reasonable measure of perfection in this art, as to compose tollerably well and commendably. It is so irregular, that (a few ordinary observations excepted) there is no certain rule to compose by. And herein this Art is more unhappy, then any other Art in the world: for Grammer, Logick, and all other sciences are drawn into rule. The want of this hath made many Composers to consult their Instruments almost in all things they doe [...]. But to compose by a rule, is a more Noble, artificial, and commendable way, by which the Composer may worke with more ease, certainty, & celerity.

His rules, he promised, would deal with

> all things, which belong to the consecution [...] of Consonants, and Dissonants in many parts: the taking of Cadences, and all wayes of Syncope: the way

---

[110]   See Chapter II.

of taking of Discords by binding or pass: the nature of counterpoint simple or compounded: the Laws of Ornate and florid Discant: the Elegant Art of Fugeing, in a few or great body of parts; the making of canons without, or uppon a plain song: and whatsoever else may be done by this Art, for the advantage of Aire and Harmony. By which Rules not onely those, who skillfully can sing or play on some Instrument, may learn to compose, but also those, who can neither sing nor play: I say, that by my said Rules such may both make good Ayre, and compose 2. 3. 4 or more parts artificially.

Three sources of the rules survive, none of which is dated. Of the three, British Library, Additional MS 4910 (fols 39–61) – which we shall call Silas Taylor's manuscript – is the best known, and probably the earliest.[111] The first leaf is helpfully inscribed: 'A Collection of Rules in Musicke from the most knowing Masters in that Science, with M[r] Birchensha's 6: Rules of Composition; & his Enlargements there-on to the Right Hon[ble] William Lord Viscount Brouncker &c: Collected by Mee, Silas Domvill alias Taylor'. As Taylor's annotations help to make clear, the section relating to Birchensha's rules was compiled in two stages. The first layer was written for Taylor by Birchensha himself, and consists of brief statements of Rules 1–3, with music examples. They undoubtedly show the rules at an early stage of development, although it is not clear whether Rules 4–6 were omitted because they had not yet been formulated or because Taylor's study with Birchensha was interrupted. The hypothesis we advance here is that Taylor got to know Birchensha in 1659–60 when he was serving in London as captain of a troop of horse and commissioner for the Westminster militia, and that the autograph layer of the manuscript is likely to date from that period. Taylor was already an amateur composer who had had pieces published in Playford's *Court-Ayres*, so in his relationship with Birchensha he may have combined the roles of disciple and friend. Sometime later, Taylor supplemented this autograph layer with a second layer transcribed by himself, in which he was able to draw upon a version of the rules made by Birchensha for Lord Brouncker. Taylor's manuscript is thus a complex but authoritative source. 1664–65 seems the most likely time both for the making of Brouncker's manuscript and for the addition of Taylor's second layer.

The second source, Brussels, Bibliothèque Royale de Belgique, MS II 4168 Mus. – which for convenience we call William Corbett's manuscript, although he was not its first owner – is a bound music notebook, almost entirely in Birchensha's hand.[112] Both ends of the notebook were used, one for the rules themselves and the other for ancillary material. Comparison of handwriting

---

[111] See Chapter VIII. This is the only source of the rules mentioned in Miller, 'John Birchensha and the Early Royal Society', and Herissone, *Music Theory in Seventeenth-Century England*.

[112] See Chapter IX.

and content with Taylor's manuscript and the 'Compendious Discourse' suggest that it probably dates from between the mid-1660s and early 1670s. William Corbett, the violinist, composer and collector, was fourteen or fifteen when he signed his name in it in 1695.

Our third source – referred to here as Francis Withey's manuscript – is the notebook which Withey, a well-known musician in Restoration Oxford, had bound with his copy of Simpson's *Compendium of Practical Musick*: together these now make up Oxford, Christ Church, Mus. 337.[113] Over a period of some thirty years, as Robert Thompson has shown, Withey used the notebook as a musical commonplace book in which to enter extracts from musical treatises, excerpts from compositions in a variety of styles and words of wisdom from contemporaries such as the young Bartholomew Isaack, a former Chapel Royal boy who was organist of St John's College, Oxford, in the early 1680s.[114] Sixteen pages of Withey's commonplace book are taken up by Birchensha's rules and their examples. At one point the name 'Mr Lenton' occurs in a heading, suggesting that his source of information may have been John Lenton, who became one of the violinists of Charles II in 1681 and a gentleman of the Chapel Royal in 1685. We tentatively infer that Withey copied out the rules at some time between 1675 and 1685. Directly or indirectly, his copy must have been based on a lost autograph.

Taylor's, Corbett's and Withey's manuscripts furnish us with three separate versions of the rules, or four if one distinguishes between Taylor's two layers. It is regrettable that Pepys's fair copy does not survive, since chronologically it would fall roughly midway between Taylor's first and second layers (if our conjectural dating of these is correct) and show how far the rules had developed by February 1661/2. Although Evelyn's phrase 'a mathematical way of composure' might suggest a rigid system, the manuscripts give a rather different impression, of a set of rules that continued to evolve and be refined throughout the 1660s, and perhaps even beyond. Like John Coprario's 'Rules how to Compose', Birchensha's rules relied as much on musical illustration as on verbal precept.[115] It is true that recurrent patterns in his illustrations can be discerned from manuscript to manuscript; but, as one would expect from any live harmony teaching, neither the examples nor the exact wording of the rules remained constant. Each source presumably reflects the instruction of an individual pupil.

---

[113]   See Chapter X.

[114]   See note 12 above.

[115]   *Giovanni Coperario: Rules how to Compose*, facsimile of the autograph MS with introduction by Manfred Bukofzer (Los Angeles, 1952); ed. Christopher R. Wilson in *A New Way of Making Fowre Parts in Counterpoint by Thomas Campion and Rules how to Compose by Giovanni Coprario* (Music Theory in Britain, 1500–1700: Critical Editions; Aldershot and Burlington, VT, 2003), pp. 79–116.

Some differences between the versions appear to be the result of Birchensha's efforts to organize his teaching in the most satisfactory way. In the first layer of Taylor's manuscript, for instance, Rule 1 is entitled 'The Rule of graduall Motion both in the upper Part and Bass', and is concerned with two parts moving by step, mainly in similar motion; but in Corbett's manuscript it is renamed the 'Rule of Two Parts Ascending or Descending together Gradualy, or By Saltation'. This is a significant change, because it allows movement by leap ('saltation') in parallel thirds or sixths to be considered under this rule. An example of leaping in parallel thirds can be seen in Taylor's second layer under Rule 1, so the change must have occurred by the time Brouncker's version of the rules was made. In Taylor's manuscript, Birchensha included 'Syncope' under the 'Rule of graduall Motion'; but in Corbett's such syncopation is dealt with under Rule 5 (the 'Dividing Rule'). In passing, it may be observed that under Rule 1 Birchensha implicitly allows descending conjunct motion from a perfect fifth to a diminished fifth:[116] examples of this progression are found in both Taylor's and Corbett's manuscripts.

Rule 2 is the 'Rule of graduall Motion in the upper part, and of Saltation in the Bass'. Birchensha reduces this procedure to three basic patterns. In each case the treble moves by step, first descending, then ascending, while the bass falls a fourth or a fifth, depending on whether the voices begin an octave, a third or a fifth apart. There was nothing very original about this, however, for it was essentially derived from Thomas Campion's *A New Way of Making Fowre Parts in Counter-point*.[117] Campion had the idea of making an aide-memoire showing the interval sequences:

But that all this may appear more plaine and easie, I haue drawne it all into these sixe figures.

8	3	5
3	5	8

This link with Campion is implicitly acknowledged in Taylor's manuscript where, alongside Birchensha's autograph example of Rule 2, Taylor has drawn Campion's six figures in a box in red and black ink, with the caption 'Regula

---

[116] See Herissone, *Music Theory in Seventeenth-Century England*, pp. 165–6.

[117] Thomas Campion, *A New Way of Making Fowre Parts in Counter-point* (London, n.d.), sig. B7ᵛ; ed. Wilson, p. 47. Campion's 'figure-box' was well known, being regularly included in editions of Playford's *A Brief Introduction to the Skill of Musick* from 1660 onwards. This connection between Campion and Birchensha was first pointed out by McDonald Emslie in an appendix to 'The Relationship between Words and Music in English Secular Song, 1622–1700' (PhD dissertation, University of Cambridge, 1957–58).

Aurea Bassi' ('the Golden Rule of the Bass'). Corbett's manuscript adds nothing of note to this rule, except to illustrate each of the three basic patterns in both a major and a minor form.

Rule 3, the 'Transverse Rule', deals with various kinds of contrary motion. When the first layer of Taylor's manuscript was written, there were only two categories: 'breaking' (or 'dividing') and 'simple counterpoint'. The former involves 'breaking' into crotchet movement either in the treble or in the bass. The pupil is here introduced to the use of passing discords, since the second crotchet of the pair may make a dissonance. (Birchensha speaks of such a crotchet as falling 'on the second Part of a Note' – meaning the second half of a minim – rather than of it being in an unstressed position.) 'Simple counterpoint' is note-against-note counterpoint, with treble and bass both moving by step in contrary motion. Only concords are used, if one counts the 'concinnous' intervals – *semidiapente* or diminished fifth as well as major and minor thirds and sixths – in that category. Withey's manuscript provides the most methodical set of examples: two-note, then three-note, then four-note patterns are shown, first with the treble part ascending, then with it descending. By the time of Taylor's second layer a third category had been added: 'Transverse motion by Saltation'. Once again, Withey's manuscript affords the most systematic and exhaustive illustration of the rule. Treble and bass, in turn, are shown first rising, then falling, in ever-widening steps from a second to an octave, while the other voice demonstrates the various possible ways of moving from an octave, third, fifth or sixth to another concord.

At some point between the writing of Lord Brouncker's book and Corbett's manuscript the numbering of the next two rules was changed. This revision was presumably intended to formalize what experience had shown was a more logical order in which to teach them. So the 'Rule of Cadences or of binding discords', which appears in Taylor's second layer as Rule 5, becomes Rule 4 in Corbett's and Withey's manuscripts; conversely the 'Rule of Division', which is Rule 4 in Taylor, becomes Rule 5 in Corbett and Withey. Under the former rule, Birchensha explains and illustrates three classes of suspended discord: 4–3, 7–6 and (in the bass) 2–3. Several of the examples in Corbett's and Withey's manuscripts show prolongation of the 'binding note' and shortening of the 'cadent note' (or note of resolution) – a sign of French baroque influence, perhaps.

In its simplest form, as set out in Taylor's second layer, the 'Rule of Division' (or 'Divideing Rule') deals with crotchet or quaver movement 'upon a holding ground or upon a moveing ground' – in other words, as counterpoint to a given part that either remains stationary or moves in minims and semibreves. Division may occur 'either in the upper part or Base at the will of the composer'. Birchensha demonstrates how the dividing part may proceed by 'graduall motion', by 'saltation' or by 'both mixed'. In the first and third, the pupil is given further practice in the use of 'passing discords', and is taught to 'lay the Discord between two concords: both when the Discord is the first & second

Part of the Note' (that is to say, whether it is stressed or unstressed). Fourths, it should be noted, are regarded as discords in two-part writing. By the time Corbett's manuscript was written, two further techniques – 'Chromatick notes' and 'Syncopation' – had been brought under the umbrella of the 'Divideing Rule'. Placing the latter there (rather than under Rule 1) had the advantage of allowing syncopation in disjunct as well as conjunct movement to be taught.

In Rule 6, the 'Fuge Rule', Birchensha introduces the pupil to canon and imitation. Only Corbett's manuscript covers this rule in any depth. Regarding the making of 'a perfect Canon', the advice given is to 'Prick out the fuge in the following Part; in what Key you please: & at what Distance you will. Then make Discant to the fuge so prick'd out. Then prick out that Discant: and so proceed as long as you please.' In imitation, on the other hand, 'you may break off the fuge when you please: & bring it in againe where the discant will beare it'; you may also sometimes imitate 'the Movement of the fuge' (that is, its rhythm) without following its melodic shape. A music example in Taylor's second layer, which reappears in a modified form in Corbett's manuscript, illustrates the possibilities for imitating a given subject at various intervals above and below.

Having grasped the six rules, the budding composer crucially has to learn how to apply them. To this end, Birchensha set out to formulate a 'Method'. Three distinct versions of this survive – one in Taylor's manuscript (presumably copied out from Lord Brouncker's book), one in Corbett's manuscript, and one in Withey's. In each case it seems to be assumed that one part – probably a treble melody – has already been composed. Taylor's version is comparatively brief and straightforward; Corbett's and Withey's are more sophisticated. The numerous differences between them suggest that Birchensha gave a good deal of thought to the best procedure and how to express it; but certain points remain constant. In every case the first two steps are the same: first, bring in any points of imitation 'as the descant will allow', and secondly, put down the cadences that involve suspended discords. Thereafter the pupil is instructed to work through the other rules and their various sub-sections in a logical order, calculating or finding out by trial and error what will work and what will not. Division, chromatic notes, syncopation or dotted rhythms may be introduced if a suitable occasion presents itself. The 'Method' thus imposes a systematic but not inflexible way of working. In Taylor's manuscript the pupil is told: 'These things observe unlesse designedly you will make use of any particular Rule, contrary to this method'; in Corbett's, a check-list is provided of situations where it may be necessary 'to Alter what you have wrought by your Method' and look for an alternative solution. If need be, 'you may forsake your designed Order, or Method, & work by any Rule which will avoid these things, which you will find out by passing through your Rules in order. which you are to go over, & over; untill you have completed, & fill'd up your song'.

Despite all the impressive talk of 'composing of two, three, four, five, six, and seven Parts', Birchensha's rules are fundamentally conceived in terms of treble-and-bass writing. Once they have been mastered, it is assumed that the ability to handle more complex textures will follow. All the music examples in Taylor's manuscript are two-part. In Withey's manuscript, several examples have a second treble part lightly sketched in. In Corbett's, a section was devoted to examples of Rules 1–4 'composed into 4 Parts', a process that usually means adding middle parts to a two-part example. Birchensha merely offers the succinct advice: 'If any of those midle Parts faile you then work by an other Rule'. He was aware of the difficulties that clefs could pose for pupils, so in order to simplify matters the inner parts are all written in the treble clef.

Although Birchensha never mentions the German philosopher and music theorist Athanasius Kircher (1601–80) in his writings, it is instructive to compare the combinatorial system of composition described in Kircher's *Musurgia universalis* with Birchensha's 'Rules' and 'Method'. In particular, the language used by the two men when crying up the merits of their respective systems is strikingly similar. Kircher claimed that his 'Nova musurgia' would 'enable anybody, however unskilled in music, to achieve quickly and easily what practising composers scarcely achieve in many years',[118] and to compose 'melodic lines, in any given harmonic style, for 1, 2, 3, 4, 5, 6, 7, 8, even up to 20 voices'.[119] Birchensha's 'few, easy, certain, and perfect rules' were designed to let somebody 'who can neither sing nor play' learn how to compose 'in a few weeks, or months at the farthest':[120] '*viz.* in two Months he may (exquisitely, and with all the Elegancies of Musick) Compose two Parts; in three Months, three Parts; and so forwards to seven Parts, [...] which otherwise cannot be done in so many Years'.[121] Both theorists lay down a procedural routine that has to be carried out. Obviously there were fundamental differences between their approaches. Kircher's was the more mechanistic way: it involved use of an 'Arca musarithmica', a chest containing boards on which were encoded chord sequences that could be utilized for setting texts to music in a variety

---

[118]   'Serio iam à multis annis huic negotio incubui, nihil non intentatum relinquendo, quo Artem aliquam reperirem, qua quavis etiam quantumvis Musicæ imperitus, id exiguo temporis spacio & sine labore consequi posset, quo practici Compositores vix multorum annorum spacio consequuntur': Athanasius Kircher, *Musurgia universalis sive Ars magna consoni et dissoni* (2 vols, Rome, 1650), vol. 2, p. 2.

[119]   'Nova Musurgia, qua universali quadam ratione, & dato quolibet harmonico stylo, quispiam etiam Musicæ imperitus impositum sibi munus implere possit, per Compositionem Melodiarum 1. 2. 3. 4. 5. 6. 7. 8. usque ad 20 Vocum, in Choros quotlibet distributarum': Athanasius Kircher, *Ars magna sciendi sive combinatoria* (Amsterdam, 1669), p. 480.

[120]   Letter to the Royal Society, 26 April 1664: London, Royal Society, Letter Book Original, vol. 1, pp. 147–8 (see Chapter II).

[121]   Animadversion for *Syntagma musicæ*, 1672: London, British Library, Add. MS 4388, fol. 69 (see Chapter V).

of rhythms and tones, and was intended to benefit Jesuit missionaries.[122] Birchensha's was aimed primarily at the British gentleman amateur and made pragmatic use of traditional didactic methods. Yet it is noteworthy that in July 1664 Hooke refers in the same breath to Kircher's *ars combinatoria* and Birchensha's success in teaching the Duke of Buckingham, who was ignorant of 'the practick part of musick', to compose.[123] It may also not have been entirely coincidental that another of Birchensha's pupils, Pepys, later acquired an 'Arca musarithmica'.[124]

Birchensha's Compositions

It appears that none of Birchensha's compositions was printed in his lifetime, nor do they seem to have circulated much in manuscript. A rare reference to him as a composer, rather than a theorist or teacher, is provided by Nicolaus Mercator, the Danish mathematician, who lived in London from 1658 to 1682 and was elected a fellow of the Royal Society in 1666. In a paper on the tuning of Birchensha's scale (discussed in more detail below) Mercator observed that for much of Birchensha's music a chromatic scale of twelve notes to the octave is all that is needed: 'many of M[r] Berchinshaw's compositions use no more then these twelve keyes, and for such compositions hee hath no other Scale, then that I have sett forth'. If nothing else, Mercator's comment reveals awareness of a body of creative work.[125] Matthew Locke, in his prefatory letter to Simpson's *Compendium*, contrived to deliver sharp criticism without actually mentioning Birchensha by name. In a single sentence Locke implicitly disparages both the Royal Society's zeal for experiments – in 1664 some

---

[122]   Kircher presented one to Duke August of Brunswick-Lüneburg-Wolfenbüttel; it is now in the Herzog-August-Bibliothek at Wolfenbüttel. See Carlo Mario Chierotti, 'Comporre senza conoscere la musica: Athanasius Kircher e la "Musurgia mirifica"', *Nuova rivista musicale italiana*, 28 (1994): 382–410.

[123]   See note 39. One English mathematician on whom Kircher's claims had made an immediate impression was Sir Charles Cavendish (1595?–1654). In a letter written from Antwerp to John Pell in Breda, dated 13 May 1650 (NS), Cavendish wrote: 'I heare Keircher the Jesuit hath latelie printed a booke at Roome wherein he teaches howe in a little time to make anie man of reasonable Capacitie to make songes of all sortes, & aires as well as expert Musitians.' Six months later Cavendish was able to report to Pell that he had obtained a copy of *Musurgia universalis* and read Kircher's chapters on combinatorial treatment of melody and rhythm. See Noel Malcolm and Jacqueline Stedall, *John Pell (1611–1685) and his Correspondence with Sir Charles Cavendish: The mental world of an early modern mathematician* (Oxford, 2005), pp. 550–51 (letter 94), 566 (letter 103).

[124]   It is now in Magdalene College, Cambridge. See R.T. Gunther, *Early Science in Cambridge* (Oxford, 1937), p. 96. Pepys bought a copy of Kircher's *Musurgia universalis* on 22 February 1668; this too is now in Magdalene College Library.

[125]   London, British Library, Add. MS 4388, fol. 44[v].

of these had taken place in the steeple of old St Paul's – and Birchensha's undertaking to the Society to formulate rules 'which shall contain all things, that appertaine to the making of excellent and good Aire in any part or kind of musick', hinting that it was this very quality, 'good Aire', that he found lacking in the latter's compositions:

> And though perchance our new Lights (of which this Age has been monstrous fruitful) who can speculate how many Hairs-bredths will reach from the Top of *Paul's* Steeple to the Center of a Full Moon, and demonstrate that the thousandth part of a Minute after, there will be so many thousand more Hairs necessary, by reason of the Earths or Moons motion; yet we poor Practical men, who *doe, because we doe,* (as they are pleas'd to censure us) are content with such Rules and Predicaments only as are, or may be useful to us, or such whose Genius incline that way: leaving the rest to those who love to busie themselves about nothing, or to no purpose; of whom I shall make bold to deliver this truth, that I could never yet see *that done* by them which they pretend to be most vers'd in, viz. *The production of Ayre*: which, in my opinion, is the *Soul of Musick*.[126]

This edition is not the place to assess Birchensha's merits and limitations as a composer. A summary of his compositions may be useful, however, in view of the patently close relationship between his music and his teaching. Perhaps the earliest of his surviving instrumental works are four fantasia-suites for 'Treble [violin] and Base [viol] to the Organ' (Oxford, Christ Church, MSS Mus. 781 and 1016–17). These belong to a genre of chamber music originally created by Coprario for Charles I as Prince of Wales, to which Birchensha may have been attracted by the possibilities it offered for rhetorical gesture, angular melody and chromatic counterpoint. So far as can be judged from the music's rough-hewn style, his particular models may have been fantasia-suites for the same ensemble by William Lawes or by Cromwell's master of music, John Hingeston. A date in the 1640s or 1650s seems plausible.[127] Probably dating from the Commonwealth years is a suite in A [minor] for two violins,

---

[126]	Christopher Simpson, *A Compendium of Practical Musick* (London, 1667), sig. A5ᵛ. One may also see an allusion here to Boyle's celebrated air-pump experiments.

[127]	There are two suites in D [minor], both with signatures of one flat, and two in D [major], both with signatures of two sharps. Each suite comprises three untitled movements: (i) [Fantasia]; (ii) [Alman]; (iii) [Galliard]. Inscriptions on the fronts of the part-books identify 'Mʳ Birchensha' as the composer. Movements are consecutively numbered from 1 to 12. The music hand may possibly be autograph, though the absence of signatures or titles and the presence of examination marks in the string parts make this far from certain. This set of part-books was part of Henry Aldrich's bequest to Christ Church (see London, Royal College of Music, MS 2125, fol. 23ʳ).

a 12-course lute using the 'flat French' tuning, bass viol and thoroughbass.[128] In the early 1660s it was copied into a set of part-books belonging to a gifted Oxford undergraduate, Richard Rhodes (Oxford, Bodleian Library, MSS Mus. Sch. E.410–14).[129] An unusual venture by Birchensha into representational writing is his suite in F [major] entitled *Threnodia*. This undated lament, reminiscent in some ways of Jenkins's 'bell pieces', is found in part-books copied in 1683–84 for Sir Gabriel Roberts (1629–1715), a London merchant (Hamburg, Staats- und Universitätsbibliothek, MS ND VI 3193). Its seven movements are headed 'Prelude', 'Passing Bell', 'Entrance', 'Entertainment', 'Knell', 'Solemnity' and 'Returne, or closeing Aire'.[130]

---

[128]   Here and elsewhere, the editors use '[minor]' and '[major]' to signify what Simpson meant when describing a key as 'either *Flat*, or *sharp*: not in respect of its self; but in relation to the *flat* or *sharp 3d.* which is joyned to it': see Christopher Simpson, *A Compendium of Practical Musick in Five Parts* (London, 1667), p. 43; Christopher D.S. Field, 'Jenkins and the Cosmography of Harmony', in Andrew Ashbee and Peter Holman (eds), *John Jenkins and His Time: Studies in English Consort Music* (Oxford, 1996), pp. 1–74, at pp. 49 and 54. The movements of the suite are: (i) Pavan; (ii) [Alman]; (iii) [Corant]; (iv) [Alman]; (v) [Corant]; (vi) [Saraband].

[129]   The six movements are nos 27–32 of a collection of 32 airs at the reverse of each part-book. Ascriptions are to 'Mr Birchingshaw' or 'J.B.' One book is signed: 'Ri: Rhodes ex Æde Christi Oxon: Sep. 7. 1660'. Rhodes, a former pupil of Westminster School, matriculated at Christ Church in 1658 and graduated in 1662. Wood, who took part in music meetings with him, considered him 'well grounded … in the practical part of music'. He played the violin, and was the author of a comedy, *Flora's Vagaries*, which was acted at Christ Church in January 1663/4 and taken up by the King's Company in London; Pepys attended a performance on 8 August 1664. Rhodes died in Madrid in 1668, and the part-books were given to Edward Lowe for the use of the Oxford Music School. See Anthony Wood, *Athenæ Oxonienses*, 3rd edn, ed. Philip Bliss (4 vols, London, 1813–20), vol. 3, col. 819; Tim Crawford, 'An Unusual Consort Revealed in an Oxford Manuscript', *Chelys*, 6 (1975–76): 61–8; Matthew Spring, *The Lute in Britain: A History of the Instrument and its Music* (Oxford, 2001), pp. 344, 359. Bodleian Library, MS Mus. Sch. C.44, fol. 99^v contains a concordant copy of the bass part in the hand of Edward Lowe, who headed it: 'The Ayres in the redd Bookes I had of Mr Rhodes'.

[130]   This piece, which bears the ascription 'Mr Birchensha', seems to have been the last music to be added to the books, the scribe having left a number of unused pages between it and the late fantasia-suites for three violins, bass viol and thoroughbass by Jenkins which precede it. No indication is given of the intended scoring of the *Threnodia*. Parts for two treble instruments, bass and thoroughbass survive, but one part-book from the set of five is lost. See Richard Charteris, 'A Rediscovered Manuscript Source with some Previously Unknown Works by John Jenkins, William Lawes and Benjamin Rogers', *Chelys*, 22 (1993): 3–29; *The Viola da Gamba Society Index of Manuscripts containing Consort Music*, compiled by Andrew Ashbee, Robert Thompson and Jonathan Wainwright, vol. 2 (Aldershot and Burlington, VT, 2008), pp. 5–6, 15–23. Jenkins's 'The Five Bells', which enjoyed great popularity in the mid-

The most progressive of Birchensha's instrumental works are two suites in the French style, one in D [minor] (with a signature of one flat) for two violins and bass (New York Public Library, Drexel MS 3849: i–iii, pp. 101–2), the other in B♭ [major] (with a signature of two flats), for which the two outer parts survive (London, Royal College of Music, MS 2087: [i], fols 187ᵛ–190ʳ; [ii], fols 178ᵛ–181ʳ). Each includes a sequence of three branles followed by a 'gavot', as well as other kinds of French dance that were fashionable at court balls in the years following the Restoration. Birchensha was familiar with 'Bransles' and 'Gavots' by the mid 1660s, since he mentions them in his 'Compendious Discourse', but the B♭ suite also includes an example of an 'Overture' in the Lully manner, which makes a date in the 1670s more likely. Royal College of Music MS 2087 was given in 1676 by Stephen Monteage to his eldest son, Deane, as is shown by an inscription in the bass part-book: 'Deane Monteage his book / given by his Father January 1676'. Stephen Monteage had been a steward to the Duke of Buckingham (Birchensha's pupil) in the 1660s before becoming agent to Christopher, second Baron Hatton (later first Viscount); when Stephen died in 1687 he was succeeded in the latter office by Deane. Both this manuscript and Drexel MS 3849 subsequently belonged to Thomas Britton, whose famous concerts in Clerkenwell began in 1678; Britton's signature in Drexel MS 3849 is dated 1680. This was evidently not the only Birchensha music that Britton owned. When his music books were sold in December 1714, lot 73 comprised '3. Sets of Sonatas, and one set by [William] Lawes, 5 and 6 parts, and 2 sets by Birchenshaw'; these items cannot now be traced.[131]

---

seventeenth century, contains movements entitled 'The Bells', 'The Mourners' and 'The Ringers', as does its companion, 'The Six Bells'; for an edition of both pieces see *John Jenkins: The Lyra Viol Consorts*, ed. Frank Traficante (Recent Researches in the Music of the Baroque Era, 67–8; Madison, WI: A-R Editions, 1992), pp. x–xi, 12–22, 129–37.

[131]   The D minor suite is headed 'Mʳ Birchenshaw Bralls' (i.e. Branles), and consists of: (i) [First] Brall; (ii) [Second] Brall; (iii) [Third Brall]; (iv) Gavot; (v) Corant; (vi) Saraband; (vii) [Ayre]; (viii) Chichoney. The B♭ suite comprises: (i) Overture; (ii) Branle 1; (iii) Branle 2ᵈ; (iv) Branle 3ᵈ; (v) Gavot; (vi) Courant; (vii) Minuet; (viii) Rondeau. The editors are very grateful to Professor Holman for making photocopies of Drexel MS 3849 available to us, although we are not persuaded that this part of the manuscript is in Birchensha's hand: see Holman, *Four and Twenty Fiddlers*, pp. 312–17, 323–6, 338–9. On Stephen Monteage, see *Oxford Dictionary of National Biography*, vol. 38, p. 784. Deane Monteage bore the maiden name of his mother, Jane Deane, and would have been about 21 in 1676; in later years he was accomptant-general to the Commissioners of Excise. For a transcription of the Gavot from the B♭ suite, see Field, 'Birchensha's "Mathematical Way of Composure"', p. 132. The Britton sale catalogue is reprinted in Hawkins, *A General History* (1776), vol. 5, pp. 80–82.

The only surviving vocal pieces that can be confidently assigned to Birchensha are settings of metrical psalms or canticles.[132] A collection compiled in 1688 of '120 or more of the Choicest Divine Hymns or Anthemnes English and Latin, that have binne Extant within this 110 or 120 yeeres' (York, Minster Library, MSS M 5/1–3 (S)) includes a group of seven such psalms for three voices. These are not cathedral part-books, however, and the settings may have been intended for domestic or educational rather than ecclesiastical use.[133] There is also a manuscript that belonged to Pepys which bears the title 'M^r: Berchinshaw's Two Parts to be sung (severally) with the Ordinary Church-Tunes of the Singing-Psalms' (Cambridge, Magdalene College, MS Pepys 2544). This contains 'common tunes' for 21 metrical psalms, the *Te Deum* and the *Veni Creator*, to each of which Birchensha has added two alternative parts in plain counterpoint. The simple style, and the fact that only treble clef is used, may reflect an educational purpose – for singing in a school, perhaps, or as specimens of composing by his rules. This score may have been copied for Pepys in the late 1670s or early 1680s.[134]

---

[132] Ian Spink has tentatively identified as Birchensha's a Service in C major ascribed to 'Beckinshaw', which is among the additional manuscript music incorporated with Lichfield Cathedral's part-books of Barnard's *Selected Church Musick* in the late seventeenth century. According to Spink, a note in the source alleges that William Lamb the younger (who succeeded his father as the Lichfield organist in 1688) tried to pass off Beckinshaw's work as his own: 'Mr Lamb stole this service and put his own name to it'. But there is otherwise no evidence of Birchensha composing for the Church of England liturgy.

[133] The compiler was a scribe identified only by his initials 'J.W.' MS 5/2 (fols 97^v–102^r) contains the two treble parts on facing pages for the first five psalms; MS 5/1 (fols 96^r–98^r) contains the bass part. The last two psalms appear in table-book layout on fols 106^r–106^v of MS 5/1. Ascriptions are to 'Mr Birkinshaw', 'Mr Birkingshaw', Mr John Birkinshaw' or 'Jn° Birkinshaw'. See David Griffiths, *A Catalogue of the Music Manuscripts in York Minster Library* (York Minster Library Sectional Catalogues, 2; [York], 1981), pp. 42, 45.

[134] *Catalogue of the Pepys Library*, vol. 4, part 1, p. 12. John Stevens, the compiler of the catalogue, suggested there that the 'skilled hand' is 'possibly Berchinshaw's', but comparison with Birchensha's authenticated autograph manuscripts does not support this conjecture. On the other hand there seems to be a distinct resemblance to the hand of Cesare Morelli, the copyist of MSS Pepys 2591 and 2802–4, who worked for Pepys between 1675 and 1682. The use of void notation inevitably gives the psalm manuscript an individual appearance.

The Mathematical and Philosophical Parts of Music

The 'Mathematical Part of Music'

We now turn to the mathematical content of Birchensha's musical theories. The following writings in particular bear on the mathematical part of his project: his letter to the Royal Society of 26 April 1664;[135] the 'Compendious Discourse';[136] the description of his 'Grand Scale' dated 9 June 1665;[137] the 'Animadversion' for *Syntagma musicæ*, dated 1672;[138] the synopsis of *Syntagma musicæ*, dated 10 February 1675/6, which is preserved among the Royal Society's 'Classified Papers';[139] and the official record of Birchensha's appearance before the Society on that day, when he demonstrated his 'Compleat Scale of Musick'.[140]

Our discussion will treat separately, below, the portions of these texts which deal with the 'Grand Scale', which apparently developed somewhat independently of *Syntagma musicæ* (and, as was suggested above, may even have been engraved and printed at one stage). In addition to Birchensha's own writings, written responses to his theories survive from the mathematicians John Wallis, John Pell and Nicolaus Mercator. The extent to which these writers had themselves received reliable information about Birchensha's ideas is difficult to establish, and the content of their writings is perhaps less significant than is the fact that three major mathematicians active in England in the 1660s took time to comment on the work of a man whose claims to eminence were in music rather than mathematics. These three sources will be discussed below; those of Wallis and Mercator after the discussion of the 'mathematical part of music' and that of Pell within the discussion of the 'Grand Scale'.

In his letter to the Royal Society in 1664, Birchensha emphasized the need to ground music on rules, in language which echoed that of his preface to *Templum musicum*. He proposed to present rules for the placing of pitches within an octave, for the finding of the numbers corresponding to intervals ranging in size from a comma to an octave, and for 'the tryall of proportions'. He would explain 'the admirable production and Generation of Proportions and consequently of Sounds', and his 'Grand System' would 'clearly and visibly demonstrate' all of this. In this text, in keeping with the audience for which he was writing – the fellows of the Royal Society – Birchensha seemed to assume a reader who would find the mathematical content of his ideas easier

---

[135] See Chapter II of this edition.
[136] See Chapter III.
[137] See Chapter IV.
[138] See Chapter V.
[139] See Chapter VI.
[140] See Chapter VII.

than the musical, and seemed to conceive the 'practical part of music' chiefly as an adjunct to the 'mathematical part', presenting the musical rudiments necessary for understanding the 'mathematical part'.

This text possessed a feature which would recur in all of Birchensha's writings about the mathematics of music: an emphasis on the unison as not just the most basic case of a musical interval but also, in some sense, the source of the other intervals. At this stage little more can be gleaned from Birchensha's text than that the unison possessed a fruitful ambiguity for him. Its nature would become clearer in the 'Compendious Discourse', where Birchensha was at pains to set out his ideas as systematically and as fully as the format of a condensed prospectus or sampler would allow. At times this led to confusion, when he misjudged the degree of compression in relation to the complexity of his material; but we should be grateful that it also provided us with both an indication of the overall shape of Birchensha's musical treatise at this stage of its development (*c*.1664), as well as a good deal of its content in a clearly structured form.

The 'Compendious Discourse' helps us to interpret certain of the lists of words which occur elsewhere in Birchensha's writings, and which might otherwise seem to be empty of meaning. Thus:

- a 'musical sound' may be an interval, as well as an individual note;[141]
- a 'ration' is a ratio, but without the distinction between ratio and fraction made by other mathematical writers around this time;
- a 'proportion' is a relationship between two or more intervals or ratios, not, usually, an individual ratio;
- 'magnitude' means the distance on a string corresponding to a particular interval, so that, for example, the magnitude of the lowest octave on a 36-inch string is 18 inches;
- the 'difference' of an interval is, usually, the difference between the two terms of its ratio, as opposed to the 'difference' between two intervals which is, as one would expect, the result of subtracting one from the other;
- the 'excess' of one interval over another is the result of subtracting the smaller interval from the larger.

---

[141] The 'Observations' which Birchensha places between the 'Practical' and 'Mathematical' parts of the 'Compendious Discourse' seem to emphasize the complexity of this term: 'A musicall Sound – Theoretically considered, is called (respectively) A musicall Being / Body / Number / Magnitude – Practically considered [is called] [A musicall] Moode / Key / Intervall / Note / Voice'.

Three terms are not elucidated even here: 'quality', which seems entirely obscure;[142] 'habitude', which may mean the set of magnitudes which a particular ratio or size of interval can take within a particular scale; and 'dimension', which is apparently another term for the size of an interval.

One source of complexity in Birchensha's terminology was a distinction, which he articulated nowhere in the surviving texts, between intervals and ratios considered abstractly – such as the perfect fourth, corresponding to the set of ratios reducible in their lowest terms to 4 : 3 – and particular instances of them – such as C–F or D–G, or the ratios 8 : 6 or 24 : 18. The English language does not, and did not in Birchensha's time, have terms with which to make this distinction, and his use of Greek, Latin and English terms for intervals, pitches and ratios does not seem sufficiently systematic to provide much help. Nearly all of the terms listed above could be applied to specific intervals and ratios, with the possible exception of 'dimension'. Most could also be applied to intervals and ratios in general, with the possible exceptions of 'magnitude', 'habitude' and 'difference'.

The 'mathematical part of music' was divided by Birchensha, after the writing of the text, into 21 sections, a division that is not always particularly natural. In outline the chapters may conveniently be divided into four groups: chapters 1–3 are introductory; chapters 4–8 deal with the definition and manipulation of musical ratios; chapters 9–14 with the naming of pitches, intervals and scales; and chapters 15–21 with 'medieties', which are, broadly speaking, certain types of relationships between ratios.

Following an initial discussion of the nature of the subject in chapter 1, Birchensha began his 'Mathematical Part of Music' with sets of 'axioms', first for the 'arithmetical' and then for the 'geometrical' part of music: chapters 2 and 3. After chapter 4 this subdivision of the 'Mathematical Part', into matters of number on the one hand and matters of magnitude or lengths of strings on the other, never reappeared. The first few of the 'arithmetical' axioms are generalities explicitly modelled on the 'common notions' found at the beginning of Euclid's *Elements*, but the later axioms state the relationships between specific sets of ratios with musical significance, for example that the ratio 2 : 1 can be considered to contain the ratios 3 : 2 and 4 : 3. Statements of this kind could have been easily verified from the general rules for the manipulation of ratios which Birchensha gave later, in chapter 5, and it is hard to understand why they were raised to the status of axioms at this stage. The 'geometrical' axioms, apart from defining some of the terms listed above, are concerned with the elusive nature of the unison. It emerges here

---

[142]   It might conceivably be related to the fact that the four steps of the tetrachord (*protus, deuterus, tritus, tetrardus*) were known as 'qualities', but there seems nothing to confirm that this is the meaning Birchensha intended. See Calvin Bower in *Cambridge History of Western Music Theory*, ed. Christensen, pp. 151, 153–6; also David Cohen, ibid., pp. 325, 348–9.

that Birchensha considered the unison in two different guises: as an interval, whose corresponding ratio is 1 : 1 and whose 'magnitude' is zero; or as a pitch, specifically the lowest pitch which can be played on a given string and whose 'magnitude' is the total length of that string. The former he called the 'unextended' unison, and the latter the 'extended' unison. One is capable of being 'extended' to produce other intervals; the other of being 'divided' to produce other pitches. Birchensha said nothing to indicate that he had clearly distinguished these two concepts in his own mind, and his phrase 'the radical unison' appears to be applied to both. But the distinction is useful for understanding Birchensha's many references to the unison and its properties, which can otherwise appear incoherent.

Chapters 4–8 introduce and discuss the correspondence between musical intervals and numerical ratios. Chapter 6 defines some of the terms discussed above; chapters 5 and 7 show how musical ratios can be manipulated arithmetically, and present a classification of them. Throughout this and his other discussions of the concept, the ratio corresponding to a particular musical interval is the ratio of the lengths of two strings, identical in respects other than length, which would produce, when struck, the interval in question. These ratios are often, but not always, considered in their lowest terms.

Addition of intervals or ratios is carried out by multiplying corresponding terms: the sum of $a : b$ and $c : d$ is $ac : bd$. To subtract we cross-multiply, so that the difference between $a : b$ and $c : d$ is $ad : bc$. Birchensha, in common with other writers on ratio theory of his time, consistently wrote of 'adding' and 'subtracting' ratios (which correspond to adding and subtracting musical intervals) when we might consider the operations in question to be more naturally characterized as multiplication and division. As a result his notions of 'multiplication' and 'division' correspond to what we would call raising to powers and taking roots. The 'multiplication' of a ratio by a number can be carried out by adding that ratio to itself repeatedly, or equivalently by raising each of its terms to the appropriate power: similarly a ratio can be 'divided' by a number by taking the appropriate root of each of its terms. (The operation which we would describe as dividing one musical interval by another is difficult to perform in this scheme, requiring the use of logarithms, and Birchensha does not attempt it.)

Ratios are subjected to a threefold classification: they are either equal to the ratio of equality, 1 : 1, or they are ratios of greater or of lesser inequality depending on whether the first or the second term is the greater. Considering only ratios of greater inequality the further classification, in modern notation, amounts to the following. A ratio $a : b$ is a multiplex ratio if a is an exact multiple of b; in a superparticular ratio a is one greater than b. In a superpartient ratio a is greater than $b + 1$ but less than $2b$. In a multiplex superparticular ratio a is one more than an exact multiple of b, and in a multiplex superpartient ratio a lies between $kb + 1$ and $(k + 1)b$ for some k.

This presentation as a whole is quite routine. It perhaps derives ultimately from the classification of ratios in Boethius' *De arithmetica* (itself dependent on Nicomachus), but we have no way to determine exactly where Birchensha had obtained his fairly standard material. In chapter 4, however, he presented an alternative classification of musical ratios which seems to be entirely his own. It is concerned, broadly speaking, with the relationship of particular musical ratios to the set of ratios which correspond to simple consonances. Such a strategy has the potential to make meaningful links between the musical and mathematical terminology in use, but Birchensha did not really pursue the matter systematically enough to achieve more than a further layer of terminological complexity.

Chapters 9–14 discuss the set of pitches that are to be placed within the octave or within two octaves. Birchensha presented several different organizing principles which bore on this placement of pitches, and did not stop to ponder how they might relate – or fail to relate – to one another. Thus chapter 9 lists the pitches which result from the extension of the cycle of fifths to include double sharps and double flats; chapter 10 discusses the division of the two-octave system into tetrachords on what is ultimately a Greek model; chapter 11 enumerates the permutations of tones and semitones within a fourth, a fifth or an octave; and chapters 13 and 14 introduce the three genera of ancient Greek music and the pitches which they add to the diatonic scale. These chapters are thematically coherent but disparate in content; the resulting proliferation of possible placements of pitches perhaps had more consequences for Birchensha's 'Grand Scale' than for his treatise.

The most striking feature of these chapters is Birchensha's insistence on a diatonic scale which is Pythagorean in the sense that every octave, fourth and fifth is pure, with ratios $2:1$, $4:3$ and $3:2$ respectively. This results in major seconds of $9:8$ and major thirds of $81:64$; but Birchensha nowhere refers to the fact that these impure thirds, and the resulting impure sixths, were almost universally considered unacceptable by theorists of this period. Nor are Pythagorean thirds, on the whole, useable in performing the music of the period, and Birchensha therefore presents us, as in the table of consonant intervals mentioned above, with the puzzle that his theoretical prescriptions were surely inconsistent with his practice as a performer.[143]

The final group of chapters within the 'Mathematical Part of Music', chapters 15–21, deals with 'medieties'. This is another section of material which Birchensha could have found in Boethius, concerned with pairs of ratios $a:b$, $c:d$. If $b = c$ the two ratios form a 'conjoined' mediety, whereas if they are unequal the mediety is 'disjoined'. If the two ratios are equal

---

[143]   This could help to explain why Birchensha had difficulty with the Royal Society's dichord, if he was accustomed in practice to something closer to equal temperament than to the Pythagorean system he espoused in theory. See Mark Lindley, *Lutes, Viols and Temperaments* (Cambridge, New York and Melbourne, 1984), pp. 9–18.

($a : b = c : d$) then they form a 'geometrical' mediety. If the differences $a - b$ and $c - d$ are equal they form an 'arithmetical' mediety. If the differences of reciprocals are equal ($1/a - 1/b = 1/c - 1/d$) then they form a 'harmonical' mediety. Birchensha on the whole gives a reasonably clear presentation of these various cases, with musical examples, although he makes some errors in the examples, and gives a very garbled presentation of one of the simpler cases, conjoined arithmetical mediety. His point in presenting this material is that such mathematical structures help to systematize the production of new musical intervals by the subdivision or stacking-up of others. This strategy matches the overall aim of the 'Mathematical Part of Music', which seems to be to use mathematics to produce musical knowledge or even to embody it: a role more usually assigned to the musical performer, who is conspicuously absent from this part of Birchensha's writings.

The next 'mathematical part of music' we have is that in Birchensha's 1672 'Animadversion'. The brevity of this text is such that it is difficult to discern more than that it refers to recognizably the same kind of treatise as the 'Compendious Discourse'. While it refers to some of the same matters as the 'Discourse' – the scale and its division, the equality, inequality and arithmetic of intervals, the three medieties, the genera and the types of ratios – its omissions are more likely to result from compressed presentation than from decisions to exclude material from the treatise.

On the other hand, certain elements appear here which do not seem to have parallels in either the 'Discourse' or the 1664 letter: sections on 'the Principles of a Musical Magnitude, what, and how manyfold they are, and how they are conjoyned', and on 'the Contact, Section, Congruity, Adscription of a Musical Body [and] Of the Commensurability thereof.' Sadly, these hints are now beyond interpretation; but they do indicate that the proposed content of the 'mathematical part of music' had undergone some development during the preceding eight or so years.

Birchensha's 1676 'Account' of *Syntagma musicæ* is rather less brief, and its similarities to and differences from the 'Compendious Discourse' are correspondingly more telling. The 'mathematical part', now divided into 19 numbered sections, still begins with a discussion of 'What it is', followed by axioms. The arithmetic of musical ratios now follows immediately, preceding Birchensha's idiosyncratic classification of the ratios as well as, apparently, the discussion of 'what they are' and their 'species', the latter probably referring to their classification as multiplex, superparticular and so on.

By the tenth section out of 19 we have reached 'musical medieties', which are now contained in a single section, by contrast with their sprawl across seven chapters out of 21 in the 'mathematical part' of the 'Compendious Discourse'. The twelfth section appears to be the longest and most complex, dealing with Birchensha's 'Perfect and Compleat Scale of Musick'; this is the only occasion when Birchensha made it explicit that *Syntagma musicæ* was to contain a commentary on the 'Grand Scale' (to be discussed below).

Sections 14 to 19 seem perhaps to deal with the 'geometrical' part of music, implying that up to this point we have been dealing with the 'arithmetical' part of music, although this is not made explicit. This contrasts with the 'Compendious Discourse', where the arithmetical and geometrical parts of music were clearly distinguished only in the two initial lists of axioms, and where the giving of these two sets of axioms consecutively implied that the two 'parts' were to be considered in parallel. This 'geometrical part' seems to have been a somewhat haphazard grouping, however, since section 16 was to deal with 'a Musical Magnitude; and what it is' and section 17 with 'the Longitude, Latitude, and Crassitude of Sounds, Physically and Relatively considered'. 'Magnitude' was Birchensha's term for the length of the portion of a musical string bounded by a particular interval, as opposed to the ratio between the two string lengths involved; while longitude, latitude and crassitude, terms which he took over from Lippius and Alsted, were probably meant to refer to the temporal duration, dynamics and pitch of musical sounds.

Chapters 15, 18 and 19 deal, tantalizingly, with a 'circular scale of sounds', which is discussed nowhere else and which seems impossible to reconstruct from the information given here. It is apparently distinct from the 'Grand Scale', and may have owed something to the derivation of musical intervals from geometrical constructions superimposed upon the circle found in the *Harmonices mundi* (1619) of Johannes Kepler. That Birchensha had by this stage been in contact with Thomas Salmon is also suggestive in this respect, since Salmon made much of the 'circulation' of the octave in his books and was probably responsible for a striking circular depiction of the octave published in 1684.[144] Circular octaves had also appeared in other sources, for example the *Compendium musicæ* of Descartes (1650) and its English translation (1653): but with so little information it is probably idle to speculate about Birchensha's intentions.[145]

The official minute of Birchensha's appearance at the Royal Society on 10 February 1675/6 adds very little to our knowledge of *Syntagma musicæ*, only some slender hints about the 'Grand Scale'. Birchensha's only comment here that bears interpretation is that all tones are the same size, likewise all

---

[144] Anon., 'The Musicall Compass', [London, 1684]. Salmon's authorship of this pamphlet is suggested by similarities of language between it and his 1688 *Proposal to Perform Musick*, notably the concept of the 'circulation' of the octave; see Benjamin Wardhaugh, *Music, Experiment and Mathematics in England, 1653–1705* (Farnham and Burlington, VT, 2008), pp. 170–71.

[145] E.g. Descartes, *Compendium*, p. 35; trans. Charleton, p. 35. See Benjamin Wardhaugh, 'Musical logarithms in the seventeenth century: Descartes, Mercator, Newton', *Historia mathematica*, 35 (2008): 19–36.

semitones, semiditones, ditones and so on.[146] This statement is, strictly, true of Birchensha's Pythagorean system, where, since no temperament is ever performed and the purity of tuning is consequently allowed to result in an inexorable proliferation of pitches, identically named intervals are always exactly equal. But such a statement could be misunderstood by taking it to refer to a division of the octave into twelve equal semitones, resulting in six equal tones, four equal minor thirds and three equal major thirds, and it is possible that this or a similar description of Birchensha's scale was responsible for the confusing passage in Baynard's correspondence discussed above.

Responses of Wallis and Mercator

As mentioned above, Birchensha's mathematical ideas attracted a number of responses. That of the Oxford mathematician and Savilian Professor of Geometry John Wallis arose during May 1664, in correspondence with Henry Oldenburg. In a letter of 4 May, now lost, Oldenburg described the letter Birchensha had recently written to the Royal Society. In reply Wallis wrote about music on 7, 14 and 25 May.[147] Wallis' second letter gave an elaborate description of a tuning system which he asserted was original, claiming not to have seen the work of modern musical theorists. This was clearly untrue, since the scheme he presented was essentially that of Zarlino, and although we cannot identify Wallis' specific source with any confidence it is clear that the content of this letter was derived from reading rather than cogitation alone. In his next letter Wallis admitted to some relevant reading; but his previous letter had meanwhile been read at the meeting of the Royal Society on 18 May. Although Wallis proved to have seen some modern mathematical music theory, there is nothing in his letters to invalidate his claim to ignorance about Birchensha's ideas in particular, and it is therefore needless to discuss them further here.

The response to Birchensha's ideas by Nicolaus Mercator, though brief, is a little more substantial, in that it seems to be based on a small amount of apparently correct information about Birchensha's musical theory. Mercator (1620–87) seems to have been interested in the mathematical theory of music since at least 1653: various manuscript texts, plus a printed prospectus, exist, most of which can be tentatively dated to the mid-1650s. Versions of some of these were seen by Robert Hooke, John Aubrey and William Holder at various times later in the century.[148] Mercator's manuscript discussion of Birchensha

---

[146]   Birch, *The History of the Royal Society*, vol. 3, p. 296.

[147]   *The Correspondence of Henry Oldenburg*, vol. 2, pp. 179–203.

[148]   Mercator's musical writings are in: Oxford, Bodleian Library, MS Aubrey 25, fols 1–25, 32–43; Oxford, Christ Church Library, MSS 1130, 1187; and London, Guildhall Library, MS 51757 21. See Wardhaugh, 'Musical logarithms'.

is independent of his other musical writings, but its existence confirms at least that his opinion on mathematical music was valued by some.

It is found in the same volume of the John Pell papers – British Library, Add. MS 4388 – which contains Pell's calculations upon the 'Grand Scale', occupying fols 39–44. The text is in Mercator's hand, and, though it is unsigned and undated, sophisticated appeals to the measurement and comparison of musical intervals point clearly to Mercator as its author. It is not strictly incomplete either grammatically or logically, but it does both begin and end rather abruptly, and could well have been part of a larger text about music – either a treatise or a letter. Perhaps Pell had solicited an opinion on Birchensha from Mercator; but Pell's papers are in such disorder that we cannot assume that the appearance of this document among them is more than accidental.[149]

The subject of the text was the sizes of the diminished fourth and the major third; specifically 'whether the Eares of our Practitioners will judge that false. Fourth of Mr Berchinshaw's, v[i]z 57344/59049, or that of mine, v[i]z 7/9, to be right'.[150] This appeal to the testimony of the ears was alien to Birchensha's approach to musical mathematics (and to Mercator's), and neither of the ratios mentioned appeared in any tuning theory of the period. The ratio 7 : 9 is baffling because the diminished fourth did not normally have a simple pure ratio, because it would have implied impure major thirds of $3 : \sqrt{14}$ (or, perhaps, one of 4 : 5 and another of 45 : 56: neither possibility is really plausible), and because of the rarity of interval ratios using the number 7 at this time. (Conceivably Mercator had become aware by some means of the unpublished musical ideas of Christiaan Huygens, who had hinted at the use of ratios involving the number 7 as consonances in a draft in 1661, and would fully articulate it in another in 1690.[151]) The ratio given for Birchensha's diminished fourth was even odder, being ludicrously narrow, smaller than half a semitone. It can be factorized into small numbers – it is equal to $7 \times 2^{13} : 3^{10}$ – which makes it unlikely to be a mere slip of the pen, but does nothing to explain it. The presence of the number 7 here as well is justified by nothing in Birchensha's surviving writings.

There followed an elaborate section of working in which Mercator purported to deduce the interval structure of Birchensha's chromatic scale from little more than the information that it contained a large number of pure fifths and pure tones. He derived a set of pitches from the cycle of fifths, and explained that any reordering of the resulting seven diatonic and five chromatic semitones would reduce the number of pure fifths and tones: a

---

[149]   London, British Library, Add. MS 4388, fols 39ʳ–44ʳ.

[150]   Ibid., fol. 39ʳ.

[151]   H. Floris Cohen, *Quantifying Music: The Science of Music at the First Stage of the Scientific Revolution, 1580–1650* (Dordrecht, 1984), pp. 214, 226–8.

curious strategy, since the suggestion of reordering the semitones rendered irrelevant the derivation of the scale from the cycle of fifths.[152]

Next, Mercator illustrated the different sizes of the intervals in his own favoured tuning compared with Birchensha's and, for reference, with equal temperament, using a diagram. Mercator's own preference seems to have been for the mean-tone scale, which he had discussed in his other musical writings. He explained that certain pairs of augmented triads and their inversions (such as c–e–g♯ and c–e–a♭), though differentiated in common musical experience, would be indistinguishable in equal temperament, and claimed, without much attempt to provide evidence, that the relative sizes of major thirds and diminished fourths in his own scale matched those of musical practice. The diagram showed that certain pitches in Birchensha's scheme were twice as distant from Mercator's positions for them as from those of equal temperament, and Mercator concluded that, since equal temperament distorted certain chords, Birchensha's scheme must distort them even more. Thus Birchensha's scale was not merely different from common practice but must be intolerable to the ear.[153]

The argument is not wholly convincing, essentially because of the questions which Mercator ignored – how did he make his diagram for the three tuning schemes and on what data was it based? what common musical experience gave detailed information about the sound of augmented triads in their various inversions? But a twelve-pitch 'Pythagorean' scale like Birchensha's was indeed problematic for use even in a small range of keys, and the mean-tone scale did produce better results in some circumstances. That Mercator's text failed to justify his conclusions in full may simply indicate that it is incomplete.

Mercator wrote that 'It is the truth I seek, and it shall be as wellcome to mee, if I find it on his side, as if I should find it on my side'. Perhaps his purpose in this text was simply to clarify for his own satisfaction the essential differences between the three tuning systems (Pythagorean, equal temperament and mean-tone) and the possibility of distinguishing between them aurally.

The 'Philosophical Part of Music'

The 1671 'Animadversion' introduced a new section into Birchensha's musical treatise: the 'philosophical part' of music, parallel to its 'practical' and 'mathematical' parts. Although the appearance of the 'philosophical part' is perhaps the most substantial overall change to occur in Birchensha's descriptions of his project, its proposed contents are regrettably obscure. In the 'Animadversion' they are as follows:

---

[152] London, British Library, Add. MS 4388, fols 39^r–42^r.

[153] Ibid., fols 42^v–44^v.

Of Sounds generated, produc'd, diffus'd in their *Medium*: Of their Deference
to the Organ of Hearing; of their Reception there, and wonderful Effects:
Of the Matter, Form, Quantity, and Quality of Musical Bodies or Sounds.
That all Musical Sounds are originally in the Radix, or Unison; and of
their Fluxion out of it: Of the General, and Special Kinds, Differences,
Properties, and Accidents of Sounds. Of the Truth and Falshood of Sounds.

All of this material was new, apart from the origin of sounds in the unison,
which had previously appeared in the 'mathematical part'. The notion that
intervals were produced by derivation from the unison had been discussed in
the 'Compendious Discourse', but the specific meaning of the word 'fluxion'
is a mystery, as are the meanings of most of the other terms in this passage.
They suggest, though, that the 'philosophical part' here was intended to be
concerned with the physical nature of musical sound, an interest which was
not to be found in Birchensha's earlier accounts of his work.

The 1676 'Account' introduced more new material to the 'philosophical
part', as well as new sections in the 'mathematical part' which seem to echo
its concerns. Music was now said to be a sister to the other arts, and was not
based on arithmetic or geometry: this was a revision of the view implied by the
'Compendious Discourse' in which there was a clear sense in which musical
rules were founded upon mathematical ones.

The origin and nature of sounds were now to be developed at length, and
we learn a little more about the relationship of other intervals to the unison:
they took their nature 'according to the quantity of its sonorous nature which
they receive from it'. And the division of the string would show how much
of the nature of the unison was in every other interval. Otherwise, we are
again faced with lists of terms which in the absence of fuller information
can only baffle. The musical scale was built up from several 'Totums', which
were the basic kinds of intervals. There were three kinds of unisons, artificial,
natural and accidental. Each sound was both flat and sharp, both correlated
and radical, depending on what it was taken to be relative to; likewise it
was at once consonant, concinnous and dissonant. Musical intervals had
being, existence and duration, each imaginarily (in our minds), audibly (in
the medium) and objectively (in a system of music). Each interval was in
itself 'one, true, good, ordinate, perfect, and beautiful'; it might be active or
passive; intervals were mutually related (Birchensha perhaps meant that each
interval could be considered either in itself or as the difference between two
others), so that each could be considered both cause and effect, measured or
measuring. Sounds had quantity, quality, place, time and motion, and could
be considered 'physically' as created by an instrument, or 'relatively' as sound
in itself. Certain items seem to deal with the physical nature of sound and
consonance. For example, 'There is a force and vertue in Sounds to work on
Recipient Bodies, and on the Affections of those who hear them'; 'the unison
in Music is as the Soul in the Body of man, sc. Totum in Toto, et in qualibet

parte'. It appears that Birchensha was trying to develop a theory of the nature of sound capable of a very detailed taxonomy, but it is extremely difficult to discern anything of its content from these headings.

Birchensha's 'Grand Scale' and John Pell

One of the sources for Birchensha's mathematical ideas, John Pell's copy of what seems to be a text authored by Birchensha and connected with a public lecture he gave in June 1665, is concerned entirely with the description of what he there called his 'Grand Scale'.[154] In his letter of 1664 Birchensha promised to 'draw a grand System, which shall containe and comprehend the whole body of the Mathematical part of Musick', and of which the Royal Society's library would receive a copy. The description of 1665, although it does no more than make promises, can probably be taken to imply that a more elaborate version of the 'Scale' now actually existed and was displayed at this lecture. Certainly by the time of Birchensha's visit to the Royal Society in February 1676 the 'Scale' existed in a developed manuscript, and it is possible that it had been engraved by that date.

The various descriptions of the 'Grand Scale' suggest that it would have been, at its most basic, a large table showing letter-names and ratios for all the notes and intervals obtained when an octave scale is transposed into a wide range of keys, probably laid out in such a way that the entire table would span a 'disdiapason' or double octave from A to aa. From the 'Compendious Discourse' (Mathematical Part, chapter 9) it appears that in order to 'complete a perfect scale of musick in the diatonic, & permixed (commonly called the Chromatic) Genus' Birchensha envisaged expanding his table of 'practicable' consonant and dissonant intervals (Figure 3.3) by allowing every note from A to G in its flat, natural and sharp positions to function as the 'assumed unison' or keynote. If the scale structure of the horizontal rows remained the same, the enlarged table would have contained 63 different pitches and 34 different pitch-classes, with every double flat and double sharp except B double sharp represented at least once.[155] He considered it important that the relative string

---

[154] On the 'Grand Scale' see particularly Leta E. Miller, 'John Birchensha and the Early Royal Society: Grand Scales and Scientific Composition', *Journal of the Royal Musical Association*, 115 (1990): 63–79.

[155] The missing pitch-class, B double sharp, would however have been needed if Birchensha had placed an extra column between his columns for the minor and major seconds, showing the apotome above the keynote. This addition would have given reversible symmetry to the array of intervals by mirroring the column for the semidiapason (which comes between the columns for the minor and major sevenths).

lengths for these notes should be shown; such numerical information would have been laborious though not particularly difficult to prepare.[156]

Birchensha's letter to the Royal Society of 1664 indicated that his 'grand System' would demonstrate not only 'the Ration, Habitude, Difference, Exces, Quality, Dimension and Magnitude' of intervals, but also 'all things, that doe concerne the Moods, Tetrachords, and Musical Genus's'. One cannot do more than speculate about how this material would have been presented. It is possible, for example, to imagine Greek note names being placed in columns to either side of a 'Disdiapasonick' table of the kind described above, from 'Proslambanomenos' (A) to 'Mese' (a) and from 'Mese' to 'Nete hyperbolaion' (aa); but incorporating the semitones of the chromatic genus and the dieses of the enharmonic genus (with their mathematical proportions) into such a table would have posed a greater challenge. Such things might have been more satisfactorily shown separately, as might the various classes of intervals produced between all of these pitch-classes. Wallis, Pell and Mercator all drew or outlined tables in which the ratios between notes were recorded in a two-dimensional array, with the notes themselves listed on two sides.[157]

By June 1665 the supplementary information had become much more elaborate, and defies summary. The text consists of a list of 33 items of information which 'My Grand Scale doth comprehend and demonstrate'. These include the positions of all notes relative to the unison, the sizes of all intervals and the different species of ratios, as well as various arithmetical relations, including the three 'medieties', showing the generation, interrelationship and

---

[156]   The 34 pitch-classes would have formed a long chain of fifths from F double flat to E double sharp, each fifth involving a decrease in string length of one third (and possibly also a doubling, so as to remain within a compass of two octaves). The smallest number which can undergo 33 such decreases without involving fractions – the smallest possible string length for F double flat – is 3^{33}, a 16-digit number.

[157]   Although it dates from fifty years later, the 'Scheme' produced by William Jackson in *c*.1726 gives an inkling of what the 'Grand Scale' might have looked like. The 'Scheme' consists of an enormous bifolio, with a musical string depicted at its left-hand edge: aligned with this, and stretching across the page to the right, are eighteen columns recording a wide range of information including the names of musical intervals, their corresponding ratios and their sizes in commas and fractions of a comma. At the top of the page, between two supplementary tables (the upper reaches of the musical string and the correct positions of pitches on a violin) appear verbal explanations of this information: an explanatory pamphlet was also produced. Despite a broad similarity of intention there is nothing to connect Jackson's work with that of Birchensha. See William Jackson, *A Scheme demonstrating the Perfection and Harmony of Sounds* ([London, *c*.1726]); idem, *A preliminary discourse to A scheme, demonstrating the perfection and harmony of sounds. / By William Jackson, M.M. [Music Master]* ([London, *c*.1735]); Jamie Croy Kassler, *The Science of Music in Britain, 1714–1830: A Catalogue of Writings, Lectures and Inventions* (2 vols, New York and London, 1979), vol. 1, pp. 572–4.

division of intervals. Birchensha also proposed to show the relationship of all this to consonance, as well as displaying certain specific relationships such as, for example, the excess of six tones over an octave.

The information given would also cover the three Greek genera, and the division of tones and the types of semitones which would result. Birchensha would also show the five tetrachords (implying that this version of the 'Scale' covered two octaves), with the names and properties of the strings that formed them. Returning to the diatonic scale, Birchensha mentioned the species of fourths, fifths and octaves, and the gamut and the modes. Finally he suggested that 'you may trie the trueth of any Monochord' using the scale.

Much of this, in fact, reads like a list of the contents of the 'Compendious Discourse', and most of it was not associated with the 'Grand Scale' in the letter of 1664. It is difficult to imagine how all of this information could have been contained actually within the 'Scale' itself: some of it would surely have been expounded in a commentary, which might well have been identical with *Syntagma musicæ*. At this stage Birchensha may have been thinking of his project as based around the 'Grand Scale'.

The suggestion of testing a monochord using the scale is striking, and it recalls the incident at the Royal Society, less than a year before the talk at which this description of the 'Scale' was presented, when Birchensha himself had been tested by the monochord and found wanting.

The later descriptions of the 'Grand Scale' are much less full than that of 1665, placing in the 'mathematical part' and 'practical part' of music much material that in the 1665 text was incorporated into the scale. The 1672 'Animadversion' innovated only by stating specifically that the scale would be in 'intire numbers', integers, a point which had not been made by Birchensha before (although it was a feature of Pell's 1666 calculations). In other respects what was described in 1672 was simply a scale of pitches upon which would be indicated the intervals and their ratios.

In the 1676 'Account' the basic contents of the scale were again the intervals with their subdivisions and ratios, and the Greek genera. Here there was, for the first time, the assertion that the scale would show 'the denominations and characters of notes': that is, their names and their notation. It would also show 'pauses, signed keys and signs of the moode'. It is hard to imagine how an exposition of musical notation could have been integrated coherently into what was still essentially a table of string lengths: Birchensha was surely envisaging a supplementary commentary when he made these promises.

The entry in the Royal Society's 'Journal Book' for Birchensha's visit in 1676 adds that the scale would show all of this information in relation to a string 36 inches long: a curious detail, but one which suggests that even at this stage the 'Grand Scale' had not wholly lost its connection with the tuning of real instruments or perhaps the demonstration of Birchensha's ideas on a real monochord.

Finally, extensive calculations, and a version of the 'Grand Scale', were made by the mathematician John Pell (1611–85) in early 1666. They are now in British Library, Add. MS 4388, with the bulk of Pell's other notes on music. On one sheet (fol. 18^v) he showed how 'Mr Berchinshaw's Scale' – in this instance a 12-note chromatic scale of A (including B♭, C♯, E♭, F♯ and a♭) – might be expressed numerically, using the ratio 2304 : 1152 ($3^2 \times 2^8 : 3^2 \times 2^7$) to represent the octave A–a, as Birchensha himself had done in the 'Compendious Discourse' (fol. 15^r; see p. 000). On fol. 20^r Pell multiplied the figures by 81, giving A–a the ratio 186,624 : 93,312 ($3^6 \times 2^8 : 3^6 \times 2^7$). His next step, on fol. 18^r (dated 'Febr. 12 1665[/6]') and fols 26^v–27^r, was to create a 21-note scale: he split each apotome into a diatonic semitone and a comma, so that F–F♯–G–a♭–a became F–G♭–F♯–G–a♭–G♯–a, and also admitted the notes E♯ (between F and G♭), B♯ (between C and D♭), F♭ (between D♯ and E) and C♭ (between A♯ and B). On fol. 30^r (dated 'Tuesday morning Febr. 13. 1666/65') he converted this into a 33-note scale by incorporating the additional pitches obtained if the lower note of each diatonic semitone is raised by a diesis. Having multiplied all his numbers again by 55,296 ($3^3 \times 2^{11}$) in order to avoid fractions, and having calculated the dieses, Pell finally produced a complete mathematical table of this 33-note scale, expressed in ten- or eleven-digit integers (fol. 37^r). The full scale runs: A, A diesis, B♭, A♯, A♯ diesis, C♭, B, B diesis, C, B♯, B♯ diesis, D♭, C♯, C♯ diesis, D, D diesis, E♭, D♯, D♯ diesis, F♭, E, E diesis, F, E♯, E♯ diesis, G♭, F♯, F♯ diesis, G, G diesis, a♭, G♯, G♯ diesis, a.[158]

Why did Pell make these calculations? The neatness of some of the working and of the final tables (some of which are carefully ruled and use different inks to distinguish string lengths from note-numbers) suggest possibly that the work was intended to be transmitted to others, and therefore that it was the result of a specific request. Conceivably that request was Birchensha's, since one page of related jottings (fol. 21^v) bears the note: 'Thirsday Febr. / I gave Mr Birchens[ha] / a coppy of this'.[159]

---

[158]   A is given the number 10,319,560,704; a, its octave, is consequently half that (5,159,780,352). On fol. 16 Pell sets out 'the way by which I found my long numbers for Mr Birchensha's scale'. Even he seems to have nodded at this late stage in his calculations, for he places the notes A♯ diesis, B♯ diesis, D♯ diesis and E♯ diesis at the arithmetical midpoints not of the diatonic semitone (A♯–B, B♯–C♯, D♯–E, E♯–F♯) but of the twice diminished third (A♯–C♭, B♯–D♭, D♯–F♭, E♯–G♭).

[159]   The date is incomplete in the manuscript: possibly 15 February 1665/6 (which fell on a Thursday) is meant. Pell's choice of words ('I gave Mr Birchensha a coppy', rather than 'I sent Mr Birchensha a coppy') is striking, and does not suggest the use of an intermediary. From July 1665 to July 1669 Pell lived at Brereton Hall in Cheshire as a guest of his former pupil William, Lord Brereton, and (unlike Brereton) he seems not to have returned to London at all during that period: see Malcolm and Stedall, *John Pell*, pp. 198–213.

This response to Birchensha's ideas displays a rather more substantial acquaintance with their content than the responses of Wallis or Mercator, but it nonetheless tells us nothing new about Birchensha himself, except possibly that the mathematical labour of actually producing the 'Grand Scale' was to be delegated to someone else; and it serves to illustrate how substantial that labour might have been.

'To reduce all the Parts of Musick to a Regularity and Just order'

What is known of Birchensha's earlier life provides little or no preparation for the minor stir he caused in intellectual and musical circles in Restoration London. Even if he studied at Trinity College, Dublin, as we have surmised he may have done, there is nothing to indicate that he excelled in the art and science of music as a young man, except perhaps for acquiring skill on the viol. Such evidence as there is, in fact, seems to point to him having come to composing and theorizing late, and being largely self-taught; and it is not unknown for self-taught late starters to display (outwardly at least) a proud and stubborn independence of mind. It is worth reflecting that when he made his first appearance before the Royal Society in 1664, he may already have been in his late fifties; when he made his last in 1676, he may have been in his early seventies.

The idea that the philosophical, mathematical and practical aspects of music are interdependent lies at the heart of Birchensha's theorizing. The synopsis that he provided for the Royal Society in 1676 of his projected book, *Syntagma musicæ*, ends with him affirming his intention 'to reduce all the Parts of Musick to a Regularity and Just order' and thereby 'bring the Philosophical, Mathematical, and Practical parts of Music to analogize and agree in all things'. Twelve years earlier, in the preface to *Templum musicum*, he had argued that 'it is as necessary for a perfect and complete Musician to understand the Proportion of Sounds, as for a curious Painter, exactly to know the Symmetry of every part of a Body'. This attitude probably helps to explain why at the beginning of Corbett's manuscript of the 'Rules of Composition' the pupil is presented with the sonorous body of material he or she has to work with, in the shape of a 'Table to find out all Consonant and Dissonant Intervals in an Octave' in a wide range of keys. It also accounts for the assiduousness with which Birchensha set out to perfect his 'Grand Scale'.

Some who knew Birchensha in the early 1660s clearly saw him as a man with interesting, original and well-thought-out ideas. One such was Captain Silas Taylor, his disciple, champion and friend, who when in London acted as an intermediary between him and the natural philosophers and 'virtuosi' of the Royal Society. Henry Oldenburg, the Society's secretary, loyally helped to spread Birchensha's name at home and abroad, by means of correspondence with fellows or in the pages of the *Philosophical Transactions*, over a period of a dozen years or more. Throughout that time the president was the music-loving mathematician, Viscount Brouncker. He, too, appears to have been supportive, though we do not know what his private views were. What is surprising is that (with the possible exception of Mercator) none of the members of the Society who might have been in a position to take issue with the mathematical aspects of Birchensha's theories or question their compatibility with the tuning of real seventeenth-century instruments – Brouncker, Boyle, Pell, Holder, Wallis, Hooke or Huygens, for example – seems to have done so, at least publicly. They can scarcely have claimed to be unaware of the Pythagorean basis of his thought. In his letter of 26 April 1664 to the Society Birchensha had openly invoked Pythagoras's name more than once; the music committee formed six days earlier had the opportunity to question him; and the 'Compendious Discourse' given to Boyle included tables of Pythagorean ratios. Instead, the Society encouraged his plan to publish *Syntagma musicæ*, and continued to treat him with respectful indulgence even as late as the mid-1670s. Though it might be argued that Pythagorean harmonic science represented more than just an antique tuning system,[160] Birchensha's letter made a point of attacking virtually all recent writing on the mathematics of music: 'the Proportions of most of those sounds, which are mentioned by all the writers of this Art, whose writings I have seene and perused (I say, Pythagoras excepted) are very much mistaken'.

Birchensha's appearance at the Royal Society during the series of musical experiments conducted in the summer of 1664 is emblematic of the promise held out by his ambivalent position as practitioner-cum-theorist, as well as of the failure of that promise, at least from the point of view of the experimentalists of the Society. Throughout this series of experiments they expressed an increasing degree of scepticism about the ability of their own ears to provide information useful in natural philosophy, which is why Birchensha was invited to the meeting on 10 August. What the Society wanted from him was to make use of his professional musical ear. The Society's Journal Book records: 'Mr Birchensha being called in, tuned the string by his ears, to find how near the practise of Musick did agree with the Theory of Proportions'. This was exactly what the fellows had been trying to find out the previous week, and they now appealed to the superior ability of Birchensha's ear to do so. But his appearance was a failure: 'The effect was, that he could not by his Ear distinguish any difference of Sounds (upon the moving of the bridge) above half an inch, especially in 4^{ths}. 3^{ds}. and Tones'. Assuming that the apparatus

---

[160]   Compare Daniel Chua's comment regarding Vincenzo Galilei's *Discorso particolare intorno all'unisono*: 'The system of equal temperament [...] is a method, whereas Pythagorean tuning is an ethos'. Daniel K.L. Chua, 'Vincenzo Galilei, Modernity and the Division of Nature', in *Music Theory and Natural Order from the Renaissance to the Early Twentieth Century*, ed. Suzannah Clark and Alexander Rehding (Cambridge and New York, 2001), pp. 17–29, at pp. 24–5.

used was the four-foot monochord (or dichord) described above, moving the bridge by half an inch from any of the intervals named would produce an error of between 20 and 25 cents, that is up to a quarter of a semitone. This is not a huge amount, but it ought to be perceptible by a competent musician. (The difference between the major and minor tones of just intonation, 8 : 9 and 9 : 10, for example, is 22 cents, and between the Pythagorean and mean-tone fourths it is 15 cents.) So Birchensha's ear – possibly not a very acute ear by musical standards – was rejected in favour of an instrument: 'it was resolved, that a Virginal should be as exactly tuned as could be done, by the Ear, and then the Monochord be examined by it'.[161]

This incident, and the recognition that the ear could not be relied upon to produce usefully precise information, was a turning point for the experimental study of musical acoustics at the Royal Society. In this sense Birchensha's failure to function as the experimental subject the Society expected – surely not a role he had planned to play – had consequences for the subsequent development of mathematical acoustics as a whole. The incident was also perhaps a turning point for Birchensha; certainly his visibility in the surviving sources declines after this point.

Oldenburg and his colleagues probably overrated Birchensha's intellectual powers and his musicianship. There are numerous places in his writings where human fallibility, either musical or mathematical, is apparent. Another problem seems to have been a compulsion to revise, redraft and reorganize his material. Signs of this can be seen, for example, in the variant versions of the 'Method' for applying the 'Rules of Composition', or in the differences between the 'Animadversion' and the subsequent synopsis of *Syntagma musicæ*. One senses that as late as 1676 Birchensha was still wrestling with the content and the organization of this *magnum opus*.

The failure of *Syntagma musicæ* to appear ultimately scotched any influence Birchensha might have had as a musical theorist. Nevertheless there must have been some – perhaps many – who valued what they had learned from their conversations and composition lessons with him. Arguably it took a society in which rational thought flourished, in which composers as skilful as Jenkins and Locke did not disdain to write two-part airs, and in which gentlemen were applauded if they could compose songs or improvise divisions, for Birchensha's rules to acquire the celebrity they did. Such a system of rules would never produce a Henry Purcell, but it had its modest place in the culture of the time. In a letter of 5 November 1700 to Arthur Charlett, the Master of University College, Oxford, Pepys expressed the view that more people would derive satisfaction from music, and invent compositions of their own, 'were the doctrine of it brought within the simplicity, perspicuity, and certainty

---

[161] Unfortunately the new strategy too had an obvious flaw: the virginal would need be tuned 'by the Ear', and would therefore be little more reliable than the ear itself. The proposed trial appears not to have been carried out.

common to all other the parts of mathematick knowledge'.[162] Another former pupil, Thomas Salmon, was undoubtedly remembering Birchensha's Second Rule of 'gradual motion in the upper part and saltation in the bass' when he wrote in 1672:

> 'Tis an incomparable pleasure to play an Airy Tune, or well contriv'd Consort; but to be Author of it, is a kind of unknown delight. I have heard many Scholars, in vain, importune their Masters for some directions to this purpose, that they would crown their pains and joys, with this last consummating kindness. [...] Did but a Scholar understand the mode of lessons, the smooth nature of a Treble, the proper movements of a leaping Base; how Consort is generally by Fifths, Thirds, and Eights, with some few directions for their use; he needs no more but to fancy what he would write down, and write down what he fancies.[163]

Such sentiments as these might almost have come from Birchensha himself.

The Sources

List of Birchensha's Writings with their Sources

Although an Editorial Note in each chapter gives detailed information on relevant sources, a consolidated list of Birchensha's writings on music with their sources may be useful here. The writings are arranged in approximate chronological order except for the 'Rules of Composition', the sources for which appear together at the end of the list; this is also the order adopted in our edition.

A. *Templum musicum* (London, 1664)

TEMPLUM MUSICUM: / OR THE / MUSICAL SYNOPSIS, / OF / The Learned and Famous / *Johannes-Henricus-Alstedius*, / BEING / A *Compendium* of the *Rudiments* / both of the *Mathematical* and / *Practical* Part of / MUSICK: / *Of which Subject not any Book is extant in our English* / Tongue. / – / Faithfully translated out of Latin / By *John Birchensha*. *Philomath*. / – / Imprimatur, *Feb. 5. 1663. Roger L'Estrange*. / – / *London*, Printed by *Will. Godbid* for *Peter Dring* at the / *Sun* in the *Poultrey* next Dore to the *Rose-Tavern*. / 1664.

---

[162]   *Private Correspondence and Miscellaneous Papers of Samuel Pepys*, vol. 2, p. 109.

[163]   Salmon, *An Essay to the Advancement of Musick*, pp. 88–9.

RISM B/VI, pp. 82–3; Wing's *Short-Title Catalogue*, A2926. Entered at Stationers' Hall, 5 February 1663/4. Contents: (a) Frontispiece, engraved by John Chantry, with verses by Birchensha (sig. A1^v). (b) 'Epistle Dedicatory' to Edward Montagu, first Earl of Sandwich (sigs A3^r–A6^v). (c) Preface, 'To all ingenious Lovers of Musick' (sigs A7^r–A8^v). (d) Translation of Book 20 of Johann Heinrich Alsted's *Encyclopædia* (Herborn, 1630; Lyons, 1649) (pp. 1–[94]). See Chapter I for (a), (b) and (c) only.

B. Letter to the Royal Society (26 April 1664)

London, Royal Society, Letter Book Original, vol. 1 (pp. 143–8): 'An Extract of / A letter / Written to the Royall Society, by Mr Bir- / shenshaw, concerning Musick'.
Not autograph. Also in Royal Society, Letter Book Copy, vol. 1 (pp. 166–73). See Chapter II.

C. 'A Compendious Discourse'

London, Royal Society, Boyle Papers, vol. 41 (fols 1–21): 'A Compendious Discourse / of the Principles of the / Practicall & Mathematicall / Partes of / Mvsick. / ∞ / Also, Directions how to make any kind of / Tune, or Ayre, without the helpe of the Voice, / or any other Musicall Instrument. / Written by John Birchensha, for the use of / the Honorable Robert Boyle Esquire.'
Contains: (a) Title page (fol. 2). (b) 'Principles and Elements of the Practicall part of Musick' (fols 3^r–6^r). (c) 'Observations' (fol. 6^v). (d) 'Principles and Elements of the Mathematicall Part of Musick' (fols 7^r–18^v). (e) Table of 'Contents' (fol. 19). (f) 'How to make any kind of Tune, Ayre, or Song, without the help of the voice, or any other Instrument' (fols 20^r–21^v). Birchensha's hand. See Chapter III.

D. Birchensha's description of his 'Grand Scale', 9 June 1665

London, British Library, Additional MS 4388 (fols 67^r–68^r): '[Mr Berchenshaw speakes] June 9. 1665.' John Pell's hand. See Chapter IV.

E. Preface to Salmon's *Essay to the Advancement of Musick* (1672)

AN / ESSAY / To the Advancement of / MUSICK, / BY / Casting away the Perplexity of / *DIFFERENT CLIFFS.* / And Uniting all sorts of Musick / *Lute, Viol, Violin,* } { *Organ, Harpsecord, Voice,* &c. / In one Universal Character. / – / *By* THOMAS SALMON, *Master* / *of Arts of* Trinity College *in* Oxford. / – / *Frustra fit per plura, quod fieri potest per pauciora.* /

LONDON, / Printed by *J. Macock*, and are to be Sold by / *John Car* at the *Middle-Temple-Gate*. 1672.

RISM B/VI, p. 749; Wing's *Short-Title Catalogue*, S417. Birchensha's preface occupies sigs A3ʳ–A5ʳ; it is headed 'THE / PUBLISHER / TO THE / READER' and signed 'Their Humble Servant / *John Birchensha.*' Not included in this edition.

F.   'Animadversion' for *Syntagma musicæ*, 1672

Printed sheet with caption title '*ANIMADVERSION.*', describing 'a Book preparing for the Press, (Intituled *SYNTAGMA MUSICÆ*)' by '*John Birchensha* Esq;'. At the foot is a subscription slip. The only known copy is in London, British Library, Add. MS 4388 (fol. 69). Its subscription slip is dated (partly in ink) 'The ⟨27.⟩ day of ⟨Dec.⟩ 1672.', and has Birchensha's signature and seal, but spaces for the subscriber's name are blank. Included in Wing's *A Gallery of Ghosts*, O B2941A. An edited version was published in *Philosophical Transactions*, 7/90 (20 January 1672/3), pp. 5153–4. See Chapter V.

G.   Synopsis of *Syntagma musicæ* for the Royal Society, 1675/6

London, Royal Society, Classified Papers, vol. 22 (1), no. 7 (fols 16ʳ–19ʳ): 'An Account / Of divers particulars remarkable in my Book; In which I will / write of Musick philosophically, mathematically, and practically'. Henry Oldenburg's hand. See Chapter VI.

H.   Birchensha's paper to the Royal Society, 10 February 1675/6

London, Royal Society, Journal Book Original, vol. 5 (pp. 141–3): secretarial minutes of the Royal Society's meeting on 10 February 1675/6, at which Birchensha 'presented himself to the Society, and shew'd them his Scale of Musick'. See Chapter VII.

I.   Rules of Composition, I: Silas Taylor's manuscript

London, British Library, Add. MS 4910 (fols 39–61): Captain Silas Taylor's 'Collection of Rules in Musicke'. The leaves containing 'Mʳ Birchensha's 6: Rules of Composition; & his Enlargements there-on to the Right Honᵇˡᵉ William Lord Viscount Brouncker' are partly in Birchensha's and partly in Taylor's hand. See Chapter VIII.

J. Rules of Composition, II: William Corbett's manuscript

Brussels, Bibliothèque Royale de Belgique, MS II 4168 Mus.: notebook containing the Rules of Composition, made for an unknown pupil. Largely or wholly in Birchensha's hand. See Chapter IX.

K. Rules of Composition, III: Francis Withey's manuscript

Oxford, Christ Church, MS Mus. 337 (fols [36–45]): Francis Withey's commonplace book, bound with his copy of Christopher Simpson's *A Compendium of Practical Musick* (London, 1667). Withey's hand. See Chapter X.

Birchensha's Autograph Hand

Among the sources listed above are four which we consider to be partly or wholly in Birchensha's hand:

C. 'A Compendious Discourse'

London, Royal Society, Boyle Papers, vol. 41 (fols 1–21). Fols 2–21 appear to be entirely autograph, including the original page numbers, but excluding the modern foliation. Fol. 2 is a title-page in formal italic hand, including the author's name. Fols 3–21 are written in a variety of styles – italic, secretary, mixtures of the two, even traces of an 'engrossing' hand (on fol. 12^v) – and contain many authorial corrections. Examples of Birchensha's music hand appear on fols 4^r–4^v and 20^r–21^v. *c.*1664–65? See Figures 3.1 (fol. 2^r), 3.2 (fol. 5^r), 3.3 (fol. 6^r), 3.4 (fol. 11^r) and 3.5 (fol. 12^v).

F. 'Animadversion' for *Syntagma musicæ*

London, British Library, Add. MS 4388 (fol. 69). This printed sheet bears Birchensha's signature and seal. December 1672. See Figure 5.1.

I. Rules of Composition, I: Silas Taylor's manuscript

London, Add. MS 4910 (fols 39–61). As Silas Taylor's annotations make clear, the first layer of his manuscript of the 'Rules of Composition' was written by Birchensha (*c.*1659–60?), and the second layer was copied by Taylor himself (*c.*1664–65). Birchensha here uses a different type of G clef from the one he adopts in Sources C and J. See Figures 8.1 and 8.2 (fols 50^v–51^r), where the top two systems of fol. 50^v and the top 18 lines of fol. 51^r – down to Taylor's note in red ink, 'Thus farre Mr Birchensha himselfe to mee S.T.' – are in Birchensha's hand; the remainder is in Taylor's hand.

J.   Rules of Composition, II: William Corbett's manuscript

Brussels, Bibliothèque Royale de Belgique, MS II 4168 Mus. As in Source C,
   the styles of handwriting employed for both text and music vary widely,
   from formal engrossing and italic hands (fol. 2^r) to a few hastily dashed-off
   music examples and comments; but most if not all appears to be autograph.
   The formal music hand here is similar to that in Source C. *c*.1667–72? See
   Figures 9.1 (fol. 2^r), 9.2 (fol. 4^r) and 9.3 (fol. 36^r inverted).

Transcription Policy

Our aim in preparing this critical edition has been to strike a balance between
fidelity to the original texts and ease of use for the reader. These texts have been
drawn from a dozen or so seventeenth-century sources, mostly manuscript.
While focussing primarily on the theoretical content of Birchensha's writings,
the editors have tried to convey something of the character of each principal
source. Additions and alterations have been kept to a minimum. Throughout
the edition, original page or folio numbers are shown in square brackets,
although their original sequence has not always been strictly followed, either
because of the need to exclude extraneous material (as in Chapters VIII
and X) or so as to present Birchensha's own material in a more coherent
and logical order (as in Chapters VI and X). For texts where more than one
source exists, as is the case with the Royal Society's journal books and letter
books and the 'Animadversion' for *Syntagma musicæ* (see Chapters II, V and
VII), priority has been given to the earliest and most authoritative. Where
more than one hand was involved in compiling a text (as in Chapter VIII),
editorial glosses have been supplied in order to make clear who wrote what.
From an editorial point of view, the largest and most challenging source is
the holograph manuscript of the 'Compendious Discourse'. Though destined
for the use of Robert Boyle, it would be an exaggeration to describe it as a
fair copy: Birchensha's handwriting is extremely variable in style, there are
numerous deletions, alterations, interpolations and even some uncorrected
mistakes, extensive use is made of contractions (some standard, others not)
and the punctuation is often erratic.

Throughout the volume, standard contractions of short words in common
use (y^e = the, y^t = that, yor = your, w^{th} = with, w^{ch} = which, w^t = what) have
been silently expanded, and any superscript letters in them lowered. The same
is true of other words in which 'th' is written as some form of the 'thorn': *they,
this, these, those, thus, there, their, then* and so on. Also expanded without
comment are many terminations indicated by a conventional symbol: for
example *frõ* = from, *Numeraõn* = Numeration, *Compendiũ* = Compendium,
diton^9 = ditonus, *Franchin^9* = Franchinus. Hyphens are shown in the edition
as -, not (as sometimes in the sources) as =. Interlineations and interpolations

found in the source are placed within angled brackets, ⟨thus⟩. For texts based on manuscript sources, distinctions in type size are used in order to make clear Birchensha's various implied grades of heading; they do not necessarily correspond to variations of script in the sources. Birchensha's headings in the 'Compendious Discourse' present distinct inconsistencies: they are frequently the subject of complex interlineations and afterthoughts, and he sometimes slips from text into chapter heading, or vice versa. It has nonetheless seemed worthwhile to try to make clear the intended hierarchy as far as possible, using four different sizes of roman type to correspond to the four levels of heading which the manuscript implies. The smallest of these is distinguished from the body of the text by being centred on the page, as indeed are all headings both in the source and in our edition.

Most other editorial interventions are clearly identified as such by means of square brackets or footnotes. Square brackets are used when expanding longer or less familiar contractions such as $mu:^{ll}$ = mu[sica]ll, $Arithm^{ll}$ = Arithm[etica]ll, eq^{ll} = eq[ua]ll, so^{ds} = so[un]ds, and abbreviations such as $tr:$ = tr[eble], $desc:$ = desc[ending], $chro:$ = chro[matic]. They also enclose words or letters apparently omitted by mistake, as well as any punctuation marks added by the editors in order to clarify sense or improve readability. Footnotes are used to record significant scribal deletions and emendations, but trifling corrections have been disregarded. Endnotes to each chapter contain editorial comments on Birchensha's texts.

Superscript characters have been retained in contractions of titles such as M^r and Honble, and in ordinal numbers. For the latter, the commonly used forms 2^d and 3^d appear as in the sources, as do 2^a (for 'secunda'), 8^a (for 'octava') and similar Latin forms; but 6^t (for 'sixth'), a less common alternative to 6th, is editorially modified to $6^{t[h]}$. Some abbreviations have been left unexpanded when their meaning seems sufficiently clear, such as *ma* (for 'major'), *mi* (for 'minor'), *ex.* (for 'example') and *sc.* (for 'scilicet'); but in Chapter IX, where Birchensha often wrote *ma* and *mi* as superscript – for instance 3ma for 'major third' or 6^{mi} for 'minor sixth' – those abbreviations have been silently lowered for the sake of greater clarity. Birchensha's capitalization and punctuation – including a tendency to use a full stop followed by a lower-case letter, where nowadays we would probably use a colon or comma – have been respected as far as possible. It is sometimes unclear whether a particular letter is intended to be upper- or lower-case, however, with *D* and *S* in particular existing in a range of larger and smaller forms that cannot always be classified with confidence. Context and comparison with nearby occurrences of the same word have guided us in doubtful cases: occasionally a capital has been silently introduced in place of an apparent minuscule at the beginning of what is clearly intended as a new sentence or paragraph. Distinctions in the sources (both printed and manuscript) between the interchangeable characters *i* and *j*, and *u* and *v*, have been retained in the edition, as have occurrences of the ampersand (&, &c.). In Chapters I and V, differentiation between roman and italic type in the edition follows that in the printed source. In Chapters II, IV and VI, underlining of words in the edition signifies underlining in the manuscript source.

In the musical examples clefs and signatures are original, unless enclosed in editorial square brackets. Note-values are unaltered. Beams connecting quavers or shorter notes are original, but the direction of note stems has usually been regularized in accordance with modern convention. Barring (including double bars) nearly always matches the source, but has occasionally been adjusted without comment for the sake of consistency or greater clarity. Any repeat sign is found in the source. Editorial ties, shown with a slash, are used to join separate notes when necessary. Some notes which appear in the source as a series of fine dots, or with slashed note-heads, are printed here with small diamond-shaped heads; their function is explained as necessary in editorial notes. Accidentals supplied by the editors are in square brackets. All other accidentals are present in the source. Redundant accidentals have usually been retained, but the ♮ sign (which Birchensha did not use) is substituted for a cancelling ♯ or ♭ wherever modern convention requires it. Birchensha employed his own form of double sharp sign, a sharp with a third cross-bar, as may be seen in Figures 3.3, 3.5 and 9.1; in the transcription this is replaced by the modern double sharp sign. Only a few examples include a time-signature; where there is no signature, common time is generally to be assumed. Most of the figuring is original, but the vertical arrangement of figuring has sometimes been adjusted from its haphazard state in the sources, to match the vertical distribution of the notes on the staves. In autograph manuscripts of the 'Rules of Composition' Birchensha's figuring is frequently punctuated by dots. Although these have no obvious didactic or musical significance, they have been retained in Chapters VIII and IX; but when transcribing musical examples from Withey's copy (Chapter X), where a scattering of similar dots is found, they have generally been disregarded. Any editorial figuring is in square brackets.

From time to time the editorial commentary uses a version of Helmholtz's system of pitch notation (*C′–B′, C–B, c–b, c′–b′, c″–b″, c‴–b‴* etc, where *c′* = middle C). It is printed in italic in order to distinguish it from systems of lettering which are found in the sources, and from the use of roman capitals to mean any note of a particular pitch-class (irrespective of octave). Clefs are indicated in the form: *c′*1 (= C clef on the lowest line of the staff), *c′*3 (= C clef on the third line of the staff, counting upwards), *g′*2 (= treble clef), *f*4 (= bass clef).

Throughout the annotations arithmetical operations on ratios are named as they were in the seventeenth century, so that 'addition' and 'subtraction' of ratios are what would now be called multiplication and division; for example, $a : b + c : d = ac : bd$.

Dates

In the seventeenth century England still used the Julian (or 'Old Style') calendar, which was ten days behind the Gregorian (or 'New Style') calendar used widely elsewhere. Moreover, although the English commonly thought of the year as beginning on 1 January (New Year's Day), for most legal purposes they reckoned it to start on 25 March (Lady Day). So what was 28 March 1660 on the Continent would in English sources typically have been shown either as 'March 18. 1659' or (with dual numbering of the year) as 'March 18. $16^{59}/_{60}$'. Throughout the present edition days and months are generally given in Old Style, except in a few instances where a date is followed by the abbreviation '(NS)' – for example with reference to letters written abroad. When referring in the Introduction or Editorial Notes to dates between 1 January and 24 March, the editors present them in the form '18 March 1659/60' in order to minimize potential ambiguity.

I

Dedicatory Epistle and Preface to
Templum musicum (1664)

Editorial Note

Templum musicum, the work which introduced Birchensha to the scholarly world as a music theorist, was entered at Stationers' Hall and licensed by Roger L'Estrange for publication on 5 February 1663/4. Its title-page reads:

TEMPLUM MUSICUM: / OR THE / MUSICAL SYNOPSIS, / OF / The Learned and Famous / *Johannes-Henricus-Alstedius*, / BEING / A *Compendium* of the *Rudiments* / both of the *Mathematical* and / *Practical* Part of / MUSICK: / *Of which Subject not any Book is extant in our English* / Tongue. / Faithfully translated out of Latin / By *John Birchensha. Philomath.* / Imprimatur, *Feb.* 5. 1663. *Roger L'Estrange.* / *London*, Printed by *Will. Godbid* for *Peter Dring* at the / *Sun* in the *Poultrey* next Dore to the *Rose-Tavern*. / 1664.

Birchensha's book consists principally of a translation of Book 20 of Johann Heinrich Alsted's *Encyclopædia*, in the revised and expanded text found in the editions of 1630 and 1649.[1] This translation takes up pages 1–[94] (sigs B1^r–G7^v). In addition, there is a frontispiece, engraved by John Chantry, with some specially written verses by Birchensha (sig. A1^v; see Figure 1.1); an 'Epistle Dedicatory' to Edward Montagu, first Earl of Sandwich (sigs A3^r–A6^v); and a preface addressed 'To all ingenious Lovers of Musick' (sigs A7^r–A8^v). The book's title, *Templum musicum*, is taken from one of Alsted's closing sentences, which Birchensha translated as follows: 'And this is the *MUSICAL TEMPLE*, whose Foundation is *Harmony*, or *Concord:* whose Covering is honest *Pleasure:* whose Wood and Stones are the Harmonical *Monads*, *Dyads*, and *Tryads.*'[2] Peter Dring, the publisher, was active as a bookseller in the Poultry from 1660 until the Great Fire of 1666; this appears to have been the only music book published by him. The printer, William Godbid, was also responsible for printing all John Playford's musical publications between 1656 and 1679.[3] More than two dozen exemplars of the original edition survive.[4] Facsimiles have been published in the series *Monuments of Music and Music Literature in Facsimile* and (on microfilm) in *Early English Books 1641–1700*.[5] The present critical edition omits the translation of Alsted, but includes Birchensha's verses for the frontispiece, his dedicatory epistle, and his preface.

Figure 1.1   The engraved frontispiece from *Templum musicum* (London, British Library, shelfmark Hirsch I. 24). © The British Library. All Rights Reserved.

It is based on inspection of the two copies of *Templum musicum* in the British Library (shelfmarks: Hirsch I. 24 and 1042.e.10) as well as the reproduction of the Harvard College Library copy available in the Wing microfilm series (item A2926).

Notes

1 'Encyclopædiæ liber vigesimus, in quo explicatur Musica': *Johannis-Henrici Alstedii encyclopædia septem tomis distincta* (Herborn, 1630), pp. 1195–1211; *Ioan. Henrici Alstedii scientiarum omnium encyclopædiæ tomus secundus* (Lyons, 1649), pp. 616–33. Book 14 of Alsted's *Cursus philosophici encyclopædia* (Herborn, 1620), cols 1533–70, is an earlier version of these ten chapters and 'peroratio'. Birchensha appears to have worked chiefly from the Lyons edition of 1649.

2 'Atque hoc est templum Musicum, cujus fundamentum est harmonia seu concordia; tectum, honesta voluptas; ligna & lapides, monas, dyas, & trias harmonica': Alsted, *Encyclopædia* (1630 edn), p. 1211.

3 Henry R. Plomer, *A Dictionary of the Booksellers and Printers who were at work in England, Scotland and Ireland from 1641 to 1667* (London, 1907), pp. 66, 83; Charles Humphries & William C. Smith, *Music Publishing in the British Isles*, 2nd edn (Oxford, 1970), p. 156.

4 The following libraries are known or believed to hold copies: Brussels, Bibliothèque Royale de Belgique; Paris, Bibliothèque Nationale de France (two copies); Cambridge, Gonville and Caius College; Cambridge, Pendlebury Library of Music; Cambridge, University Library; Glasgow, University Library (two copies); London, Royal Academy of Music; London, British Library (two copies); London, Royal College of Music; Manchester, Central Library; Dublin, Trinity College Library; Ann Arbor, University of Michigan Music Library; Boston, Public Library; Cambridge, MA, Harvard University Library; New Haven, CT, Yale University Library; New York, Public Library (three copies); Rochester, NY, Eastman School of Music; San Francisco, California State Library, Sutro; San Marino, CA, Huntington Library; Urbana, University of Illinois Music Library; Washington, DC, Library of Congress; Washington, DC, Folger Shakespeare Library.

5 *Monuments of Music and Music Literature in Facsimile*, 2nd Series, 35 (New York, [1968]); *Early English Books 1641–1700*, Reel 198 (University Microfilms International: Ann Arbor, MI [1979]).

Edition

[sig. A1ᵛ]

    To Musicks sacred Temple, Mercurie,
    And Orpheus dedicate their Harmonie
    From thence proceeding. Whose faire Handmaid's are
    Myster'ous Numbers: which, if you compare,
    The Rat'on of proport'ons you will find.
    These please the Eare, and satisfie the mind.
    For nothing, more, the Soule and sense contents,
    Then Sounds express'd by voice, and Instruments.[a,1]

[sig. A3ʳ]

To the Right Honourable
EDWARD *Lord* MONTAGU
Earl of *Sandwich*, &c.
Knight of the *most Noble Order* of
the *Garter*, and One of His
Majesties most Honourable
Privy-Council.[2]

SIR,

WHen I considered the Excellency of the Subject of this *Book*, and deserved
Fame of the learned *Author*,[3] I thought it not necessary to crave a Pro- [sig.
A3ᵛ][b] tection for this *Treatise* by a *Dedication* of it unto any: being in it self
far above the reach of detracting *Calumniators*. Yet I have made bold, humbly,
to present it to your Honour as a pleasant and delightful Divertisement from
your many and great Imployments. In all Ages *Musick* hath been acceptable to
the wisest, greatest, and most Learned men, of whom many have been famous
for their great Ability and Knowledge in this *Science* and *Art*. It was no
dispraise to *David* that he plaid *skilfully* on the *Harp*, and *Sang* well: the [sig.
A4ʳ] Compositions of divers *German* Princes are extant:[4] neither is it the least
of those Virtues which are eminent in your Lordship, that you are both a Lover
of *Musick*, and a good *Musician*.[5] The renowned *Alstedius* in this *Compendium*
(not much differing in his Judgement from the Opinion of the Generality
of modern musical *Classic's*) does present the world with a great Light and
Discovery of this Art, with the *Subject*, *Principle* and *Affections* thereof,
with the curious *Symmetry* of Proportions: the proportional Dimensions of
[sig. A4ᵛ] *Sounds*: the Variety of *Diastems*: the admirable *Series* of musical
Voices: the usefulnesse of *Tetrachords*: the several *Genus's* of *Musick*: and

---

    [a]   The following words are engraved in slightly larger characters: *Temple*, *Mercurie*,
Orpheus, *Harmonie*, *Myster'ous Numbers*, *Soule*, *Sounds*, *Instruments*.
    [b]   The running head of sigs A3ᵛ–A6ᵛ is *The Epistle Dedicatory*.

harmonical *Moods*, which being expressed by *Voice* or *Instrument* or both, do operate incredibly upon the *Affections*. Wherefore I hope that this *Book* will be accepted both by your *Honour*, and all ingenuous Lovers and Professors of this *Art*, and the *Errors* thereof favourably pardoned by your Lordship and them. The *Reason* which moved me to undertake this *Translation*, was, be- [sig. A5ʳ] cause I desired a Discovery might be made of some Principles of the *Mathematical* part of *Musick*, unto those ingenuous Lovers of this *Science*, who understand only our own Language, to the End that by this means the transcendent Virtue and Excellency that is comprehended in the due proportions of musical *Sounds* may be known unto them; which will give Satisfaction unto their *Reason* aswell as to their *Sence*. I do not think this unworthy my labour, because that many skilful Musicians have not thought it any Disparagement [sig. A5ᵛ] to publish their *Translations* of the Works of famous Men, who did write of the *Art* which they themselves professed. As *Meibomius* Translated some Fragments of *Baccheus*, *Alyppius*, *Nichomachus*, and others:⁶ the never to be forgotten *Franchinus*, the Commentaries of *Briennius*, *Aristides*, *Ptolomy*, and others:⁷ and our *English Douland*, the *Introduction* of *Ornithoparcus*.⁸ In the Author's last *Edition* of his universal *Encyclopædia*, I met with an *Appendix* to his Musical *Synopsis*, taken out of the writings of *Erycius Puteanus*;⁹ but not find- [sig. A6ʳ] ing any thing new in it, only an *ABCdary Repetition* of the first Elements of *Musick*, formerly but more judiciously and largely handled in this *Compendium*: and also some few *Questions* started by *Cardanus*,¹⁰ which are, for the most part more fully and Satisfactorily resolved by the Author; I did forbear the Translation thereof; not being willing to weary the *Reader* with the unnecessary recital of those things, nor your Lordship with too tedious an Epistle, which I here conclude, humbly craving pardon for my boldnesse, and your Honours [sig. A6ᵛ] favourable Acceptation of this Mite from your Lordships

Most humble

and devoted

Servant,

JOHN BIRCHENSHA.

[sig. A7ʳ]

To all ingenious LOVERS of
MUSICK.

GENTLEMEN,

I*T was for your Profit and Benefit that I undertook this Translation: and that you might thereby understand the Rudiments and Principles both of the Mathematical and Practical Parts of this Science. We know that there is some light into the Mathematical Part of all other Arts; but little discovery of that Part of the Theory of Musick hath been made in our Language; therefore I did suppose that this work would be gratefully accepted by you, the Author having* *more fully discovered the Precepts, Rules, and Axioms of this Science, then any other whose Works I have seen.*[11]

Since the Rumour of this Translation hath been spred abroad, I have by diverse been demanded, What Benefit and Advantage the Knowledge of the Mathematical Part of Musick does contribute to the completing of a Musician? *To which I answer, That it is as necessary for a perfect and complete Musician to* [sig. A7ᵛ][a] *understand the Proportion of Sounds, as for a curious Painter, exactly to know the Symmetry of every part of a Body: that so he may rightly understand the ground and foundation of the Art he does profess, which is, the nature of Sounds, and their due Proportion, in respect of their Ration, Habitude, Quality, Difference, Excess, Dimension, and Magnitude.*[12] *For this I dare boldly affirm, and if Occasion be offered, undertake to prove it: That such Rules may be yet further, and are already, in part, contrived (drawn from the Mathematical Principles of Musick[)]*[b] *by which, musical Consonants and Dissonants (artificially applied and disposed, according to the nature of their Proportions, and by the forementioned Canons) may afford, in* 2, 3, 4, 5, 6, 7, *or more parts, as good Musick, that is, as agreeable, artificial, and formal, as can be composed by the help of any Instrument. Yet until such Rules be known, it is commendable in any to use such helps as may Advantage their Compositions. But for any Musician to undervalue or speak slightly of the Mathematical part of Musick, is to reproach the Common Parent from whom the Art he professeth received a Being. I know that all Ingenuous persons who are Artists, will acknowledge that it is a more noble way to work by Rules and Precepts in any Art, then mechanically; And so to work in this Art. i.e. to compose regularly, will be found more advantagious then any other way in these Respects.*[13] *For by such a way of Operation the Composer shall work more certainly, firmly, readily, and with more facility then by any other way.*

If Musick be an Art, then it may be contracted [sig. A8ʳ] *and collected into certain Rules which may discover all those Mysteries that are contained in that Science, by which a man may become an excellent Musician, and expert, both in the Theorical and Practical Parts thereof. To the Completeing of such forcible Rules I have contributed my Mite, whose Certainty and Reality has been Experienced by divers, and may likewise be further known unto others, if they please or desire to understand them.*

I know that all Virtuoso's[14] *will encourage those things which conduce to the Improvement of any ingenious Art: but what shall be spoken against such things by persons rude, envious, or that do pass their Judgement rashly upon things which they know not, having neither seen, heard, nor understood them, is not to be valued. And I do assure my self that there is not any person in this Nation, that is a true Lover of this Science; or a Professour*[15] *thereof, who does truely honour and understand this Art, but could cordially wish such an Improvement thereof,*

ᵃ   The running head of sigs A7ᵛ–A8ᵛ is *To the Reader*.
ᵇ   The source has a comma rather than a bracket here.

that those things which in Musick are concealed and mysterious, might be fully discovered: those which are imperfect, completed: those which are doubtful and disputable, cleared by evident Demonstration: those which are not to be done without great trouble, facilitated: those many Observations which burthen the Memory, made few and plain: and those whose Operation and Experience do's require the study and Expence of many years, might be performed without any difficulty in a few Weeks, or Months at the farthest. And that this way is found out and effected in a great measure, I say, many persons of Worth and Quality are able experimentally to testifie.[16]

[sig. A8ᵛ]

Musick hath already flowed to a great Heighth in this Nation, for I am perswaded that there is as much Excellency in the Musick which hath been, and is now composed in England, *as in any part of the World, for Ayre, variety and Substance. But I heartily wish, that after this great Spring and Flood, there be not in our succeeding Generations[,]*[a] *as low an Ebb. For if the serious and substantial part of Harmony be neglected, and the mercurial only used: It will prove volatile, evaporate, and come to nothing. But, Gentlemen, I would not willingly weary your patience, and since the* Temple *is so small, I will not make the* Gate *too bigg; But subscribe my self as it is known I am[,]*[b] *a true Lover of Musick, and*

Your Servant

J. B.

Notes

[1] John Chantry's engraved frontispiece (see Figure 1.1) depicts the Pythagorean vision of celestial and human harmony that Birchensha's verses describe. On the highest plane, to either side of Music's temple, Mercury and Orpheus play the harp, an instrument with which each was associated in the popular mind: in Thomas Blount's *Glossographia* (London, 1656), for example, Mercury is 'the messenger of the gods, the god of Eloquence, ... also author of the Harp' (sig. Bb5ʳ), while Orpheus 'is feigned to have plaid so excellently upon the Harp, that he drew Stones, Woods and Trees after him' (sig. Ee4ʳ). Below them, the personifications of Arithmetic, Harmony and Geometry hold sets of numbers that 'please the Eare, and satisfie the mind' – respectively $2:3:4$, $3:4:6$ and $2:4:8$, representing the ratios of arithmetical, harmonical and geometrical medieties (see Introduction, pp. 52–3). On the lowest, audible level, trios of singers and instrumentalists – the latter playing cornett, violin and bass viol – perform music that 'the Soule and sense contents'. The plate is inscribed *Io. Bir.* in the lower left-hand corner and *Iohn Chantry sculp*[*sit*] in the lower right. This suggests that Birchensha himself wrote the verses, and possibly sketched the pictorial

---

[a] The source has *Generations)*.

[b] The source has *I am)*.

design too, leaving its detailed execution to Chantry. At the bottom of the plate is the publisher's imprint, *Sould by Peter Dring at the Sun in the Poultry*, which suggests that it was possible to buy the engraving separately, and helps to explain why in some copies of *Templum musicum* inspected by the editors the frontispiece is pasted in, and in others it is absent.

[2]   As joint General-at-Sea, Edward Montagu or Mountagu (1625–72) was responsible for bringing King Charles II back to England from exile in May 1660. In reward he was created first Earl of Sandwich, appointed Admiral of the Narrow Seas and given court office as Master of the Wardrobe. Montagu became a fellow of the Royal Society in 1661, and was a member of the committee formed on 20 April 1664 to hear and assess Birchensha's views on music. Samuel Pepys, his secretary, took composition lessons from Birchensha early in 1662.

[3]   The Calvinist scholar Johann Heinrich Alsted (1588–1638) was Professor of Philosophy (from 1610) and of Theology (from 1619) at Herborn in the German principality of Nassau, where his pupils included the educational reformer Comenius (Jan Amos Komenský). In 1629 the disruption brought about by the Thirty Years War caused him to move to Weissenburg (Alba-Iulia) in Transylvania, where he taught for the last nine years of his life. The first edition of his systematic and comprehensive *Encyclopædia* was published in 1620; a revised and enlarged second edition followed in 1630.

[4]   Birchensha was probably thinking especially of Moritz, Landgrave of Hesse (1572–1632), and the Holy Roman Emperor Ferdinand III (1608–57).

[5]   Montagu's love of music is attested by Pepys. He sang, played the viol, chamber organ, virginals and guitar, and composed a little, including an anthem for the Chapel Royal. There are accounts of him making music at home or on board ship with William Child, Christopher Gibbons, Henry Cooke, Humphrey Madge, Thomas Mallard, Pepys and others. See *The Diary of Samuel Pepys*, ed. Robert Latham and William Matthews (11 vols, London, 1970–83), especially at vol. 1, pp. 114–15, 285, 292, 297; vol. 2, pp. 103, 121–2; vol. 4, pp. 160, 428; vol. 6, p. 301.

[6]   Marcus Meibom (1621–1710) was the translator and editor of *Antiquæ musicæ auctores septem* (2 vols, Amsterdam, 1652), which he dedicated to his patron Queen Christina of Sweden. The passage reveals that Birchensha was familiar with this relatively recent publication, which provided reliable Latin versions (with commentaries) of Greek texts by Aristoxenus, Cleonides, Nicomachus, Alypius, Gaudentius, Bacchius, Aristides Quintilianus and Martianus Capella. Meibom visited England in 1674–77; Robert Hooke records that at Sir Christopher Wren's house on 4 March 1675/6 there was 'Much discourse [...] of Meibomius, of Musick and of Berchenshaw' (*The Diary of Robert Hooke M.A., M.D., F.R.S. 1672–1680*, ed. Henry W. Robinson and Walter Adams (London, 1935), p. 218).

[7]   In the 1490s the humanist Franchinus Gaffurius [Franchino Gafori] commissioned or encouraged Latin translations of musical treatises by Aristides Quintilianus and Manuel Bryennius, and of Ptolemy's *Harmonics*, from Gian Francesco Burana of Verona and Nicolò Leoniceno of Ferrara. Gaffurius's own treatises *Theorica musice* (Milan, 1492), *Practica musice* (Milan, 1496) and *De harmonia musicorum instrumentorum opus* (Milan, 1518) were widely influential. He is one of only two Renaissance theorists whom Birchensha cites by name in 'A Compendious Discourse' (the other being Glarean).

8   Ornithoparchus's treatise *Musicæ activæ micrologus* (Leipzig, 1517) was translated by John Dowland as *Andreas Ornithoparcus his Micrologus or Introduction* (London, 1609), in the belief that 'nothing can more advance the apprehension of *Musicke*, than the reading of such Writers as have both skilfully and diligently set downe the precepts thereof'. Interestingly, Birchensha makes no mention of another work that had lately been translated into English, though he must surely have been aware of it: the *Compendium musicæ* of René Descartes. Written in 1618 but first published in 1650 in Utrecht, it reappeared in London in 1653 as *Renatus Des-Cartes Excellent Compendium of Musick: With Necessary and Judicious Animadversions Thereupon. By a Person of Honour*. The unnamed author of the 'Animadversions' was revealed by Walter Charleton to be '*the Lord Viscount Brouncker*; (whose constant Friendship, and learned Conversation, I must profess to have been one of the chiefest Consolations of my life.)'. Brouncker, who in 1662 became the first President of the Royal Society, has often been credited with the translation of the Descartes text too; but Humphrey Moseley's preface ('The Stationer to the Ingenious Reader') clearly implies that another person – presumably commissioned by Moseley – carried out this task, and the Stationers' Register assigns the translation to Charleton himself. See Walter Charleton, *Physiologia Epicuro-Gassendo-Charltoniana: or a Fabrick of Science Natural, Upon the Hypothesis of Atoms* (London, 1654), p. 226; Jamie C. Kassler, *The Beginnings of the Modern Philosophy of Music in England* (London and Burlington, VT, 2004), p. 31; René Descartes, *Abrégé de musique: Compendium musicæ*, ed. F. de Buzon (Paris, 1987), p. 38; *A Transcript of the Registers of the Worshipful Company of Stationers; from 1640–1708 A.D.* (3 vols, London, 1913–14), vol. 1, p. 402.

9   Alsted's appendix is not in the 1620 edition of his *Encyclopædia*, but is in the editions of 1630 (pp. 1208–11) and 1649 (pp. 629–32). Erycius Puteanus [Eryck de Put] (1574–1646) was successively professor of Rhetoric at the Schola Palatina in Milan and professor of History, Roman Literature and Roman Law at Leuven University. Among his writings is a treatise on music which was first published in Milan in 1599 under the title *Modulata Pallas*; Alsted knew it in a version published at Hanau in 1602, entitled *Musathena*.

10   Cardanus [Girolamo Cardano] (1501–76) was a colourful figure who taught mathematics in Milan and gave his name to a procedure of solution for a type of mathematical problem, became professor of Medicine first at Pavia (1543) and then at Bologna (1562), travelled in 1551 to Scotland (where he treated the Archbishop of St Andrews for asthma) and England (where he cast the king's horoscope), and after being imprisoned by the Inquisition for heresy spent the last five years of his life on a papal pension in Rome. His writings reveal a lively interest in the practice of music and its effects. They include the *De subtilitate* (Nuremberg, 1550), on which Alsted drew, and two treatises on music.

11   The words 'in our language' imply a negative judgement on the English translation of Descartes's *Compendium musicæ* (see above). Birchensha never made his disapproval of Descartes's book explicit, but he may have objected to it because of its espousal of the just intonation. Again, the phrase 'more fully' seems to imply that Birchensha either had not seen the works of Mersenne and Kircher or felt it self-evidently reasonable to neglect them.

12   These specific terms recur often in Birchensha's writings: for their meanings see the Introduction, pp. 49–50.

¹³   Birchensha's opposition of 'by rule' with 'mechanically' inevitably strikes the modern reader as odd. 'Mechanically' in this context indicates something like trial and error using a musical instrument, as opposed to composing without an instrument using the rules of harmony and counterpoint.

¹⁴   According to the *Oxford English Dictionary* the two meanings of 'Virtuoso' in use at this time were: '1. One who has a general interest in arts and sciences, or who pursues special investigations in one or more of these; a learned person; a scientist, savant, or scholar. 2. One who has a special interest in, or taste for, the fine arts; a student or collector of antiquities, natural curiosities or rarities, etc.; a connoisseur; freq., one who carries on such pursuits in a dilettante or trifling manner.' In his diary Pepys sometimes referred to the Royal Society as 'the college of the Virtuosoes' (e.g. 28 April 1662) or 'the Virtuosi of Gresham College' (e.g. 5 October 1664).

¹⁵   'Professor' here probably means 'one who makes a profession of any art or science' (*Oxford English Dictionary*) – in other words, a professional musician.

¹⁶   The references to 'Virtuoso's' and 'experiment' and to the clearing of doubts by 'evident Demonstration', as well as the dedication to an F.R.S., suggest that Birchensha was already keen to cultivate the interest of the Royal Society. The relevant sense of 'experimentally' here is 'by experience'.

II

Letter to the Royal Society (26 April 1664)

Editorial Note

Following a suggestion from Silas Taylor to Sir Robert Moray, the Royal Society appointed a committee at its meeting on Wednesday 20 April 1664 to consider Birchensha's views on the theory of music. The committee met on 23 April at the lodgings of Viscount Brouncker, the president, and Birchensha was apparently asked to produce a written summary of the matters with which he intended to deal in his proposed treatise. This he did in a letter to the Society, dated 26 April. The Society's Journal Book reveals that his letter was read out at the next day's meeting, which was attended by (among others) Sir Robert Moray, Dr John Wilkins, Robert Boyle, Dr John Pell, John Evelyn, Dr Walter Charleton, Robert Hooke and Henry Oldenburg. Afterwards Birchensha 'was called in, and thanked for his respect to the Society, and assured, that the Committee, formerly appointed to hear him, and to discourse with him concerning this matter, should further consider thereof, and of wayes to encourage and promote his designe and study'.[1] Oldenburg sent an account of the meeting to Dr John Wallis in Oxford, to which Wallis responded on 7, 14 and 25 May.[2]

Birchensha's autograph letter is lost, but two official transcripts of it survive, both abridged. Unfortunately there is no way of telling how much of what Birchensha wrote was omitted from the transcripts. The earlier of these is Royal Society, Letter Book Original, vol. 1 ('The Letter-book / of the / Royall Society. / N° 1.'), pp. 143–8. It is the main source for the present edition. The other, Royal Society, Letter Book Copy, vol. 1, pp. 166–73, is an eighteenth-century copy based on the Letter Book Original, and lacks independent authority. Its variant readings have been noted in one or two places, but its many divergences in spelling, capitalization and punctuation have been disregarded.

Notes

[1]   Royal Society, Journal Book Original, vol. 2, pp. 71–4; Thomas Birch, *The History of the Royal Society of London* (4 vols, London, 1756–7), vol. 1, pp. 416, 418.
[2]   The *Correspondence of Henry Oldenburg*, eds A. Rupert Hall and Marie Boas Hall, vol. 2 (Madison, Milwaukee and London, 1966), pp. 179–82, 190–203.

Edition

[p. 143]

An Extract of
A letter
Written to the Royall Society, by Mr Bir-
shenshaw, concerning Musick.

April 26. 1664.

– In obediance to your commands, I doe here give you an account of these
things, which, by God's assistance, I shall undertake to write, concerning both
the Mathematicall and practicall part of Musick, for the good and benefit of
all men, but especially of our owne Countrymen; being a discovery of many
things, the knowledge whereoff I have purchased with the expence of many
100.ll. and of more then 20 yeares labour and study.

In the first place I shall let you understand the presant condition of this
Noble Science and Art, which, allthough for the excellency of it in it selfe it is
not inferiour to any humane science or Art, yet at this day (notwithstanding
it be highly esteemed and much used) is the most obscure, difficult, uncertain,
irregular and imperfect Science in the world. For first there are no certain
rules given by any, whose workes I have seene (Pythagoras excepted)[1] for the
finding out the proper places of those simple intervals, which are required
to the compleating of those diastems and Systems, which are to be found in
the compas of a disdiapason,[2] without which the practicall part of Musick
cannot well consist and be perfect, as the Chromatic Semitones, and other
such intervalls. 2. there are not sufficient directions for the finding out of
Numbers or termes of difference, which ought to be applyed to the respective
Intervals.[3] 3. there are no certaine rules for the tryall of Proportions, as of
the divers Rations, Habitudes, &c, of sounds.[4] 4. As there is no mention of
many hundreds of sounds, so the Proportions of most of those sounds, [p.
144] which are mentioned by all the writers of this Art, whose writings I have
seene and perused (I say, Pythagoras excepted) are very much mistaken; as the
proportions of the Semiditonus, Ditonus, sexta minor, sexta major, septima
<u>mi</u>, septima <u>ma</u>, Tritonus, and Semidiapason, acute to the Unison. For, the
Proportion of the semiditonus is only given, and the Proportion of the perfect
is not mentioned.[5] So of^a the Ditonus and the rest. And if the proportions of
sounds (which are the foundation of all musicall Harmony) or the most part
of them^b be omitted or mistaken, all the superstructure, or what is built or
depends thereupon, must of necessity come to nought: and all things, that are
so written of sounds and their proportions, in respect of their Ration, Habitude,

---

^a　Letter Book Copy has *So if.*
^b　Letter Book Copy omits *of them.*

difference, Excess, Quality, Dimension, and Magnitude,[6] and all things, that are written so of the severall species of Intervals, Moodes, Tetrachords, Musicall Genus's, & what soever els does concerne the Mathematicall part of Musick, must of necessity be disjoynted, and out of order.

And as for the Practicall part of Musick, which hath respect to Composition, it is so obscure, that few do understand it, but doe grope at their worke, as men in the darke, and therefore it is no wonder, if they fall into many errors. It is so difficult, that many after the expence of most of their lifetime in laborious practise, do not attain to such a reasonable measure of perfection in this art, as to compose tollerably well and commendably. It is so irregular, that (a few ordinary observations excepted) there is no certain rule [p. 145] to compose by. And herein this Art is more unhappy, then any other Art in the world: for Grammer, Logick, and all other sciences are drawn into rule. The want of this hath made many Composers to consult their Instruments almost in all things they doe, as to find out the consecution of sounds in single Ayres, and of Consonants and Dissonants in the Composing of many parts: which allthough it is not without its proper use, is but a low and Mechanick way. But to compose by a rule, is a more Noble, artificial, and commendable way, by which the Composer may worke with more ease, certainty, & celerity.

Having shewed your Honors the lamentable present condition of this Noble Science and Art, I shall in the next place give you an account of what I shall undertake (God assisting) for the perfecting[a] of the same.

Concerning the Mathematicall part of Musick, first I shall lay downe divers certain and easy Rules for the finding out of these Intervals, which are required to the compleating of a Diapason, and all other simple Diastems, and the placing of them in their proper seats and Cells in a Disdiapasonick system; which knowledge is requisite in a Mathematical Musitian. For, it will not be found sufficient, that we take away some part of the Proportion of an Intervall, and adde so much to another to complete any system (the great Creator of sounds having made them all perfect, and of a due and just proportion, even the least of them) but every Interval must be placed in the scale in its proper place, and have its proper terme of difference assigned to him, that the scale may be perfect, i.e. so far as the eye and ear can judge it so to be. 2. I will deliver certain Rules for the finding out of the numbers and termes of difference, which ought [p. 146] to be adscribed to every perticular Interval, from a Comma to an Octave (my scale being divided into Comma's;)[7] I say such Numbers as will shew, what proportion the Unison, first assumed, dos hold with the adjoyning Comma, Diaschisma, Diesis, Semitone, Tone, Semiditone, ditone, Diatessaron, Diapente, and all other meane Intervals within the Octave and Disdiapason;[8] So likewise, if you make the following Comma or Diesis or any other interval the Unison, the following Intervals shall, through the whole scale, agree in the like just proportion one with

---

[a] Letter Book Copy has *for the Performance.*

another.[9] 3. I will lay downe certaine Rules for the tryall of Proportions of every species, and of the Ration, Habitude, difference, exces, Magnitude, &c of sounds;[10] by which any Ingenious Person may be able rightly to judge of the Proportions of sounds given both by others and my selfe. 4. I will write of the admirable production and Generation of Proportions and consequently of sounds. 5. I will draw a grand System, which shall containe and comprehend the whole body of the Mathematical part of Musick, by which I will not onely give an account of Musical sounds and their Proportions, but I will thereby clearly and visibly demonstrate all things, that doe concerne the severall species of Intervals, and also the Ration, Habitude, Difference, Exces, Quality, Dimension and Magnitude of all such Intervals: also all things, that doe concerne the Moods, Tetrachords, and Musical Genus's, and whatsoever else dos concerne the Mathematicall part of Musick: so that not any question shall rationally be demanded concerning those things, but by that scale (the use of it being known) they shall satisfactorily and demonstratively be resolved; which scale [p. 147] I will humbly present to your honors to remaine in your library, both for the satisfaction of yourselves and others, together with directions for the use of it. And by this means the Mathematicall part of Musick, which now is in a dying and allmost lost condition, will revive, and be made the most perfect part of all the Mathematicks; the works of ancient and moderne Authors, who have written of this subject, will be understood and rightly judged of; what hath bin mistaken by them, will be rectified, and the Mathematical part of this[a] science will in all things exactly square and harmonise with the Practicall part thereof. And –

As for the practicall part of Musick, 1. I Shall write soe much of the Elementary part thereof, as will enable those, who shall peruse my booke, to understand the composition of Antient Authors, who have composed excellent Musick (allthough, as I may say, out of Fashion, in respect of the Mode of these times,) which I know many will desire to doe, and also to understand the Musathena or lection of the musick of these present times.[11] 2. As to the Melopoetical or Compositive part thereof, I shall discover a few, easy, certain, and perfect rules (never yet invented or publisht by any man) which may be understood, and made practise of, in a few weeks, or months at the farthest, by any reasonable capacity; and which shall contain all things, that appertaine to the making of excellent and good Aire in any part or kind of musick: and all things, which belong to the consecution of sounds in a single part, and of Consonants, and Dissonants in many parts: the taking of Cadences, and all wayes of Syncope: the way of taking of Discords by binding or pass: the nature of counterpoint simple or compounded: the Laws of Ornate [p. 148] and florid Discant: the Elegant Art of Fugeing, in a few or great body of parts; the making of canons without, or uppon a plain song: and whatsoever else may be done by this Art, for the advantage of Aire and Harmony. By which Rules not

---

[a]   Letter Book Copy omits *this*.

onely those, who skillfully can sing or play on some Instrument, may learne to compose, but also those, who can neither sing nor play: I say, that by my said Rules such may both make good Ayre, and compose 2. 3. 4 or more parts artificially. Also I shall give Instructions for the casting and designing of all kind[a] of Musick, and the several contrivances thereof, likewise directions for the setting of Musick out of the score, unto most of our known instruments: Lastly, to compose to words; and of the lawes of vocal musick.

And if any doe question my ability to doe this, I shall returne this answer, that there are divers persons of worth and quality, who allready have experienced these things in a great measure, and can testify the same, whose compositions shall be produced, and be exposed to the judgements of any, who desire to hear them. For what I have allready done and performed, and many have allready experienced, I dare boldly affirm and undertake. This account of my undertakeings, I doe hereby humbly offer and submit to your honors judgement and serious considerations and subscribe my selfe

Your Honors
most humble servant
John Birchensha.

Notes

[1]   Birchensha held to the belief – passed down from Nicomachus by way of Boethius to Renaissance theorists such as Gaffurius – that it was Pythagoras who first discovered and demonstrated the ratios of consonant intervals. Various editions of 'fragments' or 'verses [*carmina*]' attributed to Pythagoras were published from the early sixteenth century onwards, but Birchensha implies that he has seen a text giving 'certain rules' for music. It is conceivable that he had seen the reasonably detailed (though mathematically dubious) passage describing the musical doctrines of the Pythagoreans in Porphyry's *Commentary on the Harmonics of Ptolemy* at 107.15ff: see Andrew Barker, *Greek Musical Writings, II: Harmonic and Acoustic Theory* (Cambridge, New York and Melbourne, 1989), pp. 34–5; although this part of this text appears not to have been printed until 1699 (a Latin translation of it appeared in John Wallis, *Opera mathematica*, (Oxford, 1693–99)). It is perhaps more likely that Birchensha took some other text to represent the work of Pythagoras.
[2]   A *diastem* is a simple interval, a *system* is a compound interval, and a *disdiapason* is a double octave; all three terms were taken from Greek musical theory.
[3]   Birchensha sometimes uses the term 'difference' to refer to the difference between the two terms of a given ratio (as in the 'Compendious Discourse', Mathematical Part, chapter[a] 17); elsewhere (as in ibid., chapter 5) it simply means the difference between

---

[a]   Letter Book Copy has *all sorts*.

two intervals, the result of subtracting one from the other. 'Terms of difference' could relate to either of these usages.

4   For the meaning of these three terms, see Introduction, pp. 49–50.

5   The *semiditonus* is the minor third; the *ditonus*, the major third; the *sexta minor* and *major*, the minor and major sixth; the *septima minor* and *major*, the minor and major seventh; the *tritonus*, the augmented fourth; and the *semidiapason*, the diminished octave. (Possibly Birchensha intended to write 'Semidiapente', meaning diminished fifth, rather than 'Semidiapason'.) Butler explains the prefix 'semi-' thus: '*Semidiapente. Semi* in this word (as in *Semiditonus* and *Semidiapason*) doth not signifie half of the whole, but the whole save half a Note' (Charles Butler, *The Principles of Musik, in Singing and Setting* (London, 1636), p. 49). All these terms were known in England at least by 1609, when Dowland's translation of Ornithoparchus appeared. Birchensha lists the proportions of the intervals in his 'Compendious Discourse' (fol. 12ʳ; see p. 000); each is assigned its Pythagorean ratio. The last sentence here should probably be interpreted as meaning: 'Most writers mistakenly give the *semiditonus* its superparticular ratio 6 : 5, not its Pythagorean ratio 32 : 27'.

6   See pp. 49–50.

7   Birchensha apparently means by this that the Pythagorean comma (531441 : 524288) – the difference between D♭ and C♯, or G♭ and F♯ – is the smallest interval represented in his scale. In 'A Compendious Discourse' (fols 5ᵛ–6ʳ; see pp. 111–13) he gives a comparatively simple 14-note scale of G, followed by a table of consonant and dissonant intervals 'in All Keyes practicable by our Instruments' in which the 14-note scale appears in various transpositions. In each case, a comma separates the *semidiapente* (diminished fifth) from the tritone and the *semidiapason* (diminished octave) from the major seventh. In the 33-note version of 'Mr Berchinshaw's scale' preserved in John Pell's papers (see Introduction, p. 62) there are nine steps of a comma.

8   The sizes of most if not all of these intervals appear in the 'Compendious Discourse': see pp. 132–3. *Comma*, *diaschisma* and *diesis* are all varieties of microtone. Birchensha defined the *comma* as the difference between a diatonic semitone (e.g. C to D♭) and an *apotome* (e.g. C to C♯); he also gave ratios for two sizes of *diesis*, minor and major ('A Compendious Discourse', Mathematical Part, chapters 5, 8.) Possibly he regarded *diaschisma* (which appears nowhere else in his extant writings) as synonymous with his 'minor diesis'. Philolaus's definition of *diaschisma* as half a diatonic semitone is cited by Butler in *The Principles of Musik*, p. 23; see also Barker, *Greek Musical Writings, II*, p. 38, note 36. *Diatessaron* and *diapente* are the perfect fourth and perfect fifth.

9   The point here is that any note of his scale may serve as the 'assumed Unison', and hence generate its own scale. Birchensha illustrates this in the 'Compendious Discourse' (fol. 6ʳ; see p. 113) by using a chromatic scale of A to generate a dozen different 14-note scales (cf note 7). Thus if the unison is transposed up by a semitone from A to B♭, the minor second of the new scale becomes C♭; if transposed down by an apotome from A to A♭, the minor second becomes B♭♭. By using double flats and double sharps where necessary, the integrity of the scale's Pythagorean interval structure is preserved in every case. Birchensha's 'perfect scale of musick' will however require the use of more extreme notes such as F♭♭ and E✹ ('Compendious Discourse', fol. 12ᵛ; see p. 133), and dieses too. His claim that the principle of scale generation will hold good if the unison is transposed by a diesis is no doubt theoretically sound, but would involve cumbersome nomenclature.

10   See pp. 49–50.

[11] 'Antient' need not mean Greek or Roman ('Ancient: 1. a. Of or belonging to time past, former, earlier, bygone.' *OED*), although it is possible that it does: Athanasius Kircher had published examples of Greek musical notation in 1650 in his *Musurgia universalis* (Rome). The context suggests however that Birchensha was thinking here of music of the sixteenth and early seventeenth centuries, which, like others of his generation (including Christopher Simpson and Thomas Mace), he saw being rejected as unfashionable. The word 'Musathena' seems to have been coined by the Dutch humanist Erycus Puteanus with reference to seven-syllable solmization; he symbolically associated this with the goddess Pallas Athena, who from ancient times had been linked with the number seven. Puteanus uses the term in his treatise *Musathena, sive Notarum heptas, ad harmonicæ lectionis novum et facilem usum* (Hanau, 1602); Birchensha knew of this work through Alsted's *Encyclopædia* (see *Templum musicum*, p. 35). Alsted in turn borrowed the word in his opening precept, 'Musica est scientia bene canendi, *alias* Harmonica & Musathena *dicitur*', which Birchensha rendered as 'Musick is the Science of Singing well, otherwise called Harmonical: and Musathena' (*Templum musicum*, p. 1). Here Birchensha uses it, broadly speaking, to mean the 'reading' of music.

III

'A Compendious Discourse'

Editorial Note

The unique source of 'A Compendious Discourse', an autograph manuscript, is now the first item in London, Royal Society, Boyle Papers, vol. 41. This is a modern guard-book, containing papers on a variety of subjects that had belonged to the natural philosopher Robert Boyle. After Boyle's death, the manuscript seems to have passed into the possession of his executor, John Warr. It was among the Boyle papers subsequently collected by Henry Miles FRS (1698–1763) and presented to the Royal Society in 1769 by Miles's widow, Emma.[1]

The manuscript comprises twenty leaves (fols 2–21), measuring about 310 × 200 mm. These appear to be wholly in Birchensha's handwriting. Each pair of adjacent leaves, beginning with fols 3–4 and continuing to fols 19–20, is formed of a sheet of paper folded once. Most of these bifolios show a watermark of a posthorn on a shield, of a kind that suggests an origin in the Angoumois region of western France which produced much of the paper used in England in the 1660s.[2] Fols 2 and 21 are single leaves, without watermark. All the leaves and bifolios have been disbound in order to be mounted in the guard-book, but old stitch marks are visible close to the left-hand edge of each leaf. Fol. 1 is smaller (300 × 122 mm), and its paper – though perhaps of seventeenth-century date – is of a different kind, watermarked with the arms of Genoa.[3] It bears the following annotation in a handwriting identifiable as that of Henry Miles: 'Treatise / Music / Written By Birchensa / for Mr Boyle / & Dr Wallis on the Same / Subject / – / perhaps Valuable'.[4] This corresponds to an entry in one of the inventories of Boyle's papers drawn up by Miles (London, Royal Society, Boyle Papers, vol. 36, fols 157–60). There, on fol. 160^r, Miles described the contents of the bundle he marked 'E.a' as: 'Two Rolls[:] a Treatise on Music by Birchensa for Mr Boyle[,] another by Dr Wallis on the same subj[ect]. Q[uery] whether not valuable[.] – the other[,] part of a Tract of Nat[ural] Philos[ophy]. Q[uery] whether not DesCartes?'[5] Michael Hunter and Lawrence M. Principe date this inventory to between 1738 and 1742.[6] Miles's descriptions therefore show that by 1742 the 'Compendious Discourse' manuscript was associated with what is now the second item in the guard-book, a copy of a long letter about the ratios of musical intervals that Dr John Wallis, the Savilian Professor of Geometry at Oxford, sent to Henry

Oldenburg on 14 May 1664 (Boyle Papers, vol. 41, fols 22–31). The original of Wallis's letter, in which he refers to Birchensha by name, is in Royal Society, Early Letters, vol. W 1 (no. 8), but the copy is also in Wallis's hand and differs from the original in a number of details.[7] It is possible – though it would be rash to go further than that – that Birchensha's treatise and the copy of Wallis's letter were already kept together by Boyle before being removed after his death in 1691 from the house in Pall Mall, London, where he had lived from 1668 onwards with his sister, Lady Ranelagh.[8] The leaf bearing Miles's annotation (fol. 1) may have served as a cover or docket for the roll containing these two manuscripts.

Birchensha's manuscript consists of five main parts: first, a title-page, with an inscription to Robert Boyle (fol. 2); secondly, two bifolios devoted to principles and elements of the 'Practicall Part of Musick' (fols 3–6); thirdly, six bifolios devoted to principles and elements of the 'Mathematicall Part of Musick' (fols 7–18); fourthly, a table of contents (fol. 19); and fifthly, two leaves of 'Directions' for 'How to make any kind of Tune, Ayre, or Song, without the help of the voice, or any other Instrument' (fols 20–21). It cannot strictly be called a fair copy, for it contains many corrections and revisions. Tables and diagrams are by no means free of errors, and on some pages (especially in the 'Mathematicall Part') one can see the author still tussling with his material. On the whole, however, the handwriting – a mutable 'mixed' hand combining elements of italic and secretary styles – is clear and neat. Many of the revisions, such as the alterations to the titles of the sections, have more to do with presentation than substance. Birchensha's decision to divide the 'Practicall Part' and 'Mathematicall Part' into numbered chapters was evidently made at a late stage, after the text as a whole had already been drafted. Having squeezed in chapter headings and supplied page numbers from 1 to 32 (which he confusingly called 'folio' numbers), Birchensha went on to prepare a detailed table of contents for the 'Practicall' and 'Mathematicall' parts. By way of an appendix, he then copied out the 'Directions' on two unpaginated leaves, starting on the spare leaf of the bifolio used for the table of contents and continuing on fol. 21. Finally, before delivering the manuscript to Boyle, he wrote out a title-page for the whole work in his best italic hand (Figure 3.1). In this edition the modern foliation and Birchensha's pagination are shown side by side, where appropriate.

The manuscript is undated, but 1664–65 seems the most likely time for its production and presentation to Boyle.[9] In April 1664 a Royal Society committee was formed, with Boyle as a member, to consider Birchensha's proposals regarding the theory of music. Wallis's letters to Oldenburg of 7, 14 and 25 May 1664 were prompted by these same deliberations, which probably explains why Boyle received a copy from Wallis of one of them.[10] At several points in the 'Discourse' there are borrowings from the musical portion of Alsted's *Encyclopædia*, of which Birchensha published a translation (*Templum musicum*) early in 1664. There are also allusions to a book in preparation –

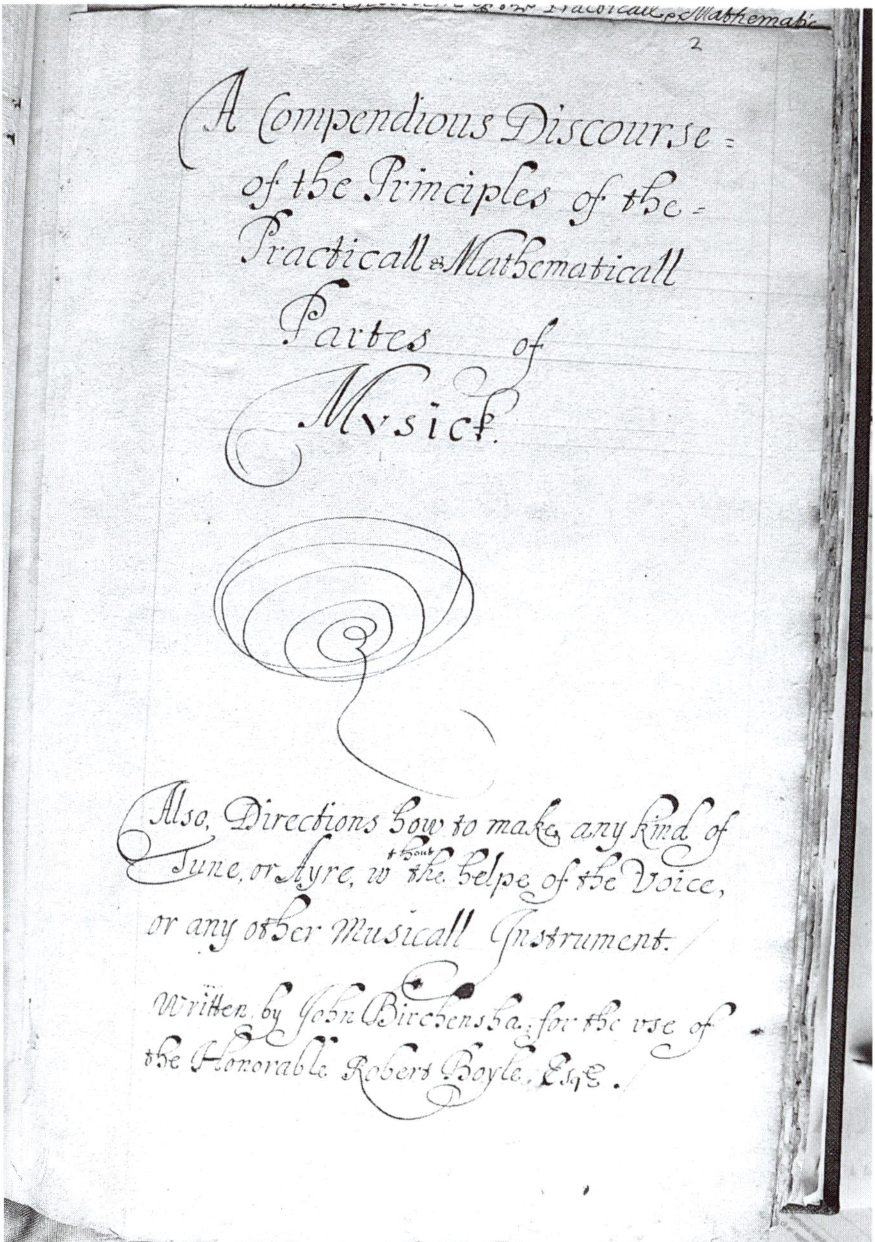

Figure 3.1 Title-page from the 'Compendious Discourse' (London, Royal Society, Boyle Papers, vol. 41, fol. 2ʳ). Autograph. © The Royal Society.

presumably the *Syntagma musicæ* – of which this manuscript seems to have been intended as a compendium or sampler.[11]

Notes

[1] R.E.W. Maddison, *The Life of the Honourable Robert Boyle F.R.S.* (London, 1969), pp. 203–5; Keith Moore (with additions by Mary Sampson), *A Guide to the Archives and Manuscripts of the Royal Society* (London, 1995), pp. 41–2; Michael Hunter (with contributions by Edward B. Davis, Harriet Knight, Charles Littleton and Lawrence M. Principe), *The Boyle Papers: Understanding the Manuscripts of Robert Boyle* (Aldershot and Burlington, VT, 2007), pp. 22–31 and 37–44. Boyle's letters and papers belonging to the Royal Society have been published in microfilm by University Publications of America [UPA], accompanied by a guide by Michael Hunter, *Letters and Papers of Robert Boyle: A Guide to the Manuscripts and Microfilm* (Bethesda, MD, 1992).

[2] Cf Edward Heawood, *Watermarks mainly of the Seventeenth and Eighteenth Centuries*, Monumenta Chartae Papyraceae, vol. 1 (Hilversum, 1950), nos 2676, 2681, 2688; Andrew Ashbee, Robert Thompson and Jonathan Wainwright, *The Viola da Gamba Society Index of Manuscripts Containing Consort Music*, vol. 1 (Aldershot and Burlington, VT, 2001), p. 296.

[3] Cf Heawood, *Watermarks*, nos 733–4, 741–2, 763.

[4] The editors have compared the hand with holographs of Miles in London, British Library, Add. MS 4229, and Royal Society, Boyle Papers, vol. 36.

[5] Michael Hunter and Lawrence M. Principe, 'The Lost Papers of Robert Boyle', *Annals of Science*, 60 (2003): 269–311, at 294; reprinted in Hunter, *The Boyle Papers*, pp. 73–135, at 108. In this quotation the punctuation and expansions in square brackets are supplied by the present editors. Hunter and Principe tentatively identify the second of the 'Two Rolls' as a commentary on parts 2–4 of Descartes's *Principia philosophiæ* (Royal Society, Boyle Papers, vol. 24, pp. 223–306).

[6] Hunter and Principe, 'The Lost Papers', 270–71; Hunter, *The Boyle Papers*, pp. 74–5. The authors suggest ('The Lost Papers', 301; *The Boyle Papers*, p. 121) that an entry in another of Miles's inventories of Boyle's papers might also refer to the manuscript of the 'Compendious Discourse'. The item in question, no. 71 in the 'List of Titles as I sort em' dated 10 February 1742/3 (Royal Society, Boyle Papers, vol. 36, fol. 141[r]), was described by Miles as 'Musical progression – not his' (i.e. not by Boyle). This description does not fit the 'Compendious Discourse', however, and it seems unlikely that Miles would have included Birchensha's treatise in his 1743 inventory – which is believed to list a batch of Boyle's papers that he obtained from William Wotton's son-in-law in November 1742 – as well as the earlier one.

[7] Letter no. 318 in *The Correspondence of Henry Oldenburg*, eds A. Rupert Hall and Marie Boas Hall, vol. 2 (Madison, Milwaukee and London, 1966), pp. 190–201. Boyle's copy, which seems not to have been used by the editors of the Oldenburg correspondence as a source, was endorsed by Miles on fol. 31[v]: 'D[r] Wallis Tract of Mus[ick]'. See Hunter, *The Boyle Papers*, p. 490, and note 10 below.

[8] Katherine, the dowager Viscountess Ranelagh (1615–91), to whom Boyle had intended to leave his papers, was the Earl of Cork's fifth daughter; Joan, Countess

of Kildare (1611–56), Birchensha's former patron, was his fourth. Robert, the Earl's youngest son, was born in 1627 and died a week after Lady Ranelagh.

9   Dr Penelope Gouk has similarly dated the manuscript to *c*.1664: see Gouk, *Music, Science and Natural Magic in Seventeenth-Century England* (New Haven and London, 1999), p. 281. Leta Miller and Albert Cohen assign it to the period 'after 1664, before 1672' in *Music in the Royal Society of London 1660–1806* (Detroit Studies in Music Bibliography, 56; Detroit, 1987), p. 182.

10   Wallis's letters of 7 and 25 May are nos 316 and 320 in *The Correspondence of Henry Oldenburg*, vol. 2, pp. 179–82, 202–3; for his letter of 14 May, see note 7. The letters of 7 and 14 May were read at the Royal Society meeting on 18 May 1664. In the first of these (a reply to one in which Oldenburg had outlined the Royal Society's recent discussions about music) Wallis recomended that 'the Gentleman' – meaning Birchensha – 'be incouraged in his design'. In the second, Wallis argued in favour of a scheme of just intonation, declaring that he could not tell 'how far this may agree with Mr Birchinsha's Thoughts or Notions concerning the same subject'. The copy made for Boyle includes the following postscript, which is not in the original: 'Since I had written this, I find that our Modern Writers of the Theory of Musick (in this, & part of the last Century,) have, upon like Principles, divided the Monochord much after the same Proportions as I have done: though our Practicall Musicians, generally, take no notice of it'. The postscript partly replicates a corrective remark in Wallis's letter to Oldenburg of 25 May; this suggests that Wallis may have written Boyle's copy at around that time. In fact Birchensha's concept of Pythagorean intonation being applied throughout a wide range of keys was at odds both with Wallis's theoretical position and (so far as one can tell) with the contemporary practice of lutenists, viol players, organ tuners and other musicians.

11   See for example chapter 11 of the 'Practicall Part', and chapters 4, 5, 9, 17, 20 and 21 of the 'Mathematicall Part'.

Edition

[fol. 2ʳ]

A Compendious Discourse of the Principles of the Practicall & Mathematicall Partes of Mvsick.

∞

Also, Directions how to make any kind of Tune, or Ayre, w^thout the helpe of the Voice, or any other Musicall Instrument.

Written by John Birchensha, for the use of the Honorable Robert Boyle Esqre.[1]

[fol. 3ʳ = p. 1]

A Compendium
⟨of the material principles, and Elements⟩
of the Practicall & Mathematic[a]ll
Part of Musick.

Before the Mathematicall Part of Musick ⟨can⟩ be rightly understood, there a⟨re⟩ Som pr[ae]cognita; sc[ilicet], som Principles and Elements of the Practicall part of Musick to be foreknown.

Principles, Axioms, Theorems &c. of practicall Musick.

1. The Series of Intension, & Remission is called the Scale of Musick.[2]
2. The Scale of Musick varieth, both according to Ancient & Modern Musicians[.][3]
3. The[a] Nature of mu[sica]ll so[un]ds is visibly perceived by diverse Markes & characters.
4. Notes are varied according to the Augmentation & Diminution of their Values: & Mutation of their Voices.[4]
5. The Markes or characters of Notes are Letters: signed Keyes: or mu[sica]ll Voices.[5]
6. The said Markes are placed & circumscribed in certaine Lynes & Spaces[.]
7. The Progression of mu[sica]ll Keyes, is either continued or Discontinued.[6]
8. Musicall voices, as they are distant from one another, are called Intervalls.
   ⟨But of these Things particularly.⟩

Elements of Practicall Musick.

To the End that a Mu[sica]ll so[un]d may be known; there is need of certaine Signes, by which the quantity, & Quality thereof may be Repr[e]-sented.[7] which signes or characters are placed ⟨in⟩ the Lines and Spaces of a mu[sica]ll System.

---

[a]　?*audible* deleted.

⟨Chap[ter] 1.⟩ Of a mu[sica]ll System ⟨or pentagramm⟩,

It ⟨is⟩ either

> The Greater. or
> The Lesser.

The Greater System is Ten Parallel Lines, thus

The Lesser System is five Parallel Lines, thus

It is called a System, figuratively, because it containeth, those mu[sica]ll Bodies which Musicians call Systems. The Thing containeing, by the Name of the thing contained.[8]

But because (in a Song of great Compass) there are more Notes then can be placed in five Lines, and their spaces; therefore musicians Add one, and somtimes two Additional or Leiger Lines:[9] placeing them somtime aboue and somtimes below the system (called also a Pentagram[10]),[a] thus

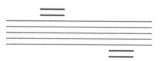

[fol. 3ᵛ = p. 2]

⟨And⟩[b] because Ten Lynes Dazel the Sight, and fiue are too few for many Parts; Musicians ⟨draw⟩ more Simple Systems in an Abacus, melopoetick chart, or Compositary.[11] According to the number of the parts. Thus

---

    [a]   Illegible words deleted.
    [b]   *But* deleted.

According to the number of parts the composer draweth his cross barrs or lines; somtimes at the End of one Time, somtimes of two; Seldom of more.[12] from hence it is called a mu[sica]ll Score. For the Musician, by these cross scores or barrs can better discern each part, and so read (by compareing one ⟨note⟩ with an other) his song.[13] Which is written by certaine[a]

        Letters. or

        Marks: characters: or Figures, called Notes.

The So[un]ds, as marked with Letters (sc, the first 7 Letters of our Alphabet, viz A. B. C. D. E. F. G.)[b] ⟨are⟩ called Keyes: Cliffes: moodes: ⟨&⟩ differing Voices. The gravest octaue is marked (as I have shewed) with Capital Letter: the second Octaue, or Lyre, with small Letter: the 3[d] octave, with geminated Letters &c.[14]

⟨Chap[ter] 2.⟩

These Keyes are either

        Natural. or

        fict.

The naturall Keyes are marked as aforesaid.

The fict Keyes are those which are, by remission of the voice or chord,[c] made flatt, and marked thus (♭) and are Graver then the natural Keys, by the greater half note; Called Apotome.[15] And

those[d] Keyes which (by the Intension of the Voice or Chord) are made sharpe, and marked thus (♯)[e] are acuter then the Natural Key⟨es⟩ by an Apotome.

These[f] Keyes, (considered as they stand Related to one another in a Scale of musick,) are[g] either

        Sharp:

        Flatt: or

        Perfect:

Sharp, as B. & E.

Flatt, as C. & F.

---

[a] MS has *certaines*.

[b] *and* deleted.

[c] *and* deleted.

[d] Illegible word deleted.

[e] *and they* deleted.

[f] *The Audible qualities of these* altered to *These*.

[g] ?*those that are* deleted.

Perfect, as A. D. & G.

Those Keys are Sharpe, which are a Ton[e] or whole note Acute from their graver proximate Key: and Graue ⟨but⟩ by a Semitone or lesser Halfe note from their proximate acuter Key.

Flat Keyes are but a Semitone acute from their grauer proximate Keye[a]: and graver by a Tone then their proximate acuter Key.

Perfect Keyes, are a Tone acute from their proximate Graver Key: & alike distant from their proximate acuter Key.[16]

[fol. 4ʳ = p. 3]

⟨Chap[ter] 3.⟩

These Keyes by the Ancients were called Moodes, and named, by Glareanus, thus.[17]

A – Hypodorius.
B – Hypophrygius.
C – Hypolydius.
D – Dorius.
E – Phrygius.
F – Lydius.
G – Mixolydius.
a – Hypermixolydius –

The Keyes in the Greeke scale, & in the Latine scale (perfected by Guido) are thus named ⟨or voiced⟩. as in this following Table.

---

[a]   *s* deleted.

⟨Chap[ter] 4⟩– Of the Denominations of Notes or Keyes[a,18]

	Denominations of Notes in the Scale of Guido.							Denominations of Notes in the Greeke Scale according to Pythagoras.	
aa								aa: Nete Hyperbolæon	
g	sol							Paranete Hyperbolæon	
f	fa		sol					Trite Hyperbolæon	
e	la		fa	sol				Nete Diezeugmenon	
d	sol		la	fa			sol	Paranete Diezeugmenon	Nete Synemmenon
c	fa	sol	sol	la			fa	Trite Diezeugmenon	Paran[e]te Synemmenon
B	mi	fa	fa	sol	sol	la		Paramese	
B♭									Trite Synemmenon.
a	la	la	mi	fa	fa	sol	sol	Mese.	
G	sol	sol	la	mi	la	fa	fa	Lychanos Meson	
F	fa	fa	sol	la	sol	la	mi	Paranete meson	
E	la	mi		sol	fa	sol	la	Hypate Meson	
D	sol	la			mi	fa	sol	Lychanos Hypaton	
C	fa	sol			la	mi		Parhypate Hypaton	
B	mi				sol	la		Hypate Meson	
A	la					sol		Proslambanomenos.	
Γ	sol								

These 4 names given by Guido, are not proper; but names common to every Keye. and, by Mutation of voices, being variously apply[e]d, do shew, that by the Addition of the (♭ cliffe or mark.) the differing Keyes do alter their nature: and are thereby Metamorphosed, and assume various formes: yet retaine one and the Same nature and Reason. which may Seeme a Paradox, that ⟨a so[un]d should be⟩ one and the Same, & yet diverse.[b]

The 4 Denominations of voices or so[un]ds are. sol. la. mi. fa.

---

[a] In the table, the denominations *Paranete meson* (alongside *F* in row 11) and *Hypate Meson* (alongside *B* in row 15) are apparently Birchensha's mistakes for *Parhypate Meson* and *Hypate Hypaton* respectively. The three occurrences of the word *Synemmenon* in the final column were originally written as *Diezeugmenon*, which Birchensha deleted and corrected.

[b] Altered from *that one and the Same should be the same yet diverse.*

Through an Octaue the notes are thus named:

$$\left\{\begin{array}{cccccccc} \text{G.} & \text{A.} & \text{B.} & \text{C.} & \text{D.} & \text{E.} & \text{F.} & \text{g.} \\ \text{sol.} & \text{la.} & \text{mi.} & \text{fa.} & \text{sol.} & \text{la.} & \text{fa.} & \text{Sol} \end{array}\right\}$$

The Keys do vary, according as they are diversly Transposed.
And their Transposition is known by the addition of the (♭ cliffe) being add⟨ed⟩ to the respective Notes.
    And this is the Rule of the Transposition of Keyes, & Mutation of mu[sica]ll Voices[:]

If there be no flatt, accidentaly, the first .Sol. ariseth from _____G.
If a flat, or (♭) be put to .B. it ariseth from _____C.
If to B. & E, it ariseth from _____F
If to B. E. & A. it ariseth from _____B♭
If to B. E. A. & D. it ariseth from _____E♭
If to B. E. A. D. and G. it ariseth from _____A♭
And if a flat bee put to B. E. A. D. G. and C. It ariseth from _____D♭.
But if to B. E. A. D. G. C. & F — it ariseth from G♭ _____G♭

Every addition of the (♭ cliffe) maketh the first .sol. to Arise from the fifth Graue. As in the following System.

[fol. 4ᵛ] = p. 4

⟨Chap[ter] 5 –⟩ Table of the Mutation of mu[sica]ll Voices[19]

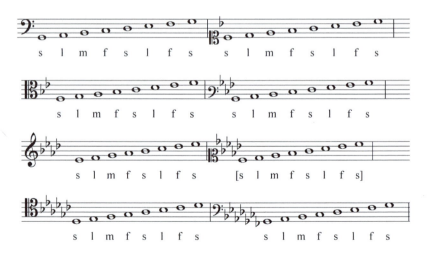

Now to the End that the places of the Notes may be known, the Signed Keyes (as in the foregoeing Table) are prefixed before every song. placed alwaies in the Lines, and are distant from one another a Diapente or Fifth. They are transposed by Reason of the Profundity & Altitude of a Song.[20]

The Signed Keyes are reduced to Three. viz;

To F. which is the signed Key of the Bass Part. and marked thus.

To C. which is the signed Key of the Meane Part. and marked thus –

And to G. which is the signed Key of the Treble Part. and marked thus –

⟨Chap[ter] 6 –⟩ Table or Type of the signed Keyes.

F. Bass.   C. meane   Treble.

Many other markes the Ancients used: but modern Musicians use onely these, and place them, as in this Type or Table.

⟨Chap[ter] 7 – ⟩ Of the characters of Notes.

The aforesaid Moodes or Keyes are expressed by diverse figures or Characters, by which their values are known. as in the following Figure.

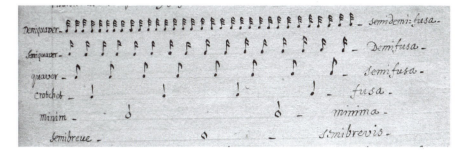

The Semibreue is without a Taile; the Rest are Caudatæ, or Tailed notes, whose Tailes may be drawn either upward or downward. As

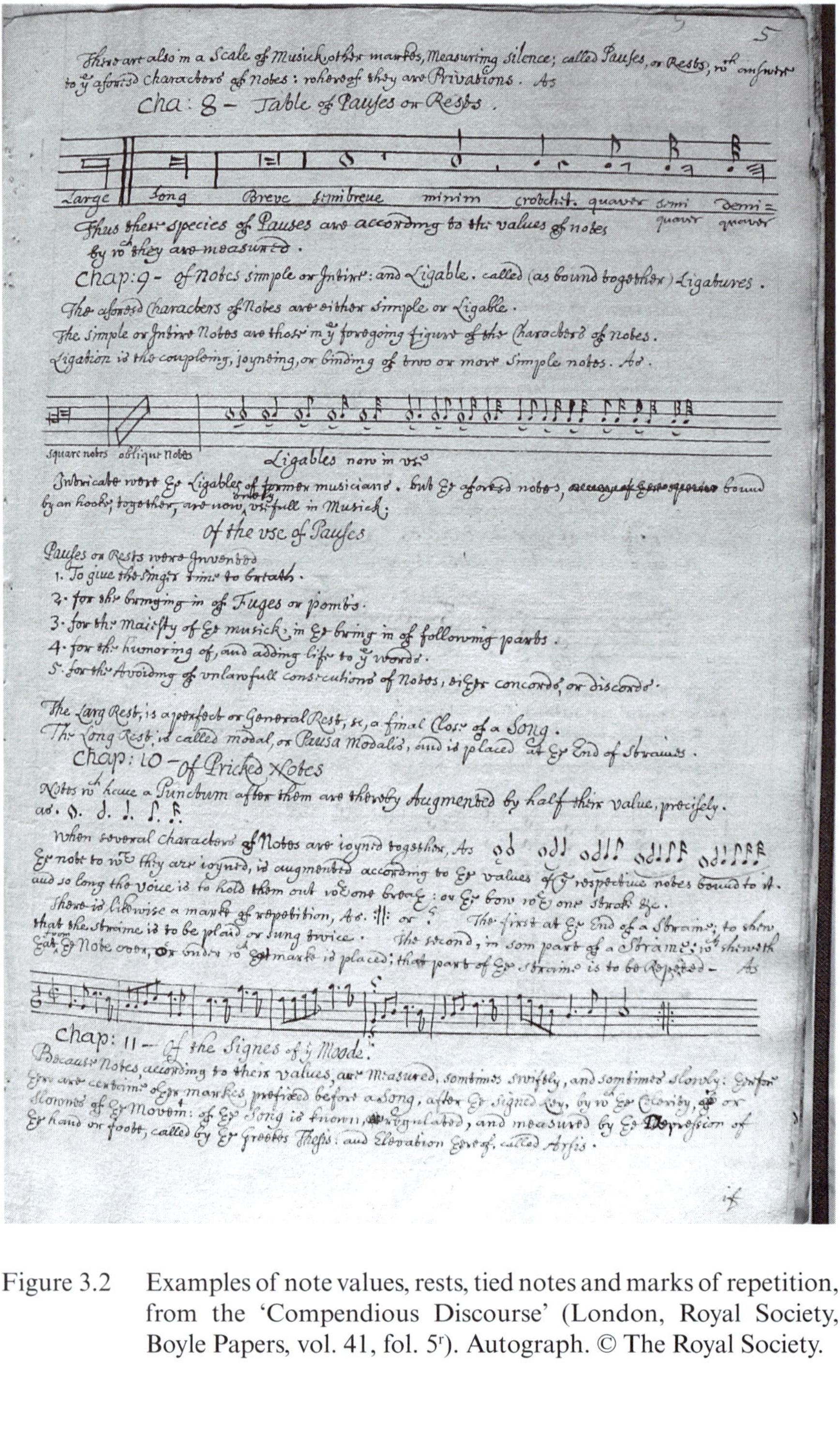

Figure 3.2　Examples of note values, rests, tied notes and marks of repetition, from the 'Compendious Discourse' (London, Royal Society, Boyle Papers, vol. 41, fol. 5r). Autograph. © The Royal Society.

There are other characters of Notes, which are not written, or prick'd in songs, but serve for the completeing the Values of notes, according to the proportions of consonant and dissonant Intervalls as I shall shew in the mathematicall Part of musick: but their figures I will giue you here.[21]

♪ 　　　　　 Semidemiquaver.

▭ 　– 　　　 Breve.

▯ 　– 　　　 Longe.

▭ 　– 　　　 Large. &c.

From the semidemiquaver to that character which is of the greatest value; a Progress is made by Multiplication, sc, duplication. And from the Note of the greatest value to the ♪ semidemiquaver, a Regress is made by Division. For every greater Note, is in value double the proximate lesser note. so that.

A quaver is in value two semiquavers. ♪♪

A crotchet is 2 quavers, & 4 Semiquavers. as in the Table. and so de ceter[is] – [fol. 5ʳ = p. 5]

There are also in a Scale of Musick, other markes, Measuring silence; called Pauses, or Rests, which answer to the afores[ai]d characters of Notes: whereof they are Privations. As

⟨Cha[pter] 8 – ⟩ Table of Pauses or Rests.

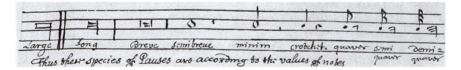

Thus these species of Pauses are according to the values of notes by which they are measured.[22]

⟨Chap[ter] 9 – ⟩ Of Notes simple or Intire: and Ligable. called (as bound together) – Ligatures.

The afores[ai]d Characters of Notes are either Simple or Ligable.
The simple or Intire Notes are those in the foregoing figure of the Characters of Notes.
Ligation is the coupleing, joyneing, or binding of two or more Simple notes. As.

square notes   oblique Notes

Ligables now in use

Intricate were the Ligables of former musicians. but the afores[ai]d notes,[a] bound by an hooke, together, are now ⟨onely⟩ vsefull in Musick.[23]

Of the use of Pauses

Pauses or Rests were Invented

1. To giue the singer time to breath[e].
2. for the bringing-in of Fuges or point's.
3. for the Maiesty of the musick, in the bring[ing] in of following parts.
4. for the humoring of, and adding life to the words.
5. for the Avoiding of unlawfull consecutions of Notes, either concords, or discords.[24]

The Larg[e] Rest, is a perfect or General Rest, sc, a final Close of a Song.
The Long Rest, is called modal, or Pausa Modalis, and is placed at the End of Straines.

⟨Chap[ter] 10 – ⟩ Of Pricked Notes

Notes which haue a Punctum after them are thereby Augmented by half their value, precisely.[25] as

---

[a]   *or any of these species* deleted.

When several characters of Notes are ioyned together, As

the note to which they are ioyned, is augmented according to the values of the respectiue notes bound to it. and so long the voice is to hold them out with one breath: or the bow with one stroke &c.

There is likewise a marke of repetition, As, ||: or 𝄋 The first at the End of a Straine; to shew that the straine is to be plaid or sung twice. The second, in som part of a Straine; which sheweth that ⟨from⟩ the Note over, or under which[a] that marke is placed; that part of the straine is to be Repeated[26] – As[b]

⟨Chap[ter] 11 –⟩ Of the Signes of the Moode.

Because Notes, according to their Values, are Measured, somtimes swiftly, and somtimes slowly: therefore there are certaine other markes prefixed before a Song, after the Signed Key, by which the Celerity,[c] or Slownes of the Movem[en]t of the Song is known, regulated, and measured by the Depression[d] of the hand or foote, called by the Greekes Thesis: and Elevation thereof, called Arsis.

[fol. 5ᵛ = p. 6]

If All the Parts move together, (haueing one and the same Time note,[e] which may be equaly divided, as a Semibreve) these are the vsual Markes.

ᵃ   *over whic[h]* altered to *over, or under which.*

ᵇ   In the MS the final note of the following example is a minim.

ᶜ   *of* deleted.

ᵈ   *Ele[vation]* altered to *Depression.*

ᵉ   *notes* altered to *note.*

C placed before pavins, and other Slow tunes
2 placed before Aires &c.
₵ placed before more active songs as Bransles &c
𝄼 placed before Gavots &c.

If the Time note be alike in All the Parts, and vnequaly divided; (as Semibreue & prick &c) these, or such like are the vsual markes

C placed before Galliards &c.
$\frac{C}{32}$ placed before corants &c.
31 – placed before Sarabands &c.
61 – Jigues &c.[27]

But if one part haue (for the Time note) an Intire note, and an other part hath a note, – vnequaly divided – Then the proportion is of Inequality. and the vsual markes are one of these.[28]

$\frac{2}{1}$ $\frac{3}{2}$ $\frac{6}{4}$ &c.

Very many are the Signes of the Moodes which were used by Ancient musicians; ⟨and they are⟩ Intricate, and difficult to be understood. of which I shall giue som Account in my practical part of musick.[29]

Of the Denomination of mu[sica]ll voices or notes I haue already writed, I will now write of their Distances. ⟨Chap[ter] 12.⟩

The aforesaid characters of notes, as they are proximately Adioyneing, are called Degrees, as

When they are more Remotely distant they are called Diastems or Intervalls. Every one of these degrees are distant from his proximate Note or Key, a Tone or whole note, except. C. and F. which are acute from the Key next below them, by a Semitone or lesser half note.[30]

The Remoter Keyes or Intervalls are these, in the following Table, in number. 14.[a]

---

[a]   *15* altered to *14*.

2ᵃ - 2ᵃ - 3ᵃ - 3ᵃ - 4ᵃ- Se[mi] - Tri- - 5ᵃ - 6ᵃ - 6ᵃ - 7ᵃ- Se[mi] -7ᵃ - 8ᵃ
mi   ma   mi   ma   Dia   tonˢ   mi   ma   mi   Dia   ma
                         pente   pason

These Intervalls are, onely, of vse in harmony. (in the diatonic & chromatick Genus) of which

Som are Consonant, as the 5th – and 8th

Som are Concinnous, as the 3ᵃ mi – 3ᵃ ma – Se[mi] Diapente – 6ᵃ mi – 6ᵃ ma – &

Som are Dissonant, as the 2ᵃ mi – 2ᵃ ma – 4ᵃ – Tritonus – 7ᵃ mi – se[mi] Diapason – 7ᵃ ma –

But on the other leafe I will giue an Account of the Denominations of the said Consonant, Concinnous, and Dissonant Intervalls in the Scale of Greeke, Latine, and English Authors, to the End that those things which they haue written of them may the better be understood.[31]
[fol. 6ʳ = p. 7]

⟨Chap[ter] 13 –⟩ Denominations of Intervalls.[32]

Keyes	Græca-Latina	Latina	English	number of Intervalls.
g	Diapason	octaua, sc, chorda	Eigth	14
F♯	Hep⟨ta⟩chordum majus	Septima maior	Greater seventh	13
G♭	Semidiapason	Octava imperfecta	Imperfect Eigth	12
F	Heptachordum minus	septima minor	Lesser Seventh	11
E	Hexachordum majus	Sexta maior	Greater Sixth	10
E♭	Hexachordum minus	Sexta minor	Lesser Sixth	9
D	Diapente	quinta	Fifth.	8
D♭	Semidiapente	quinta imperfecta	Imperfect fifth	7
C♯	Tritonus	quarta excessiva	Excessiue fourth	6
C	Diatessaron	quarta	Fourth	5
B	Ditonus	Tertia major	Greater Third	4
B♭	semiditonus	Tertia minor	Lesser or imperfect Third	3
A	Tonus	Secunda maior	Greater Second	2
A♭	Semi-tonium	Secunda minor	Lesser or imperfect Second	1
G	Proslambanomenos	chorda Assumpta or Vnisonus	Vnison	

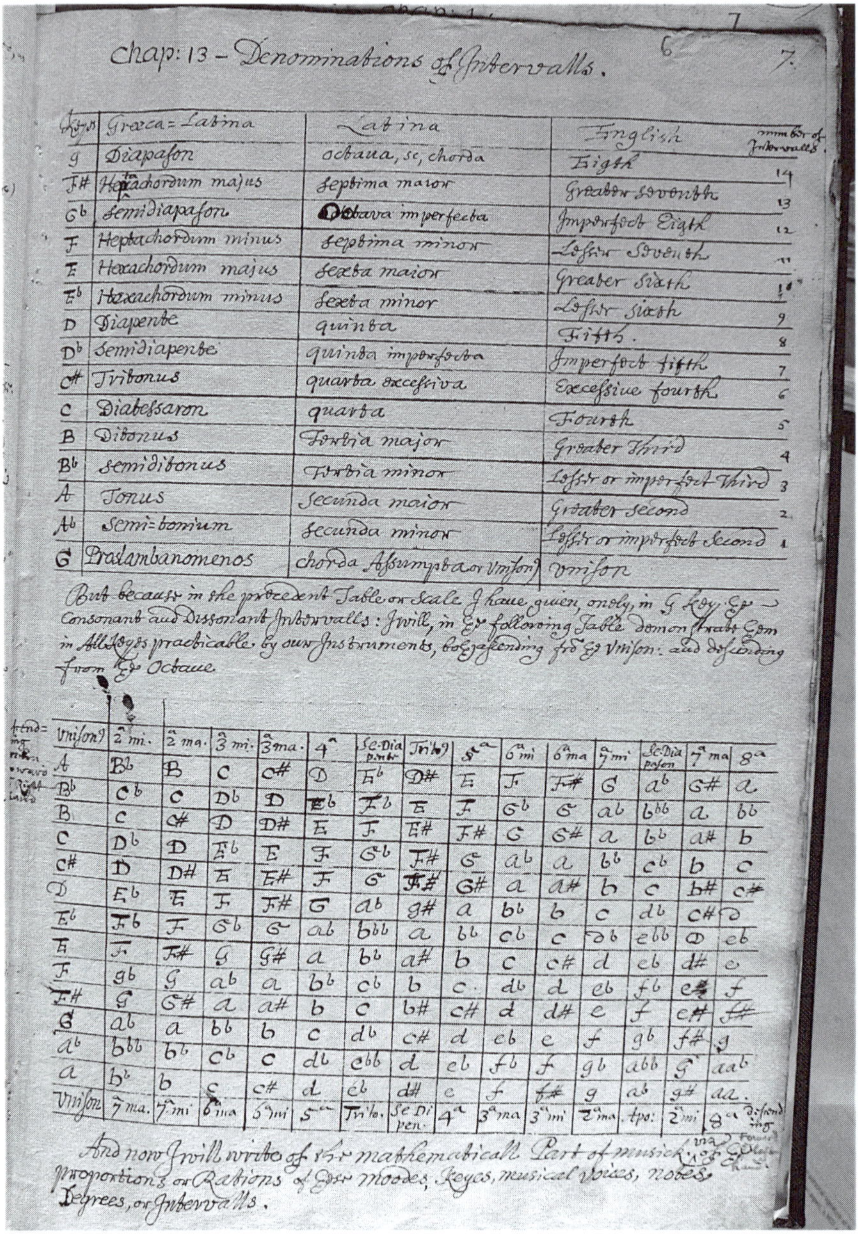

Figure 3.3   Tables of 'Denominations of Intervalls' and of 'Consonant and Dissonant Intervalls in All Keyes practicable by our Instruments', from the 'Compendious Discourse' (London, Royal Society, Boyle Papers, vol. 41, fol. 6ʳ). Autograph. © The Royal Society.

Vnisonus	2ᵃ mi.	2ᵃ ma.	3ᵃ mi.	3ᵃ ma.	4ᵃ	Se.Dia pente	Trito[n]us	5ᵃ	6ᵃ mi	6ᵃ ma	7ᵃ mi	Se.Dia pason	7ᵃ ma	8ᵃ
A	B♭	B	C	C♯	D	E♭	D♯	E	F	F♯	G	a♭	G♯	a
B♭	C♭	C	D♭	D	E♭	F♭	E	F	G♭	G	a♭	b♭♭	a	b♭
B	C	C♯	D	D♯	E	F	E♯	F♯	G	G♯	a	b♭	a♯	b
C	D♭	D	E♭	E	F	G♭	F♯	G	a♭	a	b♭	c♭	b	c
C♯	D	D♯	E	E♯	F[♯]	G	F𝄪	G♯	a	a♯	b	c	b♯	c♯
D	E♭	E	F	F♯	G	a♭	G♯	a	b♭	b	c	d♭	c♯	d
E♭	F♭	F	G♭	G	a♭	b♭♭	a	b♭	c♭	c	d♭	e♭♭	d	e♭
E	F	F♯	G	G♯	a	b♭	a♯	b	c	c♯	d	e♭	d♯	e
F	G♭	G	a♭	a	b♭	c♭	b	c	d♭	d	e♭	f♭	e	f
F♯	G	G♯	a	a♯	b	c	b♯	c♯	d	d♯	e	f	e♯	f♯
G	a♭	a	b♭	b	c	d♭	c♯	d	e♭	e	f	g♭	f♯	g
a♭	b♭♭	b♭	c♭	c	d♭	e♭♭	d	e♭	f♭	f	g♭	aa♭♭	g	aa♭
a	b♭	b	c	c♯	d	e♭	d♯	e	f	f♯	g	aa♭	g♯	aa
Vnison	7ᵃ ma.	7ᵃ mi	6ᵃ ma	6ᵃ mi	5ᵃ	Trito[nus]	Se[.] Di[a] pen[te]	4ᵃ	3ᵃ ma	3ᵃ mi	2ᵃ ma	Apo [tome]	2ᵃ mi	8ᵃ

But because in the precedent Table or Scale I haue giuen, onely, in G Key the Consonant and Dissonant Intervalls: I will, in the following Table demonstrate them in All Keyes practicable by our Instruments, both ascending from the Vnison: and descending from the Octaue[.] [see p. 113] [a,33]

And now I will write of the mathematicall Part of musick. ⟨viz⟩ of the proportions or Rations of these Moodes, Keyes, musical Voices, Notes, Degrees, or Intervalls.

[fol. 6ᵛ = p. 8]

Observations[34]

A mu[sica]ll So[un]d   —   Theoretically considered, is called,
                                                          (respectively)
                                                                    Being —
                                                                    Body —
A mu[sica]ll — — —   Number —
                                                                    Magnitude

                                                          Practically considered
                                                                    Moode
                                                                    Key
                                                                    Intervall
                                                                    Note
                                                                    Voice

---

[a]   MS has the marginal notes *Ascending* ⟨*when toward the Right hand*⟩ at the top left of the table, and *descending* ⟨*toward the left hand.*⟩ at the bottom right. It also contains the following uncorrected slips: g♯ for G♯ in row 6 (column 8); D for d in row 7 (column 14); g♭ for G♭ in row 9 (column 2); a♭♭ for aa♭♭ in row 12 (column 13); and a♭ for aa♭ in row 13 (column 13). In row 5 (column 8) Birchensha uses his distinctive form of double sharp sign, with three horizontal strokes.

[fol. 7ʳ = p. 9]

⟨A Compendium of the material⟩ Principles ⟨& Elements⟩ of the Mathematicall Part of Musick.

What it is. ⟨Chap[ter] 1.⟩

The mathematicall part of Musick, is
A Science demonstrateing the Rations of So[un]ds by the Comparation of Numbers: and the Proportions of So[un]ds, by the Comparations of their Rations[.][35]

6 —	4 –	Ratio[n].
4 —	3 –	Ratio[n].

---

24 —	12 –	Propo[rtio]n

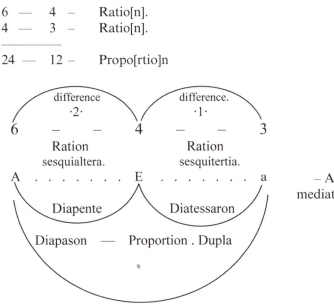

– A Diapason System mediated harmonically.[36]

It makes Inspection both into the Arithm[etica]ll and[a] Geometricall part of Musick. for[37]

1. It seeks out the Causes ⟨Natures &⟩ properties of Musicall So[un]ds, as compared with one another.

2. It considers such So[un]ds as they are perceptible by the Senses, & no otherwise.

---

[a]   *Practicall* deleted.

3. It considers them distinctly.

4. It considers[a] a So[un]d as it hath a form. (concretely.) not barely as a so[un]d (i.e. Abstractly).

5. It Respects the order, and Commensuration of[b] So[un]ds.[38]

6. It considers So[un]ds as disjoyned, divided, Related, different, measured, determined, rational, general, special, numerable, proportionate, equal, vnequal, like, vnlike, productiue, corruptible, distant, graue, acute &c[.]

7. It assumes demonstrations from knowne principles; and raiseth our minds and contemplation (in musick) to those things which are philosophicall: and stirreth ⟨them up⟩[c] from those things which are onely sensible, to those which are intellectual and Divine.

⟨Chap[ter] 2⟩ Axioms of the ⟨Arithmeticall⟩[d] Part of Musick.

1. The Unison, as extended, (which may be demonstrated by the chord of an Instrum[en]t) and divided; is greater then any part thereof. because the divided p[ar]ts thereof are contained in it.[39]

2. If to Equal Intervalls (⟨i.e⟩ equal in respect of Ration, or the parts of a chord) eq[ua]ll be added, the whole will be[e] Equal.[40]

3. If from Eq[ua]ll Intervalls, Equall be taken away, those which remaine will be eq[ua]ll.

4. Intervalls which are Eq[ua]ll or vneq[ua]ll to one & the same, are eq[ua]ll or vneq[ua]ll between themselves.

5. Intervalls which are the dimidium of the same; or equaly Lesser: are eq[ua]ll between themselves.

6 – The part of an Intervall is Less then the whole.

7 – As often as an Intervall may be substracted from any m[usica]ll System: so often that system is numerable by it.[41]

8 – Every dupla proportion, consists of a Sesquialtera & a sesquitertia proportion.[42]

9 – Every sesquitertia proportion consists of a sesquioctaua, and a super .13. partiens .243. proportion[.][43]

[fol. 7[v] = p. 10]

10 – Every sesquialtera proportion, consists of a Super .5. partiens, 27 – and a super .17. partiens. 64 – proportion.[44]

---

a   ?*such* deleted.

b   ?*such* deleted.

c   *stirreth up our Contemplations* deleted.

d   *Mathem[aticall]* deleted.

e   *Added* deleted.

11 – If a sesquitertia proportion be taken from a Diapason, a sesquialtera proportion, onely, will remaine.[45] and

12 – If a sesquialtera proportion be taken fro[m] a Diapason; a sesquitertia proportion onely will remaine.[46]

All these Axioms, are demonstrated in my Scales of the proportions of So[un]ds.[47]

⟨Chap[ter] 3 –⟩ Axioms which concerne the Geometricall Part of Musick.

1. The Radical So[un]d or Vnison (as unextend⟨ed⟩), is the Least mu[sica]ll Magnitude. but being extended, (which is demonstrated by the Intension of a Chord) it measureth every Intervall, into which it may be divided, and which is a part thereof, or which proceedeth from it.[48]
2. By the Continuation of the vnison (so extended) to a certaine and defined Terme, every Intervall is[a] formed, & made Such an Intervall.
3. A Diatessaron & a Diapente acute to that: and a Diapason acute to that Diapente, are (each of them) of the Same Magnitude, as to the proportional parts of the s[ai]d Vnison: but of different Rations. As may be demonstrated by the partition or division of a chord. as[b] I shall instance presently[.][49]
4. It is to be supposed that the radicall So[un]d may be infinitely extended. But it is necessary to bound that Infinity: which is performed, when the extended vnison is divided into 2. equal parts.
5. The vnison may not infinitely be decreased. (nay not at all) for we must not suppose that there can be a graver so[un]d then the radicall Key of a Scale of musick.[50]
6. A great⟨er⟩ mu[sica]ll Magnitude can not commensurate the Lesser: but on the contrary, great⟨er⟩ magnitudes may be commensurated by[c] ⟨those which are⟩ Lesser. as a Disdiapason is commensurated by a Diatessaron: a diapente and a diapason[51] – and so every greater System is measured by those parts of which it is constituted, and by which it is completed. as I shall presently shew[.][52]
7. The Radical So[un]d (as only emitted out of the Sonorous Instrum[en]t) is vndivided.
8. Every Intervall (considered, onely, as extended) is onely long. i.e. it hath Longitude, but not Latitude and Crassitude. It is only acute: but it hath not mollity & Asperity.[53]

---

[a] ?*constructed* deleted.
[b] *as* written twice in MS.
[c] ?*a* deleted.

9. In the progresse and division of the Radicall vnison into diverse So[un]ds or Intervalls: the gravest Terme of every specificall, i.e. Individual, & Numericall Intervall, is different, as – A – B – C – D &c.

10. The principles of a mu[sica]ll magnitude, are Matter: (i.e. The sonorous nature of the radicall vnison, which is communicated to it by the fluxion thereof) and Form, (sc, the full extent and Term thereof.) by which it is such an Intervall, sc, as 3[d]. 4[th]. 5[th] &c. So that

11 – The Material principle of every mu[sica]ll Magnitude, is the Radical vnison: But the formal principle thereof, is the Order of the Continuity of the s[ai]d vnison, to a certaine or defined Terme.

[fol. 8[r] = p. 11]

⟨Chap[ter] 4 –⟩ Of the Arithmeticall Part of musick in[a] General. ⟨and of the Division of so[un]ds.⟩

It is the Science of numbering mu[sica]ll So[un]ds (or Numbers) well.

These Numbers or So[un]ds (for the right understand[ing] of the Scale of Musicke) may be thus divided or considered –

1. Such numbers or So[un]ds are either
   Even, or
   Odd.

An Even mu[sica]ll Number or So[un]d, is that which may be divided into two Eq[ua]ll parts. ⟨Equall⟩ both in respect of Ration and the proportion[a]ll parts of the So[un]d, or chord.

No So[un]d can be thus divided but the Radicall Vnison. which is divided into two diapasons. both being of a Dupla Ration: and of eq[ua]ll magnitude – ex[empli] gra[tia] – [54]

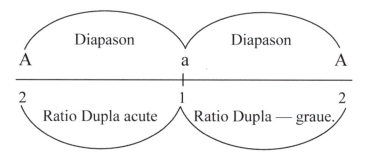

An odd Number or So[un]d is that which cannot, So, be equaly divided.

---

[a] *Special[l]* deleted.

All Intervalls are vnequaly divided – for

If they be divided into 2 Sou[nd]s, eq[ua]ll in Ration, they will be of vneq[ua]ll magnitude.
If they be divided into 2 So[un]ds, of equall magnitude: these So[un]ds will be of vneq[ua]ll Rations – [55]

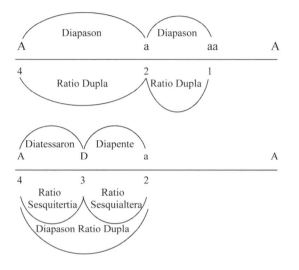

And so all other Intervalls are (in these Respects) odd numbers or So[un]ds. as will appeare, particularly, in my scale which sheweth the Rations & magnitudes of all consonant and dissonant So[un]ds usefull in musick, and of all numericall Intervalls, of which those So[un]ds are constituted – Againe

> 2. Mu[sica]ll numbers or so[un]ds ⟨are⟩ either
>> 1 – Perfect.
>> 2. Diminute. or defective[.]
>> 3. Abounding, i.e. excessive[.]

1. Every mu[sica]ll Intervall is Perfect in his Kind: or according to his due proportion.
2. A defective so[un]d is that which wanteth somthing of his true, proper, & perfect proportion – As a Tone of a sesquinona proportion. which is defective by an Intervall of a sesquioctogesima proportion as 81–80 – &c.[56]
3. Abounding or Redundant so[un]ds, are those which exceed their due proportion. As a Tone of a sesquiseptima proportion – as 8–7 – which is more the[n] a perfect Tone [(]whose true proportion is a 9–8 –) by a sesquisexagesima tertia proportion, as 64–63. But these Intervalls, and suchlike, may be seen in my permixed Scale of conjoyned systems.

3. Musicall Numbers or So[un]ds are either
Simple. or
compounded[.]

Simple or Incompounded Intervalls are those[a] whose ⟨Radicall[b]⟩ Terme is
the same; as in the foregoing Scale of conson[an]t & dissonant Intervalls – [57]

A compound⟨ed⟩ Intervall is that which is divided, by som meane part
thereof, as

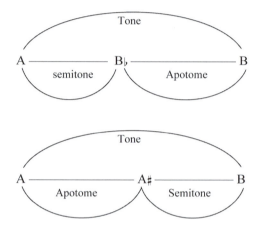

[fol. 8ᵛ = p. 12]

4 – M[usica]ll Numbers or So[un]ds, are –
1. Digite.
2. Articulate.
3. Compounded.

1. Digite So[un]ds, are all Simple Intervalls in the compasse of a Diapason,
as –

A — B — C — D — E — F — G — a

Digite so[un]ds   – called mu[sica]ll Keyes.

2. Articulate So[un]ds are those which are annexed to a diapason – as A.e –
E.g &c.

---

[a]   Altered from *A Simple or Incompounded Intervall is that*.
[b]   MS has *Radacall*.

3. Compounded So[un]ds (I meane not So[un]ds compounded as afores[ai]d) are those which are compounded of a Digite and Articulate So[un]d as A.bb – E gg &c.[58]

Now, if you demand, To what purpose mu[sica]ll Numbers or So[un]ds are thus divided, or variously (and vnder these severall Notions) considered? I answere, To the End that those materials which conduce to the makeing musicall Tunes, and Harmony, may be known, and distinguished. For.

1. So[un]ds must be first Emitted out of a Sonorous Instrument, before they can be extend⟨ed⟩ or Divided by the Art of the musician.
2. The Radicall vnison must be extended, before an Intervall can be produced, or formed.[59]
3. The Vnison must be divided into 2 eq[ua]ll parts, before a diapason be produced.
4. The diapason must be divided into 2 uneq[ua]ll parts, before a Simple Intervall can be produced.
5. If So[un]ds were not perfect in their kind, there could be no Consonancy, but all So[un]ds would be discordant.
6. If So[un]ds were not vnequal, there would be no variety in musick: for then there would be but one So[un]d.
7. If there ⟨were⟩ no So[un]ds but incompounded Intervalls, which (as I s[ai]d) have but one Radix: Terminus a quo, or common Denominator; there could be no collective System; or musicall Body, or Integral Totum of So[un]ds.
8. If there were no Digite So[un]ds, there would be no mu[sica]ll Keyes.
9. If there were no Articulate So[un]ds, the Scale of musick would extend but to a Diapason.
10. And if there were no compound⟨ed⟩ (i.e. duplicated so[un]ds) there could be no meane parts in Harmony.

So that without these various divisions, and considerations of So[un]ds, there could, neither be Tunes, nor consent of parts: and consequently no proper object for the Choicest of our Senses, sc, the Eare.

A mu[sica]ll Number or Intervall, is that, which in severall parts of my Booke, I call a Multitude, which ariseth from a conflux of vnisons. For in a strict sense the Radicall Vnison cannot be so called ⟨(sc, a multitude)⟩. But in a Larg[e] sense it may. sc, as it is so in power, not in Act. I say, although the vnison (as unextend⟨ed⟩[a] & vndivided) is not properly a mu[sica]ll number; yet as extended & divided it may be so accounted of: because, being divided, it is not looked vpon as a Monad, or abstractly considered, but as a concrete so[un]d & mu[sica]ll quantity. Therefore if we reckon from Grauity to acutenes, the

---

　　[a]　The MS has *extend⟨ed⟩*, which is surely an error.

vnison is a radicall so[un]d, not an Intervall; or a Multitude: but if we reckon from acutenes to grauity, it may be looked vpon as an Intervall or multitude. (of which I haue written chap[ter]—of the Relation of So[un]ds).[60]

Haue⟨ing⟩ written these things, concerning the Division & principles of mu[sica]ll So[un]ds as Numerable – I will write of their Affections, which haue Respect to their simple & compared Computation.

[fol. 9ʳ = p. 13]

⟨Chap[ter] 5 – ⟩ Of the Simple Computation of mu[sica]ll Numbers or So[un]ds

It is that whereby they are Treated of as void of comparison. And it is fiue-fold, viz

> Numeration.
> Addition.
> Substraction.
> Multiplication.
> Division.

1. Of the Numeration of Mu[sica]ll So[un]ds or Notes.

It is the right Notation of them: by which they are put into certaine Places. i.e. into the Lines & spaces of a System.

There they are distinguished by Degrees, which are the proximate Keyes, viz, Graue: Meane: & Acute. as

A.	B.	C.	D.	E.	F.	G —	graue. or Bass	
a —	b —	c.	d.	e.	f.	g —	meane	} Keyes
aa —	bb —	cc.	dd —	ee.	ff.	gg —	Acute. or Treble	

These Degrees of Mu[sica]ll Numbers or So[un]ds are thus Iterated by diverse Periods (sc, Octaues), and, so, put into those Ranges or Classes. (as in the following Scale of Tetrachords.[)] whose periods are noted with the Same Letters. But with this Difference; The first Octaue is marked with capital Letter: the second with minute: and the Third with Geminated Letters, as afores[ai]d. So that at the End of seven Keyes, the Octaues begin againe; the same Key begining & ending the Octaue.

The Notes are known by their figures or Characters, (as I formerly shewed) which are significatiue of their Respectiue values. And according to their severall places, (which are known by the prefixing the Signed Keyes, (sc;

to the System) such are their Distances. as one Degree is a Second: two Degrees a third, and so of the Rest. I say the second Degree is called a third; because the extreme So[un]ds are inclusiue of that distance in which there are three So[un]ds, and two Intervall[s]. as in a Fourth, there are 4 so[un]ds and but three Intervalls – et sic de ceter[is] –

The characters of Notes being thus placed in a System they may be Sung. Thus the placeing of notes in a Song is as writeing in a booke: The letters, syllables, & words must be written in their proper places, before a Sentence can be read. So that, what Delineations is in painting: Location of figures, in Arithmetick: circles, pyramids, Angles &c in Geometry: writeing in Booke; that pricking (as we call it) is in musick.

[fol. 9ᵛ = p. 14]

2. Of the Addition of Mu[sica]ll Numbers or Intervalls.

By the Addition of Intervalls, mu[sica]ll Systems, Bodies, or magnitudes are completed.

As a Semitone added to a Tone, completeth a Semiditonus.

An Apotome added to a Semiditonus, completeth a Ditonus.

Thus, every consonant and dissonant Intervall exceedes an other (i.e. its proximate so[un]d) either by a Semitone: Apotome; or Comma. I say these Distances are the differences of proximate chords or Keyes.[61]

As[a] a Semitone is the difference between
    an Apotome and Tone, or whole note.
    a Tone, & a Semiditonus.
    a Ditonus, and a Diatessaron.
    a Diatessaron, and a Semidiapente.
    a Tritonus, & a Diapente.
    a Diapente, and a 6[a] mi.
    a 6[a] ma: and a 7[a] mi.
    a 7[a] mi. and a Semidiapason. &
    a 7[a] ma. and a Diapason.
The Apotome is the difference between
    the semitone, & the Tone.
    The Semiditonus; and Ditonus.
    The semidiapente, and diapente.
    The Diatessaron, and Tritonus.
    The 6[a] mi, and 6[a] ma.
    The 7[a] mi: and 7[a] ma. &
    The semidiapason, and diapason.
The comma is the Difference, [between]

---

[a]   In the MS *As* is written twice.

The Semitone, and Apotome.
The Semidiapente and Tritonus. &
The semidiapason, and 7ª ma.
All which will appear by the foregoing Table of conson[an]t & dissonant Interv[a]lls.[62]

Intervalls more remote are different, according to their respectiue distances. As

A Tone is distant
    from a Ditonus by a Tone.
    from a Diatessaron, by a Semiditonus.
    from a Diapente, by a Diatessaron.
    from a 6ª mi. by a semidiapente.
    from. a 7ª mi – by a 6ª mi – and
    from. a diapason, by a 7ª mi –

The Addition of Intervalls, and the Sum[ma]ª or Totum, is found out by the Addition of numbers ⟨or⟩ Keyes thus.

[fol. 10ʳ = p. 15]

If I would know, what Intervall a diapente, added to a diatessaron, would produce or make.

I take the numbers assigned to the Termes of a diatessaron; and multiply them by the Termes & numbers assigned to diapente,– (sc, the major, by the major: and the minor, by the minor number) and those numbers will thereby be produced which will giue the proportion of the Intervall which will accresce by such Addition. ex[empli] gr[atia][63]

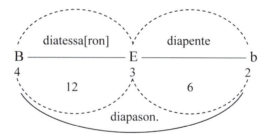

Thus I find that if a diapente be added to a Diatessaron; a Diapason will thereby be[b] produced. and in like manner, other Interv[a]lls may be found[c] out.

    ª   Written in the MS as *Sūm*.
    ᵇ   *generated or* deleted.
    ᶜ   MS has *find*.

3. of the Subst[r]action, or Subduction of Intervalls.

Hereby the Remainder of mu[sica]ll Bodies or Systems may be known.

As If I would know what would remaine of a Diapason, if a Diatessaron were substracted out of it.

The operation of this, is by multiplication crucial. sc. I take the numbers assigned to the Termes of a diapason: and multiply them by the numbers assigned to the Termes of a diatessaron; (sc. the minor of the one by the major of the other;[)] and those numbers will thereby be produced, which will giue the proportion of the Intervall which will remaine – ex[empli] gr[atia]
_64

B	b	
4	2	— diapason —

B	E	
4	3	— diatessaron —

| 12 —— | 8 | — Diapente — the remaineing part of a diapason. |

Thus I find, that if a Diatessaron be Substracted out of a Diapason, a diapente onely will remaine.

4 – of the multiplication of mu[sica]ll Numbers or So[un]ds

Hereby So[un]ds are produced or generated. and this is operated or don by multiplication of those numbers which are applyed, (as in the Addition of So[un]ds) to the Termes of the respectiue Intervalls. The major by the major, and the minor by the minor.

Thus two Intervalls, conjoyned, do procreate or ingender a third: according to the species of their proportions. (This, being seriously considered, is a wonderfull way of Generation, sc, of mu[sica]ll Intervalls) ex[empli] gr[atia][65]
[fol. 10ᵛ = p. 16]

Two dupla proportions, produce an Intervall of a quadrupla proportion – sc, two diapasons procreate, a disdiapason – as –

4 ——	2	— diapason —
8 ——	4	— diapason
32 ——	8	— disdiapason

Two Intervalls of a Tripla propor[t]ion, conioyned, ingender an Intervall of a[a] nonupla propor[t]ion – as –[b]

3 ——	1	— Diapason-diapente
3 ——	1	— diapason-diapente
9 ——	1	— trisdiapason-ad[dito] Tono.

Two sesquialtera propor[t]ions conioyned, do generate[c] Diapason ad[dito] Tono[d] – as

3 ——	2	— diapente
3 ——	2	— diapente
9 ——	4	— diapason ad[dito] Tono —

and so of others – somtimes the Intervall generated is of the same species of proportion, and Somtimes not.

as I haue written at Large, in the mathematicall part of musick, where I haue written of proportions producible both from equal and vnequal proportions.[66]

5 – of the Division of mu[sica]ll Numbers or So[un]ds.

Hereby the Musician informeth himself of the Quotus, or how often one Intervall may be taken out of an other, either precisely; or with som[e] Residuu[m] or Remainder.[67]

As out of a 7[a] minor, 2 diatessarons may be taken and nothing will Remaine – out of a Diapason ad[dito] tono, a diapente may be taken twice, or two fifths may be Substracted – without a Remainder[.]

Out of a Diapason a Tone may be taken 5 times, but then there will remaine an Intervall less then a Tone by a comma –[68]

so out of a Diapente, a Diatessaron can be but once taken: and then a Tone will remaine – Also

---

[a]   *a* written twice in MS.
[b]   *diapente* altered to *ad Tono* in the final line.
[c]   *an Intervall of a* deleted.
[d]   i.e. 'Diapason with Tone added'.
[e]   Illegible word deleted.

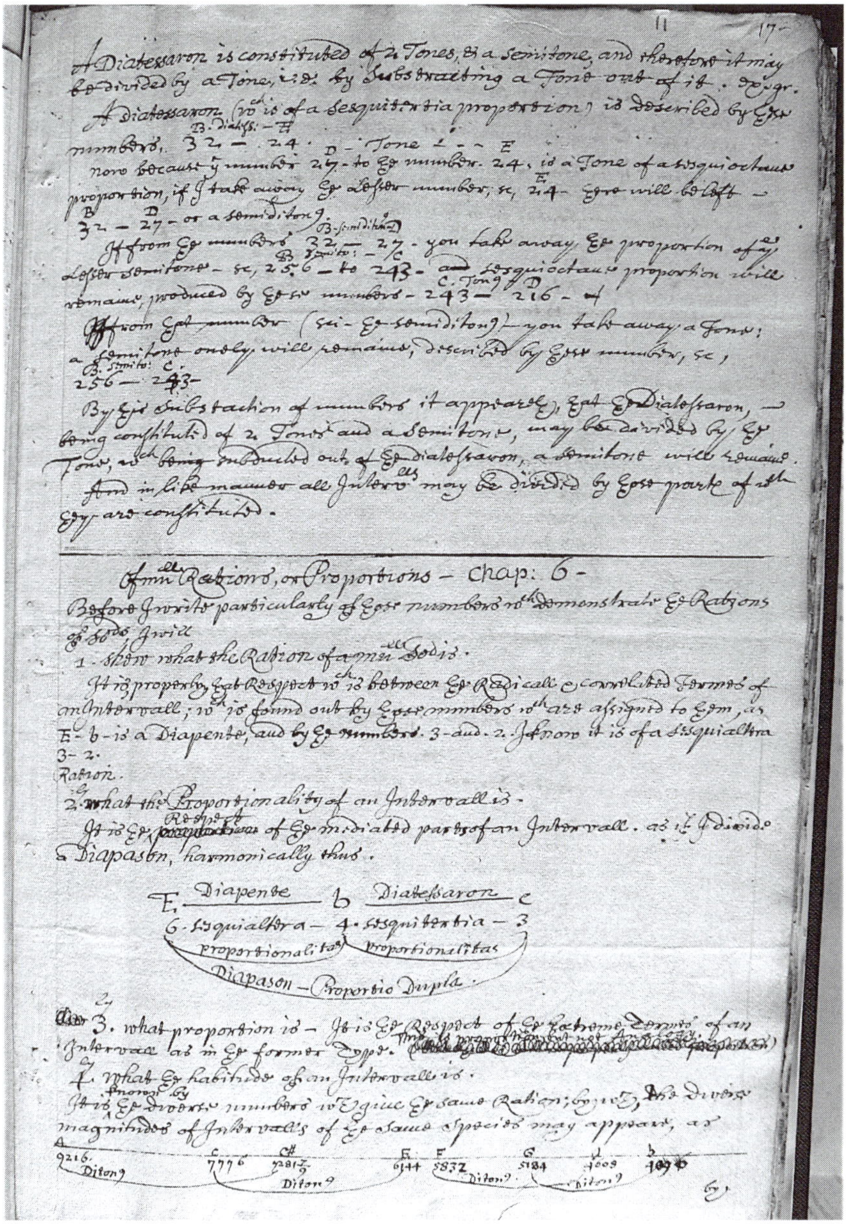

Figure 3.4 Two of Birchensha's mathematical diagrams, as well as a few of his many deletions and interlineations, from the 'Compendious Discourse' (London, Royal Society, Boyle Papers, vol. 41, fol. 11[r]). Autograph. © The Royal Society.

By this meanes the musician finds out of what parts a mu[sica]ll System, body, or Intervall is constituted. For into whatsoever parts it may be divided, of those parts it is constituted –

And this is don by su[b]straction of Intervalls, or of those numbers which are to be applyed to the parts thereof –[a] – by multiplication crutial – as afores[ai]d – or by substraction of numbers thus – or according to this Example.[69]
[fol. 11^r = p. 17]

A Diatessaron is constituted of 2 Tones, & a Semitone, and therefore it may be divided by a Tone, i.e. by Substracting a Tone out of it. ex[empli] gr[atia]

A diatessaron (which is of a Sesquitertia proportion) is described by these numbers, $\begin{array}{ccc} B & - \text{diatess:} - & E \\ 32 & - & .24. \end{array}$

Now because the number $\begin{array}{ccc} D & - \quad \text{Tone} \quad - & E \\ 27 & - \text{to the number } .24. \end{array}$ is a Tone of a sesquioctaue proportion, if I take away the Lesser number; sc, $\dfrac{E}{24}$ – there will be left – $\begin{array}{cc} B & D \\ 32 & - 27 \end{array}$ – or a semiditonus.

If from the numbers $\begin{array}{ccc} B - & \text{semiditonus} - & D \\ 32 & - & 27 \end{array}$ – you take away the proportion of the Lesser semitone – sc, $\begin{array}{ccc} B & \text{semito[nus]} - C \\ 256 & - \text{to} \quad 243 \end{array}$ – a sesquioctaue proportion will remaine, produced by these numbers – $\begin{array}{ccc} & C. \ \text{Tonus} - D \\ 243 & - \quad 216- \end{array}$

If from that number (sci[licet] – the semiditonus) – you take away a Tone: a semitone onely will remaine, described by these numbers, sc, $\begin{array}{ccc} B \ . \ \text{semito[nus] } C. \\ 256 & - & 243 \end{array}$

By this Subst[r]action of numbers it appeareth, that the Diatessaron, being constituted of 2 Tones and a Semitone, may be divided by the Tone, which being subducted out of the diatessaron, a semitone will remaine.

And in like manner all Interv[a]lls may be divided by those parts of which they are constituted.

Of mu[sica]ll Rations, or Proportions ⟨ – Chap[ter] 6 – ⟩[70]

Before I write particularly of those numbers which demonstrate the Rations of So[un]ds, I will

1. shew what the Ration of a Mu[sica]ll So[un]d is.

It is, properly, that Respect which is between the Radicall & correlated Termes of an Intervall; which is found out by those numbers which are assigned to

---

[a]   Illegible words deleted.

them, as $\dfrac{E-b}{3-2.}$ – is a Diapente, and by the numbers .3. and .2. I know it is of a

Sesquialtera Ration.

$2^{[nd]ly}$. [shew] what the Proportionality of an Intervall is.

It is the ⟨Respect⟩[a] of the mediated parts of an Intervall. as if I divide a
Diapason, harmonically thus.

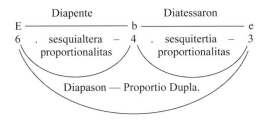

3$^{[rd]ly}$. [shew] what proportion is –

It is the Respect of the Extreme Termes of an Intervall as in the former Type.[b]
⟨This is proportion, but not Analogy.⟩

4$^{[th]ly}$. [shew] what the habitude of an Intervall is.

It is ⟨known by⟩ the diverse numbers which giue the same Ration; by which,
the diverse magnitudes of Intervalls of the Same Species may appeare, as

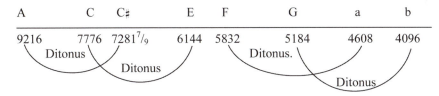

[fol. 11^v = p. 18]
By this chord it appeares, that
　　If the chord or Radicall vnison be 36 Inches long.
The Ditonus from G to b. (being, in smallest numbers, as 81–64) will be 4
Inches, and about six 8$^{th[s]}$ of an Inch.

---

　[a]　*proportion* deleted.
　[b]　*?(but this is but improperly called proportion)* deleted.

The Ditonus from ⟨A to C♯⟩, (being of the same Ration) will be 7 Inches, and about five 8[ths].

The Ditonus from .C to E. (being of the same Ration) will be 6 Inches, & about two 8[ths]. &

The Ditonus from .F to a – (being of the same Ration) will be two Inches; and ab[ou]t. seven 8[th][s].[71]

   This is fully demonstrated by my[a] scale of Inches.

So from A to D.[b] the diatessaron ⟨will⟩ be 9 Inches. ([c]if the chord be 36 Inches)[d] and the

Diatessaron from D to G – will be, 6 Inches, and six 8[th][s]. and the Diatessaron from B to E – will be 8 Inches – &c.

5[thly]. I will shew, how manyfold the Rations of sounds are.
⟨Chap[ter] 7.⟩

They are Twofold.[72]
              of Equality. &
              Inequality.

Ration (or the Reason) of Equality is between the Same Numbers, as $^2/_6$ $^2/_6$ &c.[73]
Ration of Inequality is either of the
                 greater. or
                 Lesser Inequality.

Ration of the Greater Inequality is where the Greater Terme antecedes[,] as $^2/_1$ $^3/_2$ $^4/_3$ &c.
Ration of the Lesser Inequality is when the Lesser Terme is placed first, or vppermost, as $^1/_2$ $^2/_3$ $^3/_4$ &c[e] to which the word 'sub' is joyned, as subdupla – subsesquialtera – subsesquitertia. &c.

of Ration of Inequality there are 5 species.

1. Multiplex Ration, which is the Habitude of the[f] greater quantity to the Lesser: when the greater Terme comprehends the Lesser, so that nothing wants or abounds. as $^2/_1$ $^3/_1$ $^4/_1$ &c.

---

[a] The MS has *in*.
[b] *if* deleted.
[c] *as it will be* deleted.
[d] *the* deleted.
[e] In the MS a dash separates the first two ratios.
[f] *of the* written twice in MS and deleted once.

$2^{[nd]ly}$. Superparticular Ration. – which is when the greater containeth the Lesser, and som part thereof, as. $^3/_2$ $^4/_3$ $^9/_8$ &c.

$3^{[rd]ly}$. Superpartient ⟨Ration.⟩ – which is when the greater Terme containeth the lesser once, and som parts thereof. as $^5/_3$ $^8/_5$ $^9/_5$ &c.

$4^{[th]ly}$ Multiplex Superpartient Ration. but of this species there is no vse, in the Rations of consonant & dissonant Intervalls.

5. Multiplex[a] Superparticular Ration. but of this species, likewise, there is no vse &c.[74]

Neither is the proportion of the Lesser Inequality, (or sub-proportion) in Vaine; (as some Imagine) or the same, with the proportion of the greater Inequality: but of different vse in Musick.

[fol. 12^r = p. 19]

For, this is worthy your Observation, that when a Ration of the lesser Inequality, is ioyned to a Ration of the greater Inequality, (or e contra) Then, whatsoever is produced from this Composition, will be less, then everyone of the compounded proportions. And the Reason is, because the Subproportion dissolveth or destroyeth its opposite proportion ⟨the greater number being multiply'd by the greater & the lesser &c[b]⟩. As if a ⟨sub⟩sesquialtera proportion be added to a Duplex, and you multiply the one by the other (sc, the greater Terme by the ⟨lesser of the same Intervall⟩)[c] a sesquitertia proportion, or Diatessaron onely will remaine – which is less then ⟨either⟩ a dupla or sesquialtera proportion. as[d,75]

```
B     b
4 ———— 2      — Diapason      — dupla proportion

E     b
3 ———— 2      . diapente      — subsesquialtera proportion.
———————
B     E
8 ———— 6      — Diatessaron   — subsesquialtera — proportion.
```

But if these proportions be considered by multiplication crucial, an Intervall will be formed, which will equal both the compounded proportions ioyned together, as[76]

---

[a]   *Multiplex* written twice in MS and deleted once.

[b]   i.e., '& the lesser by the lesser'.

[c]   *greater, and the lesser by the lesser)* deleted.

[d]   The second interval and ratio in this diagram should be b — E and 2 : 3 for consistency with the text. *subsesquialtera* in the last line is a mistake for *sesquitertia*.

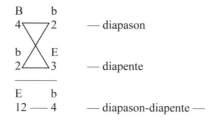

B   b
4   2   — diapason

b   E
2   3   — diapente

E   b
12 —— 4   — diapason-diapente —

Lastly, when the Termes are more then two, and betwixt them one Respect; then, properly, it is called proportion, which is defined to be the Similitude of Rations, as let there be three numbers, whereof the first hath double Respect to the Second, and the second to the third, thus – 12. 6. 3. these, or any such like, make proportion, [or][a] Analogy. and more I will, particularly, write of the Rations of All Consonant and Dissonant Intervalls.[77]

⟨Chap[ter] 8[b] –⟩

There are but ⟨7⟩[c] Numbers, which (with their duplicates) demonstrate the Rations of all consonant and dissonant Intervalls – in a Diapason ⟨(in the Diatonic Genus & chro[matic])⟩ – ⟨(besides the number assign'd to the radicall sound.)⟩
    1. 3. 9. 27. 81. 243. 729. 2187.[d,78]

The Diapason is as - - - - - - - -	2–1
The septima ma. as - - - - - - - -	243–128
The semidiapason, as - - - - - -	4096–2187
The Septima mi. as - - - - - - -	16–9.
The sexta ma. as - - - - - - - -	27–16.
The sexta mi. as - - - - - - - -	128–81
The Diapente. as - - - - - - - -	3–2
The Tritonus. as - - - - - - - - --	729–512
The semidiapente. as - - - - - -	1024–729
The Diatessaron. as - - - - - - -	4–3.
The 3[a] ma. or Ditonus as - - - -	81–64.
The 3[a] mi. or semiditonus. as - -	32–27

---

[a]   The MS is unclear.

[b]   Altered from *7*; the numbering of all subsequent chapters has been increased in the MS by one.

[c]   In the MS *7* seems to have been changed to *8*, then back to *7*.

[d]   In the following table the bracket presumably indicates that the order of the semitone (the smaller of the two intervals) and the apotome should be reversed, together with their respective ratios. It seems to have taken Birchensha two or three tries to get the final ratio, *531441–524288*, right; the deleted attempts are illegible.

The Tone or whole note — as - -	9–8–
The Semitone ⎱ as - - - - - -	256–243
The Apotome —⎰ as - - - - - -	2187–2048
The Diesis mi — as - - - - - - -	512–499
The Diesis ma — as - - - - - - -	499–486–
The Comma — as - - - - - - -	531441–524288

The Numbers which demonstrate the Rations of So[un]ds, arise from the Ternary, by the power of that number. so that. $\frac{E}{3}$ – is a Radicall So[un]d ⟨or number⟩ – $\frac{A}{9}$, is a Square So[un]d [–] $\frac{D}{27}$. is a Cube So[un]d – $\frac{G}{81}$. is a Biquadrate So[un]d – $\frac{C}{243}$. is a Solid So[un]d – $\frac{F}{729}$. is a Square of the cube so[un]d – $\frac{B\flat}{2187}$ – is a Bisolid – mu[sica]ll Number or sound –[79]

[fol. 12^v = p. 20]

And by the Order which is to be observed in placeing the respectiue numericall So[un]ds or keys (both natural and fict) in a perfect scale of musicke; (of which I haue written Chap[ter]—of the mathem[atica]ll part[a]) It will evidently appeare that the afores[ai]d proportions or Rations of conson[an]t and dissonant Intervalls are iust & proportionable: and all other Rations of So[un]ds are either defective or excessive.[80]

⟨Chap[ter] 9 – ⟩

For the completeing of all Consonant and Dissonant[b] ⟨Intervalls⟩ In All Keyes flatt and sharp: (viz. A♭. A. A♯ – B♭. B. B♯ – C♭. C. C♯ – D♭ . D. D♯ – E♭. E. E♯ – F♭. F. F♯ – G♭. G. G♯ –) it will be of absolute necessity to make all the 7 Natural keyes – double flatt: and double sharp. and then the keyes, which will complete a perfect scale of mu[sic]k in the diatonic, & permixed (commonly called the Chromatic) Genus, will be –

A♭♭.A♭.A.A♯.A✕ – B♭♭.B♭.B.B♯.B✕ – C♭♭.C♭.C.C♯.C✕ –
D♭♭.D♭.D.D♯.D✕ – E♭♭.E♭.E.E♯.E✕ – F♭♭.F♭.F.F♯.F✕ –
G♭♭.G♭.G.G♯.G✕ –

This doth partly appeare by your Table of consonant and dissonant Intervalls.

The Greatest ma'stery (that I know) in this Science, is so to place the aforesaid Individuall Intervalls in a Scale of m[usic]k that every one of them may

---

[a]   ?*of musick* deleted.

[b]   *& Dissonant* repeated in MS but deleted.

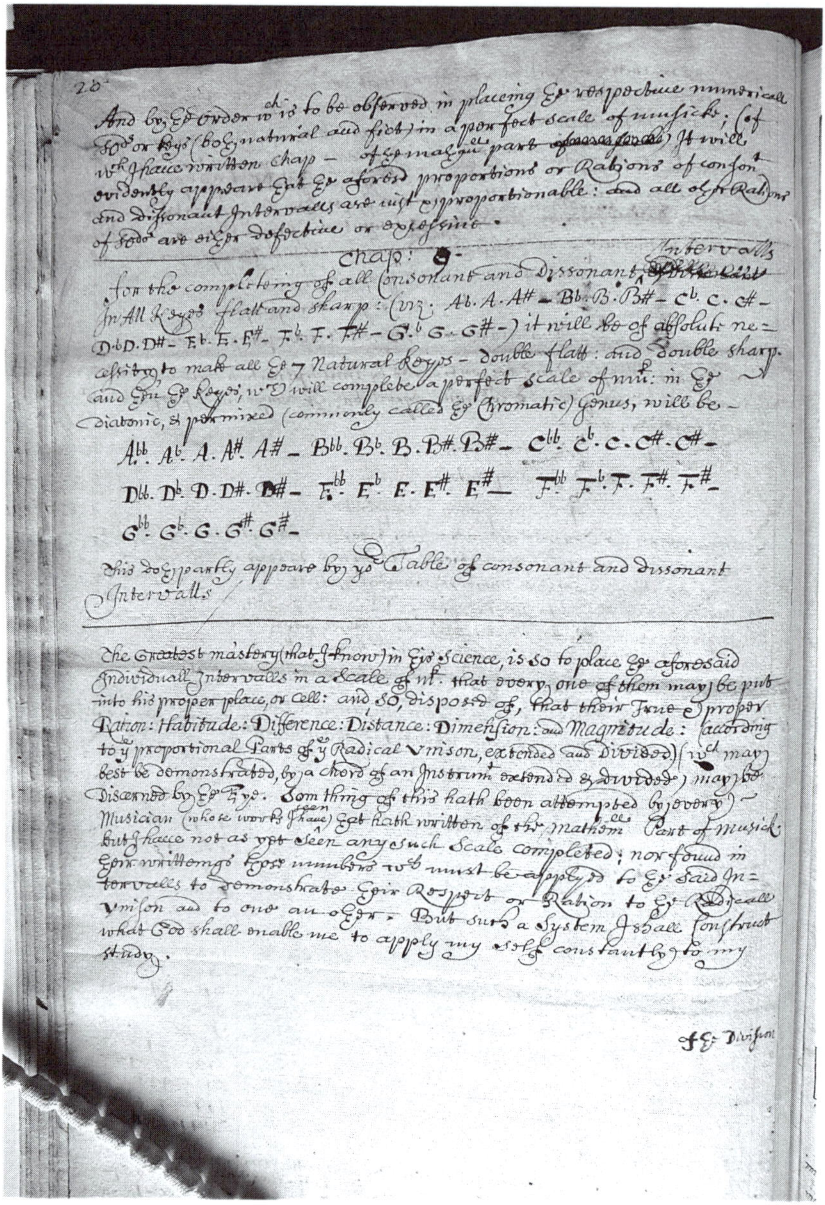

Figure 3.5 List of 'natural' and 'fict' notes necessary 'to complete a perfect scale of musick' in the diatonic and permixed genera, involving extensive use of double flat and double sharp signs, from the 'Compendious Discourse' (London, Royal Society, Boyle Papers, vol. 41, fol. 12ᵛ). Autograph. © The Royal Society.

be put into his proper place, or cell: and, so, disposed of, that their True & proper Ration: Habitude: Difference: Distance: Dimension: and Magnitude: (according to the proportional Parts of the Radical Vnison, extended and Divided.) (which may best be demonstrated, by a chord of an Instrum[en]t extended & divided) may be Discerned by the Eye. Som thing of this hath been attempted by every Musician (whose works I haue ⟨seen⟩) that hath written of the Mathem[atica]ll Part of Musick. but I haue not as yet seen any such Scale completed: nor found in their writteings those numbers which must be applyed to the said Intervalls to demonstrate their Respect or Ration to the Radicall Vnison and to one an other. But such a System I shall Construct what God shall enable me to apply my self constantly to my study.[81]

[fol. 13ʳ = p. 21]

⟨Chap[ter]: 10 –⟩ Of the Division of the Disdiapason System into Tetrachords

A Tetrachord or Quadrichord is (in a Larg[e] Sense) the same. For the Tetrachord which, anciently, was called the Tetrachord of Mercury,[82] (with his two extremes) did consonate a Diapason, according to these Keyes, & numbers, as.

sc, $\underset{12}{E} - \underset{9}{a} - \underset{8}{b} - \underset{6}{e}$ and so, any four Chords may be called a Tetrachord,

A.B.C.D – B–D.G.a – C–D–F.G &c. But in a strickt Sense, a Tetrachord is the Disposition of 4 Chords, according to a Sesquitertia Dimension, called a Diatessaron consonant.

Not that a Diatessaron is a consonant So[un]d struck ag[ains]t the first chord of the Tetrachord; but as it consonateth to the proslambanomenos of the whole Scale, – as –

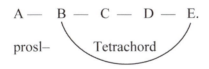

Diatessaron consonans

or to the[a] Tone graue of the Radix of the Tetrachord.

In a double Octaue they ⟨⟨(the Ancients)⟩⟩ had 5 Tetrachords, according to this following Type[:][b]

---

[a]   *or to the* written twice in MS.

[b]   This table has been editorially emended to bring it into agreement with the accompanying text: the original obscures rather than clarifies the limits of several tetrachords. Birchensha originally laid out three octaves of note names, but deleted

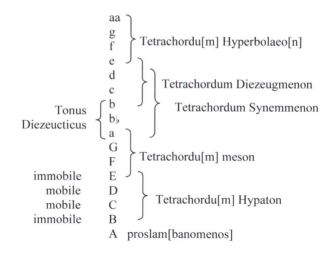

The first Tetrachord is from B. (or the Hypate chord, as in the Scale of the Greeke denomination of notes) and reacheth to E. (or Hypate Meson chord) and therefore called Tetrachordu[m] Hypaton. and it proceedeth thus, diatonicly, B–C–D–E (as in the Type) so that it did not begin from the prosl[ambanomenos] but from the first Interv[a]ll of the Scale ⟨sc, B.⟩

The second Tetrachord is from E. to a. (or the Mese chord:) therefore called the Tetrachord Meson. for it was connexed to the first, whose acutest chord, is the Gravest chord of this Tetrachord – So that these are conjoyned Tetrachords: thus E–F–G–a.

The Third Tetrachord is from b. (or the chord Paramese) and extends to .e.[a] passing over .a. (& for this cause the Tone from .a to b. is called the Diezeuctic[b] Tone, or Tone of disjoyned Intervalls.) and the Tetrachord, sc, b–c–d–e– is called the Tetrachord Diezeugmenon, or Tetrachord of disjoyned chords –

The fourth Tetrachord is from .e. to aa, (or Nete Hyperbolæon) called therefore the Tetrachord Hyperbolæon. and is ioyned to the Tetrachord[c] Diezeugmenon. thus. e–f–g–aa. as in the Type.

There was added to these ⟨four Tetrachords,⟩ an other Tetrachord, called the Tetrachord Synemmenon, or of conjoyned chords, which was from a to d. thus –a–b♭–c.d. so that it was connexed to the Tetrachord Meson – thus they interiected this Tetrachord betweene the Tetrachords Meson, & Diezeugmenon. ⟨by which meanes 3 Tetrachords were conjoyned[.]⟩

---

the highest (from *bb♭* to *aaa*). The text, to the end of fol. 13[r], was placed to the right of the table.

[a]   (⟨called⟩ *the chord diezeugmenon*) deleted.
[b]   More correctly 'Diazeuctic'.
[c]   *Hyp* deleted.

The first chord of every Tetrachord ⟨is⟩[a] stable or immoveable; – so ⟨is⟩[b] the Last: but the second & third chords ⟨are⟩[c] moueable as[d] they ⟨are⟩[e] spissated or condensed (i.e. made more or less flatt) according to the nature of the Chromatic Genus, by which[f] the 3[d] chord was made flatt by a chromatic [fol. 13[v] = p. 22] Semitone:) or the Enharmonic Genus, (by which the 3[d] and second chord were spissated by the Diesis.)

By these Tetrachords you may observe that every Diatessaron is perfected by two[g] Tones & the minor Semitone ⟨and the diapente is perfected by 3 Tones & the minor semitone⟩, and by these, the Diapason, is completed.

⟨Chap[ter] 11 –⟩ Of the species of Diatessarons: Diapentes: & Diapasons.

1 of Diatessarons.

There are three species. Sc.,[83]

$$
\left.
\begin{array}{ccccccc}
 & T & & S & & T & \\
A & - & B & - & C & - & D \\
 & S & & T & & T & \\
B & - & C & - & D & - & E \\
 & T & & T & & S & \\
C & - & D & - & E & - & F \\
\end{array}
\right\}
\begin{array}{c}
1 \\
\\
2 \\
\\
3 \\
\end{array}
$$

– if you proceed from F. acutely, they ⟨the diatessarons⟩ make the like progression.

2. of[h] Diapentes.

There a[re] 4 species[i], sc.

---

[a]   *was* deleted.

[b]   *was* deleted.

[c]   *were* deleted.

[d]   *according as* altered to *as*.

[e]   *were* deleted.

[f]   Illegible words deleted.

[g]   *?three* altered to *two*.

[h]   *Diatessarons* deleted.

[i]   MS has *spescies*.

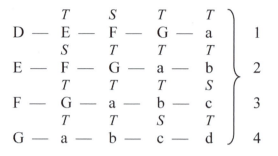

	T		S		T		T		
D	—	E	—	F	—	G	—	a	1
	S		T		T		T		
E	—	F	—	G	—	a	—	b	2
	T		T		T		S		
F	—	G	—	a	—	b	—	c	3
	T		T		S		T		
G	—	a	—	b	—	c	—	d	4

3 – of Diapasons.

which is no other, then the species of Diatessarons and Diapentes conjoyned –
by which, (as I said) the Diapason is completed – there a[re] 7. species[:]

	T		S		T		T		S		T		T		
A	—	B	—	C	—	D	—	E	—	F	—	G	—	a	1
	S		T		T		S		T		T		T		
B	—	C	—	D	—	E	—	F	—	G	—	a	—	b	2
	T		T		S		T		T		T		S		
C	—	D	—	E	—	F	—	G	—	a	—	b	—	c	3
	T		S		T		T		T		S		T		
D	—	E	—	F	—	G	—	a	—	b	—	c	—	d	4
	S		T		T		T		S		T		T		
E	—	F	—	G	—	a	—	b	—	c	—	d	—	e	5
	T		T		T		S		T		T		S		
F	—	G	—	a	—	b	—	c	—	d	—	e	—	f	6
	T		T		S		T		T		S		T		
G	—	a	—	b	—	c	—	d	—	e	—	f	—	g	7

And by[a] these Deductions it appeareth that the order of these Systems[,] sc,
the Diatessaron: Diapente: and Diapason, is varied by their Lesser part, viz,
the Semitone.

By System here, the word is not accepted as I formerly shewed, sc, for 5
parallel lines, and theire spaces.[b]

---

[a]   MS has *be*.

[b]   Despite the chapter division Birchensha later inserted into the manuscript, the
sense is continuous at this point.

⟨Chap[ter] 12. Of a mu[sica]ll System or Body⟩

[fol. 14ʳ = p. 23]

But for a Conglobation, or gathering together of many So[un]ds, into one: or ⟨a System⟩ᵃ is a mu[sica]ll Body, composed of many Diastems or Intervalls. Hence a Diatessaron and Diapente are by musicians called Systems. So that a System, in this Sense, simply considered, Is a certaine magnitude, composed of diverse Keyes, or so[un]ds; as a Consonant ⟨so[un]d⟩ is a Magnitude composed of diverse Concinnities. (or concinnous So[un]ds.) thus a Diapente is composed; sc, of a semiditonus and a Ditonus. which are two concinnous So[un]ds.

But a Diapason is a System composed ⟨of⟩ consonants, sc, a Diapente, & a Diatessaron Consonant. and a Disdiapason is composed of 2 Diapasons. Thus a Diapason is counted a perfect System, because (diatonicly dispos'd) it comprehends all the Simple species of Intervalls.

But the Disdiapason is counted a most perfect System, because it compr[e]-hends, a Diapente: Diatessaron: Diapason: Diapason-diatessaron: diapason-diapente: and so is constituted of two Diapasons. Nothing is wanting to Complete this System, and make it perfect in its kind: for it doth not in any thing exuperate,[84] neither is it in any thing defectiue. And It is called the Immutable System, because it continueth in the same disposition, without any variation. for it cannot be varied (by the various disposition of the Semitone) as the diatessaron: diapente: and Diapason are varied.

Of mu[sica]ll Genus's. ⟨Chap[ter] 13:⟩

There are 3 Mu[sica]ll Genus's, the

> Diatonic.
> Chromatic. &
> Enharmonic.

Pythagoras is the first who is Reported to dispose the Scale of Musick, most acurately, according to the Distribution of these 3 Genus's.[85]

A Mu[sica]ll Genus, is a certaine Vniversal Mode, or Manner of Melody, Demonstrateing diverse Formes of Melody. or a Certaine kind of musick, divideing the TetraChords according to the propinquity, and Longitude of Intervalls.

The Diatonic Genus is deduced, or disposed, both naturally, & artificialy, by greater Intervalls, consequently. So that, intending the voice, vehemently, it

---

ᵃ   *it* deleted.

is most convenient to naturall Pronunciation, and may easily be modulated by musicians, but meanely skilfull.[86]

The diatonic Genus proceedeth. through the Scale, (as in the foregoing Section, of Tetrachords) by 2 whole notes, and an half note, being variously disposed, according to the severall Species of Diatessarons; Diapentes; and Diapasons.

[fol. 14ᵛ = p. 24]

The Chromatic Genus, proceedes by a Semitone, a Semitone, and a

$$
\begin{array}{cccc}
& B - & C - & [D\flat] \quad\underline{\qquad}\quad E \\
\text{Semiditonus. as}^{a} & & S & [S] \quad [\text{semi-}] \\
& & & \text{dito[nu]s}
\end{array}
$$

or by Semitones, as.ᵇ

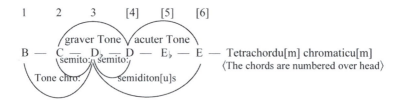

$$
\begin{array}{cccccc}
1 & 2 & 3 & [4] & [5] & [6]
\end{array}
$$

graver Tone acuter Tone

B — C — D♭ — D — E♭ — E — Tetrachordu[m] chromaticu[m]

semito: semito: ⟨The chords are numbered over head⟩

Tone chro: semiditon[u]s

The 3ᵈ chord onely, in the chromatic Genus, is varied from the Diatonic Extension, and is onely moueable. This third chord, divideth the grauer Tone of the chromatic Tetrachord into 2 Semitones. diverse from the Incision or partition of the fict or permixed Genus. (by which the Tone is divided by a Semitone, and an Apotome, as I haue shewed.) but the Third chord chromatic is so remitted, that the chromatic Semitone, doth not, pr[e]cisely, obserue the Dimension of the diatonic Semitone, nor Apotome, by reason of his smallᶜ Admixtion. Therefore, by how much acuter this third chord is made, (which is made acuter by, about the 18ᵗʰ part of a Tone) by so much that ⟨Tone⟩ which is graver, wants of the proportion of an Apotome. (as will appeare by the following Table).[87]

So That this chord produceth diverse Semitones, sc, in the Tetra[chord]: sc, A diatonic Semitone, a chromatic Semitone: and an Apotome. as in the foregoing Tetrachord.

ᵃ The diagram has been editorially emended to match Birchensha's text. In the MS the second of the two semitone steps is missing, and the interval C–E was erroneously labelled *semiditonus* before being altered to *ditonus*.

ᵇ Birchensha began numbering the semitone steps with C as 1, D♭ as 2 and D as 3, then changed his mind and starting the numbering with B as 1. He accordingly corrected C and D♭ to 2 and 3, but D remained uncorrected, and E♭ and E were left without numbers.

ᶜ MS has *smale*.

The Enharmonic Genus aboundeth with the Smallest Intervalls congruous to concinnity. This is not vsed by musicians in these daies. but of the vse of it, I will write in[a] my practicall part of M[usic]k. It is more Artificial then the Diatonic, or chromatic Genus, requireing more practise in the vse of it. It proceeds, by a diesis, a diesis, & ditonus.[88]

The Tetrachord, in this Genus, is thus disposed. ⟨The chords are numbered over head⟩[b]

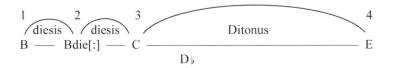

The most acute chord of the Tetrachord (viz E) is to the most Graue chord, (viz – B) a diatessaron, as 4–3 – these 2 chords, therefore, as I haue said, are immoueable; for they are the Conservatrix's of their proper System. The 2[d]. chord, which is C. (in the diatonic, and chromatic Genus's) is moued in this Genus;[c] and also the third chord chromatic, is remoued. For the Third chord being remitted (in the chro[matic] Genus) by the half of the toniæan[89] Intervall, maketh it a Semitone, by the Conversion of the diatonic, into the chromatic Genus. Againe that Chordule being depressed an other chromatic Semitone, (sc from D♭, or chromatic) the 3[d] chord[d] is remitted a Tone, (sc, from D to C.) from his diatonic Extension. And the second chord is remitted a Diesis, (sc, C. is remitted to B die[sis]) so that the diatonic Semitone from B to C. is divided by the diesis mi[nor] and diesis ma[jor] as in the next beforegoing Scale. [fol. 15[r] = p. 25]

The diatonic Genus (as afores[ai]d) is condensed as often as the chro[matic] or enharmonic Genus is adapted to it. for with cause it is said to be a densed or spissed Tetrachord.

Now a Densed System, is a Tetrachord, whose two graver proportions, are lesser then the Third, which remayneth Acute: or whose two graver termes, are lesser then that one Intervall, which remaineth Acute. For in a chro[matic] Tetrachord, the 2 grauer Intervalls, make but a Tone: and the remayneing Interv[a]ll is a Semiditon[us]. & In an Enhar[monic] Tetrachord, the two graver Termes or Intervalls make but a Semitone: but the remaineing Intervall is a ditonus. But a diatonic Tetra[chord] cannot be called densed, because the two grauer chords thereof, ioyned together, are of a greater proportion then

---

[a] MS has *is*.

[b] The physical proportions of this diagram have been editorially modified compared with the cramped original, to match its numerical content.

[c] ?*onely* deleted.

[d] *it* altered to *the 3[d] chord*.

the 3[d] acuter Intervall. For, the first two Intervalls complete a semiditonus: but the acuter or third Intervall is but a Tone. So that

The first and gravest chord of a densed or spissed Tetra[chord] is called Varipycna, i.e. grauely spissed.

The second chord, is called Mesopycna. i.e. meanely spissed. and

The Third chord is called Oxipycna. i.e. acutely spissed.[90]

⟨Chap[ter] 14 –⟩

Now followeth a Table of the diatonic: chromatic: & enharmonic Intervalls, in a diapason; with those numbers which demonstrate their proportions. The fict or semitoniæ[a]n Intervalls, and their numbers, are in the Table of the Rations of consonant & dissonant Intervalls. (before mentioned)[.][91] [See p. 143.] [fol. 15[v] = p. 26]

Of mu[sica]ll Medieties ⟨in General⟩. ⟨Chap[ter] 15 –⟩

As the Rations of So[un]ds are found by the Compareing of the Numbers ⟨assigned to them⟩: so the Proportions of So[un]ds: (i.e. of those parts of which they are Constituted) are found by the Comparation of their Rations.

Former Musicians, as Pythagoras, Plato, Aristotle, and others, (as Franchinus obserueth)[92] tooke notice onely of 3. waies, by which mu[sica]ll Numbers (or So[un]ds) were mediated. sc,[93]

> Arithmetically.
> Geometrically. &
> Harmonically.

Of Arithmeticall Mediety ⟨ – Chap[ter] 16 – ⟩

Arithmeticall Mediety (called also,[a] Mediocrity, & Proportionality) is either

> Disiunct, or
> Coniunct.

Of coniunct, or continued Arithmeticall Mediety of So[un]ds.[94]

Coniunct Proportionality, or Mediety, (called Arithmeticall Progression). is the Collection of many mu[sica]ll Numbers or So[un]ds (exceeding one an

---

[a]   ?*previously,* deleted.

Note	Values	Category
a	4608 2304 1152 576 288 144 72 36 18 9	Diatonic Immutable chr: & enhar
G	5184 2592 1296 648 324 162 81	Diatonic mutable.
G[♭] chr	5472 2736 1368 684 342 171	Chromatic mutable.
F	5832 2916 1458 729	Chromatic, & Diatonic mutable
E diesis	5988 2994 1497	Enharmonic
E	6144 3072 1536 768 384 192 96 48 24 12 6 3	Diatonic Immutable chr: & enhar
D	6912 3456 1728 864 432 216 108 54 27	Diatonic mutable
D[♭] chro	7296 3648 1824 912 456 228 114 57	Chromatic mutable
C	7776 3888 1944 972 486 243	Chromatic, & diatonic mutable.
B diesis	7984 3992 1996 998 499	Enharmonic
B	8192 4096 2048 1024 512 256 128 64 32 16 8 4 2 1	Diatonic, Immutable chr: & enhar.
A	9216 4608 2304 1152 576 288 144 72 36 18 9	Diatonic, Immutable chr: & enhar.

other by the Same Excess) into one Sum, (conglobated System) or Body. And
It is threefold. viz

> Natural.
> Of odd Numbers, or So[un]ds. &
> of Even Numbers or So[un]ds[.]

The Natural Progression of So[un]ds, is that which begins from the Vnison. In
which proceedure they follow one an other, in a Natural Order, Thus

A	—	B	—	C	—	D	—	E	—	F	—	G	—	a
Vnison	–	Tonus	–	3^a	–	dia-	–	Dia-	–	6^a	–	7^a	–	8^a
						tessaron		pente						

As I haue formerly shewed, in the Series of Consonant & dissonant
Intervalls.

The Progression of Odd mu[sica]ll Numbers or So[un]ds, begins, likewise,
from the Vnison (or radical So[un]d) but proceeds by Diapentic Habitudes, or
by Fifths,[a] ⟨grauely⟩, thus[b]

A	—	[D]	—	[G]	—	[C]	—	[F]	—	&c
Vnison	—	5	—	5	—	5	—	5th	—	&c

By the power of the Diapente. (demonstrated by the Ternary number, and
the potestas thereof) which progression is continued from the ⟨Acutest⟩[c] to the
⟨grauest⟩[d] sounds.

The Progression of Even mu[sica]ll Numbers or So[un]ds, begins, also,
from the Vnison. in which proceedure, every so[un]d exceeds an other by a
diapason. thus

8 —	4	2	
A —	a —	aa	&c
Vnison. 8^a.	8^a.	&c	

---

[a] *acutely* deleted.

[b] Birchensha originally wrote an ascending cycle of fifths, *A—E—b—f♯ —c♯* .
He later altered *b—f♯ —c♯* to *B♭ —E♭ —A♭*, having for some unaccountable reason left
the preceding notes *A—E* unchanged. The diagram has been editorially adjusted to
give a descending cycle of fifths beginning on A, the 'Vnison' that he chose for all the
examples in this chapter.

[c] *gravest* deleted.

[d] *Acutest* deleted.

[fol. 16ʳ = p. 27]

This order ariseth from the Power of the Diapason. (demonstrated by the Vnity, and the duplicates thereof, as ⟨1.⟩ 2. 4 – 8 – 16 &c)

The Respectiue Intervalls being placed in a Scale of musick, according to this Reason, (orᵃ waies of progression) the proportions. (or Rations) of All Consonant and Dissonant Intervalls, will appeare. And whatsoever Rations of So[un]ds are differing from these, will be Inept, and either excessiue or defectiue of the True proportions and Rations of mu[sica]ll Sounds or Intervalls.[95]

This conioyned Arithmeticall Mediety of So[un]ds or mu[sica]ll Numbers, is of three So[un]ds or Intervalls onely.

⟨Chap[ter] 17.⟩

I will demonstrate this by mediateing a Diapason system. Arithmetically. thus[b,96]

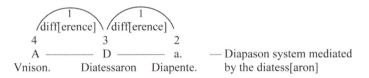

or by any other numbers which retaine the Same properties. asᶜ

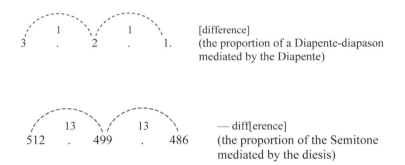

			[difference]
3	2	1.	(the proportion of a Diapente-diapason mediated by the Diapente)

			— diff[erence]
512	499	486	(the proportion of the Semitone mediated by the diesis)

The properties of this Mediety are these (inter al[ia])[:]

ᵃ   ?*Diverse* deleted.

ᵇ   In the following diagram *Diapason* was altered to *Diapente*.

ᶜ   In this and some subsequent diagrams editorial arcs (distinguishable by their dotted lines) have been added, on analogy with the preceding diagram.

1. The midle Terme is equal (as to quantity. i.e. to the proportional part of the ⟨extended vnison,[a]⟩ demonstrated by the chord of an Instrument) to the Just Dimidium of the Conjoyned Extremities.[97] (as appeares by the Example) therefore the differences are Equal.

2. The proportions of the Term's are vnequal. (in Respect of their Rations.) for, from A to D. is proportio sesquitertia: but from D to a. is proportio sesquialtera. but the difference is Equal, for betweene a 4[th] and 5[th] the difference is a Tone; by which those So[un]ds are disjoyned.

If it be demanded to what purpose So[un]ds are thus (or in any other way, sc, geometrically or harmonically) divided or mediated. I answere, first, that the Equality & Inequality of the Constituted parts thereof, (in resp[e]ct of their Magnitude) may be discerned. of which I haue written at large, & particularly, in cha[pter] -15- of my mathem[atica]ll part of M[usic]k.

⟨Chap[ter] 18 –⟩ Of the disioyned Arithmeticall Mediety of So[un]ds[98]

It is the Distraction of the Termes and Rations of So[un]ds. and it is of four or more Numbers. But if you exceed four, you will fall vpon Numbers which will giue the proportions of So[un]ds of litle or no vse in musick. And this is the Ignis fatuus, which hath misled many, both Ancient and modern Musicians: as will Appeare by my commixed scale of conjoyned Systems. for they give the proportions of so[un]ds, from this [fol. 16[v] = p. 28] Progression of Numbers, (as I haue shewed) viz. 1. 2. 3. 4. 5. 6. 7. 8 &c. Let, therefore, the Termes of discontinued Arithm[etica]ll Mediety be these[:][b]

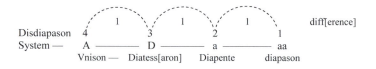

Here, the greater Terme, (which musicians call Dux) will be to the least, (which they call comes) a quadrupla proportion: to the Third, a dupla proportion: and to the ⟨second⟩[c] a ⟨sesquitertia⟩[d] Ration. That is The vnison is to the first Interv[a]ll. a Diatessaron: to the 2[d] &c as in the Example.

---

     [b]   *Disdiapason* altered to *diapason* in the final line.
     [c]   *Last* deleted.
     [d]   *Sesquialtera ⟨quadrupla⟩* deleted.

The proportions[a] are ⟨these⟩[b].

1. The proportions or Terms are vnequal, but their differences are Equal. by which is signified – that these Intervalls are (as I s[ai]d) in respect of their Magnitude, Equ[a]ll: but vnequal in respect of their Ration.

2. The two midle Termes, inclosed by the Extremes, are equall to the Extremes, as may appeare by the numbers assigned to the Intervalls ⟨in the Example⟩. For the quaternary and the vnity make .5. and so doth the Ternary and Binary, conjoynd.[99] By which is signified, that the Disdiapason contayneth in it, a Diatessar[on:][c] diapente: and diapason: which complete a Disdiapason.

⟨Chap[ter] 19 – ⟩ Of continued Geometricall Mediety of So[un]ds.

It is disposed, so, by 3 Termes, that the Same proportion which the Greatest hath to the midle: the same, the midle hath to the Least or Last Terme. And the difference of the greater Termes, hath the Same proportion to the difference of the Lesser Termes. ex. gr.[d,100]

Thus I demonstrate by dupla Habitudes. Againe[e]

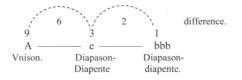

Thus I demonstrate in Tripla Habitudes ⟨by a [Tris]diapason-ad[dit]o [Tono] System⟩.[f] Againe[g] [fol. 17[r] = p. 29]

---

[a]   MS has *proporties*.

[b]   *Equal but the differences are uneq[ua]ll* deleted.

[c]   MS obscured by binding at this point.

[d]   *Disdiapason* altered to *diapason* in the final line.

[e]   *a* was altered to *e* in the centre of this diagram.

[f]   The MS has *Bisdiapason-ad[o] Diapason System*, but this must be an error, since the sum of the intervals is 3 octaves plus a tone.

[g]   Birchensha wrote *Disdiapason* (altered to *Trisdiapason*) *System* alongside the following diagram, but deleted *Disdiapason* and *Trisdiapason*.

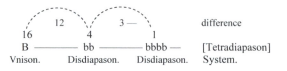

	12		3 —		difference
16		4		1	
B	——	bb	——	bbbb —	[Tetradiapason]
Vnison.		Disdiapason.		Disdiapason.	System.

Thus I demonstrate by quadrupla Habitudes, and by a Tetradiapason System.

All other conioyned Multiplex proportions proceed according to the same Reason, and Consideration. And, so in their sub-proportions, as – 1–2. 2–4. &c.

The Termes of Geometricall proportion, may likewise be these.

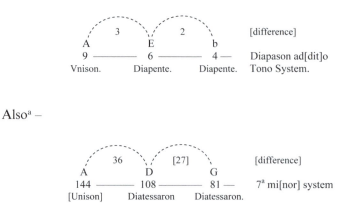

	3		2		[difference]
A		E		b	
9	——	6	——	4 —	Diapason ad[dit]o
Vnison.		Diapente.		Diapente.	Tono System.

Also[a] –

	36		[27]		[difference]
A		D		G	
144	——	108	——	81 —	7[a] mi[nor] system
[Unison]		Diatessaron		Diatessaron.	

Note[b] Thus[c] ⟨Any⟩ Two Intervalls of equall Ration being conjoyned are according to Geometricall mediety: but vnequall as to their magnitude, as appeareth by their vnequall differences. ⟨In Geometricall mediety⟩ Somtimes the proportions of the termes and differences, are Equall: and somtimes vneq[ua]ll. as in the examples: but the proportions of the Termes are alwaies equall.

⟨Chap[ter] 20 –⟩ Of Disioyned Geometricall Medietie of So[un]ds.

It is in four or more Termes.

---

   [a]   In the MS the difference between the second pair of terms is erroneously written as *17*.

   [b]   This word is written in the margin above an index hand.

   [c]   *all* deleted.

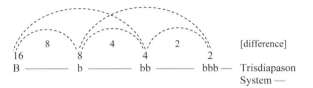

In this disposition as – bb is to bbb – so B is to b.

The proportions of the Termes are Eq[ua]ll: but the proportion[s] of the differences are uneq[ua]ll –

The proportion of the difference betweene the first and third Terme, (which is a disdiapason) is a quadrupla proportion: but the proportion of the difference between the 2ᵈ & 4ᵗʰ termes (which is also a disdiapason) is a dupla proportion.[101]

By which is Signified, that the Rations of these Interv[a]ll[s] are Eq[ua]ll: but their magnitudes are vneq[ua]ll: for if the first be 8 Inches; the 2ᵈ will be 4 Inches: and the 3ᵈ Intervall will be but 2 Inches of a chord.

[fol. 17ᵛ = p. 30]

But if you distinguish by six Termes, thus.ᵃ

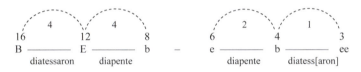

The Three Lesser Termes will not haue the same Mediety which the Three greater [have]: although the Extremes demonstrate the Same proportion, sc, a dupla proportion.

And by this is signified, (nay manyfestly Evident) that Arithmeticall and Harmonicall Mediety proceed from Geometricall-disioyned-Mediety, disposed into 6 Termes, and distinguished by twice 3 Termes, a[s] in the Example.[102]

But from whence Geometricall-mu[sica]ll-Mediety proceeds, I haue written chap[ter] -12- of my mathem[atica]ll part of M[usic]k.

Lastly, by what I haue written in that part of my Booke it will evidently Appeare thatᵇ Geometricall Mediety. proceeds not from a natural progression of numbers from the Vnity: but from the Reason of Geometricall Arithmetick, or figurate numbers.[103]

ᵃ   *16, 12* and *8* are the results of Birchensha's emendations; originally he seems to have written *8, 6* and *4*. The middle note of the three lesser terms should properly have been written as *bb*.

ᵇ   *the production of* deleted.

⟨Chap[ter] 21 –⟩ Of Harmonicall Mediety

It is diverse ⟨in som respects⟩ to Arithmeticall & Geometricall Medietie: because it is not disposed (Arithmetically) by vneq[ua]ll proportions, & Equal Differences of the Termes: nor Geometrically,[a] ⟨by⟩ Eq[ua]ll proportions both of Termes & Differences: But

The Termes are so framed or continued, that the proportion of the Graver to the Acuter is Equal to the proportion of the greater and the lesser Termes.[104]

Whereby is signified that the grauer Intervall (of the two constituted parts) is greater then the Lesser. ex. gr.

Againe, if you would dispose Tripla proportions, thus

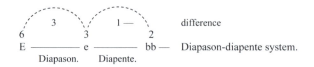

you will find the Same propriety of Mediocrity, for the senary [fol. 18ʳ = p. 31] to the Binary, is a Tripla: and the Ternary (which is the Difference of the greater Termes) to the vnity, (which is the difference of the Lesser Termes) make also a Tripla proportion. By which the parts that constjtute this System may be knowne. and this also is (by the Termes & differences) signified; that the Graver Intervall is the greater, and the[b] Acuter, is the Lesser System. Thus

This proportionality is diverse, as I s[ai]d, to the two other mediocrities.[c] But not so to Geometricall, as to Arithmeticall Mediety. For in Arithm[etica]ll Mediety the greatest Magnitude is found between the Lesser, and the Lesser between the greater Termes. But in this as in geometricall Mediety, the greater magnitude, or Interv[a]ll is found between the greater, and the Lesser between the Lesser Termes.

The Reasons, I suppose, why this Mediety is called Harmonicall, are these.

---

[a]   *of* deleted.

[b]   *Lesser, is the* deleted.

[c]   *sc. to Arithmeticall* deleted.

1. Because the numbers applyed to the Termes, ⟨being⟩[a] disposed harmonically, compr[e]hend in them (compared together) the Rations of All consonant Interv[a]lls in a Disdiapason System: and also of those Systems, which proceed from the division of the vnison, or whole chord into 4 & 9 Eq[ua]ll parts, viz, of the Diatessaron and Tone. (two dissonant Interv[a]lls) ex[empli] gr[atia][105]

The Termes of Harmonicall mediety are these, (as I shew'd)

E.	b.	e	—	dupla proportion
12	8	6		

A.	E.	e	—	Tripla proportion
9.	6.	3		

or thus, 12 . 9 . 8 . 6 . 3 .[b]

12 to 3	—	Is the Ration of a Disdiapason	—	as	E—ee.
9 to 3	—	of a Diapason-diapente	—	as	A—e.
6 to 3	—	of a Diapason	—	as	E—e
9 to 6	—	of a Diapente	—	as	A—E
12 to 9	—	of a Diatessaron	—	as	E—a
9 to 8	—	of a Tone	—	as	a—b.

2. Beca[us]e the Termes of a System, harmonically disposed, being struck together, do alwaies consonate: whereas som so[un]ds, disposed Arithmetically, do somtimes consonate: (as a diapente-diapason. sc, A–E–e.) and somtimes dissonate. (as a Diapason, sc – A. D. a)[.]

Also som so[un]ds disposed Geometrically, do somtimes consonate: as a disdiapason, (sci, A. a. aa) and somtimes dissonate, (as a 7ᵃ mi: sc, A. D. G.)[106]

But there are many Interv[a]lls (both consonants & dissonants) [fol. 18ᵛ = p. 32] which are Mediated neither Arithmetically: Geometrically: nor Harmonically, (as the 2ᵃ ma. semiditonus. Diatessaron. Diapente. Tritonus: 6ᵃ mi. Sexta ma. 7ᵃ ma. and Semidiapason) but of this no Notice is taken by any Musician, whose workes I haue seen – of which differing species of mu[sica]ll Medieties I haue written at Larg[e]. chap[ter] 14. of my Mathem[atica]ll part of Musick.

I haue insisted thus Largely vpon this Subiect, sc, the Doctrine of Mu[sica]ll Medieties, because it is a Noble, and excellent part of M[usic]k. and of great vse to the Mathematicall Musician. For hereby; (By the numbers which are to be assigned or applyd to the respectiue and before Mentioned consonant and Dissonant Intervalls) (disposed according to any Mu[sica]ll mediety) he will (without heareing the System and partes thereof struck by any Instrum[en]t:

---

[a] *be* (altered to *are*) deleted.

[b] MS has *A* altered to *a* in the final line of the following table.

or seeing it placed in a pentagramm) certainly know; onely by the numbers, so, variously deduced or disposed,

1 – The Ration of the first and second Termes[.]

2 – and of the second and third Termes.

3 – and of the Extremities. – And vnto ⟨what⟩ Keyes the numbers ought to be applyd[.]

4 – what Intervall the first constituted part is.

5 – what the Second.

6 – what the whole System.

7 – whether the parts are Eq[ua]ll or vneq[ua]ll in Respect of Ration[.]

8 – whether the parts are Eq[ua]ll or vneq[ua]ll magnitudes, and

9 – whether the first and gravest, or Acutest constituted part be the greater or Lesser Magnitude. ex[empli] gr[atia]

These Termes being put – and thus disposed.

$$6 - 4 - 3.$$

I say, by these[a] ⟨numbers, onely,⟩ (considered as afores[ai]d although the Keyes as. E. b. e. bee not expressed)[b], you may certainely Informe yourself, of All things which concerne the Reason: nature: qualities, quantity or magnitude[,] difference, distance, dimensions ⟨of so[un]ds⟩[c]: or ⟨of⟩ any thing Else, which may Reasonably be demanded concerneing any consonant or dissonant mu[sica]ll Intervall.

1.	3.	9.	27.	81.	243.	729.
B.	E.	A.	D.	G.	C.	F.

The numbers to be assigned to the Respectiue Key.[107]

---

[a]   *Termes* deleted.

[b]   *by these Numbers, onely* deleted.

[c]   Illegible words deleted.

[fol. 19ʳ]ᵃ

Contents of the most materiall Principles & Elements of the Practicall part of Musick.[108]

ᵃ   This page is ruled into two columns, of which only one is used.
ᵇ   *& of the Signed Keyes* deleted.
ᶜ   Altered from *Græka–latina*.

[fol. 19ᵛ]ᵃ

Contents of the most material Principles & Elements of the Mathematicall part of Musick

---

ᵃ This page is ruled into two columns; both are used.

ᵇ MS has *chap: 10.*

ᶜ *of mu[sica]ll* deleted.

Chap[ter] 10.

of the Division of the Disdiapason System into Tetrachords. what a Tetrachord is. of Tetrachords conjoyned: and disjoyned. of the Diezeuctic Tone – fo. 21.[a]

Chap[ter] 11.

of the species of Diatessarons: Diapentes: & Diapasons – fo: 22.

Cha[pter] 12.

of a mu[sica]ll System or Body. what it is. of a Diapason: & Disdiapason system. fol. 23.

Chap[ter] 13.

of a mu[sica]ll Genus. what it is. How many mu[sica]ll Genus's. of the diatonic-Genus – fo. 23. of the chromatic-Genus – and of the Enharmonic-Genus. How they differ. fol. 23. 24.

Chap[ter] 14.

of the Diatonic: chrom[atic] & Enharmonic Intervalls: of the numbers which demonstrate their proportions: of Intervalls mutable & Immutable. fo: 25 –

Chap[ter] 15.

of mu[sica]ll Medieties. and how many are treated of by mu[sica]ll Authors. fo: 26 –

Chap[ter] 16 –

of Arithm[etica]ll Mediety. of conjoyned Arithm[etica]ll Mediety. of natural: odd: & Even So[un]ds. & of their progression. fo. 26. 27.

Chap[ter] 17

A further Discourse of conjoyned Arithm[etica]ll Mediety: & the properties thereof. fo. 27.

Chap[ter] 18.

of disioyned Arithm[etica]ll Mediety: what it is. fol. 27. 28. The properties thereof. 28.

Chap[ter] 19.

of continued Geometricall Mediety: and how disposed. fo. 28. 29.

Chap[ter] 20.

of Disjoyned Geometricall Mediety. & what is signified by the Terms & differences of Intervalls – fo: [29–]30. from whence Arithm[etica]ll harmonicall & Geometricall mediety proceed.[b]

Chap[ter] 21.

of Harmonicall mediety.[c] How it differs from Arithm[etica]ll & Geometricall mediety. why it is so called. [fo. 30.]

[fol. 20ʳ]

How to make any Kind of Tune, Ayre, or Song, without the help of the voice, or any other Instrument.[120]

In doing this

1. Before you begin to make your Tune, there are Som Things to be Preconsidered, and Resolved on.

2. There are diverse Things which you are to take into Consideration, (being the Essentiall parts of every Airey, or Melodious Song; of which it is constituted) when you are makeing a Tune.

3. There are diverse Negative Precepts to be observed. vpon which Rocks, Musicians (being vnskilfull) often fall: and by so doeing (for want of the knowledge of the Reason of Ayre, and the true Nature of So[un]ds) they make bad Tunes, or Songs which are not good Ayre.

Concerning these Things, I will giue you particular Directions.

1. Preconsiderables

First, you must Resolve, what Tune or Aire you Intend to make, as Corant: Gavott &c.[110]
2[nd]ly. In what Key you will make it.

And these be the Keyes of common Vse. viz
A. B♭. B. C. D. E♭. E. F. F♯. G.[111]

3[rd]ly – whether your song shall be flatt or sharp, in the 3ᵈ. 6ᵗʰ. and 7ᵗʰ. vnles you will force it to be otherwise Accidentaly, by the Apposition of these markes. (♭ & ♯)[112]
Som Keyes are sharp in the 3ᵈ naturaly, as
C. is sharp in the 3ᵈ (which is E) also in the 6ᵗʰ. (or a) & 7ᵗʰ. (sc, B.)
F. is sharp in the 3ᵈ. (which is a) also in the 6ᵗʰ. (or D) & 7ᵗʰ (sc, E.)
B. is flatt in the 3ᵈ (which is D.) also in the 6ᵗʰ (or G) & 7ᵗʰ (sc, A)
E. is flatt in the 3ᵈ (which is G) also in the 6ᵗʰ (or C) & 7ᵗʰ (sc, D)
A. is flatt in the 3ᵈ (which is C) Also in the 6ᵗʰ (or F) & 7ᵗʰ (sc. G)
D. is flatt in the 3ᵈ (which is F) but sharp in the 6ᵗʰ (or B) & flatt in the 7ᵗʰ
– (sc, C)

G. is sharp in the 3ᵈ (which is B) also in the 6ᵗʰ (or E) but flatt in the 7ᵗʰ (sc. F)

But if you would haue the keyes which are naturaly flatt in the 3ᵈ. 6ᵗʰ. and 7ᵗʰ to be sharp in any of those places; you must make them so, by the Addition of this marke. (♯)

And if you would haue those Keyes which are naturaly sharp in the 3ᵈ. 6ᵗʰ. and 7ᵗʰ to be flatt in any of those places; you must make them so, by the Apposition of this marke. (♭)

4[th]ly. you must pr[e]consider the Mediations & Intermediations of your Key. And this you shall vnderstand by this following System.[113]

diapason — Arithmeticall Intermediation — Arithmeticall Mediation — Vnison

Diapason — harmonicall Mediation — harmonicall Intermediation. — Vnison

[fol. 20ᵛ]

⟨You may place your closes in all keyes. but that which is aboue or below your assumed Key.⟩

After the like manner All the other Keyes are mediated. sc.

In Arithm[etica]ll Mediation, the octaue is mediated by the 4ᵗʰ. and the Arithm[etica]ll Intermediation is the 6ᵗʰ.

In harmonicall Mediation, the octaue is mediated by the 5ᵗʰ. & the harm[onica]ll Intermediation, is the 3ᵈ.[114]

You May plant your notes in any of the Lynes, and spaces of the 8ᵗʰ, or System of 5 lynes.

But your passing, formal, & final Closes, ought to be in som of these mediations or Intermediations. and by so doing, you will not go out of your Key, or Ayre.

Your passing closes are These.

Your formall & final closes are These.

Gavot close

Gavot close.

So that a formal and final Close are all one. (in respect of the formality thereof) But this is the difference; when it is in the middle or any meane part of a song or straine; it is called a formal Close. But when it is the end of a Straine or Tune, (for som Tunes haue but one Straine) It is called a final Close.

Also before you begin to make a Tune: you must know how to make the respectiue characters of Notes, and to draw their Tailes or stroake[s]: and how to place them in the Lynes, and spaces of your pentagramm, or System.[115]

2[nd]ly – What you are to observe in making a Tune.

1. you are to obserue the proper movem[en]t of such a Tune.

2. your Tune must be formal, whether it be a Treble, or a Bass.

3. you must consider the Compass of the Instrum[en]t which must express your Tune[.]

4. you must observe the Stopps & closes proper to your Tune[.]

5. And where to end them (sc. your Tunes)[.]
    In All these Things you will be directed by your Coppy.[116]

6. you must know what the 2^d. part of a Note is. viz when a Note is divided into two eq[ua]ll parts. The first is the first part: & the 2^d, is the 2^d part of the note. as.

[fol. 21^r]
7. ⟨you⟩[a] must know what a cast off note is.
    It is an Odd note at the beginning of a Tune or straine. or where the Second part of a Note is placed with the following first part of a Note. thus. (The cast off note is marked thus (+)[.)]

begining of a Song.   midle, or end of a Song.

8. you must consider where your Tune must begin, & where it must End.
    If your Tune Be a Bass: you must Begin, & End in the Key note.

---

    a   *of* deleted.

If it be a Treble, the first must be in the Key: or in the 3ᵈ. or 5ᵗʰ. aboue the Key note.

Your Song must alwaies end in the key note.

If you haue two straines, the first may end in the Key note: (which is seldom don) but most commonly in som mediation or Intermediation of your key. The final close note must, alwaies, be in the Key.

9. you must alwaies place the
     Signed Keyes
     Marks of mollity & asperity (as ♭. ♯)[117] &
     Signe of the Moode. before the Song. as

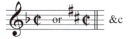

10 – you may either Retaine the movem[en]t of your Coppy, or vary it. or other waies dispose of the Notes[.]

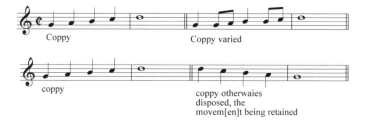

11. If your Coppy moue gradually, you may moue by saltation. or the contrary.

12. If the Coppy moue gradually in one place, you may moue gradually in an other: but the best place will be, where the Notes make the Like progression – or are alike distant –

[fol. 21ᵛ]

3[rd]ly. Negative precepts

1. you are not to rise or fall a Semidiapente, Tritone, or ⟨defective⟩ 3ᵈ.[a] unles
your following note be a Semitone ascending. as

2. you must not Rise nor fall a 5ᵗʰ, if the 2ᵈ note to the Acutest or Gravest
so[un]d be not a full 4ᵗʰ.[b]

3. com not too often to a note; especially after the Same manner. (The fault is
mark'd thus (x)[.)]

     By virtue of these Directions, and of other Observations which will Occurr
in your practise: you make a Good ⟨Ayre or Tune⟩, in any Moode; without the
help of your Voice, or of any other Instrument[.]

---

     [a]   *Excessive 3ᵈ* altered to *defective 3ᵈ*; but *defective (or imperfect) 4ᵗʰ* seems to be
meant.

     [b]   Logically the diminished fourth in the third and fourth examples should be
labelled *false 4ᵗʰ* (not *false 3ᵈ*), as in the first example.

How to form the character[s] of note[s].

Notes

[1] Robert Boyle (1627–91) was the youngest son of Richard Boyle, first Earl of Cork, and brother of Joan, Countess of Kildare (1611–56), whose husband George Fitzgerald, sixteenth Earl of Kildare, had been Birchensha's patron in Ireland. Boyle inherited his father's estate at Stalbridge in Dorset, but from 1656 lived chiefly in Oxford (where for a time he was assisted in his scientific experiments by Robert Hooke) until settling in London in 1668. By the time Birchensha wrote this treatise for him he was already highly regarded as a natural philosopher. His well known experiments using the air pump were published in 1662, and his *Experiments and Considerations Touching Colours* in 1664. He had been one of the founding Fellows of the Royal Society and served on its council, and he was a member of the music committee set up on 20 April 1664 to consider Birchensha's ideas. As a boy at Eton he had been given lessons on the viol and in singing, and he once described himself as 'very musically given', although we have no incontrovertible evidence of him as a musical performer in adulthood (see Robert Boyle, *The Usefulness of Experimental Philosophy* II, sect. 1 (London, 1663), p. 260; see also ibid., sect. 2 (1671), 'Trades', p. 20). He was interested in the phenomena of sound, and we know that musical experiments of some kind were performed in his rooms in Oxford during 1665, although the details are lost (see *The Correspondence of Henry Oldenburg*, eds A. Rupert Hall and Marie Boas Hall, vol. 2 (Madison, Milwaukee and London, 1966), p. 530, and Thomas Birch, *A History of the Royal Society of London* (4 vols, London, 1756–7) vol. 2, p. 68). The businesslike wording of Birchensha's title-page – 'Written ⟨...⟩ for the use of the Honourable Robert Boyle Esq[re]' – suggests that Boyle may have expressed a wish to see some of Birchensha's theoretical work, but there is no evidence to support R.E.W. Maddison's conjecture that Birchensha was ever Boyle's teacher (*The Life of the Honourable Robert Boyle F.R.S.* (London, 1969), p. 21 and note).

[2] Latin: *intensio* = a stretching out, an increasing of tension (hence, a raising of pitch); *remissio* = a slackening, a relaxing of tension (hence, a lowering of pitch).

[3] Birchensha took his first two 'Principles, Axioms, Theorems &c' from the first two 'theorems' concerning the musical scale in Alsted's *Encyclopædia* (Chapter 4, Rule 7): '1. *Series intensionis & remissionis, seu ascensionis à gravi sono in acutum, & descensionis ab acuto in gravem, dicitur Scala Musica. 2. Scala Musica variat apud veteres & recentiores Musicos.*' In *Templum musicum* Birchensha translated this passage as: '1: *The Series of Intension and Remission*: or of Ascension from a grave Sound into an Acute, and of the Descension from an acute into a grave, is called the *Scale of Musick*. 2. *The Scale of Musick doth vary both according to ancient and modern Musicians.*' Alsted explains his second theorem in terms both of expanding compass, from one or two octaves to three, four or more, and of differing interval structure, for example between the diatonic, chromatic, enharmonic, and 'new and perfect' syntonic (or justly intoned)

scales. Johann Heinrich Alsted, *Encyclopædia septem tomis distincta* (Herborn, 1630), pp. 1197–8; *Templum musicum*, pp. 21–3.

⁴   'Augmentation' and 'diminution' meant the lengthening and shortening of note values, usually in terms of simple mathematical proportions. 'Mutation', as used by Birchensha, in effect meant transposition: see 'A Compendious Discourse' ('Practicall Part', chapter 5).

⁵   'Letters' are the seven letter names from A to G. According to Alsted (chapter 5, Rule 6), 'These are usually called Keyes [*claves*], because that by them a Song is, as it were, opened [*cantilena veluti reseretur*]'. 'Signed Keyes' [*claves signatæ*] are the clef signs for *g'*, *c'* and *f*. 'Musical Voices' [*voces musicales*] are the solmization syllables. Traditionally there were six of these (*ut re mi fa sol la*), although Alsted cites Erycius Puteanus's *Musathena* (Hanau, 1602) as advocating the addition of a seventh syllable (*bi*) to the hexachord, and David Mostart's lost *Korte onderwysinghe van de musyk-konst* (Amsterdam, 1598) as wishing to substitute the bocedization system (*bo ce di ga lo ma ni*), while Birchensha himself follows the English practice of reducing the number of syllables to four (*sol la mi fa*). See Alsted, *Encyclopædia*, pp. 1199–1200; *Templum musicum*, pp. 32–43; 'A Compendious Discourse', 'Practicall Part', chapter 4.

⁶   Here, too, Birchensha was indebted to Alsted, who wrote of a song ascending and descending 'in a progression either continued, or discontinued [*in progressione continuâ, vel discontinuâ*]' (chapter 5, Rule 6). But Alsted was referring to solmization and mutation between hexachords, and Birchensha's principle is opaque when separated from that context. Alsted explains: 'Continued Progression is that which observeth the natural Order of *Voices*, and is called a natural Song. [Here he gives a music example consisting of the hexachord *g a b c' d' e'* ascending and descending, which could be sung to solmization syllables without mutation.] Discontinued Progression is the Mutation of a *Voice* [*Discontinua progressio est vocis mutatio*]'. See Alsted, *Encyclopædia*, pp. 1200–1201; *Templum musicum*, pp. 43–4.

⁷   Cf Alsted (chapter 5, Rule 1): 'Quia sonus nec chartæ inscribi, nec mente tantùm & semper ab homine servari potest, indiget certis signis, quibus quantitas & qualitas ipsius repræsentetur' ('Because a *Sound* can neither by any Man be written in Paper, nor kept in his Mind, neither only nor alwayes; therefore it standeth in need of certain *Signs*, by which the Quantity and Quality thereof may be represented'). Alsted, *Encyclopædia*, p. 1198; *Templum musicum*, p. 26.

⁸   Birchensha attempts to reconcile two distinct meanings of 'system': first a 'stave', and secondly a 'compound interval' or 'musical body'. For the first meaning, see his translation of Alsted (chapter 5, 'Precepts'): 'The greater System [*Systema majus*] for the most part doth consist of ten Lines: and serveth for the Composing of a Song [*cantilenæ componendæ*], called otherwise a conjoyned System. The lesser System [*Systema minus*] doth consist of five Lines, and serveth chiefly to a Song pricked out [*cantilenæ extrahendæ & notandæ*]. This is otherwise called a simple System.' (Alsted, *Encyclopædia*, p. 1198; *Templum musicum*, p. 25.) For the second meaning, see below ('Mathematicall Part', chapter 5): 'By the Addition of Intervalls, musical Systems, Bodies, or magnitudes are completed'. Cf also William Holder, *A Treatise of the Natural Grounds, and Principles of Harmony* (London, 1694), p. 145: 'By *System* they [i.e. ancient Greek writers on music] meant, a Comprehensive Interval, compounded of Degrees, or of less *Systems*, or of both'.

⁹   Birchensha anticipates by more than 30 years the appearance of the term 'Ledger-Lines' in John Playford's *An Introduction to the Skill of Musick*, 13th edn (London,

1697), p. 6. Cf Rebecca Herissone, *Music Theory in Seventeenth-Century England* (Oxford, 2000), p. 268.

[10] Although the term 'pentagram' is otherwise rare in English music theory, in Italy *pentagramma*, and in Spain *pentagrama*, have long been used to mean a five-line staff.

[11] Birchensha borrowed much of this material from his translation of Alsted, who in turn leant heavily on Lippius's *Synopsis musicæ* (Strasbourg, 1612), sigs D5ᵛ–D6ʳ. Having illustrated the greater and lesser staves, Alsted continues (chapter 5, Rule 5): 'Ambo iste systemata ponenda sunt in palimpsesto seu abaco melopoëtico, seu compositorio, ut vocant. Et prius quidem incipienti, posterius exercitato maximè convenit. Alii tamen malunt plura systemata simplicia in abaco pingere, hoc modo:' ('Both these Systems are put in a Chart, or Melopoetick *Abacus*, or Compositary as they call it. The first is convenient to a young Beginner: the latter, for a longer Practitioner: but others would rather draw more simple Systems in an *Abacus*; Thus'). As Jessie Ann Owens has shown, the terminology employed here goes back to a Renaissance practice of using an erasable tablet or *cartella* with incised or painted staves as a compositional tool. Lippius wrote of a *palimpsestus compositorius seu melopoeticus* with ruled staves; while Alsted, interestingly enough, equated *palimpsestus* with *abacus*, a term that Giovanni Spataro had used in 1529 when writing from Bologna to Giovanni del Lago in Venice with an order for 'una cartella, o vero una tabula de abaco' on which to compose. See Alsted, *Encyclopædia*, p. 1199; *Templum musicum*, pp. 31–2; Benito V. Rivera, *German Music Theory in the Early 17th Century* (Ann Arbor, MI, 1980), pp. 60–61; *A Correspondence of Renaissance Musicians*, eds Bonnie J. Blackburn, Edward J. Lowinsky and Clement A. Miller (Oxford, 1991), pp. 350–52; Jessie Ann Owens, *Composers at Work: The Craft of Musical Composition 1450–1600* (New York and Oxford, 1997), pp. 74–107.

[12] Birchensha means that a bar-length of one or two semibreves is usual. Alsted similarly wrote of staves being cut by perpendicular lines 'distantiâ duorum tactuum vel unius', i.e. at a distance of two *tactus* or one: *Encyclopædia*, p. 1199; *Templum musicum*, p. 31.

[13] Birchensha is probably correct in deriving the English term 'score' from the practice of incising or drawing vertical lines through the staves.

[14] The use of the term 'lyre octave' for the middle octave of the scale (*a* to *g'* in modern convention) seems to be rare if not unique. Perhaps it was thought of as corresponding to the seven strings of the Greek lyre: cf Alsted's comment that 'Lyra, cithara, & alia quaedam instrumenta musica quæ chordis tendebantur, antiquitus septem chordarum fuerunt proculdubio septenarum vocum causa' ('The *Lyre*, *Cithern*, and certain other musical Instruments which are strung with strings, were anciently of seven strings, without doubt, by reason of the seven Voices') (*Encyclopædia*, p. 1200; *Templum musicum*, p. 37). 'Geminated' means 'duplicated' (aa, bb, and so on).

[15] Birchensha follows mediaeval and Renaissance teaching in using the Greek term *apotome* for the greater (i.e. chromatic) semitone, which in the Pythagorean scheme of tuning exceeds the diatonic semitone by a *comma*. Compare for example Franchinus Gaffurius, *Theorica musice* (Milan, 1492), sig. f6ʳ; Thomas Morley, *A Plaine and Easie Introduction to Practicall Musicke* (London, 1597), 'Annotations', sig. ¶3ʳ. Some English writers, including Christopher Simpson, used *apotome* incorrectly for the difference between the greater and lesser semitones, though in *A Compendium of Practical Musick* (London, 1667), p. 104, Simpson adds: 'Some Authors call the

Greater Semitone, Apotome; That is (I suppose) because it includes the odd *Comma* which makes that *Apotome*'.

16   By 1660 it was becoming increasingly common in England for major and minor keys to be called 'sharp keys' and 'flat keys' respectively: see for example Christopher Simpson, *Chelys / The Division-Viol* (London, 1665), p. 16 ('Every Composition in Musick, be it long or short, is (or ought to be) designed to some one Key or Tone, in which the Bass doth always conclude. This Key or Tone is called Flat or Sharp, according as the Key-note hath the lesser or greater Third next above it. If it be the Lesser Third, 'tis called a Flat Key; if the Greater Third, 'tis a Sharp Key.') It must be emphasized, however, that this is not how Birchensha uses the terms 'sharp key' and 'flat key' here. His description of 'keys' (i.e. notes) as sharp, flat or perfect seems to stem from sixteenth-century German theory, where solmization syllables are categorized as durus, mollis or naturalis. Ornithoparchus's *Musicæ activæ micrologus* (Leipzig, 1517), as translated by Dowland in *Andreas Ornithoparcus his Micrologus* (London, 1609), p. 6, provides an example: 'Therefore of *Voyces*, Some are called ♭ *Mols, Viz. Vt Fa*, because they make a *Flat* sound. Some are called *Naturals, Viz. Re Sol*, because they make a *Meane* sound. Some are called ♮ *Sharps, Viz. Mi La*, because they make a *Sharpe* sound.' In the present passage, B and E are those notes which, in an ascending natural scale, lead to notes a diatonic semitone higher: B–C, E–F. Conversely, F and C are the notes which in a descending natural scale lead to notes a semitone lower: F–E, C–B. Birchensha used this same terminology when teaching his rules of composition (see Chapter IX, p. 247).

17   Although he invokes the name of the Swiss humanist Heinrich Glarean, whose *Dodecachordon* (Basle, 1547) may indeed have been his source, what Birchensha presents here in summary form is the system of eight modes set out by Gaffurius in his *Theorica musice* (Milan, 1492), Book 5, chapter 8, and his *De harmonia musicorum instrumentorum opus* (Milan, 1518), Book 4, chapters 11 and 12. In addition to the seven modes that Boethius had recognized, Gaffurius included in his system the Hypermixolydian mode of Ptolemy, so that (as Glarean observed) 'at least the beautiful little eightfold arrangement of the modes would not be lost'. Glarean illustrated this arrangement in *Dodecachordon*, Book 2, chapter 2, showing how the strings required to play the eight modal scales exactly encompass two octaves, before going on to propose his own enlargement of the system from eight modes to 12 (in which the Hypermixolydian had no place). Birchensha must have known something of Glarean's 12-mode system, either directly from *Dodecachordon* or – because part of his Alsted translation is concerned with the matter – indirectly through German theorists; but in the 'Compendious Discourse' he chose to pass over it in silence. Possibly he preferred to focus on the eight-mode system because of the neat way it spans the disdiapason from A to aa. See Franchino Gaffurio, *The Theory of Music*, trans. Walter Kurt Kreyszig and ed. Claude V. Palisca (New Haven, CT, and London, 1993), pp. 183–7; Heinrich Glarean, *Dodecachordon*, trans. with commentary by Clement A. Miller (2 vols, American Institute of Musicology, 1965), vol. 1, pp. 98–105; *Templum musicum*, pp. 76–87.

18   Birchensha no doubt modelled his table on similar diagrams used by humanist theorists – for example Gaffurius in *Practica musice* (Milan, 1496), sig. a ii^v, and Glarean in *Dodecachordon*, p. 4 – to show Greek note-names alongside those of the Guidonian scale. His presentation of the gamut is far from conventional, however. First, the traditional hexachords are replaced by the English system of four-syllable

solmization; hexachords are never mentioned. Secondly, to the scales starting on G, C and F he adds columns for scales starting on E♭, B♭, A♭ and D♭. He thus in effect extends the three scales taught by William Bathe to seven; compare Jessie Ann Owens, 'Concepts of Pitch in English Music Theory, c. 1560–1640', in Cristle Collins Judd (ed.), *Tonal Structures in Early Music* (New York and London, 1998), pp. 183–246, at pp. 191–215. These changes give rise to certain anomalies. Flats have to be supplied mentally, which presumably explains why he entered no syllables alongside the note B♭; even his scale starting on F has *fa* placed in the B♮ row. (The musical example in chapter 5 shows the mutations correctly notated.) He credits Guido of Arezzo with introducing the four syllables *sol la mi fa*, but passes over *ut* and *re* in silence. Treatment of the Greek denominations is more orthodox, though errors in the note-names suggest that Birchensha's command of them was still imperfect. The right-hand column is reserved for the *synemmenon* tetrachord a, b♭, c, d, with *trite synemmenon* correctly placed alongside B♭.

[19] Even in a theoretical context, most musicians would have found signatures of seven, six, five or even four flats baffling in the 1660s. Christopher Simpson's table in *Chelys / The Division-Viol*, p. 16, is perhaps the closest parallel to Birchensha's. It illustrates 16 keys (eight major, eight minor), using the eight key-notes G, A, B♭, C, D, E♭, E and F; but even Simpson's E♭ minor is given a signature of only four flats. By including abbreviated solmization syllables in his music example, Birchensha emphasizes that the scale's interval structure remains constant, no matter how remote the transposition. There is no mention at this point of sharpward transposition or sharp signatures, which in England had become increasingly familiar (especially in instrumental consort music) since the early seventeenth century; Birchensha's own compositions include fantasia-suites in D [major] with a signature of two sharps (Oxford, Christ Church, MS Mus. 781 and 1016–17). See Christopher D.S. Field, 'Jenkins and the Cosmography of Harmony', in Andrew Ashbee and Peter Holman (eds), *John Jenkins and his Time* (Oxford, 1996), pp. 1–74.

[20] Birchensha's table neatly illustrates most of the clef positions that a seventeenth-century musician was ever likely to meet: *g'*2, *c'*1, *c'*2, *c'*3, *c'*4, *f*3, *f*4. The only notable absentee is *g'*1. In his composition teaching Birchensha preferred to simplify matters, and his examples are normally restricted to *g'*2 and *f*4. Thomas Salmon's proposed clef reforms, to which Birchensha lent his support, were not published until 1672.

[21] The range of note values considered here is wider than was usual in English theoretical literature of the period; cf Herissone, *Music Theory in Seventeenth-Century England*, p. 43 (note 64). In particular, Birchensha's inclusion of what he called the 'semidemiquaver', one sixty-fourth part of a semibreve, is exceptional. Composers did occasionally use such notes (for example Giles Farnaby in his almaine for two virginals), but far more rarely than demisemiquavers. The nomenclature adopted by Birchensha for these short notes was also idiosyncratic: 'demiquaver' for demisemiquaver, 'semidemiquaver' for hemidemisemiquaver. 'Demiquaver', though found elsewhere as a synonym for 'semiquaver', occurs only seldom in the sense in which Birchensha used it – as in the dictionary *Glossographia anglicana nova* (London, 1707), sig. I 8ᵛ: '*Demi-quaver*; a Note in Musick, half a Semiquaver'. In proposing that relationships between note values are somehow analogous to the 'proportions of consonant and dissonant Intervalls' Birchensha presumably had in mind the fact that, just as the ratios of Pythagorean intervals were based on multiples of 2 and 3 (but no larger prime numbers), so musical time was generally founded on duple and triple

proportions. He was to return to this topic in his 1676 synopsis of *Syntagma musicæ*, writing of 'How the values of Notes hold proportion with the rations of Sounds' (see Chapter VI, 'Practical Part', § 25).

²²   The form of the large rest is anomalous. The usual custom was to write it as two long rests side by side: see Thomas Morley, *A Plaine and Easie Introduction to Practicall Musicke* (London, 1597), p. 9; John Playford, *A Brief Introduction to the Skill of Musick*, 4th edn (London, 1664), p. 26; and Simpson, *A Compendium of Practical Musick*, p. 13. Alternatively it could be written as a single vertical stroke extending over all four spaces: see Thomas Ravenscroft, *A Briefe Discourse* (London, 1614), p. 4; Alsted, *Encyclopædia*, p. 1199, and *Templum musicum*, p. 29. In calling the large rest a 'perfect or General Rest', indicating 'a final close of a song' (see chapter 9), Birchensha echoes Gaffurius in *Practica musice*, sig. aa vi^r: 'Maior aute[m] q[uam] trium t[em]poru[m] pausa [...] concentus declarat terminationem' ('A rest greater than three units of time [i.e. than a perfect long] signifies the end of a composition'). Its formal assimilation to a double barline is therefore presumably not fortuitous. The description of the long rest as 'modal, or Pausa Modalis', and the reference to its placement 'at the end of straines', seem to bear little relationship to seventeenth-century practice.

²³   Birchensha's treatment of obsolete or obsolescent white-note ligatures is predictably perfunctory. He follows Butler, however, in extending the term 'ligature' to cover the modern practice of joining notes with a slur or tie: see Charles Butler, *The Principles of Musik* (London, 1636), p. 37.

²⁴   This passage on 'the use of Pauses' seems to belong more naturally in chapter 8, rather than chapter 9. The reasons put forward for the invention of rests are reminiscent of similar lists given by Morley and Ravenscroft. See Morley, *A Plaine and Easie Introduction*, sig. ¶4^v ('First, to giue som leasure to the singers to take breath. The second, that the pointes might follow in Fuge one vpon another, at the more ease [...] Some restes also (as the minime and crotchet restes) were deuised, to avoid the harshnesse of some discord, or the following of two perfect concords together.'); Ravenscroft, *A Briefe Discourse*, p. 4 ('*Pauses*, or *Rests* [...] were Inuented for 3. causes. 1. For *Closes*, 2. for *Fuges*, 3. for avoyding of *Discords*, and disallowances.')

²⁵   *Punctum*: a point or dot.

²⁶   Though the *signum* of repetition had a long history, it found renewed usefulness in the seventeenth century for indicating what was known in France as a *petite reprise*, and in England as a 'small repeat', as described and illustrated here. Cf also Christopher Simpson, *The Principles of Practical Musick* (London, 1665), p. 29.

²⁷   To judge from the foregoing list, which includes so recently introduced a genre as the *gavotte*, Birchensha was abreast of the French dances that were coming into vogue in Restoration England. In 1658 the poet Richard Flecknoe had written about 'a French dancing-master in England' who 'gos a Pilgrimage to *Paris* every year, and distributes his new *Branles Gavots* and *Sarabands*, like precious Reliques amongst his *Schollars* at his return'. A few years later Pepys witnessed the custom of beginning formal balls at court by dancing 'the Bransles' (*Diary*, 31 December 1662 and 15 November 1666); on each occasion one of the chief dancers was George Villiers, second Duke of Buckingham, to whom Birchensha appears to have given composition lessons in 1663–64. The 1665 edition of John Playford's *The Dancing Master* was one of the first English publications to include examples of 'gavot' and 'bore' (bourrée). Birchensha's interest in the *goût français* is borne out by an undated suite for violin and bass by him, made up of an overture, branles, gavot, courant, minuet and rondeau (London, Royal

College of Music, MS 2087). In it, the C signature with vertical stroke appropriate to 'active songs' is used for the duple-time sections of the overture and first branle, and the reversed C signature with vertical stroke (implying a quicker speed) for the gavot. A distinction is also made between those movements in 3/2 or mixed 3/2 and 6/4 time (the second branle and courant), which have the signature '31' surmounted by C with central dot, and those in 3/4 time (the third branle, minuet and rondeau) which are given the plain '31' signature. Such notational distinctions were by no means universally observed by contemporaries, however. Birchensha's pragmatic treatment of time signatures in 'A Compendious Discourse' is in some respects innovative. The inclusion of the '2' signature, for example, predates by more than fifteen years its appearance in Nicola Matteis's *The False Consonances of Musick* (London, 1682), where it is said to indicate 'the beating of a Quick Measure after the French Fashion'. See John Harley, *Music in Purcell's London: The Social Background* (London, 1968), pp. 154–5; Peter Holman, *Four and Twenty Fiddlers: The Violin at the English Court 1540–1690* (Oxford, 1993), pp. 311–15; Herrisone, *Music Theory in Seventeenth-Century England*, pp. 65–71; *The Complete Country Dance Tunes from Playford's Dancing Master (1651–ca.1728)*, ed. Jeremy Barlow (London, 1985), nos 136, 169, 185, 190.

28   Although Birchensha was interested in how number and proportion underlie musical time and rhythm, his discussion here of proportional signs seems cursory and (in the absence of any music examples) lacking in clarity. His comment that signs such as 2/1, 3/2 and 6/4 show 'the proportion is of Inequality' harks back to Morley, who wrote about temporal proportion in *A Plaine and Easie Introduction* (p. 27): 'Proportion is either of equalitie or vnequalitie. *Proportion of æqualitie*, is the comparing of two æquall quantities togither, in which, because there is no difference, we will speake no more at this time. *Proportion of inæqualitie* is, when two things of vnequall quantitie are compared togither, and is either of the more or lesse inæqualitie. *Proportion of the more inæqualitie* is, when a greater number is set ouer and compared to a lesser, and *in Musicke doeth alwaies signifie diminution.*' Simpson, too, observed in *A Compendium of Practical Musick* (p. 34) that 'you may sometimes meet with Figures set thus 3/2 called *Sesquialtera* proportion, which signifies a *Tripla* Measure of three Notes to two such like Notes of the Common Time. The like may be understood of 6/4 or any other proportion: which proportions, if they be of the greater inequality, (that is, when the greater Figure doth stand above,) do always signifie Diminution'. For Simpson, like Morley, such signs indicate the relationship of a passage to what went before. Birchensha, on the other hand, appears to limit their application to places where one part plays three minims or six crotchets in the time of two minims or four crotchets in another part. It is difficult to see how notes should be 'unequaly divided' where the signature is 2/1.

29   This sentence evidently does not refer to the 'Practicall Part' of the present work, but to another work in preparation.

30   The abbreviations T (for 'a Tone or whole Note') and S (for 'a Semitone or Lesser half Note') were also used by Birchensha when teaching his rules of composition: cf Brussels, Bibliothèque Royale de Belgique, MS II 4168, fol. 3^r (see Chapter X).

31   Birchensha here introduces the concept of 'concinnity'. He evidently saw it as an intermediate state between consonance and dissonance, exemplified by the minor and major thirds, diminished fifth, and minor and major sixths. This may be the first appearance of the term 'concinnous' in English music theory, though the idea behind it can be traced back by way of Boethius to ancient Greece. Several sixteenth-century

German treatises, including Johannes Galliculus's influential *Isagoge de compositione cantus* (Leipzig, 1520) and Fredericus Beurhusius's *Erotematum musicæ* (Nürnberg, 1580), divide concords into those that are *æquisonæ* (octaves), *consonæ* (perfect fifths), and *concinnes* (major and minor thirds and sixths). Lippius, in his *Synopsis musicæ novæ* (1612), introduced a further subdivision: thirds *concinunt*, sixths merely *circumsonant*. (See Rivera, *German Music Theory*, pp. 80–85.) Through Birchensha's translation of Alsted, Lippius's gradations found their way into *Templum musicum* (p. 53): the octave 'doth equisonate', the fifth 'doth consonate', the ditone (major third) and semiditone (minor third) 'concent', the major and minor sixths 'circumsonate'. To Lippius and Alsted, however, the diminished fifth or semidiapente was dissonant, not concinnous (as it is in the 'Compendious Discourse'). In 1694 William Holder wrote of intervals 'which are (as the Greeks termed them) ἐμμελῆ, *Concinnous*, apt and usefull in Harmony'; but apart from the diminished fifth Holder's list of concinnous intervals was quite different from Birchensha's (it included major hemitone, minor and major tones, tritone, and minor and major sevenths), and he classified them all as discords (Holder, *A Treatise of the Natural Grounds, and Principles of Harmony*, pp. 166–70, 194). For Birchensha the concept seems to have been a purely theoretical one: when teaching pupils to compose he was happy enough to treat thirds and sixths as concords.

[32]   It may not be entirely coincidental that 'denomination' was a medieval technical term for the names given to mathematical ratios and sometimes used in ratio computations (see M.S. Mahoney, 'Mathematics' in D.C. Lindberg (ed.), *Science in the Middle Ages* (Chicago, 1978), pp. 145–78 at pp. 163–6). The letters that Birchensha gives to 'Keyes' in the following table are not quite consistent with those given in the table in chapter 4 of the 'Practicall Part', or with his guidance on the subject at the end of chapter 1. Here he marks the highest note as g (rather than G), and the lowest as G (rather than Γ).

[33]   In the first table in chapter 13, the Semidiapente (D♭) should be placed below the Tritonus (C♯), since in Pythagorean tuning C♯ is the higher note. The order is correctly shown in the second music example in chapter 12, and in the second table in chapter 13. The column in the first table headed 'number of Intervalls' simply enumerates the ascending degrees of this somewhat unusual scale, which is the same 14-note scale as shown in chapter 12. The actual steps making up the octave are as follows: (1) semitone, (2) apotome, (3) semitone, (4) apotome, (5) semitone, (6) semitone, (7) comma, (8) semitone, (9) semitone, (10) apotome, (11) semitone, (12) semitone, (13) comma, (14) semitone. The second table in chapter 13 is nearly identical with one in the autograph manuscript of the 'Rules of Composition', Brussels, Bibliothèque Royale de Belgique, MS II 4168, fol. 2ʳ (see Chapter X). In it Birchensha's signs for a 'double flatt' (♭♭, as nowadays) and 'double sharp' (a sharp sign with a third cross bar) make their first appearance: for the former, see the rows beginning on B♭, E♭ and a♭; for the latter, the row beginning on C♯. Double flats and double sharps are discussed in chapter 9 of the 'Mathematicall Part'.

[34]   Birchensha wrote these 'Observations' on the blank verso page at the end of the 'Practicall Part'. There is no entry for them in the table of contents on fol. 19, which suggests that they may have been a late addition, perhaps intended as a link between the 'Practicall' and 'Mathematicall' parts; but their presence serves to underline the importance that Birchensha attached to the concept of the 'musicall Sound'. The terms in the second list – musical 'Moode', 'Key', 'Intervall', 'Note', 'Voice' – have all been discussed in the preceding chapters, whereas musical 'Body', 'Number' and 'Magnitude' will be considered in the 'Mathematicall Part'.

35   'Rations' are simply ratios; a 'proportion' is a system of (usually equal) ratios formed by three or more numbers. 'Sounds', here as elsewhere, means intervals rather than pitches. Birchensha is quite careful to write of the ratios and proportions 'of' sounds, rather than identifying ratios with intervals.

36   This pair of diagrams is somewhat opaque at this stage in the treatise. Briefly, to mediate a ratio $a : c$ harmonically is to divide it into $a : b : c$ so that $a–b : b–c = a : c$. In this case the division of $6 : 3$ into $6 : 4 : 3$ has this property, and Birchensha displays on the right the corresponding musical division of an octave ($2 : 1$ or $6 : 3$) into a fifth ($6 : 4$ or $3 : 2$) and a fourth ($4 : 3$). The calculation at the left confirms that $6 : 4 + 4 : 3 = 24 : 12 (= 2 : 1)$.

37   In the list of items which follows, 'sound' means a musical interval, not a single pitch.

38   Although 'commensuration' could be a technical term in Euclidean geometry, it is unlikely to mean more than 'relative sizes' here.

39   This is the first hint of what will later become Birchensha's major interest in the unison as the source of all intervals. Alsted may have been the starting-point for Birchensha's ideas about the 'Radical Unison': cf *Templum musicum*, p. 16 (chapter 4, Rule 5): '*The simple Unison is the Principal and Radix of all Musical Intervals*'. Alsted's original text is: '*Unisonus simplex est principium & radix omnium intervallorum Musicorum.*' (*Encyclopædia* (Herborn, 1630), p. 1199). This is in turn indebted to Lippius, who wrote: 'Liquet etiam Unisonum Simplicem (quia habet Proportionem aequalitatis, & est principium omnis Intervalli) proprie nec consonare, ut vulgus aestimat, nec dissonare, sed aequisonare & unisonare simpliciter, atque ita Radicem esse omnis consonantiae atque dissonantiae, sicut etiam aures Monochordo attentae percipiunt inter 1. & 1.' (*Synopsis musicæ novæ* (Strasbourg, 1612), sig. E2^v–E3^r; quoted in Rivera, *German Music Theory in the Early 17th Century*, p. 104, note 5.) Birchensha's remarks about the 'Unison' in this and subsequent chapters may be compared with what Christopher Simpson wrote at about the same time in *A Compendium of Practicall Musick*, pp. 37–8: 'In reference to *Intervalls*, we are first to consider an Unison; that is, one, or the same sound; whether produced by one single Voyce, or divers Voyces sounding in the same Tone. This *Unison*, as it is the first Term to any *Intervall*, so may it be considered in Musick as an Unite in *Arithmetick*, or as a Point in *Geometry*, not divisible. As sounds are more or less distant from any supposed Unison, so do they make greater or lesser *I[n]tervalls:* upon which accompt, *Intervalls* may be said to be like Numbers, *Indefinite*.'

40   This and the following four axioms echo Euclid, *Elements*, Book I, Common Notions 2, 3, 1, 6 (spurious) and 5 respectively. See Thomas Heath, *The Thirteen Books of Euclid's Elements* (New York, 1956), vol. 1, p. 155. Birchensha would have considered Common Notion 6 genuine: see ibid., p. 223.

41   This gesture at dividing one interval by another by repeated subtraction is the closest Birchensha comes to addressing the question of how to measure and compare intervals mathematically, which exercised other mathematical theorists, including Nicolaus Mercator and Isaac Newton, around this time.

42   i.e. $2 : 1 = 3 : 2 + 4 : 3$, in other words an octave contains a fifth and a fourth. It is far from obvious why this and the remaining 'axioms' are given the same status as the quasi-Euclidean ones which precede them.

43   Birchensha presumably means *two* sesquioctavas, i.e. $4 : 3 = 9 : 8 + 9 : 8 + 256 : 243$, that is a fourth equals two tones plus a Pythagorean semitone.

[44]   i.e. 3 : 2 = 32 : 27 + 81 : 64, that is a fifth equals a Pythagorean ditone (81 : 64) plus an interval which Birchensha will elsewhere call a 'semiditone', equal to a tone plus a Pythagorean semitone.

[45]   i.e. 2 : 1 – 4 : 3 = 3 : 2, that is an octave minus a fourth equals a fifth. In this and the following 'axiom' Birchensha uses 'Diapason' where 'dupla proportion' would be expected: this is a relatively rare instance in Birchensha of a terminological slide – taking the names of ratios and of intervals as interchangeable – common in other mathematical music theorists of the period.

[46]   i.e. 2 : 1 – 3 : 2 = 4 : 3, that is an octave minus a fifth equals a fourth.

[47]   This sounds like a reference to the 'Grand Scale' (see Introduction). Nothing in the 'Compendious Discourse' demonstrates all of these axioms.

[48]   Here we meet an important feature of Birchensha's understanding of the unison: it may be an interval, with ratio 1 : 1 and 'magnitude' of zero; or it may be a pitch, the lowest pitch playable on a given string and whose 'magnitude' is the total length of that string. The former is the 'unextended' unison, capable of being extended, and the latter the 'extended' unison, capable of being divided. (The term 'radical unison' seems to be applied to both unisons.) Although many of Birchensha's subsequent references to the unison are confusing, few of them are strictly ambiguous.

[49]   'Magnitude' here means the distance on a given string which an interval occupies. On a string of length twenty-four units the bottom six units form a diatessaron (fourth, or 24 : 18 = 4 : 3), the next six a diapente (fifth, or 18 : 12 = 3 : 2) and the next six a diapason (12 : 6 = 2 : 1).

[50]   Birchensha's choice of terms in Axioms 4 and 5 is odd, but the sense of the passage seems to be this. A given note can in principle be raised in pitch ('extended') indefinitely, but for musical purposes a limit is set to this by the division of the corresponding string in two, i.e. the interval of an octave. A given note, if it is to be considered the lowest note in a musical scale, cannot be lowered in pitch ('decreased'), because it would then no longer be the lowest note under consideration.

[51]   That is, a double octave is equal to a fourth plus a fifth plus an octave.

[52]   This idea of 'measuring' a larger interval using several *different* smaller ones may seem strange: it is at odds with the Euclidean notion of measurement by a *single* smaller quantity, which was introduced as 'numeration' in Axiom 7 of the Arithmetical part. But in fact Birchensha refers here not to intervals but to *magnitudes*, in the sense defined in Axiom 3 of the geometrical part, and refers to the example given in that axiom where the *magnitude* of a double octave is equally divided into the magnitudes of a fourth, a fifth, and an octave.

[53]   In Boethius's treatise on geometry *longitudo*, *latitudo* and *crassitudo* mean length, breadth and depth. Their application to musical sounds is an idea that Birchensha owes to Lippius via Alsted: see Alsted, *Encyclopædia* (1630), pp. 1996–7; *Templum musicum*, pp. 13, 15–16. The text of Alsted's precepts, followed by Birchensha's translation, runs: 'Quantitas est triplex, longitudo, latitudo, & crassitudo. Longitudo soni Musici est, quæ cernitur in ipsius motu seu duratione: & mensuratur tactu Musico. Latitudo soni Musici est, quæ cernitur in spiritu tenui & aspero. Crassitudo soni Musici est, quæ cernitur in profunditate & altitudine ipsius.' ('Quantity is threefold, Longitude, Latitude, and Crassitude. The Longitude of a Musical Sound, is that which is discerned in the motion and duration thereof: and measured by a Musical Touch or Tact. The Latitude of a Musical Sound is that which is discerned in the tenuous and asperous spirit. The Crassitude of a Musical Sound is that which is discerned in the

Profundity and Altitude thereof.') On the derivation of this from Lippius's *Synopsis*, and the geometrical connotations of the three terms, see Rivera, *German Music Theory*, pp. 46–58. Birchensha may have got tangled up in his own terminology and have intended to write that every interval has *crassitude* only: in Lippius and Alsted it is crassitude, rather than longitude, that measures a sound's acuteness or gravity of pitch, longitude being concerned with its temporal duration (not with the string length needed to produce it), and latitude with its 'mollity & Asperity' (i.e. volume or dynamics).

54 Birchensha defines as 'even' an interval whose corresponding string length may be divided in half to produce two equal intervals. The only such interval is in fact the unison, whose string length of zero produces two more unisons when divided in half. Instead of stating this, however, Birchensha considers the 'extended' unison – that is, the whole string – and asserts that it produces two equal intervals when divided in half. Although strictly true (a string divided at its midpoint makes two half-strings whose pitches are equal) this reflects a rather different understanding of dividing a string from that found elsewhere in the treatise (the bottom half of a string as used, say, in a viol, represents a pitch range of one octave; whereas its top half represents a potentially unlimited range of pitches).

55 Here Birchensha simply observes that equal division of string lengths corresponds to unequal division of ratios, and *vice versa*. The following diagrams illustrate this for the double octave divided into equal octaves with unequal magnitudes, and the octave divided into a fifth and fourth with equal magnitudes.

56 A tone of a sesquinona proportion would be a tone of 10 : 9, the minor tone of the just intonation. Birchensha states (correctly) that it is smaller than the Pythagorean tone of 9 : 8 by 81 : 80.

57 Birchensha probably refers to the first table in chapter 13 of the 'Practical Part', or possibly to something not included in the 'Compendious Discourse'. The meaning of 'Radicall Terme' is somewhat obscure here: but it occurs again in chapter 6 of the 'Mathematicall Part', when defining the 'Ration of a Musicall Sound', where Birchensha gives 3 : 2 as an example of the 'Radicall & correlated Termes' of an interval. It seems therefore that the radical term is the larger term of an interval's ratio, and the correlated term the smaller term. Thus incompounded intervals would be those whose ratios are given in lowest terms, and compounded intervals those whose ratios may not be given in lowest terms because they are to be subdivided. For example an incompounded tone has the ratio 9 : 8, but a compounded tone divided into semitone and apotome has the ratio 2304 : 2048. (This is different from the use of 'simple' and 'compound' found, for example, in chapter 6 of *Templum musicum*, where a simple interval lies within the compass of an octave and a compound one does not.)

58 'Digite' sounds are intervals smaller than an octave; 'articulate' sounds are intervals between one and two octaves; 'compounded' sounds are intervals composed of a 'digite' sound and an 'articulate' one.

59 The distinction between 'radical unison' and 'unison' in this and the next item is that between the 'unextended' and 'extended' unison; see note 48 above.

60 Birchensha is apparently struggling in this passage with the nature of the 'extended' unison and the fact that it is a decidedly different kind of entity from other 'sounds' or intervals. Here and elsewhere in his discussions of the unison, Birchensha seems to intend an analogy with the idea of the unity as not a number but the source of all other numbers, recorded by Aristotle at *Metaphysics* 1088a6 and implied by Euclid at

Elements VII, definitions 1 and 2. For more references see Thomas Heath, *A History of Greek Mathematics* (Oxford, 1921; New York, 1981), vol. 1, p. 69. For Lippius the 'monad' seems to have been an individual note or sound considered by itself: 'Materia, ex qua Cantilena Harmonica fit, sunt ejus Partes [...] Pars simplex est Sonus, qui commodissime vocari quit Μονάς Musica' (*Synopsis musicæ novæ*, sig. B4ᵛ, as quoted by Rivera, *German Music Theory*, p. 45). Thence the term was taken up by Alsted: cf *Templum musicum*, p. 13 ('The Simple Part is called Sound: also a Musical Monad, in Greek Tonos'), or p. 56 ('*The Harmonical* Tryas [...] doth consist of three *Monads* or *Sounds*').

⁶¹   In the following catalogue of the differences between adjacent intervals, note that the prefix 'semi-' denotes diminution of an interval by a chromatic semitone or 'apotome'. The comma is the Pythagorean comma of 531441 : 524288.

⁶²   Again, Birchensha probably refers to the tables of intervals in chapter 13 of the 'Practical Part', or possibly to something not included in the 'Compendious Discourse'.

⁶³   Birchensha explains that to add intervals with ratios $a:b$ and $c:d$ one must multiply corresponding terms, constructing the ratio $ac:bd$, which will be that of the resulting interval.

⁶⁴   Birchensha explains that to subtract the interval with ratio $c:d$ from that with ratio $a:b$ one must cross-multiply, constructing the ratio $ad:bc$, which will be that of the resulting interval. The following table shows an example.

⁶⁵   Here Birchensha explains, as the following examples show, that one can multiply an interval by two by adding it to itself.

⁶⁶   This is one of the clearer indications that the full 'mathematicall part of musick' is distinct from the current text. It is not clear what exactly Birchensha means by the phrase 'species of proportion' here.

⁶⁷   Here division of one interval by another is performed by repeatedly subtracting the smaller from the larger, a method which in general will result in a remainder.

⁶⁸   This is in effect the definition of a (Pythagorean) comma.

⁶⁹   The example which follows shows that by 'substraction of numbers' Birchensha means the subtraction of ratios. His procedure would be somewhat clearer if – as he possibly intended – the second appearance of 32 : 27 were rendered as 256 : 216, showing that each subtraction involves a pair of ratios with either their lower or their higher term in common, and whose difference is therefore equal to the ratio of the non-equal terms: that is $a:c-b:c=a:b$.

⁷⁰   In this chapter we learn that the 'ration' of a sound is its ratio in lowest terms; its 'radical term' is the higher term of this ratio and its 'correlated term' the lower; the 'proportionality' of an interval is the double ratio $a:b:c$ produced when it is divided into two smaller intervals; and its 'proportion' is the ratio of the greatest and smallest terms in this case, $a:c$ (which may not be in its lowest terms). The 'habitude' of an interval is not clearly defined: it may be the set of all ratios (or at least all musically useful ratios) which can produce it, or it may be the set of all the lengths (magnitudes) it can occupy on a given string.

⁷¹   Although the more exact – and correct – numbers which follow could have been arrived at by computation, the repeated use of 'about' with approximate values in eighths of an inch in this paragraph strongly suggests that all of these figures arose from an experimental procedure using a real 36-inch string, divided and then measured using a rule with a scale of 1/8 inches. The exactly correct values would be respectively $7^5/_9$, $6^3/_8$, $4^{25}/_{32}$, and $4^3/_4$ inches (with the aid of a calculator these can easily be found

by scaling the numbers in Birchensha's diagram so that the range of 4096–9216 units becomes one of 16–36). Birchensha's own values are difficult to interpret: one is exactly correct, two show small errors in opposite directions, and one shows a very large error – $2^7/_8$ for, in his terms, about $4^6/_8$ – perhaps an error of copying rather than of experiment, since no neighbouring interval has the size which Birchensha gives. There seems no way to deduce anything about Birchensha's experimental procedure from this: it may have involved either geometric or aural division of a string, for instance.

[72] Birchensha's classification of ratios is standard: it may be derived from Boethius's *De arithmetica*, or from some more recent source.

[73] It is striking that in this chapter, by contrast with his usual practice, Birchensha writes (vertically aligned) fractions instead of ratios. No reason for this is apparent, and the implication seems to be that Birchensha considered the two to be equivalent. This was by no means universally accepted by mathematicians of the period.

[74] A ratio $a : b$ with $a > b$ is multiplex if a is an exact multiple of b; it is superparticular if b goes once into a with a remainder of 1. It is superpartient if b goes once into a with a remainder greater than 1; it is multiplex superpartient if b goes more than once into a and leaves a remainder greater than 1; and, finally, it is multiplex superparticular if b goes more than once into a and leaves a remainder of 1.

[75] Birchensha discusses the sum of a ratio $a : b$ larger than $1 : 1$ and a ratio $c : d$ smaller than $1 : 1$, apparently stating (wrongly) that the result is less than both $a : b$ and $d : c$. The only such condition which in fact exists is that the resulting ratio will lie between $a : b$ and $c : d$. The following diagram shows, or is intended to show, that $4 : 2 + 2 : 3 = 8 : 6 = 4 : 3$.

[76] Here Birchensha applies the procedure for subtracting ratios – cross-multiplication of terms – to a ratio $a : b$ larger than $1 : 1$ and a ratio $c : d$ smaller than $1 : 1$, and states correctly that the result is equal to the sum of $a : b$ and $d : c$.

[77] The numbers a, b, c are said to form a proportion if the ratios $a : b$ and $b : c$ are equal. This is sometimes obscured by the fact that, in both English and Latin, 'proportion' (*proportio*) is sometimes also used as a synonym for 'ratio'. In the original Greek of the theory of ratios and proportions 'analogia' (proportion) is not used as a synonym for 'logos' (ratio).

[78] In Birchensha's Pythagorean system all musical ratios are produced from $2 : 1$ (the octave) and $3 : 2$ (the fifth). Consequently the terms of musical ratios are always multiples of powers of two and powers of three.

[79] While the terms 'square' and 'cube' for numbers raised to the second and third powers remain in common use, 'biquadrate', 'solid', and 'bisolid' for the fourth, fifth and seventh powers are Birchensha's coinages. 'Biquadrate' derives easily enough from the squaring of a square number, but 'solid' and 'bisolid' seem wholly arbitrary.

[80] It is far from 'evident' from their order in the scale that the ratios given are the only 'just and proportionable' ones.

[81] This passage seems to refer to the 'Grand Scale' of which Birchensha wrote and spoke elsewhere. If the 14-note scale used earlier in the 'Compendious Discourse' (see Practical Part, chapter 13) is transposed into the 21 flat, natural and sharp keys listed here, every double flat and double sharp pitch-class will be needed apart from B✕. John Pell's papers show a microtonal version of 'Mr Birchensha's Scale' in which the octave is divided into 33 notes, including 12 dieses (see Introduction, p. 62); transposing this scale into the same 21 keys would involve the use not only of double flats and double sharps, but also (at extreme points) of several triple flats and triple sharps. There

is no evidence, however, to show that the 'new Scale of Musick' which Birchensha demonstrated to the Royal Society on 10 February 1675/6 went beyond the use of double flats and double sharps.

[82] The name ('Tetrachordum Mercurii') derives from the legend of the lyre invented by Mercury (Hermes) from the shell of a tortoise. According to Boethius (*De musica*, Book 1, chapter 20), the instrument was strung with four strings or 'chords' of gut which were tuned to the pattern of intervals that Birchensha gives: fourth, tone, fourth.

[83] In this and the following tables Birchensha again uses the letters *S* and *T* to mark steps of a tone and semitone respectively. His numbering of the diatessaron, diapente and diapason species corresponds to that of Gaffurius in *Theorica musice*, Book 5, chapters 7 and 8; see Gaffurio, *The Theory of Music*, trans. Kreysig and ed. Palisca, pp. 179–83. The sentence appended to the diatessaron table is unclear, however. A diatessaron beginning on F would require the fourth note (B) to be flattened; it would then match the third species in the table. A diatessaron beginning on D belongs to the first species, on E to the second, and on G to the third.

[84] i.e. exsuperate, overstep.

[85] The idea that Pythagoras formulated not only the diatonic genus, but also the chromatic and enharmonic, is found in the *Enchiridion* of Nicomachus (written around the end of the first century AD), though the accounts of the chromatic and enharmonic genera given by Nicomachus are thought to reflect Aristoxenian rather than Pythagorean teaching. See Andrew Barker, *Greek Musical Writings, II: Harmonic and Acoustic Theory* (Cambridge, New York and Melbourne, 1989), p. 258; also pp. 247, 266–8.

[86] This observation derives from Aristides Quintilianus, *De musica*, Book I, chapter 9: 'Of these [genera] the diatonic is more natural, since it can be performed by everyone, even the wholly untutored'. See Barker, *Greek Musical Writings, II*, p. 418.

[87] This passage, and the preceding diagram, though founded on classical authority, are the first real hint in the treatise of any departure by Birchensha from Pythagorean doctrine. His statement that the second interval in this chromatic progression (C–D♭) should be regarded as wider than a true diatonic semitone, but narrower than an apotome, stems from the teachings of Aristoxenus, Nicomachus and Aristides Quintilianus, rather than Pythagoras; see Barker, *Greek Musical Writings, II*, pp. 139–44, 267–8, 417–19. Birchensha specifically distinguishes between the chromatic genus, which contains such 'chromatic semitones', and the *genus permixtum* proposed by Gaffurius in his *De harmonia musicorum instrumentorum opus*, in which every tone is divided into either a diatonic semitone followed by an apotome, or *vice versa*. Increasing a diatonic semitone by one-eighteenth of a tone and reducing the apotome by a corresponding amount would not produce a good approximation to the chromatic genus, but it would in effect divide a Pythagorean tone into equal semitones of between 101 and 102 cents. This might begin to explain what appear to be terminological solecisms in Birchensha's diagram, where the interval B–D♭ is described as a 'chromatic tone' and the interval D♭–E as a 'semiditonus' or minor third. The 'Table' to which he refers is the one in chapter 14, in which proportions are given for 'chromatic mutable' D♭ and G♭ in the chromatic genus as well as for 'B diesis' and 'E diesis' in the enharmonic genus.

A further example may clarify this passage somewhat. In Birchensha's diatonic genus the tetrachord on E contains the notes E, F, G and a, with ratios 256 : 243, 9 : 8 and 9 : 8. In his chromatic genus it contains E, F, G♭ and a, with ratios 256 : 243, 81 : 76 and 19 : 16; the G♭ is found by dividing the tone F–G in arithmetic proportion.

In the enharmonic genus this tetrachord has notes E, 'E diesis', F and a, with ratios 512 : 499, 499 : 486 and 81 : 64; in this case the note 'E diesis' is found by dividing the semitone E–F in arithmetic proportion. In the permixt genus the diatonic semitone of 256 : 243 substitutes for the 'chromatic semitone' of 81 : 76 between F and G♭. Birchensha's assertion that the two differ by 1/18 of a tone is not easy to understand, both because the difference is in fact close to 1/10 of a tone and because it is not clear how Birchensha could have computed it.

88   The assertion that the enharmonic genus 'requires more practise' than the diatonic or chromatic genera suggests, perhaps deliberately and perhaps disingenuously, that Birchensha had experimented with the Greek modes in his musical practice. If this was the case he left no record of it in the form of compositions or advice for performers.

89   i.e. τονιαῖος, consisting of one tone.

90   In Greek musical theory *pyknon* denotes the cluster of three closely-packed notes at the lower end of a chromatic or enharmonic tetrachord. The lowest of these was known as *barypyknos* (βαρύπυκνος), which Birchensha calls 'Varipycna'; the next as *mesopyknos* (μεσόπυκνος); and the highest as *oxypyknos* (ὀξύπυκνος).

91   Confining his table to the lower octave of the disdiapason A–aa, Birchensha superimposes the hypaton and meson tetrachords according to his understanding of their dispositions in each of the three ancient genera: diatonic (B, C, D, E / E, F, G, a), chromatic (B, C, D♭ chr., E / E, F, G♭ chr., a) and enharmonic (B, B diesis, C, E / E, E diesis, F, a). The diezeugmenon and hyperbolaion tetrachords would have the same dispositions an octave higher; for the synemmenon tetrachord the corresponding scale would be a, b♭, c, d in the diatonic genus, a, b♭, c♭ chr., d in the chromatic, and a, a diesis, b♭, d in the enharmonic. Birchensha invites readers to compare the ratios in this table, which include the 'chromatic semitone' (243 : 228 = 81 : 76), minor diesis (512 : 499) and major diesis (499 : 486), with those that were given in chapter 8 for intervals of the permixed genus (see pp. 132–3).

92   Two passages from the *Theorica musice* of Gaffurius seem to be relevant here: in Book 3, chapter 7 he says that mathematicians are accustomed to distinguish three kinds of proportionality, namely arithmetic, geometric and harmonic; in Book 4, chapter 1, he writes 'The Pythagoreans and Platonists, therefore, conclude that the musical consonances are derived and produced from the multiple and superparticular proportions', adding that 'It appears that Aristotle himself readily agrees with these writers in Problem 41 of the section on harmony.' See Gaffurio, *The Theory of Music*, pp. 105, 117.

93   In the Boethian terminology still standard in the seventeenth century (and still standard today in the context of progressions of numbers rather than ratios), the ratio $a : b$ is divided arithmetically by $c = (a + b)/2$; geometrically by $c = \sqrt{ab}$; and harmonically by $c = 2/(\frac{1}{a} + \frac{1}{b})$. These correspond to Birchensha's 'conjunct' medieties. His 'disjunct' medieties extend the same numerical patterns to four or more terms.

Musically, arithmetic division produces an equal subdivision of the portion of string in question; geometric division produces two equal intervals; and harmonic division produces the same pair of intervals as arithmetic division, but inverted. Geometric division produces a 'proportion' in the sense discussed above (note 77): that is, the resulting two ratios are equal.

The term 'mediety' is not a common one, though its intended derivation from 'mediate' is clear. Boethius occasionally used the term *medietas* as an alternative to *proportionalitas* (see Gaffurio, *The Theory of Music*, footnote to p. 105).

⁹⁴   His diagrams show that Birchensha is confused here. Arithmetic division should result in a set of notes for which the differences between pairs of string lengths are constant; Birchensha's second and third examples, however, show notes whose string length *ratios* are constant. The first example shows a set of notes whose string lengths obey no consistent rule.

⁹⁵   This paragraph is probably intended as a gesture towards the fact that every note (of the diatonic genus) in Birchensha's Pythagorean system can be arrived at from any other using only fifths and octaves.

⁹⁶   In this chapter Birchensha displays correct examples of musical ratios divided arithmetically, that is into smaller intervals whose 'magnitudes' are equal.

⁹⁷   Birchensha means that the middle term in such a system is equal to half the sum of the outer two terms.

⁹⁸   By 'disjoined arithmetical mediety' Birchensha means the extension of arithmetic division to a set of more than three numbers with equal differences; it causes him little trouble.

⁹⁹   It is in general the case that if $a - b = b - c = c - d$, then $b + c = a + d$.

¹⁰⁰   Three numbers in geometric proportion have the property that $a : b = b : c$. This implies that $a - b : b - c = a : b$.

¹⁰¹   Here confusion reigns again. A 'disjoined geometrical mediety' contains four (or more) terms, with the property that $a : b = b : c = c : d$. As with the 'continued geometrical medieties' shown above, this has the consequence that $a - b : b - c = b - c : c - d = a : b$. When Birchensha states that 'the proportions of the differences are unequal' he can only mean that in general $a - b : c - d$ is not equal to $a : b$ or to $a - b : b - c$, which is correct. When he goes on to elaborate this statement he apparently makes a mistake, saying that the relationship between first and third term is in some way different from the relationship between second and fourth. It is very difficult to see how this could be interpreted so as to be correct. Since the phrase 'the proportion of the differences' between two terms is not itself clear, it is difficult to reconstruct what Birchensha meant to write. Possibly he meant 'the proportion of the difference between the first and third term is a quadrupla proportion, but the proportion of the differences between the second and *third* terms is a dupla proportion': that is, $16 - 8 : 4 - 2 = 4 : 1$, but $8 - 4 : 4 - 2 = 2 : 1$.

¹⁰²   This example and its discussion are somewhat impenetrable, because Birchensha does not give us sufficient information about how the sequence 16, 12, 8, 6, 4, 3 was arrived at. Apparently Birchensha has taken two geometrical medieties – 16, 8, 4 and 12, 6, 3 – and overlaid them. Since $16 : 12 \neq 12 : 8$ the following ratios of consecutive terms fall into two groups: $16 : 12 = 8 : 6 = 4 : 3$ and $12 : 8 = 6 : 4$, forming an alternating pattern. Birchensha observes that this alternating pattern means that the relationship of the first three terms is different from that of the final three terms. In this particular case the first three terms have been chosen so as to form an arithmetic progression, which in fact forces the final three to form a harmonic progression. Birchensha next asserts that this pattern is therefore the origin of arithmetic and geometric divisions ('medieties').

¹⁰³   Birchensha probably intended to point out the place of squares and cubes in geometric divisions, which in general have the form $a : ar : ar^2$.

¹⁰⁴   'Termes' should probably read 'differences': a harmonic division $a : b : c$ has the property that $a - b : b - c = a : c$. By contrast with an arithmetic division the interval between the lower two notes is larger than that between the higher two.

[105] The only intervals Birchensha recognized as true consonances were the octave and the perfect fifth (together with their compounds): when he writes here of 'All consonant Intervalls in a Disdiapason System', he presumably refers just to the four shown in the table of ratios later in this chapter: fifteenth, twelfth, octave and fifth. He passes over the 'pure' 5 : 4 major third and 6 : 5 minor third in silence, surely deliberately, although these can in fact be produced by arithmetic division of a fifth. Ignoring the tide of contemporary opinion, he would presumably have dismissed the former as defective, on the grounds that it falls short of his 'concinnous' 81 : 64 ditone, and the latter as excessive, on the grounds that it exceeds his 'concinnous' 32 : 27 semiditone. (References to mediation of the fifth in 'How to make any kind of Tune', which imply pure thirds, seem an aberration, a throwback to *Templum musicum* and Alsted: see note 114 below.)

[106] It is unfortunate that Birchensha failed to explain his criteria for categorizing intervals as consonant, concinnous and dissonant, so we can only speculate about what they were. His list of consonances could be described as a modified Pythagorean one inasmuch as it includes octave and fifth but omits thirds and sixths. The obvious departure from Pythagorean theory was his exclusion of the perfect fourth – regarded as a consonance in ancient times, but usually described as a discord or accorded an ambiguous status by Birchensha's contemporaries ('infelicissima est consonantiarum omnium', wrote Descartes). Yet while Birchensha in theory classified the fourth as a dissonance (as he reminds us in the present passage) and in practice treated it as a discord in relation to the bass, he treated it as a concord when there was another interval below it; so his teaching on this point did not differ significantly from that of Simpson and others. And his differentiation between consonance and concinnity appears to have been largely theoretical – perhaps determined by Pythagorean tradition, or by whether the interval had a superparticular ratio or not. Certainly in his composition teaching he seems to have been happy enough to treat the concinnous major and minor thirds and sixths and (up to a point) the diminished fifth as concords.

[107] This final sentence and the preceding diagram apparently refer back to chapter 14 and the large table there, the number attached to each note (or 'key') here corresponding to the lowest of the numbers assigned to that note in the earlier table. Birchensha is illustrating again the relationship between the circle of fifths and a geometric progression.

[108] Birchensha refers to the pages as 'fol[ios]'. His numbers therefore correspond to the autograph page numbers shown in the edition, not to the modern folio numbering.

[109] In the autograph manuscript of the 'Compendious Discourse', which is the only known source of them, the 'Directions how to make any kind of Tune, or Ayre' – as they are entitled on the title-page – form a kind of appendix. Birchensha may have got the idea for writing them from a passage in Alsted, which he translated as follows: 'A young Composer should first compose the most simple Melodies, which arise not from the Musical *Dyads* and *Tryads*, but from *Monads*, or a simple disposition of musical Voices' (*Templum musicum*, p. 62). Alsted's original Latin text runs: 'Omnium primò componendæ sunt tyroni hujus artis melodiæ simplicissimæ, quæ nascuntur non ex dyadibus & triadibus Musicis, sed ex monadibus, seu simplici vocum Musicalium dispositione' (*Encyclopædia*, p. 1203).

[110] The idea of pupils wanting to compose gavottes would no doubt have seemed very up-to-date in England in the 1660s: see note 27 above.

[111] Here 'key' does seem to be used in a way that approaches its modern sense of 'tonality'. Birchensha's list of 10 different key-notes or tonics was exceptionally adventurous for the time. Even during the last quarter of the seventeenth century pieces with E♭ or B as a tonic were uncommon (at least in staff notation), and those with F♯ were almost unknown. See Field, 'Jenkins and the Cosmography of Harmony', pp. 54–66; Herissone, *Music Theory in Seventeenth-Century England*, pp. 184–93.

[112] This appears to be one of the earliest uses in England of the term 'accidental' in its musical sense.

[113] This diagram transfers to a musical stave the concepts of arithmetical and harmonical mediation discussed in the 'mathematical part', but Birchensha has apparently made an error when considering the result of 'mediating' the fifth arithmetically or harmonically. Arithmetical mediation should result in a minor triad and harmonical mediation in a major triad, so that his *b'* should be *b'♭* and his *f'*, *f'♯*. Given Birchensha's lack of interest, on the whole, in pure thirds and sixths, this slip is perhaps not surprising.

[114] These two comments are remarkable in Birchensha's output for paying serious and explicit attention to *pure* thirds and sixths. While he does not explicitly state that they are musically useful, their appearance here is a surprise after their absence from the discussion of mediations in the 'mathematical part'. The incongruity can probably be put down to the influence on Birchensha of Lippius, whose theory of 'harmonically' mediated fifths producing major triads and 'arithmetically' mediated fifths producing minor triads depended however not on Pythagorean principles, but on division of the fifth into the 5 : 4 major third and the 6 : 5 minor third of just intonation: see Lippius's *Synopsis musicæ novæ*, sigs F4ʳ–F7ᵛ (quoted with English translation in Rivera, *German Music Theory*, pp. 232–6). Lippius's theory was taken over by Alsted, and thus found its way into Birchensha's *Templum musicum*, pp. 56–9.

[115] One has the impression that Birchensha may have added this paragraph on the rudiments of musical notation as an afterthought, especially as the music example illustrating it appears somewhat incongruously at the very end of the manuscript (after the section devoted to 'Negative precepts').

[116] This sentence, and the subsequent references to 'your Coppy' in clauses 10–12, seem to imply that the pupil would initially have been equipped with a pattern or model on which to base his or her own tune.

[117] To Lippius and Alsted, and to Birchensa himself in other contexts, 'mollity' and 'asperity' were gradations of 'latitude' and referred to the softness or robustness of a sound, not the remission or intension of its pitch. (See Rivera, *German Music Theory*, pp. 50–57; *Templum musicum*, pp. 13 and 16.) Here, however, 'marks of mollity & asperity' are evidently the flat or sharp signatures placed at the beginning of a staff – a meaning that was perhaps influenced by the common use of *b molle* to signify B♭.

IV

Birchensha's Description of his 'Grand Scale' (9 June 1665)

Editorial Note

Among the papers of the mathematician Dr John Pell (1611–85) which Thomas Birch gave to the British Museum in 1766 is this description of Birchensha's 'Grand Scale of Musick' in Pell's handwriting. Pell appears to have copied it from notes used by Birchensha for a talk on Friday, 9 June 1665. It is not known where or under whose auspices the event took place – and there is no independent confirmation of the date – but it was probably in London. The two leaves are now pasted into a guard-book, British Library, Additional MS 4388, as fols 67–68 (*olim* 24–25).

No exemplar of Birchensha's 'Grand Scale' in its fully developed state has come down to us, so this detailed account in his own words is valuable. As is explained in the Introduction, he seems to have conceived the 'Grand Scale' as an elaborate chart. A simpler version probably existed as early as February 1662, when Pepys was invited to Birchensha's house in Southwark and shown 'his great Card of the body of Musique, which he cries up for a rare thing'.[1] In his letter to the Royal Society of 26 April 1664 Birchensha declared his intention to 'draw a grand System, which shall containe and comprehend the whole body of the Mathematical part of Musick', and promised to present the Society's library with a copy (see Chapter II). His intention had evidently been at least partially realized by the time he gave this paper in June 1665, though modifications to design and content probably continued to be made over the following years. On 10 February 1676 Birchensha demonstrated his 'Perfect and Compleat Scale of Musick' at a full meeting of the Royal Society, and was urged to publish it (see Chapter VII).

John Pell, to whom is owed the present paper's survival, was an early member of the Royal Society. He served on several committees of the Society, including the one set up on 20 April 1664 to look into Birchensha's proposals, was present at the meeting a week later when Birchensha's letter of 26 April 1664 was read, and was a council member in 1675–76 when Birchensha demonstrated his 'Compleat Scale' to the Society. Pell had graduated BA in 1629 from Trinity College, Cambridge, and when Samuel Hartlib founded his 'little academie' in Chichester in 1630 he engaged Pell to teach there. The academy was short-lived, but Pell remained a valued member of Hartlib's intellectual circle. His *An Idea of Mathematics*, published as a broadsheet (one version in English, another in Latin) at Hartlib's expense in October 1638, attracted widespread attention.[2] That Pell was musically intelligent and literate is clear from a collection of notes on music which he began in 1635 (or perhaps earlier). These reveal a knowledge of Morley, Campion, Kepler, Butler and Mersenne, and an inquiring, down-to-earth approach.[3] He was interested in psalmody and hymnody,[4] and devised a simple numerical system of notation which he hoped would reduce the need to learn solmization and prove a useful way of writing out psalm tunes.[5] One of his letters to Mersenne, dated 29 March 1640 (NS), refers to the latter's *Harmonicorum libri* and to John Saris's account of music-making in Japan.[6] In 1650 he copied out the whole of Descartes's *Compendium musicæ* from a manuscript in the Netherlands.[7] Pell was appointed Professor of Mathematics at the Amsterdam Athenaeum in April 1644, and in July 1646 accepted an offer from the Stadholder, Frederick Henry, of a chair at the newly founded Illustre School in Breda; he held this post until 1652, when the imminence of war between the English and Dutch forced him to return to London. In 1654 he was sent as Cromwell's envoy to Switzerland, returning to London in 1658 in time to attend the Protector's funeral. After the Restoration he took holy orders and was presented with two livings in an 'infamous and unhealthy' part of Essex, and when Gilbert Sheldon became Archbishop of Canterbury in 1663 Pell was made one of his personal chaplains and awarded a Lambeth doctorate of Divinity. Nevertheless he was frequently in financial straits. In 1662 he was excused from paying his subscription to the Royal Society, a waiver confirmed in May 1663 when the original list of fellows appointed under the Society's second charter was formalized.[8]

By June 1665, when Birchensha gave this talk on his 'Grand Scale', the Great Plague was causing grave concern in London, and from 28 June until 14 March 1665/6 full meetings of the Royal Society were suspended. Like many others, Pell left the city. He set off on 6 July for Brereton Hall in Cheshire, the seat of his friend and former pupil William, third Baron Brereton – an able amateur musician who had been a member of an earlier Royal Society committee formed to examine Birchensha's ideas – and more than four years were to elapse before he returned to London.[9] Even so, in February 1665/6 we find Pell taking a renewed interest in 'Mr Birchensha's Scale': he made detailed calculations for scales of 12, 21 and 33 notes, culminating in a complete mathematical table of the 33-note scale, expressed in ten- or eleven-digit integers. An accompanying note seems to indicate that he gave a copy of this to Birchensha.[10]

Notes

[1]   *The Diary of Samuel Pepys*, ed. Robert Latham and William Matthews (11 vols, London, 1970–83), vol. 3, p. 35. See also Leta E. Miller, 'John Birchensha and the

Early Royal Society: Grand Scales and Scientific Composition', *Journal of the Royal Musical Association*, 115 (1990): 63–79, at p. 76. The chart seen by Pepys may have been a table of 14-note scales showing the consonant and dissonant intervals 'in all practicable Keyes', similar to the ones in 'A Compendious Discourse', fol. 6[r], and Brussels, Bibliothèque Royale de Belgique, MS II 4168 Mus., fol. 2[r] (see Figures 3.3 and 9.1).

2   Much the most reliable and detailed biography of Pell (by Noel Malcolm) is to be found in Noel Malcolm and Jacqueline Stedall, *John Pell (1611–1685) and his Correspondence with Sir Charles Cavendish: The Mental World of an Early Modern Mathematician* (Oxford, 2005), pp. 11–244. Among earlier accounts of Pell's life, John Aubrey's (Oxford, Bodleian Library, MS Aubrey 6, fols 51[v]–55[r]) is valuable: the best edition is in *'Brief Lives', Chiefly of Contemporaries, Set down by John Aubrey, between the Years 1669 and 1696*, ed. Andrew Clark (2 vols, Oxford, 1898), vol. 1, pp. 121–31. On Pell's years as a schoolmaster, see Malcolm and Stedall, *John Pell*, pp. 25–48, 61–2; on *An Idea of Mathematics* and its publication history, see ibid., pp. 66–76.

3   British Library, Add. MS 4388, fols 45–66; fol. 45[r] is headed 'Musicke. August. 18. 1635'. There are references to Morley's *Plaine and Easie Introduction* (fols 45[r], 47[r]), Campion's *New Way of Making Fowre Parts in Counter-point* (fols 50[r]–50[v]), Kepler's *Epitome astronomiae Copernicanae* (fol. 52[r]), Mersenne's *Harmonicorum libri* (fol. 49[r]) and Butler's *Principles of Musik* (fol. 52[r]). It seems that even before Butler's book appeared in 1636 Pell knew the 'Belgian' system of bocedization (see fol. 45[r]), perhaps from Calvisius's *Exercitationes musicae duae* or Kepler's *Harmonices mundi libri V*. Notes by Pell on Campion's 'rules of counterpoint' are also found in British Library, Add. MS 4423, fol. 379: see Malcolm and Stedall, *John Pell*, p. 130. The 1636 re-issue of Mersenne's *Harmonicorum libri* was dedicated to Sir Charles Cavendish, who became Pell's friend and patron.

4   Add. MS 4388 includes Dowland's second setting of Psalm 100, neatly scored in Pell's hand (fol. 101), and an arrangement of Psalm 1 in cittern tablature (fol. 90); on the latter, see John M. Ward, '"Sprightly and Cheerful Musick": Notes on the Cittern, Gittern and Guitar in 16th- and 17th-Century England', *Lute Society Journal*, 21 (1979–81), at pp. 171–3. On fol. 53[v] Pell made notes about Orlando Gibbons's settings for Wither's *Hymnes and Songs of the Church*, working from the undated 'alternative edition' (STC 25910a).

5   See Add. MS 4388, fols 47[r], 50[r]–50[v], 54[r], 61[r], 63[r], 92[r], 93[r], 95[r], 98[v]. Pell numbered the semitones in ascending order, usually from CC (i.e. *C*) as 1 to ddd (i.e. *d'''*) as 51, that being the compass of a typical virginal or chamber organ. On fol. 92[r] eight metrical psalm tunes are given in numerical notation, with the heading: 'J[ohn] P[ell]. A new and more easy forme than usuall of expressing / The 79 tunes appointed for the Psalmes and Hymnes, printed by W. S[tansby] at London 1631 in 16°.'

6   *Correspondance du P. Marin Mersenne, Religieux Minime*, ed. Cornelis de Waard and others, vol. 9 (Paris, 1965), pp. 228–35 (letter 844). Pell dated his letter 'Martij [19]/[29] 1640'. In it he quotes from Saris's journal, as published in Samuel Purchas's *Hakluytus Posthumus, or Purchas his Pilgrimes* (London, 1625). Saris led the East India Company's voyage to Japan of 1611–14; see Ian Woodfield, *English Musicians in the Age of Exploration* (Stuyvesant, NY, 1995), pp. 21–2, 159–65.

7   British Library, Add. MS 4388, fols 70–83. Pell sent his manuscript from Breda to Sir Charles Cavendish in Antwerp on 14 December 1650 (NS), describing it as hastily

transcribed 'out of an imperfect and ill-written copy' of Descartes's treatise; in a reply two days later Cavendish revealed that he already possessed a print of the first edition (Utrecht, 1650) and promised to send one to Pell, which he duly did when returning the manuscript on 20 December. Pell then added a postscript in Latin to the manuscript, noting that the treatise appeared in print in 1650 shortly after his transcript was made. He may have used the printed version to correct his transcript in places, but spaces for several diagrams were left unfilled. The transcript cannot have been directly based on the lost autograph archetype which Descartes took with him to Stockholm in 1649; nor (to judge from its variant readings) can his source have been Leiden, Rijksuniversiteit, MS Hug.29.a, a copy that belonged to the Stadholder's secretary Constantijn Huygens, whose son Christiaan Huygens attended Pell's mathematics lectures as a student in Breda in 1646–49. Matthijs van Otegem has argued that both the printed edition of 1650 and Pell's transcript stem from a lost copy hypothetically owned by Alphonse Pollot, though this proposition is somewhat weakened by the revelation that Pell did not know a printed edition was imminent when he made his transcript. Van Otegem's assertion that Pell's Descartes transcript was 'part of the collection of papers that belonged to John Birchenshaw' has no foundation. See *Œuvres de Descartes*, ed. Charles Adam and Paul Tannery, vol. 10 (Paris, 1974), pp. 79–169; René Descartes, *Abrégé de musique: Compendium musicæ*, ed. F. de Buzon (Paris, 1987); Matthijs van Otegem, 'Towards a Sound Text of the *Compendium musicæ*, 1618–1683, by René Descartes (1596–1650)', *LIAS: Sources and Documents relating to the Early Modern History of Ideas*, 26 (1999), pp. 187–203, especially at pp. 193–4, 197–8, 202; Malcolm and Stedall, *John Pell*, pp. 569–74 (letters 105–109).

[8]   Malcolm and Stedall, *John Pell*, pp. 102–3, 121–38, 148–77, 182, 186, 188–9; Aubrey, *'Brief Lives'*, vol. 2, p. 123.

[9]   Malcolm and Stedall, *John Pell*, pp. 198–213. Brereton had studied mathematics with Pell in Breda, and music with Henry Cooke. Aubrey described him as 'an excellent musitian, and also a good composer', and commented: 'Never was there greater love between master and scholar then between Dr Pell and this scholar of his'. An early member of the Royal Society, Brereton was appointed to the committee set up 'to examine the synopsis of Mr Berchensha' on 23 April 1662. Curious musical instruments seem to have been one of his interests: he arranged demonstrations for the Royal Society on 5 and 12 October 1664 of an 'archiviole' (a keyboard instrument whose gut strings were excited by the friction of strips of parchment), and in 1666 Dr John Worthington, the former Master of Jesus College, Cambridge, sent him a 'polyphon' or poliphant. Pepys describes a dinner party at Sir George Carteret's house on 5 January 1667/8 at which 'my Lord Brereton very gentilely went to the Organ and played a verse very handsomely'. See Penelope Gouk, *Music, Science and Natural Magic in Seventeenth-Century England* (New Haven and London, 1999), pp. 27, 62, 190; Aubrey, *'Brief Lives'*, vol. 1, pp. 122, and vol. 2, p. 125; *The Diary of Samuel Pepys*, vol. 5, p. 290, and vol. 9, pp. 10–11; *The Diary of John Evelyn*, ed. E.S. de Beer (6 vols, Oxford, 1955), vol. 3, p. 378; *The Correspondence of Henry Oldenburg*, ed. A. Rupert Hall and Marie Boas Hall, vol. 2 (Madison, Milwaukee and London, 1966), pp. 251–4; *The Diary and Correspondence of Dr. John Worthington*, vol. 2, part 1, ed. James Crossley (Chetham Society, 36; Manchester, 1855), pp. 206–9.

[10]   See Introduction, p. 62. For a comparable instance of Pell carrying out mathematical calculations on behalf of a friend – a table of the areas of circles from 1 inch to 100

inches in diameter, made at Sir Samuel Morland's request in 1682 – see Malcolm and Stedall, *John Pell*, pp. 237–8.

Edition

[fol. 67ʳ]

[Mʳ Berchenshaw speakes]ᵃ June 9. 1665.ᵇ

My Grand Scale doth comprehend & demonstrate

1. All those sounds and Intervalls which are apt for Harmony & concinnity with their minuter Intervalls.
2. It sheweth what Intervalls onely are apt to express Harmony, according to the three musicall Genuses.
3. It containeth the Greek scale.
4. It sheweth the Latine Scale of Guido, called by us the Scale of Gamut, adapted to the Greeke Scale[.]
5. It sheweth the true Proslambanomenos.
6. The onely fit numbers to shew the true Proportions of Intervalls are heere assigned to them.
7. You have here the names of the Chords according to Pythagoras & his disciples and other Ancient Authors of Musick[.]
8. You may here discerne the severall species of Proportions: as multiplex, superparticular, superpartient, multiplex superparticular and multiplex superpartient.¹
9. You have the severall musicall Genus's; as the Diatonic, chromatic, Enharmonic & Syntonic or permixed Genus[.]
10. By this Scale you may discerne the proper places of the severall Keyes, with their true distances from the assumed Unison, and every other Intervall in an Octave[.]
11. You have the Scale divided (according to the nature of every musicall Genus) into five Tetrachords. viz. the Tetrachord Hypaton, Meson, Diezeugmenon, Hyperbolæon and Synemmenon.
12. Here is also a way for the finding out and placeing in the Scale the <u>Chordules</u> or half notes, [(]i.e. the sharp of flat notes & the flat of sharp notes) with their Relation to their contiguous Chords[.]
13. Here are the number of Diatessarons in an immutable System or Disdiapason, both such as arise from the Proslambanomenos, or gravest Chord of every Tetrachord.
14. Here are the severall species of Diatessarons, Diapentes & Diapasons, in a double octave. By which the Various progressions, that the severall Keyes do make through the Scale, doth appeare.
15. Here is the true division of the Tone, according to the severall Genus's.

ᵃ These square brackets and the enclosed gloss are in the manuscript.
ᵇ The numeral *5* may possibly be an alteration from an illegible original.

16. Here are the severall species of Tones; both[a] incompounded & of the Epogdoan disposition.[2]

17. Here you may see what proportions are producible from two equall Proportions, & from two unequall proportions: and so, in part, discern the wonderfull generation of intervalls.

18. Here you may finde the <u>Excess</u> of Intervalls, when the lesser Proportion is taken from the greater; and the <u>residue</u> or remaining part, when the greater is taken from the lesser.

[fol. 67ᵛ]

19. This Scale doth shew that an Intervall of a Sesquisexta Proportion doth not exceed a Sesquioctave, by the same Proportion that a Sesqui-octave doth exceed an Intervall of a Sesquidecima Proportion.[3]

Also that six Tones do exceed a Diapason Consonant, onely by one Comma.[4]

Also that the Proportions sesquivigesima tertia, & sesquiquadragesima quinta, do exceed the minor Semitone by a Sesquioctogesima proportion.[5]

Also that an Intervall of a sesquiquinta Proportion, is more then a Tone & minor Semitone, by a Sesqui80ᵃ proportion.[6]

Also that a Diapente with a Tone is more then a Superbipartiens[b] tertias proportion, by a sesqui80ᵃ proportion[.][7]

Also that a Diapente with a minor Semitone is less then a Supertripartiens quintas proportion by a sesqui80ᵃ proportion.[8] This being known, the many Errors of many Modern musicians may be discerned.

20. Here are the Epimorion Proportions of Ptolomy.[9] And by this Scale you may finde how diversly Pythagoras & Ptolomy did dispose of their Tetrachords, in the severall Genus's, with the difference of their Intervalls.

21. Here you may finde the true Ration, Habitude, Difference, Excess, Dimension, and magnitude of Intervalls, according to the proportionall Parts of a Chord, & according to the severall Genus's.

22. Here are the mutable & immutable Chords in the Dis-Diapasonic Systeme.

23. Here are the Chromatic Semitones, which do exceed the Semitones of the permixed Genus: with their Relation to their proximate Chords.[10]

24. Here you have the Distinction between Arithmetical, Geometrical and Harmonicall Medieties, and Proportionalities with their Proprieties.[11]

25. Here you may see the Consonancy & dissonancy of sounds, as disposed according to those medieties.

26. Here you have the full & perfect Extension of all Intervalls (necessary for harmony) in respect of Gravity & Acuteness[.]

27. Here you have the Moodes, viz. Hypodorius etc properly placed, according to Glareanus & other Authors.

---

[a]   Illegible word deleted.

[b]   *ter-* written twice in MS.

28. Here you have the severall kinds of Moodes. viz: authent, plagal & spurious.[12]

29. Here you may discern the Reason of Consonancy and Dissonancy.

30. Also the Reason of the Mollity & Asperitie of Sounds. A Secret never yet fully discovered in writing, or demonstrated.[13]

31. By this Scale you may discern all things comprehended in, & that may be expressed by a Monochord. and by it you may trie the trueth of any Monochord[.]

32. By this Scale it doth appeare that no superparticular Intervall can be divided into Equall parts.[14]

33. By this Scale you may trie the trueth of all the Axioms, Postulates, Definitions, Divisions, Propositions, Problem's, Theorem's, Porismas & Lemma's of all Mathematicall & practicall Musicians, who have written of the Quantity, Magnitude, Ration and number of Sounds apt for Harmony.

[fol. 68ʳ]

There are 100 Particulars more, which do concern the Mathematicall part of Musick comprehended in, and demonstrated by this Scale: necessary to be knowen, without which this Art would be very imperfect.

By this Scale I will make any rationall Man understand more of the mathematicall part of Musick in 3 moneths, then can be knowen by him in 7 yeares by reading & studying of all the Bookes, which have been written concerning this Art.

By this Scale one may easily understand all that hath been written by any Author concerning the Mathematicall part of Musick & be able to put a Difference between that which is true & that which is false.

And if any Friend desire to be satisfied of the Trueth of my Scale in any of these Particulars, I will discover it unto him, and direct him so farr in the use of it, that hee shall clearly receive satisfaction of what he demands.

Notes

[1]   See Chapter III, note 74 for an explanation of these terms. Note that here 'proportion' is taken to mean 'ratio'.

[2]   Birchensha's wording is confusing here. In the 'Compendious Discourse' (fol. 8ʳ, section 3) he indicates that a tone can be regarded either as simple and incompounded (that is, expressible by the ratio 9 : 8), or as compounded of a diatonic semitone (256 : 243) and an apotome (2187 : 2048). Here, however, he seems to differentiate between, on the one hand, the 'epogdoan' tone of 9 : 8 and, on the other, those 'defective' or 'abounding' species of tone which have the incompounded ratios 10 : 9 or 8 : 7 (cf 'Compendious Discourse', fol. 8ʳ, section 2).

[3]   i.e. $7 : 6 - 9 : 8$ is not the same as $9 : 8 - 11 : 10$.

[4]   i.e. $(9 : 8)^6 > 2 : 1$, the difference being the Pythagorean comma of 531441 : 524288.

[5]   i.e. 24 : 23 + 46 : 45 > 256 : 243, the difference being 81 : 80. This division of the semitone into two unequal quarter-tones, 24 : 23 + 46 : 45, is that of Ptolemy's

enharmonic genus: see Andrew Barker, *Greek Musical Writings, II: Harmonic and Acoustic Theory* (Cambridge, New York and Melbourne, 1989), p. 347.

[6]   i.e. $6 : 5 > 9 : 8 + 256 : 243$, the difference being $81 : 80$. In other words a pure minor third is larger than a pure tone plus a Pythagorean semitone, by a syntonic comma.

[7]   i.e. $3 : 2 + 9 : 8 > 5 : 3$, the difference being $81 : 80$. In other words, a fifth plus a tone exceeds the pure major sixth of just intonation by a syntonic comma.

[8]   i.e. $3 : 2 + 256 : 243 < 8 : 5$, the difference being $81 : 80$. In other words a fifth plus a Pythagorean semitone is less than a pure minor sixth by a syntonic comma.

[9]   Epimorian or epimoric ratios are superparticular ratios: they were privileged in Ptolemy's *Harmonics*, though not as drastically as by the Pythagoreans. See Barker, *Greek Musical Writings, II*, p. 290 with n. 67.

[10]   The chromatic genus and the 'chromatic semitone' are discussed in Chapter III, 'Mathematicall Part', Chapter 13, and note 87 there.

[11]   See pp 52–3 for the three kinds of medieties.

[12]   In the 'Compendious Discourse', Practical Part, chapter 3, Birchensha lists eight modes in ascending order of their octave species, with the Greek names assigned to each, but does not mention their classification as authentic or plagal, or which modes he considered to be 'spurious'. The eight are: A[–a], Hypodorian; B[–b], Hypophrygian; C[–c], Hypolydian; D[–d], Dorian; E[–e], Phrygian; F[–f], Lydian; G[–g], Mixolydian; a[–aa], Hypermixolydian. There, as here, he cites the authority of Glarean, but his list is essentially the eight-mode system as imparted by Glarean's precursor Gaffurius, the formulation of which can be traced back as early as the ninth-century anonymous treatise *Alia musica*. See Chapter III, note 17; David E. Cohen, 'Notes, Scales, and Modes in the Earlier Middle Ages', in Thomas Christensen (ed.), *The Cambridge History of Western Music Theory* (Cambridge, 2002), pp. 307–63, at pp. 331–8.

[13]   On the 'latitude' of sounds – i.e. their relative 'mollity' and 'asperity' – see Chapter III, note 53. Birchensha may have envisaged that his 'Grand Scale' would tabulate gradations not only of pitches and intervals ('crassitude'), but also of dynamics ('latitude') and note-lengths ('longitude'; see Chapter VI, note 16), although it is not clear exactly how this would have been done. Apart from *Templum musicum*, the only English treatise of the period to consider the question of 'latitude' is A.B.'s *Synopsis of Vocal Musick* (London, 1680), which observes: 'Signs of the latitude or breadth of sounds are [those] which ought to shew whether a sound must be sung with a clear and full, or with a soft and small spirit, and are by Artists less carefully expressed, who leave that to the text, and to the things themselves which in a Song are to be expressed. *Italians* only, and some that them do follow, do use these two words, *Forte* and *Piano*, signifying that such part of a song must be sung clearer and fuller, under which is written *Forte*, but softer and smaller, under which is written *Piano*. See *Templum musicum*, p. 30; *Synopsis of Vocal Musick by A.B. Philo-Mus.*, ed. Rebecca Herissone (Aldershot and Burlington, VT, 2006), pp. 42, 96, 165.

[14]   This observation is quite fundamental to the complexity of musical ratio theory: an interval whose ratio is superparticular cannot be divided into any number of equal parts without the use of irrational ratios. See Euclid, *Sectio canonis*, 152 in Barker, *Greek Musical Writings, II*, p. 195 with n. 12: the theorem is proved by Boethius in *De musica* III, 11, who attributes it to Archytas.

V

'Animadversion' for *Syntagma musicæ* (1672)

Editorial Note

This 'Animadversion' is both a prospectus for Birchensha's treatise *Syntagma musicæ* and an appeal for subscribers. It was originally issued in 1672 as a printed sheet. Subscribers were promised a bound copy of the book before Lady Day (25 March) 1675 in return for every 20 shillings paid in advance.[1] Only one exemplar of the sheet is known to survive; it measures approximately 330 × 230 mm, and is fol. 69 (*olim* 47) in the guard-book British Library, Additional MS 4388.[2] The date 27 December [1672] is written on the receipt form at the foot of the sheet, above Birchensha's signature and seal,[3] but the space for the subscriber's name is empty. The sheet appears to have been among the papers of John Pell which Thomas Birch presented to the British Museum in 1766 (see Chapter IV), and may have been intended either for Pell's own use – notwithstanding the fact that for much of his life Pell was notoriously hard up – or for him to pass on to a friend. The verso is blank, apart from a British Museum stamp.

Shortly after the 'Animadversion' was issued, an advertisement couched in similar terms appeared in the Royal Society's journal the *Philosophical Transactions*, 7, no. 90 (20 January 1672/3): 5153–4. The style of its wording suggests that Henry Oldenburg, the journal's editor, was responsible for adapting it from the printed sheet. Our edition gives the original text of the 'Animadversion', but shows the most significant variants in the *Philosophical Transactions* (designated 'PT') as textual notes. Minor differences of orthography have been disregarded. We have not attempted to annotate every term used in this brief text whose meaning presents difficulty.

Notes

[1]   This may be compared with Mace's undertaking to deliver an unbound copy of *Musick's Monument* to subscribers in 1676 for every 12 shillings paid: see Thomas Mace, *Musick's Monument; or, A Remembrancer of the Best Practical Musick, both Divine and Civil* (London: printed for the Author, 1676), sigs c1ʳ–d1ʳ, d2ᵛ. Mace listed the names of 301 subscribers, who included Isaac Newton and Birchensha's pupil Thomas Salmon.

2   The left-hand margin has been trimmed.

3   The armorial wax seal, small though it is, may perhaps provide a clue to Birchensha's lineage. If he was a son of Sir Ralph Birchensha (*c*.1565–1622), Comptroller of the Musters in Ireland, as Grattan Flood stated, his arms ought to correspond closely to Sir Ralph's, which are recorded as 'Argent semée of estoiles and a pegasus passant gules'. But while the arms on the seal appear to show a field that is 'semée of estoiles' (strewn with stars), the principal charge is a bend, not a pegasus or winged horse. Above the shield, however, is a crest surmounted by what could possibly be a pegasus. See W.H. Grattan Flood, *A History of Irish Music*, 3rd edn (Dublin, 1913), p. 214; Sir Bernard Burke, *The General Armory of England, Scotland, Ireland and Wales; Comprising a Registry of Armorial Bearings from the Earliest to the Present Time* (London, 1884), p. 145 (two entries, s.v. 'Burdenshaw or Birchenshaw').

ANIMADVERSION.

THAT there is a Book preparing for the Press, (Intituled *SYNTAGMA MUSICÆ*) Being an Hypothetical Discourse of Musical Sounds and Harmony: In which the Author *(John Birchensha* Esq;) Treats of Musick Philosophically, Mathematically, and Practically.

And because the Charge of bringing the said Book to the Press will be very great (and also because the several Cuts therein, with their Printing off, will amount to more than 500 *l.* besides other great Expenses for the Impression of the said Book, &c.) divers Persons (for the Encouragement of the said Author) have Advanced several Summs of Money; who for every 20 *s.* so advanced, are to receive one of the said Books, fairly bound up, (the Price of which Book will be 20 *s.*) And,

Therein will be a Discovery of the Reason, and Causes of Musical Sounds, and Harmony. The Scale of Musick (which hath never yet been perfected) will be completed. The Proportions of all Consonant and Dissonant Sounds, useful in Musick, demonstrated by Intire Numbers, (which hath not been done by any.) The differing Opinions of Musical Authors are reconciled.

Of Sounds generated, produc'd, diffus'd in their *Medium:* Of their Deference to the Organ of Hearing; of their Reception there, and wonderful Effects: Of the Matter, Form, Quantity, and Quality of Musical Bodies or Sounds. That all Musical Sounds are originally in the Radix, or Unison; and of their Fluxion out of it: Of the General, and Special Kinds, Differences, Properties, and Accidents of Sounds. Of the Truth and Falshood of Sounds.

Of the Principles of the Mathematical Part of Musick. Of the Whole, and Parts of the Scale of Musick. Of Sounds Equal, and Unequal. Of the Numeration, Addition, Subtraction, Multiplication, and Division of Musical Sounds. Of Musical Proportions, and their various Species. What a Musical Body or Sound (Mathematically considered, *sc.* as Numerable) is. Of Musical Medieties, *sc.* Arithmetical, Geometrical, and Harmonical: And of eight other Musical Medieties, of which no mention is made by any Musical Author. Of the Radix's of Musical Numbers; and that by their Powers all those Numbers (and no other) which demonstrate the Proportions of Sounds do arise. Of Musick Diatonic, Chromatic, and Enharmonic. Of the Principles of a Musical Magnitude, what, and how manifold they are, and how they are conjoyned. Of the Contact, Section, Congruity, Adscription of a Musical Body. Of the Commensurability thereof. In what respect a Musical Sound may be said to be Infinite, and how to bound that Infinity.

Of a Musical System, Character, Voice, or Key. Of the Transposition of Keys. Of the Mutation of Musical Voices. Of Musical Pauses and Periods. Of the Denomination of Notes. Of the Moods, *viz. Doric, Phrygian, Lydian, &c.* Of Intervals Simple, or Compounded; Single, or Duplicated. Of the Dignity of Musical Sounds. Of pure and florid Counterpoint. Of Figurate Musick. Of Fuges, Canons, Double-Discant, Syncope. Of the Mensuration of Sounds (called Time), and the Reason thereof. Of Choral Musick, both *Roman,* and *English.* Of the Rhythmical Part of Musick, or Movement of Songs. Of Solmisation, and the Reason thereof. Also in this Book the abstruse and difficult Terms of this Science are explained. The unnecessary and mystical Subtilties, into which the Causes both of the Theory and Practique of Musick were reduc'd, (by which this Art hath been much obscured) are omitted. The Principles of Philosophy, Mathematicks, Grammar, Rhetorick, and Poetry, are applied to Musical Sounds, and Illustrated by them. The Generation of such Sounds (for there is a Generation of Sounds, as of other Creatures; every Consonant and Dissonant Sound being generated by the mutual Conjunction of two other Sounds) is discoursed of, and particularly demonstrated. An easie way is by the said Author invented for making Airy Tunes of all sorts by a certain Rule, (which most Men think impossible to be done) and the Composing of two, three, four, five, six, and seven Parts; which by the Learner may be performed in a few Months; *viz.* in two Months he may (exquisitely, and with all the Elegancies of Musick) Compose two Parts; in three Months, three Parts; and so forwards to seven Parts, (as many Persons of Honour and Worth have often experienc'd): which otherwise cannot be done in so many Years. Whatsoever is grounded upon the several *Hypotheses* and *Postulat's* in this Book, are clearly demonstrated by Tables, Diagrams, Systems, Examples, &c. And many other things (which are either not at all, or imperfectly Treated of by Musical Authors) are discover'd, for the Publick Benefit of all ingenious Practitioners and Lovers of this Science and Art.

The   27. —— day of *Dec* —— 1672.

REceived of   the Sum of
Advanced for bringing my said Book to the Press, and defraying other Charges thereof, for which I shall deliver to the said   or his Assigns, one of the said Books, fairly Bound up, at or before the Twenty fourth day of March, 1674. Witness my Hand, the Day and Year first above written.

                                                              John Birchensha

The Bearer of this Paper will fill up the Blanks, and receive
the Money for the Use of the Author.

Figure 5.1   The 'Animadversion' for *Syntagma musicæ*, with Birchensha's signature and seal, dated December 1672 (London, British Library, Add. MS 4388, fol. 69[r]). © The British Library. All Rights Reserved.

Edition

[fol. 69ʳ]

ANIMADVERSION.[a]

THAT there is[b] a Book preparing for the Press, (Intituled *SYNTAGMA MUSICÆ*) Being an Hypothetical Discourse of Musical Sounds and Harmony:[c] In which the Author[d] (*John Birchensha* Esq;) Treats of Musick Philosophically, Mathematically, and Practically.

And because the Charge of bringing the said Book to the Press will be very great (and also because the several Cuts therein,[e] with their Printing off, will amount to[f] more than 500 *l*. besides other great Expenses for the Impression of the said Book, &c.)[g] divers Persons (for the Encouragement of the said Author) have Advanced several Summs of Money; who for every 20*s*. so advanced, are to receive one of the said Books, fairly bound up, (the Price of which Book will be 20*s*.)[h] And,

Therein will be a Discovery[i] of the Reason, and Causes of Musical Sounds, and Harmony. The Scale of Musick (which hath never yet been perfected) will be completed.[j] The Proportions of all Consonant and Dissonant Sounds, useful in Musick, demonstrated by Intire Numbers, (which hath not been done by any.)[k,l] The differing Opinions of Musical Authors are[l] reconciled.

---

[a] PT: *Another Advertisement.*

[b] PT: *There is.*

[c] PT omits *Being an Hypothetical … Harmony.*

[d] PT: *the Eminent Author.*

[e] PT: *great, especially the several Cuts therein.*

[f] PT: *amounting by Computation to.*

[g] PT omits *&c.*

[h] PT: *fairly bound up; the Author engaging himself under his Hand and Seal to deliver to each of the Subscribers, and Advancers of so much money, one of the said Books at or before the 24th of March 1674.*

[i] PT: *In which Excellent Work there will be, 1. A Discovery.*

[j] PT: *A compleat Scale of Musick (never before perfected:).*

[k] PT: *(which the Author saith hath not been done by any:).*

[l] PT omits *are.*

Philosophical Part.[a]

Of Sounds generated, produc'd, diffus'd[b] in their *Medium*: Of their Deference[c] to the Organ of Hearing;[2] of[d] their Reception there, and wonderful Effects: Of the Matter, Form, Quantity, and Quality of Musical Bodies or Sounds. That all[e] Musical Sounds are originally in the Radix, or Unison; and of their Fluxion out of it:[3] Of the General, and Special Kinds, Differences, Properties, and Accidents of Sounds. Of the Truth and Falshood of Sounds.

Mathematical Part.[f]

Of the Principles[g] of the Mathematical Part of Musick. Of the Whole, and Parts of the Scale of Musick. Of Sounds Equal, and Unequal. Of the Numeration, Addition, Subtraction, Multiplication, and Division of Musical Sounds. Of Musical Proportions, and their various Species. What a Musical Body or Sound (Mathematically considered, *sc.*[h] as Numerable) is. Of Musical Medieties, *sc.* Arithmetical, Geometrical, and Harmonical: And of[i] eight other Musical Medieties, of which no mention is made by any Musical Author.[4] Of the Radix's of Musical Numbers; and that by their Powers all those Numbers (and no other) which demonstrate the Proportions of Sounds do arise. Of Musick Diatonic, Chromatic, and Enharmonic. Of the Principles of a Musical Magnitude, what, and how manifold they are, and how they are conjoyned. Of the Contact, Section, Congruity, Adscription of a Musical Body. Of the Commensurability thereof. In what respect a Musical Sound may be said to be Infinite, and how to bound that Infinity.[5]

Practical Part.[j]

Of a Musical System,[k] Character, Voice, or Key. Of the Transposition of Keys. Of the Mutation of Musical Voices. Of Musical Pauses and Periods. Of the Denomination of Notes. Of the Moods, *viz. Doric, Phrygian, Lydian, &c.* Of Intervals Simple, or Compounded; Single, or Duplicated.[l] Of the Dignity

---

[a]   Printed in margin; PT omits.

[b]   PT: *generated, and diffused.*

[c]   PT: *difference*, but corrected to *deference* in list of Errata: see *Philosophical Transactions*, 7, no. 91 (24 February 1672/3), p. 5172.

[d]   PT: *together with.*

[e]   PT omits *all.*

[f]   Printed in margin; PT omits.

[g]   PT: *2. Of the Principles.*

[h]   PT has *viz.*

[i]   PT: *together with.*

[j]   Printed in margin; PT omits.

[k]   PT: *3. Of a Musical System.*

[l]   PT shortens these two sentences to *Of the Moods, and Intervals.*

of Musical Sounds.[a,6] Of pure and florid Counterpoint. Of Figurate Musick. Of Fuges, Canons, Double-Discant, Syncope.[7] Of the Mensuration of Sounds (called Time), and the Reason thereof. Of Choral Musick, both *Roman*, and *English*.[8] Of the Rhythmical Part of Musick, or Movement of Songs.[b] Of Solmisation, and the Reason thereof. Also in this Book the abstruse[c] and difficult Terms of this Science are explained. The unnecessary and mystical Subtilties, into which the Causes both of the Theory and Practique of Musick were reduc'd, (by which this Art hath been much obscured)[d] are omitted. The Principles of Philosophy, Mathematicks, Grammar, Rhetorick, and Poetry, are applied to Musical Sounds, and Illustrated by them. The Generation of such Sounds (for there is a Generation of Sounds, as of other Creatures; every Consonant and Dissonant Sound being generated by the mutual Conjunction of two other Sounds)[e] is discoursed of, and particularly demonstrated. An easie way is by the said Author[f] invented for making Airy Tunes of all sorts by a certain Rule, (which most Men think impossible to be done)[9] and the Composing of two, three, four, five, six, and seven Parts; which by the Learner may be performed in a few Months; *viz.* in two Months he may (exquisitely, and with all the Elegancies of Musick) Compose two Parts; in three Months, three Parts; and so forwards to seven Parts, (as many[g] Persons of Honour and Worth have often experienc'd): which otherwise cannot be done in so many Years.[10] Whatsoever[h] is grounded upon the several *Hypotheses* and *Postulat's* in this Book, are[i] clearly demonstrated by Tables, Diagrams, Systems, Examples,[j] &c. And many other things (which are either not at all, or imperfectly Treated of by Musical Authors) are discover'd, for the Publick Benefit of all ingenious Practitioners and Lovers of this Science and Art.[k]

---

[a] PT omits this sentence.

[b] PT omits *or Movement of Songs*.

[c] PT: *4. The Abstruse*.

[d] PT: *reduced to the great obscuring of this Art*.

[e] PT omits the words in brackets.

[f] PT: *5. An easie way is by this Author*.

[g] PT: *and so forward; as he affirms many*.

[h] PT: *6. Whatsoever*.

[i] PT: *Postulata in this Book, is*.

[j] PT omits *Examples*.

[k] PT omits the last sentence and the subscription form below.

The 27. *– day of* Dec *–* 1672.[a]

R*Eceived of*   *the Sum of*
Advanced for bringing my said Book to the Press, and defraying other Charges
thereof; for which I shall deliver to the said   *or his*
Assigns, one[b] *of the said Books, fairly Bound up, at or before the Twenty fourth*
day of March, 1674.[11] *Witness my Hand, the Day and Year first above written.*

John Birchensha[c]

The Bearer of this Paper will fill up the Blanks,
and receive the Money for the Use of the Author.

Notes

[1]   On Birchensha's 'Grand Scale', see Introduction ('Birchensha's "Grand Scale" and John Pell'), Chapter III (note 81), and Chapters IV, VI and VII. 'Intire numbers' are whole numbers; as noted in the Introduction, John Pell took pains to avoid fractions in his 33-note version of Birchensha's scale, with the result that the whole numbers he produced had up to eleven digits.

[2]   That is to say, musical vibrations 'defer' or 'yield' to the ear. Birchensha would have been aware of the work done by Walter Charleton and others on the phenomena of hearing; cf Jamie C. Kassler, *The Beginnings of the Modern Philosophy of Music in England* (Aldershot, 2004), pp. 5–8.

[3]   The special nature of the unison was introduced in the 'Axioms' of the 'Geometricall Part of Musick' in the 'Compendious Discourse' (see pp. 117–18), the first of which probably gives his meaning here, namely that the unison string can be divided so as to make any interval we desire with the unison pitch.

[4]   In the 'Compendious Discourse' Birchensha dealt only with arithmetic, geometric and harmonic mediety; but he mentioned that there were further ways of mediating intervals, 'of which differing species of mu[sica]ll Medieties I have written at Larg[e]. chap[ter] 14. of my Mathem[atica]ll part of Musick' (fol. 18v; see p. 151). This lost chapter presumably would have formed the basis for the treatment of the 'eight other Musical Medieties' in *Syntagma musicæ*.

[5]   The 'Axioms' of the 'Geometricall Part of Musick' in the 'Compendious Discourse' (see pp. 117–18) may help to explain Birchensha's comment about a musical infinity: a given note can in principle be raised indefinitely, but for musical purposes it is limited to the compass of an octave.

[6]   By the 'dignity' of musical sounds Birchensha may have meant the hierarchy of intervals as consonant, concinnous or dissonant.

---

[a]   *27. —* and *Dec —* are written in ink.

[b]   *one* is written in ink.

[c]   Autograph signature followed by Birchensha's seal.

[7]   According to Christopher Simpson, 'Figurate Descant [...] is that wherein Discords are concerned as well (though not so much) as Concords [...]; and These are the Two Materials which must serve you for the raising of all Structures in Figurate Musick': *A Compendium of Practical Musick* (London, 1667), pp. 116–17. 'Double Descant' is defined by Simpson as 'when the Parts are so contrived, that the *Treble* may be made the *Bass*, and the *Bass* the *Treble*' (ibid., p. 169): in other words, invertible counterpoint. '*Syncope*, or Driving a Note, is, when after some shorter Note which begins the Measure or Half-measure, there immediately follow two, three, or more Notes of a greater quantity, before you meet with another short Note (like that which began the driving) to make the number even; As, when an odd *Crochet* comes before two, three, or more *Minims*; or an odd *Quaver* before two, three, or more *Crochets*' (ibid., p. 25).

[8]   '*Roman*' here presumably means 'for the Latin rite'.

[9]   For Birchensha's 'Directions how to make any kind of Tune, or Ayre', as appended to the 'Compendious Discourse' (fols 20–21), see pp. 156–61.

[10]   Editions of surviving versions of the 'Rules of Composition' appear below in Chapters VIII–X. Among the 'Persons of Honour and Worth' known or believed to have been taught by Birchensha are Captain Silas Taylor (*c*.1659–60); Samuel Pepys (January–February 1662); George Villiers, second Duke of Buckingham (*c*.1663–64); and Thomas Salmon (*c*.1669–70): see Christopher D.S. Field, 'Birchensha's "Mathematical Way of Composure"', in Barra Boydell and Kerry Houston (eds), *Music, Ireland and the Seventeenth Century* (Irish Musical Studies, 10; Dublin, 2009), pp. 108–34, at pp. 117–20.

[11]   i.e. the last day of the year 1674/5.

VI

Synopsis of *Syntagma musicæ* for the Royal Society (February 1675/6)

Editorial Note

Birchensha appears to have produced this detailed synopsis of his treatise *Syntagma musicæ* for the Royal Society's ordinary meeting on Thursday, 10 February, 1675/6, at which he had been invited to speak. The annotation at the head of the manuscript – 'read Feb: 10: [16]75' – is slightly misleading, however. The official minutes reveal that Birchensha's presentation at the meeting was in fact limited to demonstrating his 'Compleat Scale of Musick'.[1]

For somebody who was not an elected fellow, to address the Society personally in this way was a rare honour. At the same time, Birchensha must have been acutely aware that more than ten months had elapsed since the promised publication date of *Syntagma musicæ*, whose subscribers (if, indeed, his promises had succeeded in attracting any subscriptions) may well have included members of the audience on this occasion.[2] One purpose of this chapter-by-chapter epitome may have been to reassure them, but his use of the future tense at several points suggests that the book was still some way from completion.

The manuscript (London, Royal Society, Classified Papers, vol. 22 (1), no. 7) is in a hand identifiable as that of the Royal Society's indefatigable secretary, Henry Oldenburg (*c*.1619–77).[3] It consists principally of a sheet folded to form two leaves (fols 16 and 19), each measuring approximately 300 × 187 mm. The philosophical, mathematical and practical parts of the book occupy one page each; fol. 19ᵛ is blank apart from the endorsement, 'Birchenshaws project about Musick'. In addition there is a smaller sheet, again folded into two leaves (fols 17–18), each measuring approximately 147 × 105 mm. The text on fol. 17ʳ was possibly intended for insertion as an addendum at the foot of fol. 16ʳ, where a cross appears in the margin: this is the solution adopted here. The rest of the smaller sheet is blank except for fol. 18ᵛ, which is endorsed 'Birchenshaw'. Since the eighteenth century the manuscript has been kept in a guard-book with reviews and summaries of other books from the period 1660–1740.

The notes do not repeat explanations of terminology found elsewhere, particularly in the 'Compendious Discourse' (Chapter III above), but are limited to points which appear to be new in this text.

Notes

[1]   A transcription of those minutes (London, Royal Society, Journal Book Original, vol. 5, pp. 141–3) appears in Chapter VII. It is possible that the annotator was mistaken in associating the document with that meeting, which could explain the dissimilarity between the descriptions given of the 'Compleat Scale' in the synopsis and in Birchensha's talk. The present manuscript must however date from before Oldenburg's death in September 1677.

[2]   See the Editorial Note to Chapter V.

[3]   A native of Bremen, Oldenburg studied at the Gymnasium there (where he graduated as a Master of Theology in 1639) and, briefly, at the University of Utrecht. He went on to travel widely, working as a tutor and becoming an accomplished linguist. In 1653 he was sent as an envoy from Bremen to England, where he remained for four years and was befriended by such prominent figures as John Milton, Robert Boyle and his sister Lady Ranelagh, and John Wilkins (Warden of Wadham College, Oxford). After further travel abroad as tutor to Lord and Lady Ranelagh's son, he returned to England at the Restoration. He became active in the newly formed Royal Society, served as its secretary until his death in 1677, was a tireless correspondent on the Society's behalf, and was the creator and first editor of its *Philosophical Transactions*. He seems to have formed a favourable opinion of Birchensha early on, and continued to encourage him in his work. See Marie Boas Hall, 'Oldenburg, Henry', in *Oxford Dictionary of National Biography*, ed. H.C.G. Matthew and Brian Harrison (60 vols, Oxford: 2004), vol. 41, pp. 673–7.

Edition

[fol. 16ʳ]
read Feb:
10: [16]75.[a]

An Account

Of divers particulars, remarkable in my Book; In which I will write of Musick philosophically, mathematically, and practically: but of many things therein contained, litle or no mention is made by ⟨any⟩ Musical Author[.]

Philosophical Part.[1]

1. Of the Principles of the Philosophical part of Musick; whereof 26. are particularly mention'd, and of which I haue fully treated in their due and proper Places; and upon which I shall ground my Discourse, and shew

2. That Musick is a Sister, and not (as some imagin) a Handmaid to other Sciences (as to Arithmetic, Geometry etc) and in that respect subservient and subalternat to them.[2] For, altho shee hath the same principles with them; yet she hath them not from them; because the Inferior parts of Music (as the Arithmetical, Geometrical parts thereof, etc.) receiue their principles, subject, and affections from the Philosophical part thereof; and from no other Science or Art.

3. That All Musical Intervalls proceed from the Fluxion or extension of the Radicall Unison (which may be demonstrated by the Intension of a Chord) of which no notice is taken by Musical Authors.[3]

4. That every Interval (as a 3ᵈ, 4ᵗʰ, 5ᵗʰ etc) is what it is by the s[ai]d Radical Sound, and according to that quantity of the Sonorous Nature thereof, which it receiues from it (sc. f[rom][b] the s[ai]d radical sound,) it receiues its Numerical form.

5. How much of the nature of the radical sound is in every Consonant and Dissonant Interval, (usefull in music) which may be demonstrated by the Division of a Chord into proportional parts; as may be seen by my scale of the Proportion of Sounds.

---

[a]   i.e. 10 February 1675/6. The annotation is in a different hand from the synopsis.
[b]   MS has *for*.

6. Of the Several Totums (sc. the Totum general, subalternat general, Integral, Individual etc.) which are the Parts of which the whole System, Body, or Scale of music is constituted: And are no other, than the several sorts of Sounds, (diverse, in their kinds, from one another,) without whose mutual concurrence there would be no musical Harmony.[4]

7. That there are 3 Radix's, or 3 sorts of radical Sounds, in a Scale of Music, viz. the Artificial, Natural, and Accidental radix; as appears by my compleat scale of musick.[5]

8. That there could be no Musical Harmony, if (in a System of many Parts) one and the same sound were not, at one and the same time (by the force of relation) Grave and Acute; Flat and Sharp; consonant, concinnous and dissonant; a correlated, and yet a radical Sound.[6]

9. That, when 7 Chords or Parts are struck together, there are (for the propagation of Harmony) at one and the same time, more than 20 Sounds or Intervals actually struck, and distinguishable: which are of differing rations, habitudes, and magnitudes, from the s[ai]d 7 Chords of the Heptachord, or System of 7 Parts.[7]

10. That the Production of Intervals, from the division of the radical sound extended; the Numbers which (being applied to them) demonstrate their Proportions; and the Characters of Notes, (by which their Values are signified) proceed from the same Reason: And How?[8]

11. That every Musical Interval hath a Being, Existence, and duration; imaginarily, in our minds; audibly, in the Medium; and objectively, in a System of Musick.

12. Of the Quantity, Quality, Place, Time, and Motion of Musical sounds, consider'd physically, (as emitted by a Sonorous Instrum[en]t,) and also relatively, viz. either meerly as a Sound, or ⟨as⟩ Such a Sound.

13. That every related Sound or Interval is in itself, One, True, Good, ordinat, perfect, and beautifull: And in what respects it is so?

14. Of the Identity and Diversity of Intervals, both in their own Natures; and of their Relation to one another.

15. Of the Active and Passive nature of Intervalls: And what it is?

16. Of the Mutual Relation of Harmonical Sounds, i.e. Intervals; what it is? How many sorts of relative Sounds there are? Of the prop[er]ties of such

Sounds; of their subject, foundation, and terms: And that such Sounds, and every individual Interval (in a System of many Parts) is both the sup[er]-structure and foundation to another sound; a contrary, and yet a mutual Relate; a special, and yet a general sound; a Subject, and an adjunct; a Cause, and an Effect; Equal, and Vnequal; Like, and vnlike; Measur'd, and measuring; by Itself, and by Accident: yet those contraries assent,[a] and consent to harmonize. For, their concord is discord; and discord, Concord: And they are so equally temp[er]ed,[9] that all the variety which is in musical harmony, is by this strange metamorphosis or Alteration of Sounds effected: I say, by this mutual opposition, and opposite reciprocation.[b]

[fol. 17[r]]
[17.] When[c] I shall write of those sounds which are only convenient to harmony viz. of consonant and dissonant Intervals.[d] I will treat

1. Of Consonant and Dissonant Sounds, and shew what they are.

2. I will make it appear, that conson[an]t and dissonant intervals, the numb[er]s which demonstrat their proportions, and the characters, by which they are denoted, proceed from the same reason.[10]

3. What musical consonancy and dissonancy is?

4. From whence they proceed?

5. How they are made?

6. That they are made and have a being, before they arrive at the Eare.[11]

---

[a]   This word is unclear in the MS because of ink having seeped through the paper from fol. 16[v].

[b]   The MS has a cross in the margin, probably an indication that the text on the inserted leaf (fol. 17[r]) should follow at this point. Its numbering here as Chapter 17 is editorial.

[c]   This word could also be read *Where*.

[d]   After *Intervals* the MS adds *in my next chapter* in square brackets.

[f. 16ᵛ]

Mathematicall Part.

1. What it is?

2. Of the Particular Principles and Axioms thereof.

3. Of the Numeration, Addition, Substraction, Multiplication, and Division of Musical Intervals.

4. Of Sounds, Even, odd; Perfect, diminute; Simple, compounded; digit, Articulate: What they are? And that, if there were not Sounds of such divers kinds, and natures, musical Harmony would ⟨be⟩ defective, nay, it could not be made.

5. That there are 7 Sounds, which, being duplicated, demonstrate the Rations of all consonant and dissonant Intervals, usefull in Musick: And what they are?[12]

6. Of the Ration's of Sounds: What they are? And of their several species.

7. From whence the Numbers, which demonstrate the proportions of Sounds, proceed; viz. not from the Principles of General, but of Special Arithmetick.[13]

8. Directions how to place Sounds so in a Scale of Music, that their just and prop[er] ration, habitude, difference, dimension, and magnitude may appear, and be discover'd by the Eye.

9. Of the mystery of the Septenary number in music; and that all things that appertain to musical Sounds, and haue respect, to the Natural keys and Fict, to the species of diatessarons, diapentes, and diapasons, to consonant and dissonant Intervals, to the Audible qualities of Sounds, to the Transposition of keys, to the Mutation of musical voyces, to the various ways by which the keys make their progressions through an Octave, to the Characters of Notes etc; are according to the Septenary number; as I haue p[ar]ticularly observ'd in my Observations on that number, ch.[14]

10. Of the doctrine of Musical Medieties: Of the 3 usual ways of mediating Sounds, sc. Arithmetically, Geometrically, and Harmonically. And of other ways of mediat[in]g sounds; of which no notice is taken by any musical

authors, whose writings I haue seen or heard of. Of which I haue written ch.[15] of my Mathem[atical] part. And of the use and Benefit of musical medieties.

11. That every individual Sound hath a prop[er] and peculiar Number, to be assign'd to it: What those numbers are? And how, and to what Intervals, to be assigned? That it is irrational, to apply two or more numbers to one and the same Sound. Into which error many, both Antient and Modern musical Authors haue fallen; as will appear by my Annotations on my Scale of Conjoined Systems.

12. Of my Perfect and Compleat Scale of Musick, which comprehends

1. Keys Natural, Fict, and Enharmonic.

2. All Consonant and Dissonant Intervals of use in Music, with

3. All Individual Intervals or Sounds by which they are completed.

4. The denominations[a] of Notes.

5. Characters of Notes.

6. Pauses.

7. Signed Keys.

8. Signes of the Moode.[16]

9. Those Numbers, and no other, which demonstrate the Rations of Sounds.

10. The keys therein are so placed, that their distance, proportions, and magnitudes may be known; And in it –

11. There are neither more nor fewer Intervalls than those that are of use in Musick.

12. The reason of the Generation of Sounds; Of the Numbers which declare their proportions; and of the Characters of Notes, is by this Scale to be found out and known.

13. The Radical Unison is fixed in one certain Key.

---

a   MS has *demoninations*.

14. One number, and no more, is assign'd thereunto.

15. Every particular Interval hath one number, and no other, assigned to it.

16. And all Intervalls of the same species, are of the same Ration.

13. Of the doctrine of Moodes: What a musical moode is? Of the Dorian, Lydian, Phrygian Mood etc. That there is a force and vertue in Sounds to work on Recipient Bodies, and on the Affections of those who hear them: But the right use and application of them to use is not known.

14. Of the Geometrical part of Musick: of the particular Principles thereof.

15. Of my Circular Scale of Sounds.[17]

16. Of a Musical Magnitude; and what it is?

17. Of the Longitude, Latitude, and Crassitude of Sounds, Physically and Relatively considered.

18. That the Diapason (in a Circular Scale) is the Center of the Hemisphere; but the Unison, of the whole Sphere of Sounds: which shews, that the Unison in Music is as the Soul in the Body of man, sc. Totum in Toto, et in qualibet parte.[18]

19. By my Circular Scale it will appear, that Sounds haue their Termination, Section, Symmetry, and Ration: And that some Sounds, as they are, properly, placed in the Scale, are unto others, of a Triangular, to others, of a Square forme: And of the proportion of divers Geometrical Bodies and Figures.[19]

[fol. 19ʳ]

Practical Part.

1. Of the Keys or Moodes Natural, Fict, and Enharmonic.

2. Of what parts every Sound is formed.

3. Of Musical Voices, which in Music are as Syllables in words.

4. Of Characters of Notes; of their Values, Reason, and Distance.

5. Of Choral Music, and Lection.[20]

6. Of divers Barbarisms, which are to be avoided in the Singing and playing of Songs.

7. Of Musical Stopps, or Closes.

8. Of Consonant and Dissonant Intervals.

9. Of the species of 4[ths], 5[ths] etc.

10. Of Sounds Simple, and Compounded, and of their various Natures.

11. Of all the ways of going to, and from, Intervals, viz. from Concords to concords; from Concords to discords; from discords to discords; and from discords to concords.

12. Of the dignity of Intervalls, and various orders of Sounds.

13. Of the Signes of the Moode.

14. Of signed Keys or Cliffs; and of the marks of Mollity and Asperity.[21]

15. Of Pauses or Rest[s], of the use of them, and why they were invented?

16. Of the Compounding of Sounds, for the making of Harmony, or of the Art of composition; which I haue comprehended in 6 Canons or Rules: Of their Examples, Variations, Observations; general and special order; when they are to be observed and kept, and when to be altered: Of the Transposing of the Treble into the Bass; and Bass into the upper part.[22]

17. Of Counterpoint, and figurat Discant.

18. Directions how to compose Artificially and skilfully in a few weeks; and better, than by any way, yet known, a man may attain vnto in many years.

19. How to make a Tune without the help of an Instrum[en]t; with a Definition, and discovery of the Parts, of which Melodious Tunes, call'd Aires, are constituted: with Directions and Rules, by which good Aires or Tunes (of any sort or Mood) may be made: Which skill and art is, by most Musitians, thought impossible to be attained vnto.

20. Of the Rhetorical part of Music: In which I shall shew, that in Music there are the like Elegancies that are found in Rhetoric, and do answer the figures thereof: illustrated by Examples.[23]

21. How Notes are to be adapted to words: of pronouncing words in singing:

22. Of the Rhythmical part of Music: of Musical quantities or feet (as Sponde's, Dactils &c.) and the use of them, both in Vocal and Instrumental Music.

23. Of the Difference, Transposition, Attraction, and Conexion[a] of the keys: Also, of the Idiom of Singing, proper to divers Nations.

24. Of Time; of the Movem[en]t of Tunes, and Proportion of Songs, as to the measuring of Time.

25. How the values of Notes hold proportion with the rations of Sounds;[24] and of many other things which appertain to the practical part of Musick; with

26. Directions how to play of a Bass continual (without offence to the Intended Discant of the Composer) either on the Theorbe, Harpsicon etc.[25]

Thus I shall endeavor to reduce all the Parts of Musick to a Regularity and Just order, without too strict a Limitation of the Musitians Fancy or Invention; my rules for effecting these things being grounded on the Principles of the Philosophical and Mathematical Parts of Music, and on the True reason of the natures of Sounds, consider'd Physically, and Artificially, viz. as related to one another: And by this means I will bring the Philosophical, Mathematical, and Practical parts of Music to analogize[26] and agree in all things: Which, I trust, will be a work acceptable to all prudent and Ingenious Lovers of Musical Harmony[.]

Notes

[1]   Comparison with the 'Animadversion' of 1672 seems to show that a considerable expansion of the 'Philosophical Part' had occurred over the intervening three years.
[2]   Through Alsted, Birchensha was familiar with Lippius's dictum, 'Musica est scientia Mathematica subalternata Arithmeticæ', which he translated as 'Musick is a Mathematical Science, subalternate to Arithmetick' (*Templum musicum*, p. 2). Isaac Barrow, in his lectures in 1664–66 as Lucasian Professor of Mathematics at Cambridge,

---

[a]   This word is unclear in the MS: it could also read *Concision*.

had varied this by speaking of 'that Part of Mathematics termed Music, Harmonics or Canonics, which (as some love to speak) is subaltern to Arithmetic; but perhaps it would be more rightly subordinate to Geometry'. Barrow's lectures were not published until after his death, first in 1685 in Latin, and then in 1734 in English, but they would have been discussed in mathematical circles when Birchensha was working on his book. See J.C. Kassler and D.R. Oldroyd, 'Robert Hooke's Trinity College "Musick Scripts", his Music Theory and the Role of Music in his Cosmology', *Annals of Science*, 40 (1983): 559–95, at p. 561.

3   Compare *Templum musicum*, p. 16 ('So in Sounds, the Simple Unison is the principal and Radix of all Musical Intervals'); 'A Compendious Discourse', Mathematical Part, chapter 3 ('The Radical So[un]d or Vnison [...] being extended, (which is demonstrated by the Intension of a Chord) it measureth every Intervall, into which it may be divided, and which is a part thereof, or which proceedeth from it').

4   The term 'totum' occurs twice in the 'Compendious Discourse', once denoting the totality of sounds in a musical 'system', and once denoting the sum resulting from the addition of musical intervals (see Mathematical Part, chapters 4 and 5). The assertion that totums are 'parts' makes the word's meaning here unclear, but Birchensha may intend it to refer to a set of three or more pitches and the set of intervals between them, which would relate to both of its meanings in the 'Compendious Discourse'.

5   A 'sound' is typically an interval, for Birchensha. The most common use of 'radix' or 'radical' for him was in the phrase 'radical unison'. The only use of 'radical sound' elsewhere which could be relevant seems to be that in chapter 8 of the Mathematical Part of the 'Compendious Discourse', where it denotes the correlation of the note E with the number 3 and is the first in a sequence which continues with 'square sound' (A correlated with 9) and 'cube sound' (D with 27) – that is the cycle of fifths and the corresponding sequence of powers of 3. It therefore seems conceivable that the three 'radical sounds' here are three ways of generating a scale, as in chapter 16 of the Mathematical Part, where 'conjunct mediety' is divided into three forms: 'natural' (the diatonic scale), 'odd' (the cycle of fifths) and 'even' (a series of octaves). But the three terms 'artificial', 'natural' and 'accidental', which are not linked elsewhere in Birchensha's writings, seem extremely difficult to relate to this interpretation, and the citing of the 'Compleat Scale of Musick' may suggest instead that the 'Natural' radices are the notes of the natural scale (A, B, C, and so on); the 'Accidental', when one of these notes is flattened or sharpened (A♭, B♭, C♯); and the 'Artificial', when it is made double flat or double sharp, or raised by a diesis.

6   On 'concinnous' sounds, see the 'Compendious Discourse', Practical Part, chapter 12 (p. 111), with note 31.

7   While glancing at ancient Greek theory and the tuning of the 'heptachord' or seven-stringed lyre, Birchensha here uses 'sound' in the sense of 'interval' – as he does frequently in the 'Compendious Discourse' – remarking on the large number of intervals (21, in fact) produced by the sounding of seven pitches simultaneously.

8   That the division of the unison string can be taken to generate the numbers which Birchensha assigned to pitches is unproblematic, but it is a mystery how this was to be made to apply also to the 'characters' of notes, that is to musical notation. The assertion that this would be demonstrated is repeated in chapter 17 (subsection 2) below, and in chapter 9 of the Mathematical Part.

9   Long before being applied to division of the octave into equal (or near-equal) semitones, 'equally tempered' had a more general meaning of 'equable', as in Fulke

Greville's phrase 'a quiet and equally tempered people' (before 1628: see *OED*, s.v. 'tempered', §2.a). Here it should probably be understood in the sense of truly or fairly attuned.

10   See section 10 above.

11   As the writings of Hooke, Holder, Francis North and others show, the question of how musical sounds are received by the ear and why they are perceived as consonant or dissonant was a topic of current concern among natural philosophers. Birchensha may have been influenced partly by Pietro Mengoli's *Speculationi di Musica* (Bologna, 1670), a book which he had been keen to acquire: see Oldenburg's letter of 7 June 1673 to Marcello Malpighi (*The Correspondence of Henry Oldenburg*, eds A. Rupert Hall and Marie Boas Hall, vol. 10 (London, 1975), pp. 6–9), and his review of Mengoli's book (*Philosophical Transactions* 8, no. 100 (9 February 1673/4): 6194–7002 [recte 6194–6202]); Gouk, 'The Role of Acoustics and Music Theory in the Scientific Work of Robert Hooke', *Annals of Science*, 37 (1980): 573–605, at 595–6; Benjamin Wardhaugh, 'The Logarithmic Ear: Pietro Mengoli's mathematics of music', *Annals of Science*, 64 (2007): 327–48.

12   Cf. chapter 8 of the Mathematical Part in the 'Compendious Discourse', where 'there are but 7 Numbers, which (with their duplicates) demonstrate the Rations of all consonant and dissonant Intervalls in a Diapason.' The numbers are given there and are the powers of 3 from 3 to 2187 (= 3^7), implying that the '7 Sounds' of this passage were the intervals occurring in the cycle of fifths. In both cases the appeal to duplication presumably means that Birchensha intended to disregard differences between intervals and their compounds.

13   Although a distinction between 'general' and 'special' arithmetic is not a common one, it seems clear that by the latter Birchensha means the arithmetic of ratios.

14   There is no chapter number in the manuscript. In seventeenth-century music theory 'septenary' often meant the set of seven note-letters A B C D E F G (Birchensha's 'natural keys'). John Playford, for example, described the gamut as containing 'Three Septenaries [of Letters] ascending one above the other, *G* being put first' (*An Introduction to the Skill of Musick*, 7th edn (London, 1674), p. 2). 'Mutation of musical voyces' could well have been illustrated in *Syntagma musicæ* by transpositions of a seven-note diatonic scale, as was done in the 'Compendious Discourse', Practical Part, chapter 5. But Birchensha may also have had in mind the '7 Sounds' mentioned earlier in his synopsis and the apparently related passage in the 'Compendious Discourse', Mathematical Part, chapter 8 (see note 12 above), inasmuch as the latter's series of ternary numbers, when preceded by 'the number assign'd to the radicall sound', yields the seven natural notes – B (1), E (3), A (9), D (27), G (81), C (243) and F (729) – before coming to the first flat note in the cycle of fifths, B flat (2187). Christopher Simpson, too, reflected upon the 'Mysterious number of seven' and the 'Seven Gradual Sounds or Tones, from whose various positions and Intermixtures [...] Concords and Discords do arise': see *The Division-Violist* (London, 1659), p. 17; *Chelys / The Division-Viol* (London, 1665), p. 23.

15   The manuscript again gives no chapter number. Regarding a lost chapter on 'other ways of mediating sounds', see the 'Compendious Discourse', Mathematical Part, chapter 21, where Birchensha alludes to 'chap[ter] 14. of my Mathem[atica]ll part of Musick' (p. 151), and also the 1672 'Animadversion' for *Syntagma musicæ* (p. 195, note 4).

16   Sections 5–8 deal with the notation of note values, rests, clefs and time signatures, all of which are to be covered in the 'Practical Part' also. This is the only intimation that Birchensha's 'Compleat Scale' will embrace such matters, and reflects his desire that it should encapsulate 'the whole body of the Mathematical part of Musick' (letter to the Royal Society, 26 April 1664; see p. 88).

17   Chapters 15, 18 and 19 appear to provide the only references we have to Birchensha's 'Circular Scale of Sounds'. Other theorists devised circular scales of various kinds, including Erycius Puteanus (*Musathena* (Hanau, 1602), p. 76) and Johannes Lippius (*Synopsis musicæ novæ* (Strasbourg, 1612), sig. F3ʳ (see Benito V. Rivera, *German Music Theory in the Early Seventeenth Century* (Ann Arbor, MI, 1980), pp. 88–102), and, in Britain, Charles Butler (*The Principles of Musik in Singing and Setting* (London, 1636), p. 13) and the anonymous author of *The Musical Compass* (London, 1684; see Rebecca Herissone, *Music Theory in Seventeenth-Century England* (Oxford, 2000), pp. 84–5). Puteanus placed the seven solmization syllables from *ut* to *bi* at points on a circle which was divided into seven segments of two sizes, the larger representing a tone and the smaller a diatonic semitone. Lippius placed the seven bocedization syllables from *bo* to *ni* at points on a circle, but spaced them roughly proportionally according to the just intonation of the syntonal diatonic scale – so that *bo–ce* represents a greater tone (9 : 8), *ce–di* a lesser tone (10 : 9), *di–ga* a diatonic semitone (16 : 15), and so on – and assigned appropriate numbers to each, with linear chords connecting each of the seven points to every other point. An accurate proportionate representation of the sizes of the different intervals, in diagrams which are also circular, first appeared in manuscript versions of René Descartes, *Compendium musicæ* (Utrecht, 1650), probably around 1635. See Benjamin Wardhaugh, 'Musical Logarithms in the Seventeenth Century: Descartes, Mercator, Newton', *Historia mathematica*, 35 (2008): 19–36. Birchensha's scale may have been similarly designed to demonstrate Pythagorean proportions.

18   i.e. 'the whole within the whole, and in each and every part'.

19   This passage could conceivably indicate that Birchensha's 'circular scale' owed something to Kepler's geometrical manipulations in *Harmonices mundi*, where the overlaying of polygons onto a circle representing the musical string was used to generate the musical divisions of that string.

20   'Lection' ('reading') may here refer to some aspect of vocal style or technique, such as enunciation of the words.

21   By 'marks of Mollity and Asperity' Birchensha may mean flat and sharp signatures, as in his 'Directions how to make any kind of Tune' (see Chapter III, note 117). On the other hand, since *mollis* (soft) and *asper* (rough) were among the gradations by which Lippius (*Synopsis musicæ novæ*, sig. B6ʳ) and Alsted (*Encyclopædia* (Herborn, 1630), p. 1197) measured a sound's 'latitude', he may perhaps be referring to dynamic markings. For examples of these in practice, he would not have needed to look any further than Locke's Curtain Tune for the Dorset Garden Theatre production of *The Tempest* (March or April 1674), which contains the directions 'soft', 'lowder by degrees', 'violent', 'soft', 'lowd', and 'soft and slow by degrees', or his 'Song of Ecchoes' for the production there of *Psyche* on 27 February 1674/5, in which 'lowd' is echoed by 'soft', 'softer' and 'softest'. Both pieces were published in score in Matthew Locke, *The English Opera* (London, 1675): for a modern edition, see *Matthew Locke: Dramatic Music*, ed. Michael Tilmouth (Musica Britannica, 51; London, 1986), pp. 27–9, 104–8. One of the principal singers in *The Tempest* was James Hart, identified above as an admirer of Birchensha's teachings (see Introduction, pp. 22–4). The

earliest English theory book to mention Italian dynamic markings was A.B.'s *Synopsis of Vocal Musick* (1680): see Chapter IV, note 13.

[22]   Perhaps surprisingly, Birchensha proposes to give his six 'Rules of Composition' before his directions 'How to make a Tune' (chapter 19).

[23]   On the treatment of rhetorical figures by English musical theorists, see Christopher D.S. Field, 'Formality and Rhetoric in English Fantasia-Suites', in *William Lawes 1602–1645: Essays on his Life, Times and Work*, ed. Andrew Ashbee (Aldershot, 1998), pp. 197–249, particularly at pp. 214–17.

[24]   In the 'Compendious Discourse' (Practical Part, chapter 7) Birchensha hinted at an affinity between the proportions of string-lengths (i.e. intervals) and those of note-lengths (i.e. rhythmic durations), but did not develop the idea. See Chapter III, note 21.

[25]   This is the first time any treatment of thoroughbass playing in *Syntagma musicæ* has been mentioned. Birchensha must have been aware that he would be venturing into territory covered recently by Matthew Locke in *Melothesia: or, Certain General Rules for Playing upon a Continued-Bass* (London, 1673). On the 'theorbe', see Lynda Sayce, 'Continuo Lutes in 17th- and 18th-Century England', *Early Music*, 23/4 (1995): 666–84. The word 'harpsicon' occasionally occurs elsewhere as a variant of 'harpsichord' – for example in Oxford, Bodleian Library, MS Mus. Sch. C.84 ('Mr Jenkins: his Ayres for the Harpsecon, Lyra Vyole, Base Vyole and Vyolin', copied probably in the late 1650s for Jenkins's patron Dudley, third Baron North), or in John Playford's *Musick's Hand-Maide Presenting New and Pleasant Lessons for the the Virginals or Harpsycon* (London, 1663).

[26]   In Greek 'analogia' may denote equality of ratios, and it is plausible that Birchensha's choice of the word here reflected his belief, expressed repeatedly in this text, that the same ratios govern every aspect of music.

VII

Birchensha Demonstrates his 'Compleat Scale of Musick' to the Royal Society (10 February 1675/6)

Editorial Note

Birchensha's appearance at the Royal Society's ordinary meeting at Gresham College on Thursday, 10 February 1675/6 provided an opportunity for him to demonstrate and explain his 'Perfect and Compleat Scale of Musick', a project that had occupied him on and off for more than a decade and which he intended to make a centrepiece of the 'Mathematical Part' of *Syntagma musicæ*.[1] The fullest account of this appearance – transcribed below – is to be found in the official minutes of the meeting (London, Royal Society, Journal Book Original, vol. 5, pp. 141–3). These show that proceedings began with the election of four new fellows,[2] and that, apart from Birchensha's paper, the main business was the reading of the final instalment of Isaac Newton's 'Observations' on light and colours. Henry Oldenburg, the secretary of the Society, subsequently sent accounts of the meeting to certain members, including Newton and Martin Lister, the physician and naturalist. Oldenburg's letter to Newton, written on or about 12 February 1675/6, is unfortunately lost, but Newton's reply from Cambridge, dated 15 February, survives. In it he modestly wrote: 'I thank you for your account of Mr Berchhenshaw's scale of Musick though I have not so much skill in that science as to understand it well'.[3] Four months later, on 10 June 1676, Oldenburg sent a letter to Lister containing what was essentially a précis of the minutes:

> That famous and extraordinary Musician, Mr Birschinshaw, presented to the Society his new Scale of Musick, containing first, a Table of all Consonant and dissonant Intervals, convenient to Musical harmony, which are practicable, and may be expressed by the voyce and other Instruments; and assigning unto these Intervals, apt and proper Numbers, by which their rations and proportions are demonstrated: Secondly, a system of all the keyes, by which the s[ai]d Intervals are completed; Thirdly, the magnitude, dimension and proportion of the s[ai]d keyes exactly demonstrated, according to the proportional parts of a Chord, the Chord being supposed 36 inches long.[4]

In his *History of the Royal Society of London* Dr Thomas Birch (1705–66), the Society's secretary, included edited but faithful transcripts of the minutes of this and other meetings from the period 1660–87. Our edition provides the original text of the Journal Book, but records the more significant differences between this and Birch's text.[5]

Notes

[1]   It is just possible that by February 1675/6 Birchensha's 'Compleat Scale of Musick' had already been engraved. After his talk, it was suggested by the Royal Society (presumably through Lord Brouncker, the president) that Birchensha might consider publishing the 'Compleat Scale' separately, with an explanation of it; but there is no evidence that this was ever done.

[2]   One of these, John Mapletoft, the Gresham Professor of Physic, was present and was admitted to the Society.

[3]   *The Correspondence of Isaac Newton*, ed. H.W. Turnbull (7 vols, Cambridge, 1959–77), vol. 1, pp. 417–21; *The Correspondence of Henry Oldenburg*, eds A. Rupert Hall and Marie Boas Hall, vol. 12 (London and Philadelphia, 1986), p. 192. Though Newton's response might be thought disingenuous in view of the interest he had shown in musical scales in the 1660s, he expressed regret also to Dr John North on 21 April 1677 that he lacked the 'combination of musical & mathematical skill' needed to comment usefully on the treatment of 'Tunes, the scale of Music, & consort' in Francis North's *Philosophical Essay of Musick*. See *The Correspondence of Isaac Newton*, vol. 2, pp. 205–8; Penelope Gouk, *Music, Science and Natural Magic in Seventeenth-Century England* (New Haven, 1999), pp. 224, 233–7, 246–8; Jamie C. Kassler, *The Beginnings of the Modern Philosophy of Music in England* (Aldershot, 2004), pp. 94–104 and 175–8.

[4]   *The Correspondence of Henry Oldenburg*, vol. 12, pp. 332–5.

[5]   Thomas Birch, *The History of the Royal Society of London* (4 vols, London, 1756–57), vol. 3, pp. 295–6.

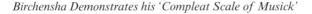

Edition

[p. 141]

February 10. 1675/6

[…]

Mr. Birchenshaw presented himself to the Society, and shew'd them his Scale of Musick, wherein is contained, first, A Table of all Consonant and Dissonant Intervalls convenient to[a] Musical Harmony which are practicable, and may be express'd by the voyce and other Instruments: Unto these respectiue Intervals, apt and proper Numbers are assigned, by which their rations[b] and proportions are demonstrated.[1]

[p. 142]

Secondly, a systeme of all the Keys, by which the aforesaid Intervals are completed: of which keyes some are Natural; some are intended to the first degree of Acutenesse; some are remitted to the first degree of Gravity; some are twice spissated, some are twice asperated.[2]

Thirdly, in this Scale the Magnitude, Dimension and proportion of the said keyes are exactly demonstrated, according to the proportional parts of a Chord, the Chord being supposed thirty six inches long.[3]

If it be demanded, whether there is any thing in this Table and Systeme, that is not to be found in the Scales and Writings of other Musicians, he answers:

1. That the Intervals in this Table are perfect and complete; there is not one too many, nor one wanting, which may conduce to the making of Harmony.

2. That the Sounds or Musicall numbers contained in this Systeme, arise out of the Unison, and from one another, according to the reason of Figurate, not simple Numbers, (as, he said, he could demonstrate by numbers assigned to the respectiue Intervals in the Table;) for that so the Reason of the Scale of Musick[c] did require.[4]

3. That there are neither more nor lesse keyes in this Systeme, than will complete the aforesaid Intervals.

4. That in this Scale all the Tones are of the same Ration; and that so are all the Semitones, Semiditones, ditones and other Intervals.

5. That the true Magnitude and dimension of every one of the said Keyes are demonstrated, according to the Proportional parts of a Chord.

---

[a]   Birch has *suitable to*.

[b]   Birch has *ratio's*.

[c]   Birch has *state of music*.

[p. 143]

6. That the natural, genuine and true Reason of the Excellency and Fulnesse of the Harmony of 3. 4. 5. 6 and 7. parts, may clearly be discerned by the Sisteme of seven parts.[5]

He added, that many other things were to be found in this Table and Scale; of which litle or no mention is made in the Scales and writings of either moderne or ancient Musical Authors: which he said he intended to discover, and to write of them at large, as he should be inabled thereunto.

He had the thanks of the Society given him for this respect and kindness, and[a] was exhorted to finish his[b] Work, or at least, to publish this Systeme with an Explanation thereof.

Notes

[1]   In this minute three distinct aspects of Birchensha's 'Scale' are described. The first of these, 'A Table of all Consonant and Dissonant Intervalls convenient to Musical Harmony', was probably similar to, but larger and more elaborate than, the tables in the 'Compendious Discourse' (Practical Part, chapter 13; see Figure 3.3) and William Corbett's manuscript of the 'Rules of Composition' (see Figure 9.1). If the same 14 intervals as feature as in those tables were to have been transposed – as the 'Compendious Discourse' (Mathematical Part, chapter 9; see p. 133) implies they may have been – into 'All Keyes flatt and sharp: (viz. A♭. A. A♯ – B♭. B. B♯ – C♭. C. C♯ – D♭. D. D♯ – E♭. E. E♯ – F♭. F. F♯ – G♭. G. G♯ –)', every double flat and double sharp note except B𝄪 would have been required. Thus in the most extreme sharp key, where B♯ is the 'assumed Unison', the scale would have run B♯, C♯, C𝄪, D♯, D𝄪, E♯, F♯, E𝄪, F𝄪, G♯, G𝄪, a♯, b, a𝄪, b♯; in the most extreme flat key, where F♭ is the 'Unison', it would have run F♭, G♭♭, G♭, a♭♭, a♭, b♭♭, c♭♭, b♭, c♭, d♭♭, d♭, e♭♭, f♭♭, e♭, f♭. The minute suggests that alongside the name of each interval its ratio was shown.

[2]   i.e. some notes are natural, some sharp, some flat, some double flat, some double sharp. This second aspect of the 'Scale', described as a 'systeme of all the Keys', may have been a 'system' in the sense of a musical staff or staves, on which every natural and 'fict' note required in the preceding table was notated. Assuming that the system covered at least the double octave from A to aa, it might also have shown the Greek note names from *proslambanomenos* to *nete hyperbolaion*, and the dieses belonging to the five tetrachords of ancient Greek theory in the enharmonic genus (B diesis, E diesis, a diesis, b diesis and e diesis); see Chapters IV and VI for indications of Birchensha's intention to incorporate such information into his 'Grand Scale'.

[3]   'Chord' here means a string (as of a monochord). This third aspect of the 'Scale', described as an 'exact demonstration' of magnitudes and proportions, may have taken

[a]   Birch omits *had the thanks … kindness, and.*

[b]   Birch has *this.*

the form of a diagram illustrating how a 36-inch string would have been systematically divided in order to produce the necessary set of pitches and intervals.

4   'Figurate' here probably bears the same sense as in 'Compendious Discourse', Mathematical Part, chapter 20, where 'figurate numbers' are those forming geometric rather than arithmetic series, such as a series of powers of 3: 1, 3, 9, 27, etc.

5   Compare Birchensha's reference to the '7 Chords of the Heptachord, or System of 7 Parts', and the sounding together of these seven strings, in his synopsis of *Syntagma musicæ* (Philosophical Part, chapter 9; see Chapter VI, p. 200). In the present context, seven-part harmony seems to be accorded special significance.

VIII

Rules of Composition, I: Silas Taylor's Manuscript

Editorial Note

In *Syntagma musicæ* Birchensha intended to make public his '6 Canons or Rules' of composition – rules which he claimed had enabled many a pupil 'to compose Artificially and skilfully in a few weeks' – together with examples and directions for their use;[1] but, as we have seen, the book failed to appear. A printed 'Sheet of plain Rules and Directions for Composing Musick in parts, by Mr. John Birchenshaw' could be bought in 1682 from John Playford's shop in London for sixpence; but no copy of it is known to survive, so we cannot tell how authoritative or useful it was.[2]

Our knowledge of the rules therefore rests on three manuscripts, of which at least two can claim real authority. The best known, but in some ways most complex, of these forms part of a collection of musical papers – British Library, Additional MS 4910, fols 39–61 (*olim* [41]–69) – originally owned by Captain Silas Taylor (1624–78), the antiquary, military store-keeper and composer.[3] On fol. 39 is an inscription in Taylor's hand, partly in black and partly in red ink:

> A Collection of Rules in Musicke from the / most knowing Masters in that Science / with M[r] Birchensha's 6: Rules of Com- / position; & his Enlargements there-on to / the Right Hon[ble] William Lord Vis- / count Brouncker &c: / Collected by Mee. Silas Domvill al[ia]s Taylor.[4]

The 23 surviving leaves from this collection are individually mounted in a guard-book. Those containing Birchensha's rules are alternately ruled for music and unruled, and probably formed part of a notebook measuring approximately 305 × 200mm.[5] The music paper has a foolscap watermark. It was ruled with rastra, giving 12 five-line staves to a page, with marginal verticals in red. The unruled paper is more lightweight, and has a posthorn watermark. Instructions and examples for each rule are written on facing pages, with music examples always on the left and instructions on the right, except for Rule 6, for which there is a music example on a recto page but no heading or explanatory text. After every rule the next opening (consisting of unruled *verso* and ruled *recto*) was generally left empty.

Thanks to Taylor's annotations, it is clear that this manuscript of Birchensha's rules was formed in two layers. The first layer consists of instructions and examples for the first three rules only, written out for Taylor's benefit by Birchensha himself.[6] The second layer, which is made up largely of Birchensha's 'enlargements' for the benefit of Viscount Brouncker (1620–84), the president of the Royal Society, is in Taylor's hand, and presumably drew upon a lost manuscript made by Birchensha for Brouncker.[7] This additional material comprises further instructions and examples relating to Rules 1–3, instructions and examples for Rules 4–5, an example for Rule 6 and – valuably – Birchensha's 'method' for putting the rules into practice.

Neither of the layers is dated. Leta Miller has proposed c.1668, Rebecca Herissone c.1673, as the approximate date of the manuscript.[8] There are features, however, that point to an earlier date for the writing of the first layer at least. They include the style of Birchensha's musical handwriting, as well as the content of the rules themselves. Nowhere here do we find the distinctive form of *g'* clef that Birchensha adopted in Corbett's manuscript and the 'Compendious Discourse' (compare Figure 8.1 with Figures 3.2 and 9.3). Early in 1664 Birchensha described his Rules of Composition as 'already, in part, contrived' – the implication being that two years after teaching Pepys he still considered them capable of further development and improvement.[9] In the autograph first layer of Taylor's manuscript Rules 1–3 are expressed in a concise, almost lapidary form that suggests they had not yet undergone the process of ramification evidenced by other sources (see Chapters IX and X). Rule 1 is here entitled 'The Rule of graduall Motion both in the upper Part and Bass', whereas in Corbett's manuscript it is called the 'Rule of Two Parts Ascending or Descending together Gradualy, or By Saltation' – a significant change which allowed disjunct movement in parallel thirds or sixths to be brought within this rule. In Taylor's manuscript syncopated conjunct motion is introduced under Rule 1, but in Corbett's manuscript it is dealt with under Rule 5 (the 'Dividing Rule'). When Birchensha first gave Taylor Rule 3 (the 'Transverse Rule'), it covered just two categories of contrary motion ('breaking', and 'simple counterpoint'); only later did he add a third category ('Transverse motion by Saltation'). A possible time for Taylor to have studied these newly devised rules with their author would have been between his move to London in August 1659 and his posting to Dunkirk late the following year. On this basis, we suggest a conjectural date of 1659–60 for the first layer.

Taylor's transcript shows that by the time Lord Brouncker received his version of the rules they had benefited from a certain amount of revision. One change is the inclusion of 'saltation' under Rule 1, an example of which may be found in Taylor's second layer. In Rule 3 greater attention is paid to 'moveing transversly by Simple counterpoint', though the possible ways of doing this are less systematically exemplified than in other sources. Clearly the scope for modification and refinement was not yet exhausted. 'Syncope' is still included under Rule 1. The 'Rule of Division' is only concerned with crotchet or quaver movement on a slow-moving or stationary ground, whereas in Corbett's manuscript it embraces 'Syncope' and 'Chromatick notes' too. Taylor's numbering of the 'Rule of Division' as Rule 4 and the 'Rule of Cadences' as Rule 5 was presumably taken from Brouncker's book, but in other sources they appear as Rules 5 and 4 respectively. The 'method' for applying the rules is considerably less sophisticated than the version in Corbett's manuscript.

From a chronological point of view, we know that during 1664 Taylor encouraged the Royal Society to take an interest in Birchensha's work. The Society's Journal Book records that on 20 April of that year

> S^r. Robert Moray suggested, that Capt. Taylor had mentioned to him, a Gentleman [Birchensha], who did pretend to discover some Musical Errors, generally committed, by all moderne Masters of Musick, touching the Scales, and the proportions of Notes, and desired to be heard by some Members of this Society, versed in Musick.[10]

A committee chaired by Lord Brouncker was formed to examine the matter, and a letter from Birchensha to the Society was read out at the next meeting on 27 April (see Chapter II). Although his letter did talk about scales and proportions, it is noticeable that the minute of the meeting focused less on Birchensha's mathematical ideas than on his rules of composition:

> M^r. Berchinsha's Musical paper was read, wherin he gives an account of the desiderata in Musick, and undertaketh to bring the Art of Musick to that perfection, that even those, who can neither sing nor play, shall be able by his Rules, to make good Air and compose 2, 3, 4 or more parts Artificially.[11]

It may not be too fanciful to imagine Birchensha being asked by the President in those circumstances to provide him with a copy of his rules – the result being the manuscript which Taylor calls 'my Lord Brounckers booke'. A few weeks later, Pepys found Taylor full of enthusiasm for Birchensha's method:

> Thence into the parke and met and walked with Captain Sylas Taylor, my old acquaintance while I was of the Exchequer, and Dr. Whore – talking of music and perticularly of Mr. Berchenshaw's way, which Taylor magnifies mightily, and perhaps but what it deserves – but not so easily to be understood as he and others make of it.[12]

Does this suggest a familiarity with Birchensha's rules on Taylor's part that already went beyond the early, incomplete version found in the first layer of his manuscript? Later that summer Brouncker, Moray, Taylor and Pepys were all present at one of Birchensha's concerts.[13] Viewed against this general background, 1664–65 – more specifically, the period between Taylor's return from Virginia early in 1664 and his departure for Harwich towards the end of

1665 – is perhaps the likeliest time both for Birchensha to have prepared a text of his rules for Brouncker, and for Taylor to have used this to amplify his own manuscript.

After 1665 Taylor's 'Collection of Rules' became more eclectic in character. Sometimes he would utilize vacant space in his Birchensha notebook. On the reverse of instructions for Birchensha's Rule 3 and music examples for Rule 4 (fols 51^v–52^r), for instance, he wrote out examples from Simpson's *Compendium of Practical Musick* (1667).[14] On fol. 40^r, immediately beneath Birchensha's 'method', he added two paragraphs, both unconnected with Birchensha's rules. The first is concerned with the precept that the addition of a flat to a scale alters its solmization but the addition of a sharp does not;[15] the second is an example from Matthew Locke (perhaps communicated personally) of an imitative sequence rising and falling. That the precept about solmization of sharps was not universally accepted is evident from 'A Scale for the right denomination of Notes in Musicke' on fol. 42. This tabulates a scale of G with the proper four-syllable solmization to use for signatures from three flats to two sharps. According to Taylor's note, it was 'invented & made by Mr Allison of the Covent-Garden & [...] presented to mee in the yeare 1668'.[16] Particularly interesting are the contributions which Taylor got from his friend Locke. They include two examples of 'Syncopated or Driving Canon' given to him by Locke in 1669 (fol. 60^r). These had been used in Simpson's *Compendium* (1667), where they are acknowledged as being 'by the excellent Mr *Matthew Lock*', but Taylor's copy of the first canon is three semibreves longer than the printed version.[17] There are also three pages of 'Rules for playing from a Basso continuo' (fols 43^r–44^r) – a pre-publication version of Locke's rules and examples in *Melothesia*, with many differences from the version published in 1673.[18] Lastly, there is a page of anonymous 'Generall Rules for a Thorough Base' (fol. 61^r). These have been attributed to Birchensha, but it seems unlikely that they have anything to do with him.[19]

Although Aubrey and Wood mention that when Taylor died in 1678 'his creditors seised on his goods and papers', it seems possible that his 'Collection of Rules in Musicke' remained in his family for a time.[20] It was later acquired by Sir John Hawkins, the author of *A General History of the Science and Practice of Music* (4 vols, London, 1776), who presented it to the British Museum in 1778 along with other theoretical writings on music.[21]

In the present edition only the material relating to Birchensha's '6 Rules of Composition' is included. Because of the way the manuscript is laid out, each double-page opening has generally been treated as a single unit, in order that the music examples may be more conveniently placed in relation to the text. Editorial rubrics indicate which passages are in Birchensha's hand (i.e. first layer) and which are in Taylor's.

Notes

[1]   See Chapters V (p. 194) and VI (p. 205).

[2]   In Playford's *Musick's Recreation on the Viol*, Lyra-Way, 2nd edn (London, 1682), sig. A4ᵛ, this sheet is the last item in a list of 'Musick Books Printed for John Playford'. Anthony Wood also mentions it in his manuscript note on Birchensha: Oxford, Bodleian Library, MS Wood D 19 (4), fol. 19.

[3]   Taylor, a native of Shropshire, entered New Inn Hall, Oxford, in 1641, but left to join the Parliamentary army, in which he rose to the rank of captain. During the Commonwealth he was a sequestration commissioner for Herefordshire, an office that involved him in controversy but allowed him to pursue his interests in antiquities and music. He became a friend of Matthew Locke, despite the latter's Catholic persuasion, and held music meetings in Hereford in which Locke took part. Aubrey records that Taylor 'had a very fine chamber organ in those unmusicall dayes', and Wood notes that towards the end of the interregnum he attended music meetings at William Ellis's house in Oxford (along with his younger brother Sylvanus, a fellow of All Souls), where he would 'play and sing his part'. Two suites by him were published in Playford's *Court-Ayres* (1655), and according to Wood some of his lessons 'were tried and played' in the Oxford Music School during John Wilson's professorship (1656–61). In August 1659 Taylor moved to London as captain of a troop of horse and commissioner for the Westminster militia, and it may have been then that he became interested in Birchensha's teaching. He was keeper of armaments at Dunkirk from 1660 to 1662, made a voyage to Virginia in 1663–64, and became keeper of the king's storehouse at Harwich in 1665. Though never elected a fellow, he took a keen interest in the Royal Society, and was admitted to its discussions and committees, had papers published, donated items to the library and museum, and pledged money towards the proposed new college. Taylor's antiquarian writings include a historical survey of Herefordshire (London, British Library, Harley MS 6726), his *History of Gavel-kind* (London, 1663) and a 'description of Harwich and all its appurtenances and antiquities' which was posthumously published by Samuel Dale (London, 1730). Among his musical compositions are a setting of Abraham Cowley's Anacreontic ode 'The thirsty Earth soaks up the Rain', published in Playford's *Catch that Catch can* (London, 1667); he also wrote several anthems, including one 'of six and seven parts' which was sung in the Chapel Royal on St Peter's Day, 1668. See Anthony Wood, *Athenæ Oxonienses*, 2nd edn (London, 1721), vol. 2, cols 623–5; Thomas Birch, *The History of the Royal Society of London* (4 vols, London, 1756–57); Anthony Wood, *The Life and Times of Anthony Wood*, ed. Andrew Clark, vol. 1 (Oxford Historical Society Publications, 19; Oxford, 1891), p. 274; John Aubrey, *'Brief Lives', Chiefly of Contemporaries*, ed. Andrew Clark (2 vols, Oxford, 1898), vol. 2, pp. 254–6; *The Correspondence of Henry Oldenburg*, eds. A. Rupert Hall and Marie Boas Hall, vols 2–3 (Madison, Milwaukee and London, 1966), letters 285, 289, 510, 514, 518 and 525; *The Diary of Samuel Pepys*, ed. Robert Latham and William Matthews (11 vols, London, 1970–83) vol. 1, p. 63; vol. 5, pp. 174–5, 258; vol. 6, pp. 80–81, 88, 318; vol. 9, pp. 151–2, 251, 271, 546–7; Michael Hunter, 'The Social Basis and Changing Fortunes of an Early Scientific Institution: An Analysis of the Membership of the Royal Society, 1660–1685', *Notes and Records of the Royal Society of London*, 31/1 (1976): 9–114, at pp. 12–13; Jack Westrup and Ian Spink, 'Taylor, Silas', in *The New Grove Dictionary of Music and Musicians*, 2nd

edn, ed. Stanley Sadie (29 vols, London, 2001), vol. 25, pp. 141–2; David Whitehead, 'Taylor, Silas', in *Oxford Dictionary of National Biography*, ed. H.C.G. Matthew and Brian Harrison (60 vols, Oxford, 2004), vol. 53, pp. 982–4.

4   Throughout the 'Collection of Rules' Taylor styles himself 'Silas Domvill al[ia]s Taylor'. He also uses this form in an autobiographical note which he wrote on 30 November 1673 for Anthony Wood (Oxford, Bodleian Library, MS Wood F.39, fol. 237; Aubrey, *'Brief Lives'*, vol. 2, p. 246); but in letters he signed himself 'Silas Taylor', and Wood noted that he was 'commonly called Captain Taylor' (*Athenæ Oxonienses*, vol. 2, col. 624).

5   Birchensha's rules occupy fols 40^r, 46^v–47^r, 48^v–49^r, 50^v–51^r, 52^v–53^r, 54^v–55^r, 56^r (*olim* 42^r, 50^v–51^r, 52^v–53^r, 54^v–55^r, 56^v–57^r, 58^v–59^r, 60^r). Of these, fols 46, 48, 50, 52, 54 and 56 are ruled, and fols 40, 47, 49, 51, 53 and 55 are unruled. Comparison of the two sequences of folio numbers shows that a number of leaves must have been removed from the collection before or during binding.

6   Immediately beneath the first-layer material on fol. 47^r Taylor wrote: 'This Rule & the 5: examples on the other leafe were written by Mr Birchensha himselfe for Silas Domvill al[ia]s Taylor'. Similarly on fol. 49^r he noted, 'Thus farre by Mr Birchensha himselfe', and on fol. 51^r, 'Thus farre Mr Birchensha himselfe to mee S.T.'

7   Below the second-layer material on fol. 47^r, for instance, Taylor wrote: 'These foregoeing observations were wrote out of my Lord Brounckers booke and transcribed by mee Silas Domvill al[ia]s Taylor'. Brouncker held the presidency of the Royal Society continuously from 1663 to 1677. He had inherited the title of Viscount Brouncker of Lyons in 1645 from his father, a Gentleman of the Privy Chamber to Charles I and Vice-Chamberlain to the future Charles II. In 1647 he graduated as a Doctor of Medicine at Oxford, but his scholarly achievement lay mainly in the field of mathematics. His 'Animadversions' on Descartes's *Compendium musicæ*, in which he put forward his own scheme of logarithmically calculated equal temperament, were published in 1653; the translation of Descartes's treatise however was not by him, as has often been asserted, but by Walter Charleton (see Chapter I, Edition, note 8). In 1662 Brouncker was appointed chancellor to the queen, and from 1664 to 1679 he was a Navy Commissioner. There is no evidence that he was a practical musician himself, but he hosted concerts in his house. Pepys described one of these on 12 February 1667 at which Giovanni Battista Draghi, a member of the king's consort of Italian musicians, sang part of an opera he had composed, accompanying himself on the harpsichord. Five days later Pepys heard 'the whole Quire of Italians' perform there under the direction of the composer Vincenzo Albrici, including Albrici's sister Leonora and two castratos; among those present were Sir Robert Moray, Christopher Wren, Robert Hooke and Sir George Ent (all fellows of the Royal Society) and Thomas Killigrew, the manager of the Theatre Royal in Drury Lane. See *The Diary of Samuel Pepys*, vol. 8, pp. 54–7 and 64–5, and vol. 10, pp. 46–7; Margaret Mabbett, 'Italian Musicians in Restoration England (1660–90)', *Music & Letters*, 67 (1986): 237–47; Susi Jeans and Penelope Gouk, 'Brouncker, William', in *New Grove*, vol. 4, p. 436; G.S. McIntyre, 'Brouncker, William, second Viscount Brouncker of Lyons', in *Oxford Dictionary of National Biography*, vol. 7, pp. 998–9.

8   Leta E. Miller, 'John Birchensha and the Early Royal Society: Grand Scales and Scientific Composition', *Journal of the Royal Musical Association*, 115 (1990): 63–79

at p. 64; Rebecca Herissone, *Music Theory in Seventeenth-Century England* (Oxford, 2000), pp. 96, 124, 165, 231, 250.

9   *Templum musicum*, sig. A7[v]; see Chapter I (p. 80).

10   London, Royal Society, Journal Book Original, vol. 2, pp. 71–2 (minutes of the meeting of 20 April 1664).

11   Ibid., p. 73 (minutes of the meeting of 27 April 1664).

12   *The Diary of Samuel Pepys*, vol. 5, pp. 174–5 (10 June 1664). 'Dr Whore' was the physician William Hoare, an FRS and amateur composer.

13   Ibid., p. 238 (10 August 1664): 'by agreement with Captain Sylas Taylor (my old acquaintance at the Exchequer) to the post-office to hear some Instrument Musique of Mr. Berchenshaws before my Lord Brunkard and Sir Rob. Murrey'. The concert seems to have been given in a room near the junction of Threadneedle Street and Cornhill, and been timed so that members of the Royal Society could go on to it after their meeting at Gresham College. (This was the meeting at which Birchensha took part in an experiment with a monochord.) A week previously John Evelyn attended a similar 'Consort of Excellent *Musitians* espe[c]ialy one Mr. *Berkenshaw*': *The Diary of John Evelyn*, ed. E.S. de Beer (6 vols, Oxford, 1955), vol. 3, p. 377. As an intermediary between Birchensha and the Society, Taylor may have helped to arrange and promote these concerts. On Sir Robert Moray's interest in music, see *The Diary of Samuel Pepys*, vol. 8. p. 64; *Letters of Sir Robert Moray to the Earl of Kincardine, 1657–73*, ed. David Stevenson (Aldershot and Burlington, VT, 2007), pp. 93, 117, 185, 187–8, 195; *Œuvres complètes de Christiaan Huygens* (22 vols, The Hague, 1888–1950), vol. 3, p. 313. Pepys called Moray 'a most excellent man of reason and learning, and understands the doctrine of Musique and everything else I could discourse of very finely'.

14   These are taken from part 2, chapters 4 ('Passage of the Concords') and 8 ('How to joyn a Treble to the Bass'): Christopher Simpson, *A Compendium of Practical Musick* (London, 1667), pp. 42, 51–3.

15   As Rebecca Herissone points out, this precept continued to be widely taught in Restoration England (*Music Theory*, pp. 99–100). See for example John Playford, *An Introduction to the Skill of Musick*, 7th edn (London, 1674), p. 9: 'But these two Rules you are to observe of them both: First the *B fa*, or *B flat*, doth alter both the name and property of the *Notes* before which it is placed, and is called *Fa*, making it half a *tone* or *sound* lower than it was before. Secondly, the *B mi*, or *B sharp*, alters the property of the *Notes* before which it is placed, but not the Name; for it is usually placed either before *Fa* or *Sol*, and they retain their Names still, but their Sound is raised half a *tone* or *sound* higher'. Taylor's paragraph states: 'For the denomination of Notes observe 1st. all ♯[s] alter not the denominations. 2. that where the key is with a flatt third, the note below the key is sol: & soe you must proceed in your denomination sol. la. mi. fa. sol. la. fa. sol. as suppose your key were g. & the 3[d] .♭. in B. then were your sol: in F: below G. & soe proceed. if your key were in C. & the 3[d] ♭ in E. then were your sol: B.♭. & your mi in D.' Herissone assumes this passage to be by Birchensha (*Music Theory*, pp. 96, 100), but there is no compelling reason for thinking that this is so.

16   The hand appears to be Taylor's, but the paper (watermarked with the arms of Amsterdam) is different from that used for Birchensha's rules. Nothing seems to be known of Allison beyond what Taylor says here.

17   See Simpson, *A Compendium*, pp. 161–2.

18   The manuscript is in Taylor's hand, using the same type of paper as Allison's scale (see note 16), and bears the ascription: 'By M[r] Matthew Locke composer in ordinary to

the King given to mee Silas Domvill al[ia]s Taylor'. It is mentioned in the introduction to Matthew Locke, *Melothesia*, ed. Christopher Hogwood (Oxford and New York, 1987), p. iv, but few of its variants are recorded there.

[19]   Compare Herissone, *Music Theory*, p. 182.

[20]   Among a number of later jottings is a poem signed by 'Elinor Taylor', who may have been a relation. It is written on a spare page of music paper (fol. 45); the reverse has a musical scrawl with the date 'January the 7th. 1704'.

[21]   See Samuel Ayscough, *A Catalogue of the Manuscripts Preserved in the British Museum hitherto Undescribed* (2 vols, London, 1782), vol. 1, p. 397. The guard-book containing the manuscript is labelled on the spine: 'Musical / Treatises / Brit. Mus. / Presented / by / Sir J. / Hawkins. / Additional / 4910'.

Edition

[fol. 39ʳ]
[*Taylor's hand:*]

A Collection of Rules in Musicke from the most knowing Masters in that Science with Mʳ Birchensha's 6: Rules of Composition; & his Enlargements there-on to the Right Honᵇˡᵉ William Lord Viscount Brouncker &c:

Collected by Mee. Silas Domvill al[ia]s Taylor.[a,1]

[fol. 40ʳ]
[*Taylor's hand:*]

The method for the Rules[b] following made by Mʳ John Birchensha.

1: Bring in your Fuge or any part of it, as the descant will allow[.]
2. Marke where you take any cadence [discord][c] or 5[th] Rule.
3. See where you can operate by your 2ᵈ or ⟨[3ʳᵈ]⟩ᵈ Rule.
4: Then worke by your first Rule.
5: Where any holding notes remaine make use of the dividing or 4th Rule.

These things observe unlesse designedly you will make use of any particular Rule, contrary to this method.[2]

---

[a] The last line is written in red ink.
[b] *for the* repeated after *Rules*, but deleted.
[c] MS has *descant*.
[d] Taylor's MS has a puzzling interlineation here which looks like *6* altered to *G*. The editors offer the conjectural emendation *3ᵈ* mainly on the grounds that there is otherwise no mention of the Third Rule.

[fols 46ᵛ–47ʳ]
[*Birchensha's hand:*]

1. Rule. called
The Rule of graduall Motion
both in the vpper Part and Bass.³

of which there are 5: Examples.ᵃ

1. A. – 3ˢ·
2. B. – 6ˢ·
3. C. – 5 & tritone.⁴
4. D. – Syncope. 5 & 6. or 6. & 5.ᵇ
5. E. – 6 & 5.

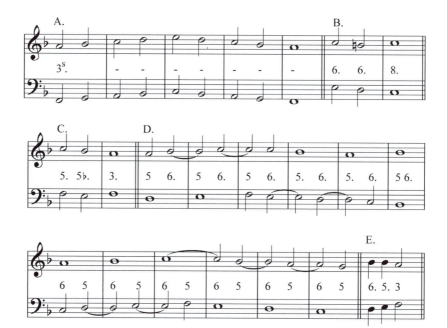

[*Taylor's hand:*]

ᵃ   Altered (by Taylor?) from *4: Examples.*
ᵇ   Birchensha's figuring *56.* in bar 6 of the example is presumably a mistake for *8.*

This Rule & the 5: examples[a] on the other leafe[b] were written by M[r] Birchensha himselfe for Silas Domvill al[ia]s Taylor[.][c]

From a 6[t[h]] you passe to the 8[tht] or 3[d]. from the 5 & Tritone to the 3[d]. as in the examples[.][d]
In Syncope, if the measure note be intire in the Basse & the parts ascend then they move by a 5[t[h]] & 6[t[h]]. But if they ascend & the measure note be in the upper part then they move by a 6[t[h]]. & 5[t[h]].
If the parts descend & the measure note be in the upper part they move by a 5[t[h]] & sixtht but if the measure note be in the Basse then they move by a 6[t[h]]. & 5[t[h]]. as in example.

2: when both parts ascend or descend together, it may be performed by Saltation[5] & then they move by thirds.

These foregoeing observations were wrote out of my Lord Brounckers booke & transcribed by mee Silas Domvill al[ia]s Taylor[.][e]

[fols 48[v]–49[r]]
[*Birchensha's hand*:]

2. Rule. called the Rule of graduall Motion in the vpper part, and of Saltation in the Bass.[f]

of this there are .3. Examples.[6]

---

[a] Altered from *4: Examples.*
[b] i.e. Examples A–E above.
[c] This sentence is in red ink.
[d] Taylor sometimes wrote 'sixth' as 'sixtht', and quite often used such contractions as 6[tht] and 8[tht], as here.
[e] This sentence is in red ink.
[f] In the MS two lines have been erased after the heading.

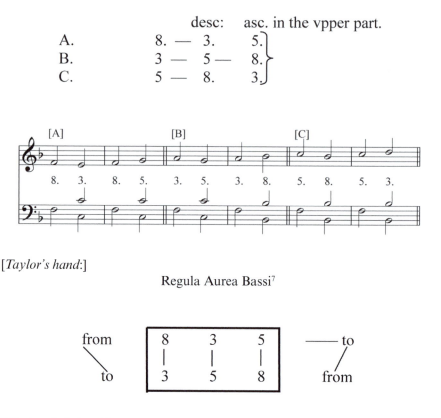

desc: asc. in the vpper part.

A.	8. — 3.	5.
B.	3 — 5 —	8.
C.	5 — 8.	3.

Regula Aurea Bassi[7]

from ↘ to	**8 3 5**	—— to
	│ │ │	
	3 5 8	from ↗

[*Birchensha's hand*:]
But if you make an vpper Part to a Bass, then observe the motion of your Bass, which will either fall a 4th (or rise a 5th) or fall a 5th (or rise a 4th[)].[8]

Bass   4 — 3. or 5.
       5 — .3. [or] 8.

[*Taylor's hand*:]
Thus farre by Mr Birchensha himselfe.[a]

of Graduall motion in the upper part & Saltation in the Basse.[9]

In workeing by this generall Rule (as by all others) you must consider whither you are to make a Basse to an upper part or an upper part to a Basse.

---

[a]   This annotation is in red ink.

When you make a Basse to an upper part: observe

1: The motion of the upper part, which will either descend or ascend a note[.]

2: The first note will be either an 8th. 3[d]. or 5th. & soe will the second note.

3:[a] if you be on the 8th & descend you goe to the 3[d]. & the Basse will fall a 4th (or rise a 5th:)

if you be on the 8th & ascend, you goe to the 5th. & the Basse will fall a 4th. or rise a 5th.

if you be on the 3[d] & descend you goe to the 5th & the Basse will fall a 4th. or rise a 5th.

but if you be on the 3[d] & ascend you goe to the 8th. & the basse will fall a 5th or rise a 4th.

– if you be on the 5th & descend, you goe to the 8th. & the basse will fall a 5th. or rise a 4th.

But if you be on the 5th. & ascend you goe to the 3[d] & the Basse will fall a 5th. or rise a 4th. as in the example.

or briefly thus[:][10]

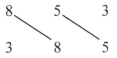

When you make an upper part to a Basse by this Rule observe.

1: if your Basse fall a 4[th] or rise a 5[th]. your first note will be either an 8[th]. or a 3[d]. if it be an 8. then (ad libitum) you may either fall a note & come to the 3[d] or rise a note & come to the 5[th].

But if the first note be a 3[d] you must fall a note in your upper p[ar]t & come to the 5[th].

2: if your Basse fall a 5[th]. or rise a 4. then the first note may either be a 3[d] or 5[th].

if a 3[d] your upper p[ar]t must rise a note & come to your 8.

But if your first note be a 5. then your upper p[ar]t (ad libitum) may fall a note, and come to the 8[th]. or rise a note & come to the 3[d].

These out of my Lord Brounckers booke & others[11] by me Silas Domvil al[ia]s Taylor.[b]

---

a   Paragraph breaks within this item are editorial.

b   This annotation is in red ink.

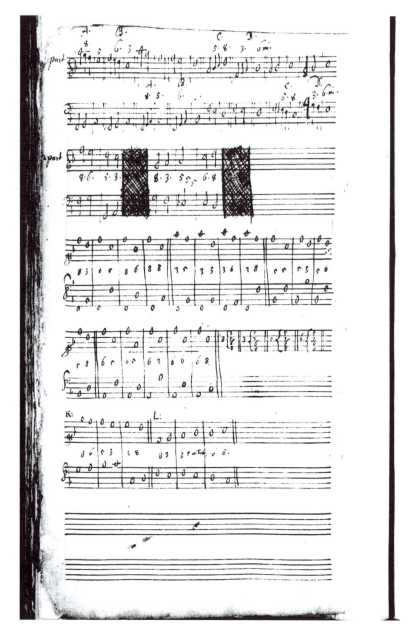

Figure 8.1   Examples of Birchensha's third Rule of Composition from Silas
Taylor's manuscript, showing Birchensha's hand in the upper
two systems and Taylor's in the lower three (London, British
Library, Add. MS 4910, fol. 50ᵛ). © The British Library. All
Rights Reserved.

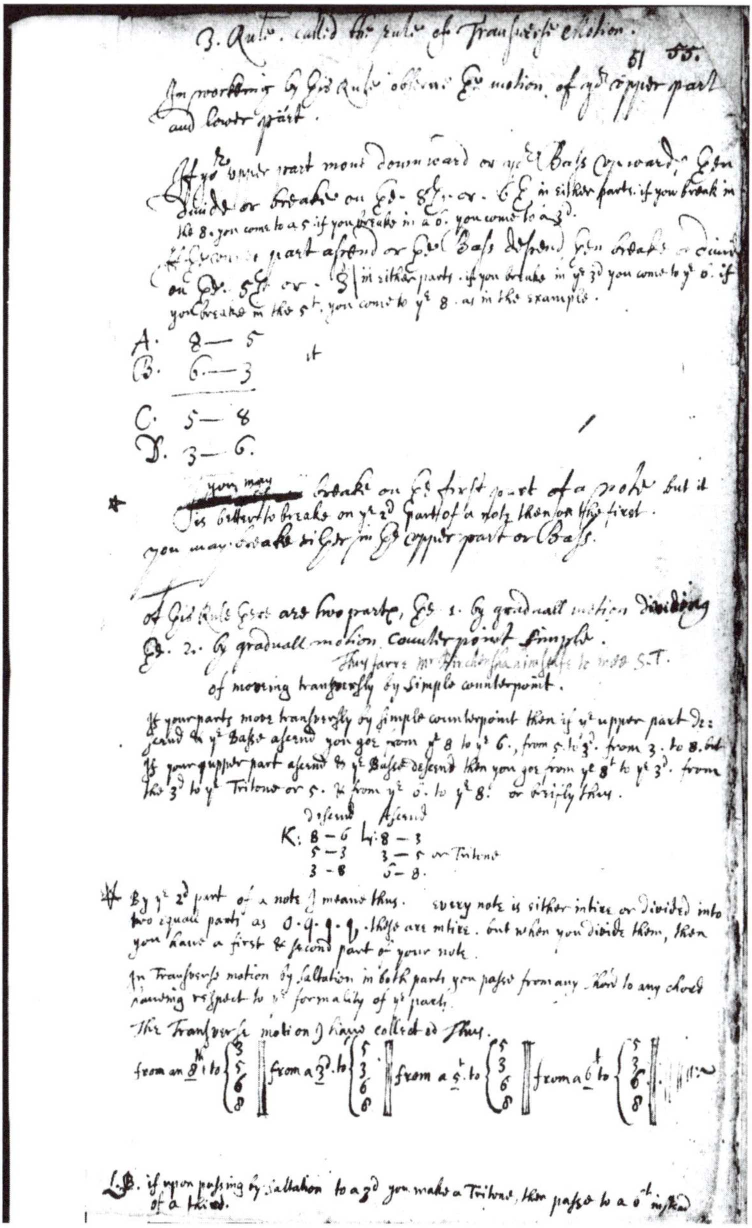

Figure 8.2   Instructions for Birchensha's third Rule of Composition from Silas Taylor's manuscript, the upper portion being in Birchensha's hand and the lower in Taylor's (London, British Library, Add. MS 4910, fol. 51ʳ). © The British Library. All Rights Reserved.

[fols 50ᵛ–51ʳ]
[*Birchensha's hand*:]

3. Rule. called the rule of Transuerse Motion.

In workeing by this Rule observe the motion of your vpper part and lower part.
If your vpper part moue downward or your Bass vpward, then diuide or breake on the .8ᵗʰ. or .6ᵗʰ ⟨in either parts. if you break in the 8. you come to a 5. if you breake in a 6. you come to a 3ᵈ.⟩
If the vpper part ascend or the Bass descend, then breake or diuide on the .5ᵗʰ. or .3ᵈ ⟨in either parts. if you breake in the 3ᵈ you come to the 6. if you breake in the 5ᵗ⁽ʰ⁾. you come to the 8. as in the example.⟩ᵃ

A.	8	—	5
B.	6.	—	3
C.	5	—	8
D.	3	—	6.

⭐ ⟨you may⟩ᵇ breake on the first part of a note ⟨but it is better to breake on the 2ᵈ part of a note then on the first.⟩
you may breake either in the vpper part or Bass.

ᵃ   In this and the preceding paragraph, the interlineated words were added by Taylor.
ᵇ   Illegible words deleted. The star is Taylor's, and points to the starred explanation on p. 233. Both interlineations in this sentence are in Taylor's hand.

Of this Rule there are two parts, the .1. by graduall motion dividing[,] the .2. by graduall motion counterpoint simple.[a]

[*Taylor's hand*:]
Thus farre M[r] Birchensha himselfe to mee S. T.[b]

Of moveing transversly by Simple counterpoint.

If your parts move transversly by Simple counterpoint then if the upper part descend & the Basse ascend you goe from the 8 to the 6., from 5. to 3[d]. from 3. to 8. but
If your upper part ascend & the Basse descend then you goe from the 8[t[h]] to the 3[d]. from the 3[d] to the Tritone or 5. & from the 6. to the 8. or breifly thus.

	descend				Ascend	
K:	8	—	6	L:	8 — 3	
	5	—	3		3 —	5 or Tritone
	3	—	8		6 —	8.

⭐ By the 2[d] part of a note I meane thus. Every note is either intire or divided into two equall parts as ○ ❘ ♩ ❘ ♩ ❘ ♩ ❘ these are intire. but when you divide them, then you have a first & second part of your note.

In Transverse motion by Saltation in both parts you passe from any Chord to any chord haveing respect to the formality of the parts.
The Transverse motion I have collected Thus.[12]

---

[a] In the following example bars 3 and 7 are cancelled in the MS.
[b] This annotation is in red ink.

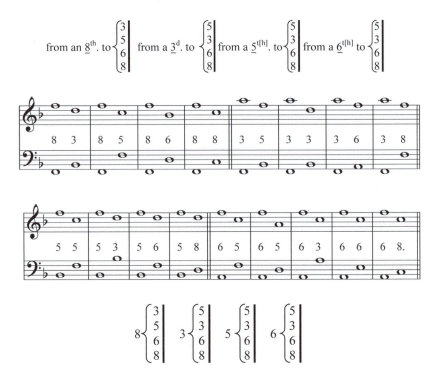

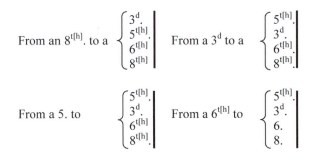

L.B.[a] if upon passing by Saltation to a 3[d] you make a Tritone, then passe
to a 6[t[h]] instead of a third.

[fol. 51[v]]
[*Taylor's hand*:][b]
M[d]: under the 3[d] Rule the Transverse motion is allowed Thus.

From an 8[t[h]]. to a   { 3[d].
                          5[t[h]].
                          6[t[h]].
                          8[t[h]]

From a 3[d] to a   { 5[t[h]].
                      3[d].
                      6[t[h]].
                      8[t[h]].

From a 5. to   { 5[t[h]].
                  3[d].
                  6[t[h]]
                  8[t[h]].

From a 6[t[h]] to   { 5[t[h]].
                       3[d].
                       6.
                       8.

---

[a]   The abbreviation *L.B.* possibly stands for *lege bene*.
[b]   The following table is written in red ink. The abbreviation *M[d]* probably stands
for *Memorandum*.

[fols 52ᵛ–53ʳ]
[*Taylor's hand*:]

4 Rule: called the Rule of Division.

This collected out of Mʳ Birchensha's workes by me Silas Domvill al[ia]s Taylor[.]ᵃ

Division is either in the upper part or Base at the will of the composer
 And that either upon a holding ground or upon a moveing ground[.]

1: upon a holdingᵇ ground upon which the divideing part doth moue
 1: by graduall motion. A.
 2: by Saltation. B
 3: by both mixed. C.ᶜ

2. upon a moueing ground
 Then you must passe from one chord of the ground to another by yourᵈ other rules: thus:
 you must lett your last note of your holding chord passe into the first note of your moveing ground or Subject (whither it bee in the Base or the upper part) by some of your Rules.

[1.] In graduall motion A:
 Note that the first part of the note must be a concord[,] the next or 2ᵈ a discord (which is called a passing discord) untill you come to a 5 & 6. or 6. & 5. & then you have 2 concords together, after which the first part of the note is a discord & the 2ᵈ a concord. Soe that still the discord must ly between two concords[.]ᵉ

 ᵃ This annotation is in red ink.
 ᵇ MS has *moveing*.
 ᶜ In the second bar of Example C, upper part, note 7, the *a'* is possibly a copying error.
 ᵈ *rules* deleted.
 ᵉ In the MS the following example, Example A, is misplaced at the foot of fol. 52ᵛ after Example E.

2. of Saltation in the dividing p[ar]t.

   This is p[er]formed 2. wayes.

   1: when you proceed by concords – B. thus you may proceed from any concord to any concord respect beeing had to the formality of the part.

   2: when you proceed by concords & discords the movement beeing mixed, that is sometimes graduall & sometimes by Saltation as .C.[13]

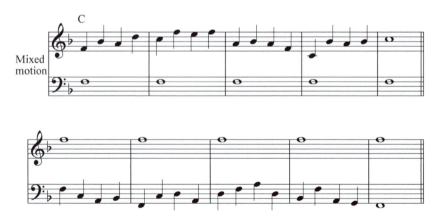

But if the ground or holding notes remove & you continue to breake on any such notes, then you must observe, how your notes doe remove either gradually or by Saltation, & lett your dividing part remove from one note to another by your first, second & third Rules. as – D.

As you must breake upon a holding note soe you must know how to hold upon a breaking note.

breifly – The Ground doth either hold or remove.

If it hold (in Basse or Treble) you move upon it gradually or by Saltation.

If it remove you remove with it according to your other Rules.

If you hold to swift notes, you lay such a note as will hold to diverse of them as .a. & when it will hold noe longer, you then place other notes that will hold as b: and c. in the letter E.[a]

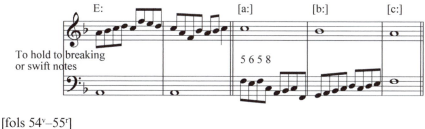

[fols 54ᵛ–55ʳ]
[*Taylor's hand:*]

---

[a]　Taylor mistakenly wrote the letters *a: b: c:* above bars 5–7 of Example A instead of bars 3–5 of Example E, where they are required by the text.

5th Rule: called the Rule of Cadences or of binding discords.

Collected alsoe fr[om M]ʳ B[i]rche[nsha's] workes.[a]

There are in an Octave 3 discords the 2. 4. & 7. & consequently 3 cadences. viz:

> 1: of the 4. & 3.
> 2. of the 7. & 6. major
> 3. of the 2. & 3.

Although these cadences are called finall because they end a Song yet they are alsoe called formall, because they may be taken in any part of a Song.

The forme[s] of the Cadences are these.

1: of the 4. & 3. – A: – the first note is called the binding note which is double (at least) the valew of the second – the second note is called the cadent note which is halfe the value (or sometimes lesse) of the binding note. the 2ᵈ note is a semitone from the first grave. the Basse doth alwaies fall a 5 or rise a 4. if the close be an 8.

2: of the 7. & 6 maj[or] B. – This cadence is formed as the other is, therefore the componist may ad placitum take upon these notes which cadence he pleaseth. The Basse doth fall a chord sometimes a Tone, sometimes a Semitone. you never end a Song with this close, but sometimes a first or 2ᵈ straine thereof, & sometimes it is used for a meane close.

3. of the 2. & 3. – C – This close is of the same forme in the Basse as the closes of the 4. & 3. & 7. & 6. is in some superiour part & endeth in the 8. or 3.

The close of the 4. & 3. doth sometimes end in the 3, but then there is an alteration of the Basse. as in D.
The close of the 4 & 3. dos sometimes end in the 6. minor. then alsoe is the Basse varied. as in E.

---

[a] Annotation in red ink. The paper is damaged at this point.

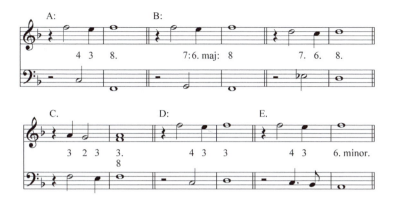

The Cadence may be a Semibr[eve] minim & close. or minim crotchet & close or crotchet quaver & close, but seldome in more minute notes.

The close note (except at the end of a Song) may be of what value you please but at the end of a Song it must be […][a]

---

[a]   The text breaks off at this point.

[fol. 56ᵛ]
[*Taylor's hand:*]

[6. Rule, called the Fuge Rule.]¹⁴

Notes

¹   Other annotations on fol. 39ʳ were made in the eighteenth and nineteenth centuries. These include the figure '3', which refers to the numbering of Sir John Hawkins's gift ('1' being the excerpts from Clüver's *Disquisitiones philosophicæ* at fols 1–10 of this volume, '2' the anonymous treatise on sound at fols 11–38, '3' Taylor's 'Collection of

Rules', and '4' Böhmer's 'Tractat von der Musicalischen Composition' at fols 62–83). Samuel Ayscough, *A Catalogue of the Manuscripts Preserved in the British Museum*, vol. 1, p. 397, shows that these numbers had already been assigned by 1782. Thomas Oliphant (1799–1873) added a brief note in pencil about Taylor ('Silas Taylor wrote the History of Gavel K[ind and] was intimate with Matthew Locke'), with a reference to John Hawkins, *A General History of the Science and Practice of Music* (4 vols, London, 1776), vol. 4, p. 425.

2   Although it is placed first in the manuscript, the 'method' would presumably not have been taught until the student had mastered each of the rules individually. This version of the method should be compared with the more elaborate ones in Corbett's and Withey's manuscripts (see Chapters IX and X).

3   To begin with, the student is taught how to handle conjunct movement in two parts, using only consonant and concinnous intervals. Through the examples, he or she learns that the figure 3 may also represent the interval of a tenth, 5 a twelfth, 6 a thirteenth and 8 a fifteenth, as in figured bass. In order to keep things as simple as possible, none of Birchensha's composition examples uses clefs other than $g'2$ (treble) and $f4$ (bass).

4   Birchensha uses 'tritone' loosely here: strictly speaking, the *semidiapente* or diminished fifth is meant. Unlike the tritone, this is a concinnous interval in his classification (see Chapter III, p. 111).

5   i.e. by leap. Saltation had no place in Rule 1 as originally formulated, but by the time the version given to Lord Brouncker was written it had been admitted. In Corbett's manuscript (see Chapter IX) Birchensha describes Rule 1 not as the 'Rule of graduall Motion both in the upper Part and Bass', but as the 'Rule of Two Parts Ascending or Descending together Gradualy, or by Saltation'.

6   In this rule the upper part is restricted to moving by step. In Example A the harmonic progression is from an octave to a third where the upper part descends, and to a fifth where it ascends; in Example B, from a third to a fifth where it descends, and to an octave where it ascends; in Example C, from a fifth to an octave where it descends, and to a third where it ascends.

7   The 'golden rule of the bass'. This diagram, which encapsulates the harmonic progressions illustrated in the preceding music examples, derives ultimately from one in Campion's *A New Way of Making Fowre Parts in Counter-point* (see Introduction, p. 39). It is drawn mainly in red ink, though the outline of the rectangular frame and the figures are black. The lines connecting the figures in each column indicate the progressions. Thus when the treble part descends the progression may be from octave to third (column 1) or third to fifth (column 2) or fifth to octave (column 3), and when it ascends it may be from third to octave (column 1) or fifth to third (column 2) or octave to fifth (column 3).

8   The meaning of the diagram that follows is that when the bass falls a fourth, the stepwise progression in the upper part is to a third or fifth above it; when it falls a fifth, the progression is to a third or octave above it.

9   This was presumably the title of Rule 2 in Lord Brouncker's book. What follows is essentially an amplification of what has gone before.

10   The diagram that follows is clearly related to the 'Regula Aurea' (see note 7). The two diagonal lines (one running between 5 and 5 and the other between 8 and 8) are not explained in the text, but are probably intended to show how a series of progressions can be constructed by using the diagram. For example, a treble part may ascend by step from a 3 to an 8 (column 1), and from that 8 to a 5 (column 2), and from that 5 to

another 3 (column 3); conversely, it may descend by step from a 3 to a 5 (column 3), and thence to an 8 (column 2), and thence to another 3 (column 1).

[11] Taylor's use of the words 'my Lord Brounckers booke & others' suggests that he may have drawn on other sources of the rules besides Brouncker's. The possibility that these included the book into which Pepys copied Birchensha's 'rules all in fair order' on 27 February 1662 cannot be ruled out; see *The Diary of Samuel Pepys*, vol. 3, p. 37.

[12] Under the heading of 'Transverse motion by saltation in both parts', Birchensha allows consecutive octaves or consecutive fifths in contrary motion even in two-part writing, as the table and music examples show. Such consecutives were also allowed by Simpson, but only in 'composition of many parts' (*A Compendium of Practical Musick*, pp. 41–2). Taylor highlights Birchensha's table on fol. 51^r by using red as well as black ink; the same table also appears in concise form alongside the music example (fol. 50^v), and yet again in red at the foot of fol. 51^v.

[13] The only type of discord occurring on the 'second part of a note' (i.e. unaccented) which Birchensha names is a 'passing discord'; but he seems to have interpreted this term widely so as to include, for example, unaccented discords which are approached or quitted by leap. Since he treated the fourth as a discord in two-part writing, it follows that he would have regarded the second crotchets of bars 1, 3, 4, 6 and 7 in Example C as 'passing discords'. The third crotchet of bar 2 (which makes a seventh with the bass) is an instance of a discord being allowed in a relatively accented position so long as it lies between two concords and is approached and quitted by step.

[14] Though it lacks any heading or explanatory text in the source, the music example is closely related to an illustration of the 'Fuge Rule' found in Corbett's manuscript (see Chapter IX, p. 264). There is therefore no doubt that it is by Birchensha, and that its purpose was to exemplify the last of his '6: Rules of Composition'. The ten lines are of course not intended to be sounded together. Stave 4 is the dux, or leading voice, which introduces the fugue subject. In the manuscript it is distinguished by an index hand, a star and a segno in the left-hand margin. Each of the other nine staves demonstrates a way of bringing in an imitative entry above or below it, and how far the imitation can be maintained. The figure in the margin indicates the interval at which the imitation occurs. Figures above staves 1, 2, 3, 5 and 10 show the interval structure in relation to the leading voice. The cross below stave 7 (bar 4) is not explained. Perhaps it was really meant to apply to stave 8, where the imitation breaks down prematurely.

IX

Rules of Composition, II:
William Corbett's Manuscript

Editorial Note

The second source of the 'Rules of Composition' – Brussels, Bibliothèque Royale de Belgique, MS II 4168 Mus. (formerly Fétis 6689) – valuably supplements and illuminates Silas Taylor's manuscript. For convenience we call it William Corbett's manuscript, although Corbett was not the original owner. It is a musical notebook made up of 12 unruled leaves, followed by 33 leaves ruled with a rastrum to give eight five-line staves to a page, and a final unruled leaf. Each leaf measures approximately 270 × 210 mm. The book was used from both ends, and is almost wholly autograph. At the unruled front end are 'A Table to find out all Consonant and Dissonant Intervals in an Octave' (fol. 2), a list of 'Things Necessary to be Observed by those who Compose by my Rules' (fol. 3) and a 'Method' for applying the rules (fol. 4). At the reverse end are the rules themselves (fols 46^r–38^v inverted), the text of each rule generally being written on the left-hand page of an opening and the music examples relating to it on the right-hand page. To conclude, there is a section illustrating how examples of Rules 1–4 may be 'Composed into 4 Parts' (fols 37^r–35^r inverted). Approximately half the pages in the book remained unused.

Despite having been in the Bibliothèque Royale since 1872, this important and well-preserved source of the rules has received surprisingly little attention from scholars.[1] The handwriting ranges from the formal calligraphy of the table of intervals (see Figure 9.1) to casual additions that were perhaps dashed off in the course of a lesson.[2] For the most part, however, Birchensha worked neatly and carefully, writing his instructions in a predominantly italic script and his examples in a clear, firm music hand. The manuscript is unlikely to have been a master copy intended for his personal use, and was almost certainly made for a student. There is no indication of when it was written, or for whom, but certain features suggest a date between about 1667 and 1672. It is noticeable that the numbering of the rules has undergone revision since Lord Brouncker's version (transmitted by Silas Taylor) was written, with the 'Rule of Binding Cadences' here becoming Rule 4 and the 'Rule of Division' Rule 5. The section of Rule 3 concerned with transverse motion by saltation is more systematically treated than in Taylor's manuscript, while the 'Method' for composing by the rules has become distinctly more sophisticated. The publication in 1667 of Simpson's *Compendium of Practical Musick* may have prompted Birchensha to include instructions for composing a two-part canon. At the same time, there are distinct points in common between this manuscript and the autograph of the 'Compendious Discourse'. Birchensha uses the same simple and distinctive form of treble clef here as he does there (see Figure 9.3), and the tables of intervals in the two manuscripts are strikingly similar.

The earliest evidence of specific ownership is a dated signature on fol. 1, followed by a title (apparently in the same hand): 'Will: Corbett his Booke 1695 / – / Berkinshaw / Rules of Composition'. This owner may confidently be identified as the violinist, composer and collector William Corbett (1680?– 1748).[3] Corbett's family belonged to the parish of St Margaret's, Westminster, where a 'Will[ia]m Corbett' was baptized on 18 July 1680. Assuming that this child was the musician, he would have been about 15 years old when he signed the Birchensha manuscript. Nothing is known of Corbett's musical education, but Peter Holman has credibly conjectured that he may have studied in London during the 1690s with Gottfried Finger.[4] His acquisition of the manuscript was perhaps prompted more by curiosity and a general interest in the craft of composition than by a resolve to follow Birchensha's rules. Corbett was evidently a precocious musician. On 17 March 1698/9, aged 18, he held his first benefit concert at York Buildings, the fashionable concert hall in Villiers Street (close to where Pepys was then living). By January 1699/1700 he was writing music for Thomas Betterton's theatre company at Lincoln's Inn Fields, and in 1700 his Opus 1, *XII Sonate à Tre*, was engraved by the Amsterdam firm of Estienne Roger.[5] When the Queen's Theatre, Haymarket, opened in April 1705 he was appointed leader of the band, and from 1709 until his death he was a member of the royal Private Music, continuing to draw pay despite long absences in Italy. It is not known how long the manuscript of Birchensha's rules remained in Corbett's possession. Possibly it was one of the items in a 'choice collection' put up for auction 'at his lodgings near the Nag's Head Inn in Orange Court' on 16 May 1724, which according to an announcement in the *Daily Journal* included 'valuable books on the Theory of Musick' as well as violins by Amati, Maggini, Stainer and Stradivari, a spinet by Celestini and 'several hundreds of original Manuscripts' of music 'never heard or seen in England'.[6]

Later in the eighteenth century the manuscript found its way into the library of one of the earls of Donegall – most likely Arthur Chichester (1739– 99), the fifth Earl and first Marquess, who was an avid book-collector. It may have been he who gave it its brown leather binding, which is stamped on the spine in gold letters: 'J. BIRCHENSHA / RULES OF COMPOSITION / MSS. ORIGINAL'.[7] Pasted on the marbled endpaper inside the front cover is the earl's engraved armorial bookplate. The book must therefore have been bound before 1791, when the earldom was raised to a marquessate. In 1851 it was bought by the musicologist François-Joseph Fétis from Calkin & Budd, the antiquarian booksellers, whose shop was at 118 Pall Mall, London; the Bibliothèque Royale acquired it with the rest of Fétis's library in 1872.[8]

In the edition that follows, some double-page openings in the manuscript have been treated as single units in order to allow musical examples to be juxtaposed with the relevant text.

Notes

[1]   Robert Eitner was one of the few to notice it, in his *Biographisch-Bibliographisches Quellen-Lexikon der Musiker und Musikgelehrten* (10 vols, Leipzig, 1900–04; 2nd edn, Graz, 1959), vol. 2, pp. 49–50. For a preliminary survey of its significance, see Christopher D.S. Field, 'Birchensha's "Mathematical Way of Composure"', in *Music, Ireland and the Seventeenth Century*, ed. Barra Boydell and Kerry Houston (*Irish Musical Studies*, 10; Dublin, 2009), pp. 108–34.

[2]   Material written in styles markedly different from the autograph hand normally used in this manuscript is found on fols 42^r, 38^v and 37^r (three music examples almost certainly written by the same person, one of which is closely related to the 'Fuge' example in Taylor's manuscript), and on fol. 41^r (supplementary notes on syncopation, with additional music examples). Birchensha's chameleon-like ability to vary his script makes it difficult to be sure that any or all of these were written by him; but their content suggests that they probably were.

[3]   A later example of Corbett's signature may be found in a letter (London, British Library, Add. MS 23782, fols 23–4) that he wrote from Milan on 13 June 1731 to Sir Thomas Robinson, the British Ambassador in Vienna, about the abscondence of his wife (the singer Anna Lodi, née Signoni) and their 18-year-old daughter.

[4]   See Holman's introduction to the facsimile edition of Corbett's *XII Sonate à Tre*, Op. 1 (Alston, 2003). Information on Corbett's life and compositions is to be found in Philip H. Highfill, Kalman A. Burnim and Edward A. Langhans, *A Biographical Dictionary of Actors, Actresses, Musicians, Dancers, Managers and Other Stage Personnel in London, 1600–1800* (16 vols, Carbondale and Edwardsville, IL, 1973–93), vol. 3, pp. 487–90; Owain Edwards, 'Espionage, a Collection of Violins, and *Le Bizzarie Universali*: A Fresh Look at William Corbett', *The Musical Quarterly*, 73 (1989): 320–43; *A Biographical Dictionary of English Court Musicians 1485–1714*, compiled by Andrew Ashbee and David Lasocki assisted by Peter Holman and Fiona Kisby (2 vols, Aldershot, Brookfield, VT, Singapore and Sydney, 1998), vol. 1, pp. 299–302; Owain Edwards, 'William Corbett', in *The New Grove Dictionary of Music and Musicians*, 2nd edn, ed. Stanley Sadie (29 vols, London, 2001), vol. 6, p. 446.

[5]   The title-page is dated 1700, although it was not until 18 August 1702 that Corbett's sonatas were advertised for sale by Roger's London agent Francis Vaillant, along with other music 'lately brought over from Amsterdam'. The work was dedicated to William, fourth Baron Byron (1669–1736), a Gentleman of the Bedchamber to Prince George of Denmark and an amateur composer and violinist.

[6]   The advertisement is reprinted in William Henry Hill, Arthur F. Hill and Alfred Ebsworth Hill, *Antonio Stradivari: His Life and Work (1644–1737)* (London, 1902; reissued Great Missenden, 1980), pp. 251–2. Corbett held a further 'sale of curious compositions and musical instruments' in March 1741, and there is a detailed

inventory of the instruments, music and pictures which he left to Gresham College in his will, dated 3 March 1747; after the college rejected his bequest, the music books and manuscripts were auctioned 'at his house in Silver-street, Golden-square' in 1751.

[7]   Information kindly provided by Marie Cornaz, head of the Music department at the Bibliothèque Royale.

[8]   François-Joseph Fétis, *Biographie universelle des musiciens*, 2nd edn (8 vols, Paris, 1860–65), vol. 1, pp. 422–3; *Catalogue de la bibliothèque de F.-J. Fétis acquise par l'état belge* (Brussels, 1877), no. 6689.

Edition

[fol. 2^r]

A Table to find out all Consonant and Dissonant Intervalls in an Octaue, both Ascending, and Descending.[a,1]

[see Table on p. 249]

Per Johannem Birchensha

[fol. 3^r]

Diverse Things Necessary to be Observed by those who Compose by my Rules.

1[.] There are in the Scale of Musick 7 natural Keyes.[b,2] of which
Two are flatt. as C F
Two are sharp. as B E
Three are Perfect. as A D G
By thes audible qualities of Sounds, the greater & Lesser seconds: thirds: fourths: fifths: sixes: & eights are known.[3]

2[.] Sharp notes are the greater vpward: & the Lesser downward:
Flatt notes are the greater downward: & the Lesser vpward.[4]
The 2^d Aboue is a 7th below – A 2^d below is a 7th aboue.
The 3^d Aboue is a 6th below – A 3^d below is a 6th aboue.
The 4th Aboue is a 5th below – A 4th below is a 5th aboue.

3[.] When 2 notes of the same Value com together, (as ♬ ♩♩ &c) the first is the first part of the Note: & the 2^d is the second Part thereof.
an intire Note, as ♩ ♩ ♩ &[c,] may be Imagined to be so divided.[5]

4[.] Marks in my pricking[6]
T. signifieth a Tone or whole Note
S. a Semitone or Lesser half Note
A. an Apotome or greater half Note

---

^a   Birchensha wrote the heading in a formal 'engrossing' hand, and his name in calligraphic italic script. In the table itself the columns and rows are separated by vertical and horizontal lines ruled in red ink. An entire row, running from E to e, was accidentally omitted; it is supplied editorially here.
^b   The MS has 7ⁿ (for 'seven').

A Table to find out all Consonant and Dissonant Intervalls in an Octaue, both Ascending, and Descending.

Vnison	2ᵐⁱ	2ᵐᵃ	3ᵐⁱ	3ᵐᵃ	4ᵃ perfect	5ᵐⁱ	4ᵐᵃ	5ᵃ perfect	6ᵐⁱ	6ᵐᵃ	7ᵐⁱ	8ᵐⁱ	7ᵐᵃ	8ᵃ
A	Bb	B	c	c#	D	Eb	D#	E	F	F#	G	ab	G#	a
Bb	cb	c	Db	D	Fb	Fb	E	F	Gb	G	ab	bbb	a	bb
B	C	C#	D	D#	E	F	E#	F#	G	G#	a	bb	a#	b
C	Db	D	Eb	E	F	Gb	F#	G	ab	a	bb	cb	b	c
C#	D	D#	E	E#	F#	G	F#	G#	a	a#	b	c	b#	c#
D	Eb	E	F	F#	G	ab	G#	a	bb	b	c	db	c#	d
Eb	Fb	F	Gb	G	ab	bbb	a	bb	cb	c	db	ebb	d	eb
F	Gb	G	ab	a	bb	cb	b	c	db	d	eb	fb	e	f
F#	G	G#	a	a#	b	c	b#	c#	d	d#	e	f	e#	f#
G	ab	a	bb	b	c	db	c#	d	eb	e	f	gb	f#	g
ab	bbb	bb	cb	c	db	ebb	d	eb	fb	f	gb	aabb	g	aab
a	bb	b	c	c#	d	eb	d#	e	f	f#	g	aab	g#	aa
Vnison	7ᵐᵃ	7ᵐⁱ	6ᵐᵃ	6ᵐⁱ	5ᵃ perfect	4ᵐᵃ	5ᵐⁱ	4ᵃ perfect	3ᵐᵃ	3ᵐⁱ	2ᵐᵃ	Apotome =	2ᵐⁱ	8ᵃ

Per Johannem Birchensha

Figure 9.1　'Table to find out all Consonant and Dissonant Intervalls in an Octave', from William Corbett's manuscript (Brussels, Bibliothèque Royale de Belgique, MS II 4168 Mus., fol. 2ʳ). Compare Figure 3.8. Autograph. By permission of the Bibliothèque Royale de Belgique.

Vnison	2 mi	2 ma	3 mi	3 ma	4ᵃ perfect	5ᵃ mi	4ᵃ ma	5ᵃ perfect	6 mi	6 ma	7ᵃ mi	8 mi	7 ma	8ᵃ
A	B♭	B	C	C#	D	E♭	D#	E	F	F#	G	a♭	G#	a
B♭	C♭	C	D♭	D	E♭	F♭	E	F	G♭	G	a♭	b♭♭	a	b♭
B♭	C	C#	D	D#	E	F	E#	F#	G	G#	a	b♭	a#	b
C	D♭	D	E♭	E	F	G♭	F#	G	a♭	a	b♭	c♭	b	c
C#	D	D#	E	E#	F#	G	F✕	G#	a	a#	b	c	b#	c#
D	E♭	E	F	F#	G	a♭	G#	a	b♭	b	c	d♭	c#	d
E♭	F♭	F	G♭	G	a♭	b♭♭	a	b♭	c♭	c	d♭	e♭♭	d	e♭
[E	F	F#	G	G#	a	b♭	a#	b	c	c#	d	e♭	d#	e]
F	G♭	G	a♭	a	b♭	c♭	b	c	d♭	d	e♭	f♭	e	f
F#	G	G#	a	a#	b	c	b#	c#	d	d#	e	f	e#	f#
G	a♭	a	b♭	b	c	d♭	c#	d	e♭	e	f	g♭	f#	g
a♭	b♭♭	b♭	c♭	c	d♭	e♭♭	d	e♭	f♭	f	g♭	aa♭♭	g	aa♭
a	b♭	b	c	c#	d	e♭	d#	e	f	f#	g	aa♭	g#	aa
Vnison	7 ma	7 mi	6 ma	6 mi	5ᵃ perfect	4ᵃ ma:	5 mi	4ᵃ perfect	3 ma	3 mi	2 ma	Apotome	2 mi	8ᵃ

S_{pen}D. Semidiapente, or the Lesser fifth
Tri: Tritonus or the greater fourth
S_{pa:}D. Semidiapason, or the Lesser Eighth.

[fol. 3ᵛ]
5[.] After gradual Motion Ascending, you must not ascend by Saltation.[7] – A
    After gradual Motion Descending, you [must] not descend by Saltation.
– B.
    After saltation Ascending, you must not ascend by gradual Motion. – C
    After saltation descending, you must not descend by gradual Motion. D
as in the Example

If you work contrary to this Observation, you must do it very warily.

6[.] The Closes of the Examples of All your Rules must be on the first Part of
a Note, except the Closes of the Example of the 2ᵈ Rule, which may be either
vpon the first or second part of a Note.

[fol. 4ʳ]

Method[8]

1. Work by your Fuge Rule.
2. By your Cadence Rule.
3. By the 2ᵈ & 3ᵈ Examples of your first Rule[.]
4. By the Transverse Rule Counterpoint. viz. 6 mi[nor]. 8. 3 ma[jor]. (in sharp
Keyes:) and 6 ma[jor]. 8. 3 mi[nor]. in flatt Keyes[.]
5. By your Transverse Rule Breaking.
6. By your 2ᵈ Rule.
7. By the first Exa[mple] of the first Rule[.][9]
8. By the Transverse Counterpoint. viz. 5. 3. 8. ⟨tr[eble] desc[ending]⟩ or 8. 3.
5. ⟨tr[eble] asc[ending].⟩

    But when you see the form of the fifth Rule, and haue an Occasion to
Breake an holding Note, or hold to many Notes: when you see any Chromatic
Notes: or Syncopation: or Prickd Notes: you may work on them either before
or after your designed Method. that is, after you haue brought in your fuge;
and put down your Cadences.[10]

4

Method

1. Work by your Fuge Rule.
2. By yo(r) Cadence Rule.
3. By the 2(d) & 3(d) Examples of yo(r) first Rule.
4. By the Transverse Rule Counterpoint. viz. 6.8.3. (in sharp Keys:) and 6.8.3. in flatt Keys
5. By yo(r) Transverse Rule Breaking.
6. By yo(r) 2(d) Rule.
7. By the first Exa: of the first Rule
8. By the Transverse Counterpoint. viz. 5.3.8. or 8.3.5.

But when you see the form of the fifth Rule, and have an Occasion to Breake an holding note, or hold to many Notes: when you see any Chromatic notes: or Syncopation: or Prickd Notes: you may work on them either before or after yo(r) designed Method. that is, after you have brought in yo(r) fuges and put down yo(r) Cadences.

When to Alter what you have wrought by your Method.

1. When you are brought to y(e) 3(d) or 6 mi. instead of y(e) 3(d) & 6ma: or y(e) contrary.
2. When you are brought to a 8: midiapent, or Triton: instead of a full 5(th) & 4(th)
3. When you fall or rise a 5 D. or Tri: instead of a 5(th) or 4(th) in the same Part.
4. When you are brought too soon to the same note, or chord.
5. When you are brought out of yo(r) Key, or Ayre.
6. When you are brought to a note that cannot will be exprest'd by y(e) voice or hand.

Upon these, and like occasion you may forsake yo(r) designed Order, or Method, & work by any Rule w(ch) will avoid these things, w(ch) you will find out by passing through yo(r) Rules in order. w(ch) you are to go over, & over; untill you have compl-ted, & fill'd up yo(r) song.

Figure 9.2   Birchensha's 'Method' for composing by his Rules, from William Corbett's manuscript (Brussels, Bibliothèque Royale de Belgique, MS II 4168 Mus., fol. 4r). Autograph. By permission of the Bibliothèque Royale de Belgique.

When to Alter what you haue wrought by your Method.

1. When you are brought to the 3ᵈ or 6 mi. insteade of the 3ᵈ & 6 ma: or the contrary.
2. When you are brought to a Semidiapente ⟨5 mi⟩, or Tritone ⟨4 ma.⟩, instead of a full 5ᵗʰ. & 4ᵗʰ ⟨betwene the parts⟩[.]
3. When you fall or rise a S~pen~D. or Tri: in stead of a 5ᵗʰ or 4ᵗʰ. in the same Part.
4. When you are brought too soon to the same Note, or chord.
5. When you are brought out of your Key, or Ayre.
6. When you are brought to a note that cannot well be express'd by the Voice or hand.

Vpon these, and like occasion you may forsake your designed Order, or Method, & work by any Rule which will avoid these things, which you will find out by pass⟨ing⟩ through your Rules in order. which you are to go over, & over; vntill you haue completed, & fill'd vp your song.

[fols 46ʳ–45ᵛ inv.]

First Rule.
Of Two Parts Ascending or De[s]cending together Gradualy. or   A.
By Saltation   B.

When the Parts Ascend & Descend gradually, there are 3 Notes in every Example. the first is the Preparatory Note. The 2ᵈ is the Example of the Rule: And the Thirdᵃ is the Close Note.
    In this, & in All the other Rules, you are to Obserue
    The form of the Treble & Bass in every Example.
    The Relation of the Parts.
    The Notes marked with. S. T.¹¹
    The Variation of the Examples. marked thusᵇ

ᵃ   MS has *Thrid*.

ᵇ   In the MS there is an index hand at this point, matching that in the following example.

When the Parts Ascend or Descend together by Saltation, they Moue either by 3ds or 6 mi[nor]. according as they Lye most convenient for the Composers purpose. as in the example

The Rules are never Varied but vpon som extraordinary Occasion, as to bring in, or maintaine a fuge: to avoid coming too often to a Note; or to the like chord &c[.]

[fol. 45ʳ inv.]

Second Rule
When the vpper Part moveth Gradualy,
& the Bass by Saltation.

In this Rule there are three Examples,

Every Example doth Ascend & Descend.

In every Example there are but two Notes.

The first Note is the Example of the Rule[.]

The second Note is the close, or coming to note[.]

The first note of the first Example both ascending & descending, is an 8ᵗʰ[.]

The first note of the 2ᵈ ex[ample] both asc[ending] & desc[ending] is a 3ᵈ.

The first Note of the 3ᵈ ex[ample] both Ascend[ing] & desc[ending] is a 5ᵗʰ.

The vpper part descends or ascends to the next Key, as in the Example.

The Lower Part descends a 4ᵗʰ three times: & a 5ᵗʰ three times. as in the Example.

The Parts are thus Related.

In the first ex[ample] desc[ending]. The first note is an 8ᵗʰ. it desc[ends] in the Tre[ble] a Semito[ne] & comes to a 3ᵈ. ma[.] the Bass falleth a 4ᵗʰ or Riseth a 5ᵗʰ.[12]

In the first ex[ample] asc[ending] The first note is an 8ᵗʰ. it asc[ends] a Tone, and coms to a 5ᵗʰ. the Bass falls a 4ᵗʰ[.]

In the second ex[ample] desc[ending] the first note is a 3ᵈ ma: it desc[ends] a To[ne] & coms to the 5ᵗʰ. the Bass falls a 4ᵗʰ[.]

In the 2ᵈ ex[ample] asc[ending] the first note is a 3ᵈ ma: it asc[ends] a se[mitone] & coms to the 8ᵗʰ. the Bass falls a 5ᵗʰ[.]

In the 3ᵈ ex[ample] desc[ending] the first Note is a 5ᵗʰ. it desc[ends] a To[ne] & coms to the 8ᵗʰ. the Bass falls a 5ᵗʰ[.]

In the 3ᵈ ex[ample] asc[ending] the first Note is a 5ᵗʰ. it asc[ends] a To[ne] and coms to the 3ᵈ ma. the Bass falls a 5ᵗʰ[.]

[fol. 44ᵛ inv.]

[fol. 44ʳ inv.]

Third Rule, called the Transverse Rule.¹³ which is
By Breaking
By Counterpoint
By Saltation

By Breaking

In the Breaking Part there are 3 notes. viz the Preparatory Note: the Example of the Rule: & the Close, or coming to Note.

When the Treble Descends, you breake in 8ᵗʰ, & com to the 5ᵗʰ: or in the 6ᵗʰ ma: & com to the 3ᵈ ma: either in the Treble or Bass. the Breaking is always on the second Part of a Note. as in the [first] Example.

The holding Part is of Intire Notes.

When the Treble Ascends you breake on the 3ᵈ maior, & com to the 6 mi. or on the 5ᵗʰ & com to the 8ᵗʰ. or on the 7ᵗʰ & com to the 3ᵈ mi. [as in the second Example.]

The first 2 notes of the Breaking Part, are of Equal or Equivalent value to the note Broken vpon.

You never break on the 7ᵗʰ but onᵃ som extraordinary ⟨occasion⟩. As to avoid 8ᵗʰˢ or fifths: coming to a discord, or too often to the same Note or chord: to maintaine the Point: &c.

[fol. 43ᵛ inv.]

   1st ex[ample,] tr[eble] desc[ending]

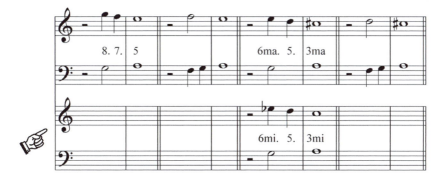

ᵃ   MS has *but vpon but on.*

2nd ex[ample,] tr[eble] asc[ending]

[fols 43^r–42^v inv.]^a

Third Rule, Transvers & counterpoint.

When you work transversly & by Counterpoint, you go
  (when the Treble descends)
        from the 5th to the 3^d
        from the 3^d to the 8th
        from the 8th to the 6th
  when the Treble ascends. you go
        from the 6th to the 8th
        from the 8th to the 3^d
        from the 3^d to the 5th
When the treble ascends, & the Bass descends the greater 3^d, then you go

---

   ^{a} At the foot of fol. 44^r inv. Birchensha wrote *verte fol[iu]m* to indicate that Rule 3 continues overleaf.

6 mi. 8. & third maior, in sharp keyes. but
when the treble ascends, & the Bass descend the Lesser 3[d]. then you go:
6 ma: 8[th]. & 3[d] minor, in flat Keyes.
But seldom work transversly & counterpoint, between the treble & Bass when
the treble descends: but to mayntaine [a] fuge,[a] or on som great occasion[.]

Transver[s]e & counterpoint Tr[eble] descending & Ascending, gradually[b]

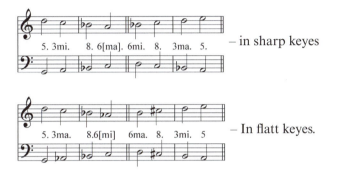

– in sharp keyes

– In flatt keyes.

Third Rule Transvers & by Saltation

When you work Transversly & by Saltation then ⟨you⟩ may go from any
concord to any concord that is most convenient for you. as in the Example[.][14]

Transverse & counterpoint, Tr[eble] Ascend[ing] & [Bass] desce[nding] by
Saltation

---

[a] MS has *& fuge.*
[b] In the second and sixth bars the MS interchanges *6 mi* and *6 ma.*

[fols 42ʳ–41ᵛ inv.]

Fourth Rule of Binding Cadences.

There be 3 Binding Cadences[:]

1. of the 4ᵗʰ & 3 ma[jor]

2. of the 7ᵗʰ & 6 ma[jor]   These cadence[s] are alwaies in the
                                    vpper Part

3. of the 2 ma[jor] & 3ᵈ minor —   this cadence is alwaies in the Bass
                                    Part or som Lower Part.

The cadence of the 4ᵗʰ. ends in the 8. 6 mi[nor]. or 3ᵈ
The cadence of the 7ᵗʰ. ends in the 8. or 6 mi[nor]
The cadence of the 2ᵈ. ends in the 8. or 3ᵈ.

In the cadent Part there are 3 Notes[:]
1. The Binding Note. which is more then the value of the Cadent Note[15]
2. The cadent note. which is the next key below the bynding note
3. The close note[.] which stands in the place of the Binding note

In the cadence of the 4ᵗʰ. the Bass falleth a 5ᵗʰ[.]
In the cadence of the 7ᵗʰ. the Bass descends to the next Key.
In the cadence of the 2ᵈ. the Bass hath the form of the treble, in the cadence of
the 7ᵗʰ & 6ᵗʰ. and the treble hath the form of the Bass.

The first Part of the Binding note may be what concord you please[.]

The form of all the Cadence Parts is the sam[e.][a]

---

[a]   An index hand at the end of the next example guides the reader to a supplementary example of 'binding cadences' at the foot of fol. 42ʳ, which in this edition appears after the other examples of the Fourth Rule. Both the index hand and the supplementary example were later additions.

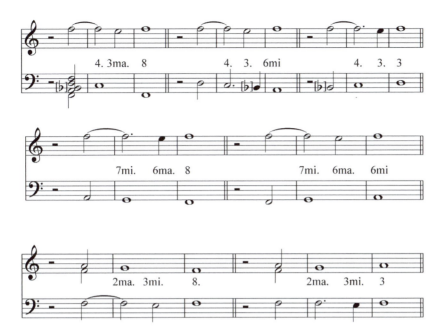

There are two Cadences of use[a] in Instrumentall Musick.

1. A Breaking cadence.
2. A Dragging Cadence[.][16]

Example. of ⟨Binding⟩ Cadence[s:][17]

---

[a] MS has *out of use*.

[fols 41^r–40^v inv.]

Fifth Rule called the Divideing Rule.

1. By Graduall Motion – A.

2. By Saltation & gradual Motion mix'd – B.

3. By chromatick notes. – C.

4. By Sy[n]copation graduall & saltation. – D[.]

When you divide by graduall motion, you must lay the Discord between two concord[s]: both when the Discord is the first & second Part of the Note.[18]

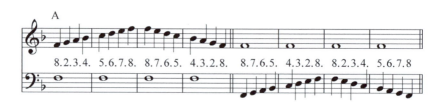

When you divide by saltation, you may Go from any concord to any Concord on[a] the second part of a note, provided that a concord follow it.[19] but it is best to divide, somtimes gradually, & somtimes by saltation.

---

[a] MS has *or.*

Chromatick notes are born out by a 3[d] or 6th. either holding: or by saltation as in the Example.

[Syncopation, gradual and by saltation.]

Syncope which belongeth to the 5[th] Rule.[20]
When the vpper part ascendeth and is the Syncope and the Bass the intire no[te] you clime by a 5[th] and a 6[th] and may Com of[f] as in the example[;]
but when the vpper part de[s]cendeth and is the Syncope part then you goe by a 6[th] and a 5[th] and may close as in the ex[ample] or wher you please, so it be by som [?rule.][a]

---

[a]   The binding of the MS is tight at this point, making the text difficult to read in this and the next paragraph.

When the vpper part ascendeth by Intire notes & the Bass [is] the Syncope you ascend by 6 [& 5,] but when the upper part d[es]cendeth by Intire notes you proceed by a 5th and a 6th[:]

[fols 40^r–39^v inv.]

Of Pricked notes

Pricked notes[21] are somtimes expressed by a Note bound as [=]

Somtimes the Parts com in together, & then they moue by 3^{ds}[.]
Somtimes they com in after a crochet[,] somtimes after a minim ⟨& crochet⟩ Rest. as in the Example.[22]

so that 4 part[s] may moue by Prickd notes, driueing by way of a fuge.

[fols 39ʳ–38ᵛ inv.]

Of the fuge Rule.

A fuge or Point is, when one Part leads and an other part followeth in the same or some other Key.

The fuge may com in at what Distance the Musician pleaseth as after a

♩　　♩　　♩·　　○ or at any other further Distance.

The fuge may com in vpon an 8. 3ᵈ. 5. or 6 mi[.][23]

The[a] fuge is best followed in the 8. 4. or 5th.[24] next in the 3. 6. 7. & 2ᵈ[.]

The fuge should be followed before the Point do end.

If you continue a fuge, do thus. Prick out the fuge in the following Part; in what Key you please: & at what Distance you will. Then make Discant to the fuge so prick'd out. Then prick out that Discant: and so proceed as long as you please.[25]

If a Subiect or Song be made, bring in the point where the discant will, & so long continue it, that is, so long as the Discant will beare it: as in the example[b,26]

If you intend not to make a perfect Canon, you may break off the fuge when you please: & bring it in againe where the discant will beare it.

Somtime the Movement of the fuge may be imitated, although the point be not directly followed.[27]

---

[a]　*The best distance*, followed by two or three more illegible words, deleted.

[b]　In the MS there is an index hand at this point, matching that in the following example.

[fol. 37ʳ inv.]

In the following Leafes you have all your Rules & their Examples composed into 4 Parts. But if any of those midle Parts faile you then work by an other Rule.[a]

[fol. 36ᵛ inv.]

1 Rule.[28]

---

[a] Written in Birchensha's 'engrossing' hand.

[fol. 37ʳ inv.]

[fol. 36ʳ inv.]

2 Rule[29]

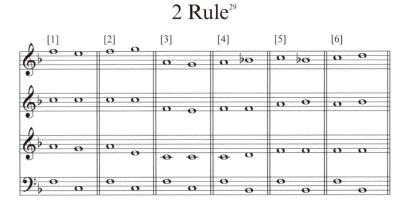

3 Rule. Transverse & Breaking[:] Treble Desc[ending][30]

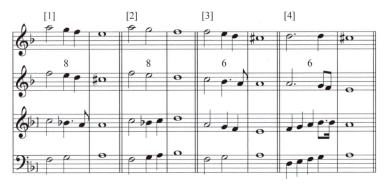

Figure 9.3   Examples of Birchensha's second and third Rules of Composition 'composed into 4 Parts', from William Corbett's manuscript (Brussels, Bibliothèque Royale de Belgique, MS II 4168 Mus., fol. 36ʳ). Compare Figure 8.1. Autograph. By permission of the Bibliothèque Royale de Belgique.

[fol. 35ᵛ inv.]

3 [Rule.] Transverse & Breaking[:] Treble Ascending[31]

[3ʳᵈ Rule. Transverse & Counterpoint][32]

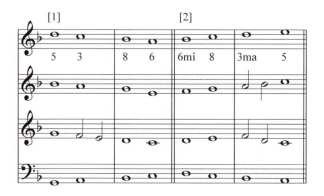

[fol. 35ʳ inv.]

4 Rule of Binding Cadences[33]

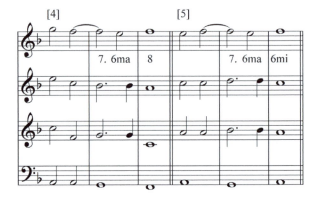

Notes

[1] A similar table of intervals appears in the 'Compendious Discourse' (Practical Part, chapter 13), the main differences being in the names attached to some of the intervals. Instead of 'Se[mi]-Diapente' for the diminished fifth, Birchensha here writes '5 mi[nor]'; instead of 'Tritonus' for the augmented fourth, he writes '4ᵃ ma[jor]'; and instead of 'Se[mi]-Diapason' for the diminished octave, he writes '8 mi[nor]'. (Somewhat inconsistently, on the very next leaf he does use the terms 'Semidiapente', 'Tritonus' and 'Semidiapason', even assigning an abbreviation to each of them.) In row 5, column 8, he employs a special sign for the double sharp, exactly as in the 'Compendious Discourse' (see Figure 9.1).

[2] Compare the 'Compendious Discourse', Practical Part, chapter 2 (see p. 101). The 'natural Keyes' ('natural' as opposed to 'fict') are the uninflected notes A B C D E F G.

C and F are regarded as flat because only a semitone separates them from their lower neighbours B and E; conversely, B and E are regarded as sharp because only a semitone separates them from their upper neighbours C and F.

3 It is not clear why sevenths are not included in this list.

4 Birchensha here considers inversion of intervals. For example, F♯ makes a greater (i.e. major) third with the D below, but a lesser (i.e. minor) sixth with the D above; whereas B♭ makes a major third with the D above, but a minor sixth with the D below.

5 The concept of any 'entire note' being divisible into two parts is important to Birchensha's teaching of passing-note discords, cadential suspensions and rhythmic structure generally. It should not be assumed that the 'first part' of a note always carries the greater stress, however. In cadential suspensions, where the pupil learns that the 'first part of the Binding note may be what concord you please', it is the second, discordant part of the note that falls on an accented part of the measure, as the examples of Rule 4 show.

6 To a greater extent than in Silas Taylor's manuscript, Birchensha is at pains to distinguish between the diatonic 'Semitone or Lesser half Note' and the chromatic 'Apotome or greater half Note' and between the 'Semidiapente' and the 'Tritonus', thus emphasizing the Pythagorean basis of his teaching.

7 'Gradual Motion' (literally 'movement by step') and 'Saltation' ('leaping') are Birchensha's usual terms for conjunct and disjunct motion.

8 This version of the 'Method' for composing by Birchensha's rules should be compared with the simpler and presumably earlier version in Taylor's manuscript.

9 i.e. treble and bass ascending or descending by step in thirds.

10 In other words, the first two steps in the Method must always be given priority.

11 Indicating where one of the parts moves by a step of a semitone or a tone respectively.

12 This description only applies to the example in the upper system. The lower system, indicated in the manuscript by an index hand, contains a minor-mode variant, in which the first note in the treble descends a tone and comes to a minor third (incorrectly marked '3 ma' in the source). Similar variants are also given for Example 2 (descending) and Example 3 (ascending). It is noteworthy that even at this early stage in the tuition Birchensha does not see the introduction of a note from the four-flat scale, $d''♭$, as requiring special comment.

13 'Transverse motion' was Birchensha's term for what was more generally known, then as now, as 'contrary motion'. Each of the three categories within this rule is concerned with contrary movement between treble and bass.

14 The notes in the lower stave of the first system and the upper stave of the second system are not chords, but alternative consonances that may be quitted or approached by leap in contrary motion. In bar 2 of the second system the f'' is present in the source but is probably a mistake, as it makes a fourth with the bass.

15 Particularly striking among the examples of cadential suspensions that follow are three in which the 'binding note' (and consequently the discord) is prolonged and the 'cadent note' delayed and shortened by a crotchet: see the third example of a 4–3 cadence, the first example of a 7–6 cadence, and the second example of a 2–3 cadence. This idiom perhaps reflects the influence of French music in Restoration England. Silas Taylor's manuscript explains that the binding note should be 'double (at least) the value of […] the cadent note', and the cadent note 'halfe the value (or sometimes lesse)

of the binding note' (see Chapter IX, p. 238) – but none of the examples given there actually illustrates the idiom.

16   The second example shown of a 'dragging cadence' (a 6–5 progression) calls for comment, inasmuch as it does not conform to any of the '3 Binding Cadences' which Birchensha has described and there is no suspended discord, although it could of course be combined with the first example (a 4–3 progession) in three-part writing. Its appearance here seems to add weight to Rebecca Herissone's comment in *Music Theory in Seventeenth-Century England* (Oxford, 2000), p. 161, on the 'general confusion about the nature of suspensions' in seventeenth-century England.

17   These supplementary examples of binding cadences, written in an informal hand at the foot of fol. 42^r, were added after the other examples. Though not spelt out, their purpose was evidently to illustrate crotchet suspension sequences, in which the duration of the 'binding note' is a minim rather than a semibreve. Indices imply that they should come between the main examples of cadences of the seventh and cadences of the second, but in order to avoid breaking up the sequence the editors have preferred to place them here at the end of the section.

18   Though he does not explicitly say so here, Birchensha taught that fourths (like seconds and sevenths) are discords in two-part writing. Bars 2, 4, 6 and 8 of Example A show seconds and sevenths (both major and minor) that fall on 'the first part of a note' at minim level; bars 4 and 6 show perfect fourths that do so at both minim and semibreve level.

19   In bar 2 of Example B, Birchensha appears to break his own rule by leaping from *d''* (a concord) to *b'♭* (a discord).

20   Christopher Simpson similarly writes of '*Syncope*, or *Driving* a Note' in *The Principles of Practical Musick* (London, 1665), p. 30. Birchensha initially wrote out examples of such syncopation (Example D), but no explanatory text. The explanation and examples that follow were added later in vacant space on fol. 41^r, probably by Birchensha himself, but using a form of secretary hand (rather than italic) and a less refined style of musical script. 'Come off' is here used in the sense of 'finish', i.e come to a cadence. It may incidentally be noticed that the second example in Example D ends with a cadence in which the 'binding note' is introduced as a fourth above a stationary bass (the 'consonant fourth' idiom), although no reference has been made to this in Rule 4, which states that the 'first Part of the Binding note may be what concord you please'; and at the end of the section there is an example of ascending syncopation in the bass which contains a 'pathetic' falling leap of a diminished fourth in the upper part.

21   'Pricked notes' was common terminology in seventeenth-century England for dotted notes. (Playford, for example, refers to the dot as the '*Prick of Perfection or Addition*': see *An Introduction to the Skill of Musick*, 7th edn (London, 1674), p. 27.)

22   Birchensha may have thought of this example as a neat way of reviewing lessons learnt in Rule 1 (two parts ascending by step in thirds) and Rule 5 (use of passing discords) at the same time as introducing the pupil to imitative counterpoint and canon ('driving by way of a fuge'), which is to be covered in Rule 6, and to composition in more than two parts. As in the four-part examples found later in this manuscript, Birchensha uses only two clefs – *g'*2 (treble) for the three upper parts, and *f*4 for the bass.

23   That is to say, the answering voice should make a concord of an octave, third, fifth or sixth at its point of entry.

²⁴ i.e. the subject is best answered at the octave, fourth or fifth, either above or below.

²⁵ This paragraph introduces the student to the technique of writing a simple two-part canon. To 'continue a fuge' here apparently means to contrive a canon from a given opening; to 'prick out' is to write out in musical notation; 'make Discant to' means 'compose a counterpoint to'. Birchensha's advice may thus be paraphrased as: 'Write out the opening notes of the canon (suitably transposed) for the second voice, having decided at what interval above or below the first voice you will bring it in, and how long a rest you will leave between the entries. Then extend the first voice part by writing a counterpoint to the opening notes of the second voice. Then transpose that counterpoint into the second voice part; and so on.' Christopher Simpson, who devoted the final part of *A Compendium of Practical Musick* (London, 1667) to 'The Contrivance of Canon', observed that although English musicians had composed excellent and intricate canons he knew of none who had published instructions on how to do so (ibid., p. 147). Birchensha's inclusion of the topic here is noteworthy, therefore, even if the procedure he describes is not materially different from the one elucidated by Simpson. There are one or two similarities of phraseology (Simpson wrote of 'making new Descant to the last removed Notes', and explained that 'In this manner you may continue Two Parts in One, to what length you please') which may suggest that Birchensha wrote this passage after the *Compendium* appeared.

²⁶ Here Birchensha turns to the adding of an imitative counterpoint to a given melodic line. With its boldly handled sevenths in bars 2 and 4, however, his example leaves something to be desired as a model of how to continue a point 'so long as the discant will beare it'. Perhaps he meant to start with a minim rest in the bass, rather than a semibreve, but decided to press on regardless.

²⁷ The next example, written in an informal hand, has the appearance of a quickly dashed-off sketch; but it is closely related to the elaborate fugue example in Silas Taylor's manuscript (see Chapter VIII, p. 240), so its credentials are not in question. In this version the leading part is transposed up a fourth, and occupies stave 3. The other staves show how an imitative answer can be brought in at the fourth or fifth above, or at the fourth or fifth below. Staves 1 and 2 correspond in essence to staves 1 and 2 of Taylor's version, and staves 4 and 5 to staves 6 and 10.

²⁸ All the examples of Rule 1 that follow are based on examples of 'Two Parts Ascending or Descending together Gradualy' in the earlier part of the manuscript (see p. 253), and are designed to show how a treble-and-bass texture may be expanded to four parts – a compositional procedure not uncommon in the seventeenth century. Here the outer parts are the original treble and bass, usually unchanged. Both inner parts use the $g'2$ clef, and sound at written pitch. Though the procedure for devising the inner parts is not explained in detail, a pupil would presumably have been encouraged in this instance to make use of Rule 3 (the Transverse Rule), as well as Rule 1. Birchensha's general advice is to 'work by an other Rule' when in difficulty. Occasionally one may see in the manuscript that an inner part has been emended: in Example 9, for instance, the second part seems to have been altered from dotted minim g' / crotchet f' to the reading shown. Some part-writing of which Morley would almost certainly have disapproved because it involves 'hitting the eight on the face' or doubling a sharpened bass note at the octave is allowed to stand, however (Examples 2 and 3). Like Simpson, Birchensha permits parallel fifths if one of them is diminished and the other is perfect (Examples 1 and 8), and has no objection to parallel fourths between upper parts (Example 5), notwithstanding Alsted's ruling against them (*Templum musicum*, p. 66); but the

parallel octaves in Example 5 may have been an oversight. Example 10 is fragmentary sketch, perhaps added during a lesson, in the same informal handwriting as the fugue example on fol. 38ᵛ (see note 27). It is a transposed version of Example 1, marked to draw attention to the way the second line moves in sixths with the bass and in a semidiapente–diapente progression with the treble.

29   These are harmonically filled-out versions of the six main examples on fol. 44ᵛ inv. (see p. 254), which showed a treble part descending and ascending by step and a bass moving by leap of a fourth or fifth.

30   Using examples of 'Transverse Breaking' from fol. 43ᵛ inv. as a basis, Birchensha provides four-part versions that are not only filled out, but also slightly extended, in order to show how the breaking may be typically approached. The first group consists of examples in which the treble part descends and the bass ascends by step, with the breaking occurring alternately in treble and bass; figures beneath the treble line indicate whether the breaking is from an octave to a fifth or from a sixth to a third. In Example 1 consecutive fifths between the first and third parts are escaped by means of the quaver anticipation, which (though dissonant with the bass) is consonant with the treble.

31   The second group of examples of 'Transverse Breaking' consists of those in which the treble part ascends and the bass descends, the breaking being from a third to a sixth, or from a fifth to an octave, or from a seventh to a tenth. Example 5 is striking because the seventh occurs not as a passing note in the treble, but as a dissonant prolongation of a harmony note; something similar also occurs in the second bar of Example 2 between the two lowest parts. Example 6 provides a further instance of parallel movement from a perfect fifth to a diminished fifth.

32   Birchensha omitted to provide any heading for the following examples of 'Transverse Counterpoint', which are based on two 'sharp key' examples of contrary conjunct motion given on fol. 42ᵛ inv. (see p. 257). In Example 2, bar 2, the second part boldly moves in minims from a seventh to a tenth above the bass by the rule of 'Transverse Breaking', so that the discord falls on the first part of a semibreve. As the pupil has been taught that 'you never break on the 7th but on som extraordinary occasion' (fol. 44ʳ inv.), this presumably rates as such an occasion.

33   The only four-part examples given of 'Binding Cadences' are of 4–3 or 7–6 suspensions, where the binding note is in the top part. Interestingly enough, each of the 4–3 examples shows 'consonant fourth' preparation, the binding note being introduced as a fourth above a stationary bass, though this is not explained anywhere in the text, and none of the two-part examples on fols 42ʳ–41ᵛ inv. does this. Example 5, though admittedly not a final cadence, is remarkable for having the seventh resolve onto a 6/5 chord.

X

Rules of Composition, III:
Francis Withey's Manuscript

Editorial Note

Oxford, Christ Church, MS Mus. 337 consists of two books bound together in a seventeenth-century leather case stamped with the initials of the owner, 'FW'. Signatures identify him as the musician and teacher Francis Withey (*c*.1645–1727). The first book is Christopher Simpson's *A Compendium of Practical Musick*, which Withey bought in Worcester a few weeks after its publication in 1667 for two shillings and a penny. On one of the front endpapers he wrote in red ink, 'baught of / Mr Jons in / Worster', adding an ornate signature, 'Francis: Withey / His: Booke / October ⟨12⟩ 1667'. The second is a manuscript commonplace book, comprising nearly 100 leaves and measuring approximately 154 × 100 mm. Robert Thompson has shown that over a period of some thirty years – between about 1668 and 1698 – Withey copied into it extracts from theoretical works ranging from Morley's *Plaine and Easie Introduction* (1597) and Elway Bevin's *Briefe and Short Instruction of the Art of Musicke* (1631) to Locke's *Melothesia* (1673) and the 1694 edition of Playford's *Introduction to the Skill of Musick*, as well as advice gleaned from elders and contemporaries such as Benjamin Rogers, Henry Hall and Bartholomew Isaack. There are excerpts from compositions by Tallis, Bull, Jenkins, Henry Lawes, Christopher Gibbons, Locke, Michael Wise, Purcell, Lully, Corelli, Bassani and others. Withey evidently considered Birchensha's 'Rules of Composition' worthy of study, for he devoted sixteen pages to them.[1]

Withey's family belonged to Worcester, where his father and uncle were both professional musicians. (The family spelt its name variously as Withy, Withie, Withey and Wythie.) His uncle, Humphrey Withey (1596–1661), was a chorister and for many years a lay clerk at the cathedral, and also served as its sub-treasurer and clerk of works. Thomas Tomkins, the cathedral organist, dedicated one of his *Songs* of 1622 to him. John Withey (*c*.1600–85), Francis's father, became a lay clerk at Worcester in 1621 but seems to have relinquished the post three years later, perhaps because of his recusancy. Anthony Wood characterized him as 'a Rom[an] Cath[olic] & sometime teacher of musick in the citie of Worcester – Father to Franc[is] Withie of Oxon. – […] excellent at the Lyra-viol & improv'd the way of playing thereon much'.[2] Tomkins, who apparently took part in music-making with the Witheys in the 1640s, composed two pavans for him.[3] John's compositions include an In Nomine of five parts, airs for two bass viols and organ, and a song for Richard Brome's play *The English Moore*, which was staged in London by Queen Henrietta Maria's company in 1637–38.[4]

It was presumably John who gave Francis his early musical training. On the first leaf of his commonplace book Francis wrote: 'Jhon Withey / My Dear F[ather] / died Janu: 3ᵈ /85'. In the late 1660s Francis moved to Oxford, where from June 1670 until his death in December 1727 he was a 'singing man' at Christ Church. Besides his work in the cathedral choir, he was skilled on the viol and violin, as Edward Lowe, the professor of Music in the University and organist of Christ Church, seems to have been quick to recognize. On 4 May 1669 Prince Cosimo de' Medici of Tuscany, who was visiting Oxford, was taken 'to the Musick Schoole, where he heard a song sung by [Stephen] Crespine an undergraduate-student of Ch[rist] Ch[urch] and a division by Mr Withie on the base viol'.[5] When Wren's Sheldonian Theatre was officially opened two months later, 'Mr Withye' was one of the violinists who played in an ode specially composed by Lowe, 'Nunc est canendum', followed by a sonata for three violins and bass by Lambert Pietkin.[6] Francis was also active as a teacher and as a musical scribe who was capable of fine and elegant penmanship.[7] One pupil, 'his loving Scholler' Henry Knight of Wadham College, made him a gift of a vellum-bound manuscript book (now Oxford, Bodleian Library, MS Mus. Sch. C.61) in December 1687.[8] Elizabeth Hyde, a gifted singer who was the second wife of Thomas Hyde (Bodley's librarian and professor of Arabic and Hebrew in the university), also seems to have been taught by him.[9] Withey's lively interest in music of both the past and the present is reflected in the works he copied out for his own use.[10] He also made manuscript copies for others, which no doubt helped to augment his modest pay as a singing man. In the 1670s he assisted Lowe in building up the University Music School collection,[11] and in the 1680s (as Thompson has discovered) he was paid by Christ Church for 'pricking out' three of Henry Aldrich's 'recomposition' anthems into the cathedral choir-books.[12] He copied music for Aldrich's private library too – an important example being the part-books of Locke's 'Consort of Two Parts' (Oxford, Christ Church, MSS Mus. 409–10)[13] – and almost certainly took part in the music meetings that Aldrich, as tutor, canon and (from 1689 until his death in 1710) dean of Christ Church, held in his rooms in the college. When Withey died in 1727 he seems to have left his music manuscripts for the use of the Music School, but his copy of Simpson's *Compendium*, with the attached commonplace book containing Birchensha's rules, went to Christ Church.[14]

Withey's commonplace book lacks any pagination or foliation. For the purposes of the present edition a sequence of folio numbers has been assumed, starting at the leaf immediately following Simpson's *Compendium*, so that fol. 1ʳ of the notebook faces p. 176 of the *Compendium*. The collation of the first six gatherings of the notebook is: A⁸ (A4 removed), B–F⁸. Thereafter it is less clear, but probably continues as G–M[8]. The pages containing Birchensha's rules belong to gatherings E and F, and extend from fol. 36[v] to fol. 45[v].

Because of the character of the source – a miscellaneous collection of musical excerpts and didactic examples for Withey's personal use – it is not always immediately apparent what is by Birchensha and what is not. Comparison with Taylor's and Corbett's manuscripts is usually enough to dispel doubt, although it is clear that neither of those manuscripts can have been Withey's source. Since the policy in this edition is to include only material known or believed to be by Birchensha, some extraneous material on fols 36[v], 38[v]–39[r], 41[v]–43[r] and 44[v]–45[r] has been rejected; the reasons for its exclusion are generally given in a note at the appropriate point. Withey used a rastrum to rule staves on his blank pages as required – usually eight staves to a page in the Birchensha section, with marginal lines in red ink or pencil. He copied out his Birchensha examples neatly and attentively, but not always in the most rational order, and often without any explanatory directions; in such cases the editors' aim has been to present the material in a logical sequence, providing clarification where necessary. From time to time, readers may wish to refer back to Chapters VIII and IX. There is virtually no text here relating to the first rule, for instance, and nothing at all about the sixth ('Fuge') rule. For some rules there are copious examples, however, with the third ('Transverse') rule receiving particularly thorough illustration. Several of the examples are in three parts. Withey also includes a version of Birchensha's method for putting his rules into practice, which he seems to have obtained from the violinist and composer John Lenton (?1657–1719). Whether Lenton was Withey's source for the rules themselves is unclear, but the possibility that he studied composition with Birchensha in the 1670s cannot be ruled out. Directly or indirectly, Withey's transcript must have been based on a lost autograph source. Thompson considers that the position of Birchensha's rules in the commonplace book 'makes it unlikely that they were copied there very early';[15] on the other hand they were evidently present before the excerpts from Christopher Gibbons, Lully, Purcell and Corelli in their immediate vicinity, and must originally have been surrounded by numerous blank pages. It seems possible that Withey could have copied out the rules sometime between about 1675 and 1685.

Notes

[1]   Robert Thompson, '"Francis Withie of Oxon" and his Commonplace Book, Christ Church, Oxford, MS 337', *Chelys: The Journal of the Viola da Gamba Society*, 20 (1991): 3–27. 'Mr Jons' is probably to be identified as the Jones who was a bookseller in Worcester in 1663, and possibly the John Jones who is named as a bookseller there in publications of 1681 and 1698: see Henry R. Plomer, *A Dictionary of the Booksellers and Printers who were at Work in England, Scotland and Ireland from 1641 to 1667*

(London, 1907), p. 108; *A Dictionary of the Booksellers and Printers who were at Work in England, Scotland and Ireland from 1668 to 1725* (Oxford, 1922), p. 175.

2   Oxford, Bodleian Library, MS Wood D 19 (4), fol. 136.

3   As shown by Francis's annotations ('Made for J: Withy') in Oxford, Bodleian Library, MSS Mus. Sch. E.415–18, an incomplete set of part-books apparently compiled in Worcester in the early 1640s mainly by Humphrey Withey, and later owned by Francis. The pavans are nos 23–4 in *Thomas Tomkins: Consort Music*, ed. John Irving (Musica Britannica, 59; London, 1991). See also John Irving, 'Consort Playing in Mid-17th-Century Worcester: Thomas Tomkins and the Bodleian Partbooks Mus. Sch. E.415–18', *Early Music*, 12/3 (1984): 337–44.

4   For a summary list of John Withey's compositions, see Robert Thompson, 'Withy [family]', *The New Grove Dictionary of Music and Musicians*, ed. Stanley Sadie, 2nd edn (29 vols, London, 2001), vol. 27, pp. 451–2.

5   Anthony Wood, *The Life and Times of Anthony Wood, Antiquary, of Oxford, 1632–1695, Described by Himself*, ed. Andrew Clark, vol. 2 (Oxford Historical Society Publications, 21; Oxford, 1892), p. 158. In the course of the day the prince also heard Benjamin Rogers play on the organs of Magdalen and New College and Dr John Wallis lecture in the Geometry School. Several sets of divisions for bass viol by Francis survive (see note 8). Stephen Crespion matriculated from Christ Church on 13 July 1666, aged 17, and took his BA degree in 1670; he became a gentleman of the Chapel Royal in 1673. Withey's collection of 'Ayres for 3 parts Composed by severall Masters' (Oxford, Bodleian Library, MSS Mus. Sch. E.447–9) includes some pieces by him.

6   Peter Holman, 'Original Sets of Parts for Restoration Concerted Music at Oxford', in *Performing the Music of Henry Purcell*, ed. Michael Burden (Oxford, 1996), pp. 15–16. The performing material for Lowe's ode, in which Stephen Crespion (see note 5) sang the bass solos, is in Oxford, Bodleian Library, MS Mus. Sch. C.141. Pietkin was maître de chapelle of the cathedral in Liège; part-books in Lowe's hand containing the sonata are in Bodleian Library, MS Mus. Sch. C.44. John Evelyn, who attended the ceremonies on 9 July, commented on the 'excellent Musique both vocal, & Instrumental'.

7   For a facsimile of a page from Oxford, Christ Church, MS Mus. 8, showing Withey's score of a fantasia-suite by Christopher Gibbons, see Peter Holman, '"Evenly, Softly, and Sweetly Acchording to All": The Organ Accompaniment of English Consort Music', in *John Jenkins and his Time*, ed. Andrew Ashbee and Peter Holman (Oxford, 1996), p. 371.

8   Knight matriculated in 1682, aged 19, and took the BA degree in 1686 and the MA in 1689. He was subsequently rector of West Knighton, Dorset, and a canon of Hereford Cathedral. Music copied into the book by Withey included divisions for bass viol of his own composition, airs for two bass viols by his father and by Jenkins, a recently composed anthem by Henry Purcell ('My song shall be alway') with the copying date 9 September 1690 and an overture-suite by Daniel Purcell (organist of Magdalen College from 1689 to 1696) to which he appended the note, 'Sent this to Wo[r]c[ester]'.

9   A note by Withey on one of the end-papers of Mus. Sch. C.61 states, 'Mrs Elizabeth Hide was my Scholler April 2^d 1697'. Her identification here as the Elizabeth Oram whom Thomas Hyde married in 1688 does not appear to have been made before. Hyde became a canon of Christ Church in 1697 on being appointed Regius Professor of

Hebrew. See P.J. Marshall, 'Thomas Hyde', in *Oxford Dictionary of National Biography*, ed. H.C.G. Matthew and Brian Harrison (60 vols, Oxford, 2004), vol. 29, pp. 156–7.

[10] Besides the music mentioned in note 8, we find Withey for instance writing out playing parts of Alfonso Ferrabosco II's *Ut re mi fa sol la* – a work whose circular modulations continued to fascinate Oxford musicians in the late seventeenth century – and, from contemporary France, some of Marin Marais's *Pièces à une et à deux Violes* (Paris, 1686). He had acquired the Ferrabosco half copied in Bodleian Library, MSS Mus. Sch. E. 437–42, a set of old part-books which he bought for 6 shillings: see *Alfonso Ferrabosco the Younger: Consort Music of Five and Six Parts*, ed. Christopher Field and David Pinto (Musica Britannica, 81; London, 2003), no. 1a–b. Marais's *Tombeau de M. Meliton* and other duos are in MSS Mus. Sch. E.428a–b.

[11] See for example the anonymous airs in Oxford, MS Mus. Sch. C.44, fols 99–105, for which Withey wrote out the violin parts and Lowe the bass part, or the three movements from Locke's 'Second Part of the Broken Consort' at fols 136–41 of the same manuscript, which Withey may have copied for use at an Oxford Act or similar ceremony. A more substantial contribution to the Music School library was his set of part-books of Christopher Simpson's 'Little Consort', MS Mus. Sch. E.430, on which Lowe wrote: 'Prickt & given mee by Mr Francis Withye 11 Jan: 1672/3'.

[12] Robert Thompson, 'A Fallacy in Duration? Musical Survival and Revival in Late Seventeenth-Century Oxford', paper read at the Sixth Biennial Conference on Baroque Music, Edinburgh, 10 July 1994. Five of the choir-books survive (Oxford, Christ Church, MSS Mus. 1220–24). The anthems copied by Withey were 'Why art thou so vexed' (after Palestrina, 'Ave Maria'), 'I look for the Lord' (after Tallis, 'Absterge Domine') and 'Be not wroth' (after Byrd, 'Civitas sancti tui'); he was paid 9 shillings for the first two in 1686, and 6 shillings for the third in 1689.

[13] Christopher D.S. Field, 'Matthew Locke and the Consort Suite', *Music & Letters*, 51/1 (1970): 15–25, at 18–20; Robert Thompson, 'The Sources of Locke's Consort "for seaverall freinds"', *Chelys*, 19 (1990): 16–43. The exceptional quality of the music paper used suggests that Aldrich may have acquired it with the music manuscripts that had belonged to Christopher, first Baron Hatton, who died in 1670; the leather binding of Mus. 409–10, stamped on the spine 'FANT[asias]: A / 2. B[ooks]', matches those which Aldrich gave to many of his Hatton manuscripts and prints. On Hatton's music collection and Aldrich's acquisition of it, see David Pinto's articles 'The Music of the Hattons', *Royal Musical Association Research Chronicle*, 23 (1990): 79–98, and 'Placing Hatton's Great Set', *Chelys: The Journal of the Viola da Gamba Society*, 32 (2004): 1–20.

[14] The music manuscripts probably included Bodleian Library, MSS Mus. Sch. C.59–60, C.61, D.217, E.415–18, E.428, E.437–42 and E.447–9. None of these items is identifiable in the 1682 catalogue of the Music School collection (see Margaret Crum, 'Early Lists of the Oxford Music School Collection', *Music & Letters*, 48/1 (1967): 23–34), or in transcripts made of it by Richard Goodson the younger (London, British Library, Add. MSS 30493 and 33965). Withey's commonplace book (described as 'Manuscript directions for Composing') is shown as part of 'M[r]. R[d]: Goodsons Collection Of Manuscript Music' in a catalogue of the Christ Church music collection made by J.B. Malchair in 1787 (London, Royal College of Music, MS 2125, fol. 14[r]). Presumably all these items would have gone through the hands of Goodson who, like his father, combined the duties of professor of Music and organist of Christ Church (1718–41).

[15] Thompson, '"Francis Withie of Oxon" and his Commonplace Book', p. 8.

Edition

[fol. [37]ʳ]

Mr Joh: Birchensha's [Rules]

[Things necessary to be observed]

Perfect Notes[1]

Flat notes

Sharp [Notes]

Notes made flat

Notes made ♯

[fol. [36]ᵛ]

[First Rule: Of two parts ascending or descending together]

[Examples of] Mid Closes
1 Rule [1ˢᵗ Example]

2ᵈ Ex:²

3[ʳᵈ] Ex:³

[fol. [37]ʳ]
[Further examples of treble and bass ascending or descending together gradually:]

[Examples of treble and bass ascending or descending together by saltation:]

[fols [36]ᵛ–[37]ʳ]

[Second Rule: When the upper part moves gradually and the bass by saltation]

Rules of Making a Basse to a Treble[4]

1 Ex:

When your Treble fall's a Semitone the Basse descends a fourth 8 to a 3.
When the Treble riseth a Tone, the Base riseth a fifth[a] from a[n] 8 to a 5.[5]
1 Example

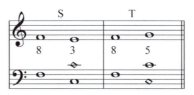

2ᵈ Ex:

When y[o]ur ⟨Tr[eble]⟩ fall's a Tone the Basse fall's a fourth from a 3ᵈ to a 5ᵗʰ[.]

When the Treble rises a Semitone the Basse rises a fourth from [a] 3ᵈ to a[n] 8[.]

ᵃ   MS has *fif⟨e⟩th*.

2ᵈ Ex:

3 Ex:

When y[o]ur Treble fall's a Tone f[r]omª C to B♭, the Basse falleth a fifth from ⟨a⟩ 5 to an 8[.]

When y[o]ur Treble rises a Tone the Basse rises a fourth from a 5 to a 3ᵈ[.]

3ᵈ Ex.ᵇ

[Example of a cadence in which the treble falls by two steps of a tone and the bass falls by a fourth and a fifth:]

[fols [37]ᵛ–[38]ʳ]

[Third Rule, called the Transverse Rule]

Third rule Transverse by Saltation[,] by Mr Bergen[sha]

[1. Examples of treble ascending or descending by increasingly wide intervals, from a second to an octave, with alternative harmonic possibilities indicated for the lower part:]⁶

ᵃ *the* altered to *f*[r]*om.*

ᵇ *8* altered to *3.*

[(a) Voices initially an octave apart:]⁷

[(b) Voices initially a third apart:]

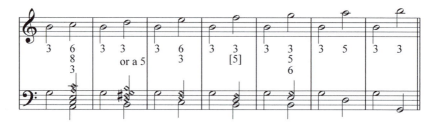

[(c) Voices initially a fifth apart:]

[(d) Voices initially a sixth apart:]

[fol. [39]ᵛ]

[2. Examples of bass ascending or descending by increasingly wide intervals, from a second to an octave, with alternative harmonic possibilities indicated for the upper part:]

A Treble made to the Basse by J:B:

[(a) Voices initially an octave apart:]

[(b) Voices initially a third apart:]

[fol. [40]ʳ]
  Saltation ⟨or leaps⟩ in the Basse by Mr Berchen[sha]

[(c) Voices initially a fifth apart:][a]

[(d) Voices initially a sixth apart:][b]

---

[a]   Bar 12, second minim: figured 5 in MS; emended editorially to 6.
[b]   Bar 1, treble, 2nd minim: upper note *e″* in MS, but figure 6 added above it. Bar 11, 2nd minim: figured 6 in MS.

[fols [38]ᵛ–[39]ʳ]

3d Rule of Transvers breaking

[Examples of] 3 Rule Transverse & breaking[:][8]

Breaking in the Treble from the	<u>6 to a 3</u>	[Ex. A]
Breaking in the Basse from the	<u>6 to a 3</u>	[Ex. B]

[Ex. A][a]

[Ex. B]

Breaking in the Treble f[r]om the	8 \ 7 & \ 5	[Ex. C]
Breaking in the Basse from the	<u>8 / 7 & / 5</u>	[Ex. D]

[Ex. C]

---

    [a]   In the first example Withey originally copied the bass a third lower (as in Ex. C).
He corrected this, but without deleting the figuring *3 8 7 5*.

[Ex. D]

Breaking in the Tr[eble from the]   3 / 4 to a / 6   [Ex. E]
Breaking in the Ba[sse from the]   <u>3 \ 4 to a [\] 6</u>   [Ex. F]

[Ex. E]

[Ex. F]

[Breaking in the Treble from the]   5 / 6 [to an] / 8   [Ex. G]
[Breaking in the Basse from the]   <u>5 \ 6 [to an \] 8</u>   [Ex. H]

[Ex. G]

[Ex. H]

[Breaking in the Treble from the]   5 / 7 / 8 [to a] / 3   [Ex. J]
[Breaking in the Basse from the]   5 \ 7 \ 8 [to a] \ 3   [Ex. K]

[Ex. J]

[Ex. K]

[fols [40]ᵛ–[41]ʳ]

3d Rule

Transvers & Counterpoint by Graduall motion; is either of one Note ascending or des[c]ending

[Examples of] 3ᵈ Rule Transverse Counterpoint by Graduall Motion
Ascending one Note ⟨or⟩ 4 Notes or ⟨3⟩ Notes[:]

If you ascend in your Treble ⟨to⟩ the next key you go

1	From the 6th to the 8th or
2	From the 8th to the 3d [or]
3	From the 3d to the 5th

} A

A 1 Note

If you ascend in the Treble to the 3d Note you goe a 6. 8. 3. or 8. 3 5.

1	From the 6 to the	—	8th
	From the 8th to the	—	3d
	or		
2	From the 8th to the	—	3d &
	From the 3d to the	—	5th

B

B [3 Notes]

If [you] ascend in y[o]ur Tr[eble] [a] 4th you go

From the 6 to the 8
From the 8 to the 3
From the 3 to the 5

} C

C [4 Notes]

If y[o]u descend in the Tr[eble] to the nex[t Note you go]

1	From the 5 to the 3^d	
2	From the 3 to the 8	D
3	From the 8 to the 6	

D Descending one Note

If y[o]u descend a 3^d [you go]

From the 5 to the 3	
From the 3 to the 8	E
From the 8 to the 6	

E or 3 Notes

If [you] Descend 4 Notes [you] go

From the 5 to the 3[d]
From the 3 to the 8th   } F
From the 8 to the 6th

F [4 Notes]

[fol. [37][r]]
Transvers Counterpoint[9]

6 8 3 5 | 5 3 8 6 | 8 3 5 | 3 8 6

[fols [41][v]–[42][r]]

4th Rule [of Binding Cadences]

Binding Cadences[a] there are 3[:][10]
   The 4th & 3
   The 7 & 6
   The 2[d] & 3

4th Rule Cadences

---

[a]   MS has *Cadedences*.

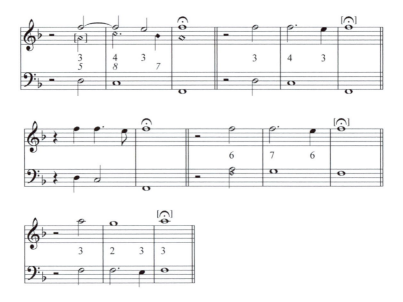

[fols [43]ᵛ–[44]ʳ]

5th Rule

Called the Division Rule

When one part holds, and the other divides on the holding Note.
First Gradually[;] 2ᵈly By Saltation

1st Gradu⟨a⟩lly .... A
2ᵈ By Saltation .... B
3[r]dly Mixd C

When y[o]u work gradually, you go a Concord & a Discord. A[.]
A [Gradual motion]

When you divide by Saltation you go from a Concord to a Concord[.] B[.]
  B Saltation

When y[o]u work both waies you go by the same Rule.
  C [Gradual motion and saltation mixed]

(D) By this Rule you may know how to hold one Note to many Notes.
  D [Gradual motion and saltation against a moving part]ᵃ

  ᵃ In the example bar 2 is problematic, though the MS is clear enough. Perhaps
Birchensha wrote (or intended to write) the last three quavers as *f´ g´ a´*, but these were
miscopied and then clumsily altered.

[fol. [43]^r]
   A 5th Ru[le]
   [Examples of syncopation]¹¹
[a. Gradual]

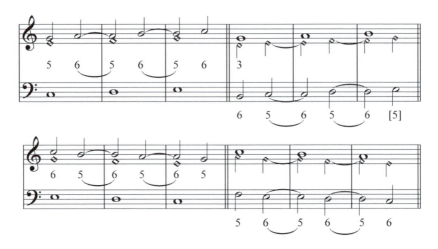

[b. By saltation]

[fol. [41]ʳ]

[Example of chromatic notes][12]

in A

[fol. 45ᵛ]

[Method]
by Mʳ Lenton[13,a]

First[,] follow a point where the descant will bear it[,][14]

2ᵈly[,] put down the Cadences[,] leaving out the preparitory or binding Note[,][15]

3ᵈly[,] put down the transverse counterpoint [(]Example ⟨of rule⟩[)]ᵇ and close not[e,][16]

4ᵗʰly[,] put down the examples of the transverse bre⟨a⟩king, leaving out the preparatory Note,[17]

5ᵗʰly[,] ⟨put⟩ down the 3ᵈ Example of the first Rule [(]Ex[ample] of rule[)] and Close not[e],[18]

6ᵗʰ[,] [put down] the 2ᵈ [Example] of the first rule descending [(]Exam[ple] of the rule[)] and Close not[e],[19]

7ᵗʰ[,] [put down] the 2ᵈ Exam[ple] of the first rule ascending, [(]Exam[ple] of the rule[)] and Close not[e],[20]

and in all these Eminent Exam[ples] leav out the preparatory Note, till you find if the precedantᶜ des⟨c⟩ant will bear it in smooth working and avoiding Tautologi[;][21] what remains fill up with transvers saltation[,] fir[s]t rule saltation[,] 3ᵈ or 5ᵗʰ Rule holding[.][22]

variations wan⟨t⟩ing[23]

ᵃ   Paragraph breaks in what follows are editorial.

ᵇ   Originally there must have been music examples here and in clauses 5, 6 and 7 below, but none are present in Withey's copy.

ᶜ   Altered from *preparatory*.

Notes

[1]   For Birchensha's classification of the seven uninflected notes of the scale as perfect, flat or sharp, see also Chapter III, pp. 101–2, and Chapter IX, p. 247. Here music examples help to make his meaning clear.

[2]   Notes printed small appear in the source as dots.

[3]   Withey corrected the figuring of the first interval from 5 to 6; but Birchensha may well have intended a minim g (not f) in the bass in order to illustrate conjunct descending motion from a perfect fifth to a diminished fifth. For similar examples of the latter progression in this context, see Taylor's and Corbett's manuscripts (p. 226 and p. 253).

[4]   A restatement of the 'Regula Aurea Bassi', or golden rule for making a bass, found in Taylor's manuscript. Immediately above, at the top of fol. 36^v, Withey wrote out a music example showing '12 Semitones in an Octave' with the statement, 'A Greater 6th & a Lesser 7th [are] all one as From G to E soe from G♯ to F naturall the same Number of semitones'; these were apparently later additions to the manuscript. The example shows a 12-note chromatic scale from g' to g'' (including g'♯, b'♭, c'♯, d''♭ and f''♯), with the semitones numbered from g'♯ as 1 to g'' as 12 and from g'♯ as 0 to f'' as 9. Apart from the misuse of the term 'lesser seventh' (which to Birchensha meant a minor seventh), the notion that a major sixth and diminished seventh are identical is alien to the Pythagorean view of musical intervals which inspired Birchensha's mathematical and practical teaching. Withey's example implies an advocacy of equal temperament, or at least the pragmatic attitude of a viol player for whom the number of frets spanned by an interval was the most important consideration. (In Corbett's manuscript, by way of contrast, the composition pupil is shown at the outset that the semitone G–a♭ is smaller than the apotome G–G♯.) Similar examples showing intervals divided into numbered semitones occur on fols 9^r, 33^v and 44^v of Withey's commonplace book. For these reasons, the example on fol. 36^v is not included in our edition.

[5]   In this and the next two examples, notes printed small appear in the source with a stroke through them.

[6]   In the second layer of Taylor's manuscript, transverse motion by saltation was illustrated by a more or less random selection of ways of leaping in contrary motion from an octave, third, fifth or sixth to another concord. In Corbett's manuscript, the illustration was more methodical. First, various possibilities were shown of moving from concord to concord against a treble ground which made progressively wider upward leaps from f', ranging from a third to an octave; then the same was done against a bass ground which made progressively wider downward leaps from f. In Withey's manuscript, Birchensha goes through a similar routine, but even more systematically and exhaustively. The bass always begins each bar on g or G. In example 1(a), treble and bass are initially an octave apart, and the treble ground ascends, then descends, in increasingly wide intervals ranging from a second to an octave. Examples 1(b), 1(c) and 1(d) repeat the demonstration, but with treble and bass initially a third, fifth or sixth apart. In examples 2(a)–(d) the ground is transferred from treble to bass. Notes printed small in these examples appear in the source lightly sketched in with fine dots.

[7]   In the manuscript, consecutive octaves by contrary motion in bars 3–4 are marked with red dots in the centre of the lower note (g–c, g–d); perhaps these were Withey's own addition. In bar 11 the treble e'', though intrusive, is in the source.

8   In the following musical examples Withey wrote a dot immediately above or below the figure relating to the first crotchet of each pair: the 6 in examples A and B, the 8 in examples C and D, the 3 in examples E and F, the 5 in examples G and H, and the 7 in examples J and K. There is no certainty that these marks originated with Birchensha, however; Withey used similar marks elsewhere, including a Purcell example on fol. 39^r. In the explanatory text accompanying examples C–K, upward-slanting and downward-sloping strokes (shown here as / and \) indicate whether the voice in question ascends or descends. Withey occasionally muddled the signs, however; in such cases the correct stroke has been substituted in editorial square brackets. In several of the examples the possibilities for adding a third voice are shown by the use of broken note-heads (printed here as small notes) and/or figuring. Ex. C also indicates by figures how a fourth voice may be added. Withey subsequently squeezed in further music examples in the remaining space on fol. 39^r. One of these is ascribed to H[enry] P[urcell], others are unattributed, but there seems to be no reason to connect any of them directly with Birchensha. At the foot of the unruled fol. 38^v Withey wrote out two cadences, using a system of figured-bass shorthand; these are ascribed to 'M.M.' (perhaps Marin Marais).

9   These examples, which appear on an earlier page of the manuscript – fol. 37^r – merely repeat Examples C and F and the second bars of Examples B and E from fol. 41^r.

10   As in Corbett's manuscript, Birchensha shows a fondness for prolonging the 'binding note' and shortening the 'cadent note': see the second, third, fourth and fifth examples. (In the source Withey copied out the third example twice.) On the remainder of the unruled fol. 41^v Withey went on to write out a number of cadences by Purcell ('H:P.') in his figured-bass shorthand, while the unused staves of fol. 42^r were filled up with examples of cadences by 'Se[nior] Bap[tist]' (Lully) and 'Dr [Christopher] Gibbons'.

11   In Taylor's manuscript Birchensha included 'syncope' within Rule 1 (the 'Rule of graduall Motion'); but here and in Corbett's manuscript it appears under Rule 5, as a species of 'division'. This allowed for the teaching of syncopation not only in 'gradual' motion (see Ex. (a)) but also in 'saltation' or disjunct motion (Ex. (b)). In Withey's manuscript the examples of the former are in three parts, the second treble part being written in pencil (partially overlaid with fine ink dots). At a later date Withey added at the foot of fol. 43^r an unrelated excerpt by 'Se[nior] Bap[tist]'.

12   In the manuscript this example of two parts moving chromatically follows a series of examples of transverse counterpoint by gradual motion (Rule 3, Examples A–F). Although it is not certainly by Birchensha, it seems close enough in style to the example in Corbett's manuscript of dividing 'by chromatick notes' – a subdivision of Rule 5 – for it to be included here.

13   After the examples of Birchensha's Rule 5, Withey left two blank pages, fols 44^v–45^r, which he later filled up with calculations of the number of semitones in various intervals, and with part of the last movement of Corelli's Sonata in D minor, Op. 3, No. 5 (first published in 1689), before copying out the following instructions. Although these are ascribed to 'Mr Lenton', and Birchensha's name does not appear, they are closely akin to the 'Method' for composing by his rules which Birchensha laid down on fol. 4 of Corbett's manuscript. Lenton was evidently not the author of the instructions, therefore, but merely communicated them to Withey. He is almost

certainly to be identified as the John Lenton who was sworn as one of Charles II's violinists in 1681 and as a gentleman extraordinary of the Chapel Royal in 1685. As a composer he published jointly with Thomas Tollett *A Consort of Musick, in Three Parts* (1692), and its sequel (1697), and wrote music for the Lincoln's Inn Fields theatre; he was also the author of a violin tutor, *The Gentleman's Diversion* (London, 1693). Withey's manuscript is the only evidence connecting Lenton with Birchensha, but raises the possibility that he may have studied with him.

14   The wording is reminiscent of the version of the 'method' given by Silas Taylor: '1. Bring in your Fuge or any part of it, as the descant will allow'. Although there is nothing about Rule 6 (the 'Fuge' rule) in Withey's manuscript, the pupil is directed to begin by determining where imitative entries should go, just as in Taylor's and Corbett's versions.

15   The second step, likewise, is basically the same in all three versions of the method: the pupil must decide where to place cadences involving suspended discords. Withey's is the only source, however, which advises that the binding note should be left out at this stage.

16   This version of the method differs from the one in Corbett's manuscript by applying 'Transverse Rule Counterpoint' and 'Transverse Rule Breaking' before the second and third examples of Rule 1, rather than after them.

17   To judge from the examples of 'Transverse Breaking' in Withey's manuscript, 'preparatory Note' may here mean the minim that precedes the pair of 'breaking' crotchets, whereas in Corbett's manuscript it appears to mean the first crotchet itself. It would make more sense to omit the former than the latter.

18   i.e. descending by step from perfect fifth to diminished fifth.

19   i.e. descending by step in sixths.

20   i.e. ascending by step in sixths.

21   'Tautology' probably here means 'coming too often to the same Note or chord', which in Corbett's manuscript Birchensha warns the student to avoid.

22   As in Corbett's manuscript, the pupil learns to refrain from applying the 'Division Rule' ('when you see the form of the fifth Rule, and have an Occasion to Breake an holding Note, or hold to many Notes') until this late stage. Withey's is the only version of the method to refer specifically to the use of saltation, whether in parallel (Rule 1) or 'transverse' motion (Rule 3). The apparent reference to '3ᵈ Rule holding' is obscure; the 'Transverse Rule' contains no such section. What is most obviously missing is any reference to Rule 2, which in Corbett's version of the method receives a clause to itself, and in Taylor's is invoked as soon as the imitative entries and cadences have been settled.

23   These words in the lower right-hand corner of fol. 45ᵛ bear no relation to anything on the following page, and possibly refer to the absence of the 'examples' mentioned in clauses 3, 5, 6 and 7.

Bibliography

Alsted [Alstedius, Alstedt], Johann Heinrich, *Cursus philosophici encyclopædia libris XXVII complectens* (Herborn: Christoph Corvin, 1620); revised and enlarged 2nd edn as *Johannis-Henrici Alstedii encyclopædia septem tomis distincta* (Herborn, 1630); 3rd edn as *Ioan. Henrici Alstedii encyclopædia universa, in quatuor tomos divisa* (Lyons: Jean-Antoine Huguetan & Marc-Antoine Ravaud, 1649); English translation by John Birchensha of Book XX ('In quo explicatur Musica') as *Templum musicum: or the Musical Synopsis, of the Learned and Famous Johannes-Henricus-Alstedius, being a Compendium of the Rudiments both of the Mathematical and Practical Part of Musick* (London: William Godbid for Peter Dring, 1664; facsimile edn, Monuments of Music and Music Literature in Facsimile, 2nd series, 35, New York: Broude Brothers, [1968]).

Alumni Dublinenses: A Register of the Students, Graduates, Professors, and Provosts of Trinity College, in the University of Dublin, ed. G.D. Burtchaell and T.U. Sadleir (London: Williams & Norgate, 1924).

Ammann, Peter J., 'The Musical Theory and Philosophy of Robert Fludd', *Journal of the Warburg and Courtauld Institutes*, 30 (1967): 198–227.

Antiquæ musicæ auctores septem, ed. with Latin translations by Marcus Meibom (2 vols, Amsterdam: Lodewijk Elzevir, 1652).

Arber, Edward, *The Term Catalogues, 1668–1709 A.D.* (3 vols, London: privately printed, 1903–1906).

Atcherson, W.T., 'Symposium on Seventeenth-Century Music Theory: England', *Journal of Music Theory*, 16 (1972): 6–15.

Aubrey, John, *'Brief Lives', Chiefly of Contemporaries, Set down by John Aubrey, between the Years 1669 and 1696*, ed. Andrew Clark (2 vols, Oxford: Clarendon Press, 1898).

Ayscough, Samuel, *A Catalogue of the Manuscripts Preserved in the British Museum hitherto Undescribed* (2 vols, London: John Rivington, 1782).

Barker, Andrew, *Greek Musical Writings: I. The Musician and his Art; II. Harmonic and Acoustic Theory* (2 vols, Cambridge, New York and Melbourne: Cambridge University Press, 1984 and 1989).

—— *The Science of Harmonics in Classical Greece* (Cambridge and New York: Cambridge University Press, 2007).

Barnett, Gregory, 'Tonal Organization in Seventeenth-Century Music Theory', in Thomas Christensen (ed.), *The Cambridge History of Western Music Theory* (Cambridge: Cambridge University Press, 2002), pp. 407–55.

Bathe, William, *A Briefe Introduction to the Skill of Song*, ed. Kevin C. Karnes (Music Theory in Britain, 1500–1700: Critical Editions; Aldershot and Burlington, VT: Ashgate, 2005).

Bevin, Elway, *A Briefe and Short Instruction of the Art of Musicke* (London: Robert Young, 1631); ed. Denis Collins (Music Theory in Britain, 1500–1700: Critical Editions; Aldershot and Burlington, VT: Ashgate, 2007).

A Biographical Dictionary of English Court Musicians 1485–1714, compiled by Andrew Ashbee and David Lasocki assisted by Peter Holman and Fiona Kisby (2 vols, Aldershot, Brookfield, VT, Singapore and Sydney: Ashgate, 1998).

Birch, Thomas, *The History of the Royal Society of London* (4 vols, London: A. Millar, 1756–57).

Birchensha, John (the tractarian), *The History of Divine Verities* (London: T.C. for John Wright, 1655; reissued with cancel title-page as *The History of the Scripture: [...] By J.B. a lover of peace and truth in Christ Jesus* (London: for William Rands, 1660).

—— *The Eagle Prophesie. Or, an Explanation of the Eleventh and Twelfth Chapters of the Second Booke of Esdras* (London: T.C., to be sold by Jeremy Hierons, 1656).

Birchensha, John, *Templum musicum*: see Alsted, Johann Heinrich.

Blasius, Leslie, 'Mapping the Terrain', in Thomas Christensen (ed.), *The Cambridge History of Western Music Theory* (Cambridge: Cambridge University Press, 2002), pp. 27–45.

Boethius, Anicius Manlius Severinus, *Opera omnia* (Basle: Heinrich Petri, 1570).

—— *De institutione musica*, trans. with introduction and notes by Calvin M. Bower and ed. Claude V. Palisca as *Fundamentals of Music* (New Haven, CT, and London: Yale University Press, 1989).

Bower, Calvin M., 'The Transmission of Ancient Music Theory into the Middle Ages', in Thomas Christensen (ed.), *The Cambridge History of Western Music Theory* (Cambridge: Cambridge University Press, 2002), pp. 136–67.

Boydell, Barra, 'The Earl of Cork's Musicians: A Study in the Patronage of Music in Early Seventeenth-Century Anglo-Irish Society', *Records of Early English Drama*, 18/2 (1993): 1–15; reprinted with minor revisions in Barra Boydell and Kerry Houston (eds), *Music, Ireland and the Seventeenth Century* (Irish Musical Studies, 10; Dublin: Four Courts Press, 2009) , pp. 81–91.

Boyle, Richard, 1st Earl of Cork, *The Lismore Papers (First Series): Autobiographical Notes, Remembrances and Diaries of Sir Richard Boyle, First and 'Great' Earl of Cork*, ed. Alexander B. Grosart (5 vols, privately printed, 1886).

—— *The Lismore Papers (Second Series): Selections from the Private and Public (or State) Correspondence of Sir Richard Boyle, First and 'Great' Earl of Cork*, ed. Alexander B. Grosart (5 vols, privately printed, 1887–88).

Boyle, Robert, *Some Considerations touching the Usefulnesse of Experimental Naturall Philosophy* (2 vols, Oxford: Henry Hall for Richard Davis, 1663–71).

—— *The Works of the Honourable Robert Boyle* [...] *To which is prefixed The Life of the Author*, ed. Thomas Birch (5 vols, London: for A. Millar, 1744).

—— *The Works of Robert Boyle*, ed. Michael Hunter and Edward B. Davis (14 vols, London: Pickering & Chatto, 1999–2000).

—— *The Correspondence of Robert Boyle*, ed. Michael Hunter, Antonio Clericuzio and Lawrence M. Principe (6 vols, London: Pickering & Chatto, 2001).

Burney, Charles, *A General History of Music, from the Earliest Ages to the Present Period* (4 vols, London: for the author, 1776–89).

Burke, Bernard, *The General Armory of England, Scotland, Ireland and Wales; Comprising a Registry of Armorial Bearings from the Earliest to the present Time* (London: Harrison, 1884).

Butler, Charles, *The Principles of Musik, In Singing and Setting: with The Two-fold Use therof, [Ecclesiasticall and Civil]* (London: John Haviland for the Author, 1636); facsimile edition with introduction by Gilbert Reaney (New York: Da Capo Press, 1970); ed. Jessie Ann Owens (Music Theory in Britain, 1500–1700: Critical Editions; Farnham and Burlington, VT: Ashgate, forthcoming).

Calvisius, Sethus, *Exercitationes musicæ duæ* (Leipzig: Jacob Apel, 1600; facsimile edn, Hildesheim: Georg Olms, 1973).

Campion, Thomas, *A New Way of Making Fowre Parts in Counter-Point* (London: Thomas Snodham, n.d.); ed. Walter R. Davis in *The Works of Thomas Campion: Complete Songs, Masques and Treatises with a Selection of the Latin Verse* (Garden City, NY: Doubleday, 1967; London: Faber & Faber, 1969); ed. Christopher R. Wilson in *A New Way of Making Fowre Parts in Counterpoint by Thomas Campion and Rules how to Compose by Giovanni Coprario* (Music Theory in Britain, 1500–1700: Critical Editions; Aldershot and Burlington, VT: Ashgate, 2003).

Catalogue de la bibliothèque de F.-J. Fétis acquise par l'État belge (Brussels: C. Muquardt, and Paris: Firmin-Didot & Cⁱᵉ, 1877).

Catalogue of the Pepys Library at Magdalene College, Cambridge, ed. Robert Latham (16 vols, Cambridge: D.S. Brewer, 1978–94), vol. 4, part 1 ('Music', compiled by John Stevens).

Charleton, Walter, *Physiologia Epicuro–Gassendo–Charltoniana: or A Fabrick of Science Natural, Upon the Hypothesis of Atoms* (London: Thomas Newcomb for Thomas Heath, 1654).

Charteris, Richard, 'A Rediscovered Manuscript Source with some Previously Unknown Works by John Jenkins, William Lawes and Benjamin Rogers', *Chelys: The Journal of the Viola da Gamba Society*, 22 (1993): 3–29.

Chenette, Louis F., 'Music Theory in the British Isles during the Enlightenment' (PhD dissertation, Ohio State University, 1967).

Chester, Joseph Lemuel (ed.), *The Marriage, Baptismal, and Burial Registers of the Collegiate Church or Abbey of St Peter, Westminster* (Harleian Society, 10; London, 1876).

Chierotti, Carlo Mario, 'Comporre senza conoscere la musica: Athanasius Kircher e la "Musurgia mirifica"', *Nuova rivista musicale italiana*, 28 (1994): 382–410.

Chua, Daniel K.L., 'Vincenzo Galilei, Modernity and the Division of Nature', in *Music Theory and Natural Order from the Renaissance to the Early Twentieth Century*, ed. Suzannah Clark and Alexander Rehding (Cambridge and New York: Cambridge University Press, 2001), pp. 17–29.

Cohen, David E., 'Notes, Scales, and Modes in the Earlier Middle Ages', in Thomas Christensen (ed.), *The Cambridge History of Western Music Theory* (Cambridge: Cambridge University Press, 2002), pp. 307–63.

Cohen, H. Floris, *Quantifying Music: The Science of Music at the First Stage of the Scientific Revolution, 1580–1650* (Dordrecht: D. Reidel, 1984).

Cooper, Barry, 'Englische Musiktheorie im 17. und 18. Jahrhundert', in F. Zaminer (ed.), *Geschichte der Musiktheorie, 9: Entstehung nationaler Traditionen: Frankreich, England* (Darmstadt: Wissenschaftliche Buchgesellschaft, 1986), pp. 141–314.

Coprario [Coperario], John [Giovanni], *Rules how to Compose*, facsimile of the autograph MS with introduction by Manfred Bukofzer (Los Angeles: Ernest E. Gottlieb, 1952); ed. Christopher R. Wilson in *A New Way of Making Fowre Parts in Counterpoint by Thomas Campion and Rules how to Compose by Giovanni Coprario* (Music Theory in Britain, 1500–1700: Critical Editions; Aldershot and Burlington, VT: Ashgate, 2003).

Corbett, William, *XII Sonate à Tre* [...] *Opera Prima* (Amsterdam: Estienne Roger, 1700; facsimile edn with introduction by Peter Holman, Alston: JPH Publications, 2003).

A Correspondence of Renaissance Musicians, ed. Bonnie J. Blackburn, Edward J. Lowinsky and Clement A. Miller (Oxford: Clarendon Press, 1991).

Crawford, Tim, 'An Unusual Consort Revealed in an Oxford Manuscript', *Chelys: The Journal of the Viola da Gamba Society*, 6 (1975–76): 61–8.

Crocker, Richard L., 'Pythagorean Mathematics and Music', *The Journal of Aesthetics and Art Criticism*, 22/2 and 22/3 (1963–64): 189–98 and 325–35.

Crum, Margaret, 'Early Lists of the Oxford Music School Collection', *Music & Letters*, 48/1 (1967): 23–34.

Damschroder, David, and Williams, David Russell, *Music Theory from Zarlino to Schenker: A Bibliography and Guide* (Harmonologia, 4; Stuyvesant, NY: Pendragon Press, 1990).

Descartes, René, *Musicæ compendium* (Utrecht: Gisbertus à Zÿll & Theodorus ab Ackersdÿck, 1650); English translation by Walter Charleton, with commentary by William, second Viscount Brouncker, as *Renatus Des-Cartes Excellent Compendium of Musick: With Necessary and Judicious Animadversions Thereupon. By a Person of Honour* (London: Thomas

Harper for Humphrey Moseley, 1653); ed. Frédéric de Buzon as *Abrégé de musique: Compendium musicæ* (Paris: Presses Universitaires de France, 1987).

—— *Œuvres de Descartes*, ed. Charles Adam and Paul Tannery, rev. edn (11 vols, Paris: Librairie Philosophique J. Vrin, 1974).

Edwards, Owain, 'Espionage, a Collection of Violins, and *Le Bizzarie Universali*: A Fresh Look at William Corbett', *The Musical Quarterly*, 73 (1989): 320–43.

—— 'William Corbett', in *The New Grove Dictionary of Music and Musicians*, 2nd edn, ed. Stanley Sadie (29 vols, London: Macmillan, 2001), vol. 6, p. 446.

Eitner, Robert, *Biographisch-Bibliographisches Quellen-Lexikon der Musiker und Musikgelehrten* (10 vols, Leipzig, 1900–04; 2nd edn in 11 vols, Graz: Akademische Druck- und Verlagsanstalt, 1959).

Emslie, McDonald, 'Pepys's Songs and Songbooks in the Diary Period', *The Library*, 5th series, 12 (1957): 240–55.

—— 'The Relationship between Words and Music in English Secular Song, 1622–1700' (PhD dissertation, University of Cambridge, 1957–58).

—— 'Pepys, Samuel', in *The New Grove Dictionary of Music and Musicians*, 2nd edn, ed. Stanley Sadie (29 vols, London: Macmillan, 2001), vol. 19, pp. 327–8.

Evelyn, John, *The Diary of John Evelyn*, ed. E.S. de Beer (6 vols, Oxford: Clarendon Press, 1955).

Ferrabosco, Alfonso, *Alfonso Ferrabosco the Younger: Consort Music of Five and Six Parts*, ed. Christopher Field and David Pinto (Musica Britannica, 81; London: Stainer & Bell, 2003).

Fétis, François-Joseph, *Biographie universelle des musiciens*, 2nd edn (8 vols, Paris: Librairie de Firmin Didot Frères, Fils et Cⁱᵉ, 1860–65).

Field, Christopher D.S., 'Matthew Locke and the Consort Suite', *Music & Letters*, 51/1 (1970): 15–25.

—— 'Jenkins and the Cosmography of Harmony', in Andrew Ashbee and Peter Holman (eds), *John Jenkins and His Time: Studies in English Consort Music* (Oxford: Clarendon Press, 1996), pp. 1–74.

—— 'Formality and Rhetoric in English Fantasia-Suites', in Andrew Ashbee (ed.), *William Lawes (1602–1645): Essays on his Life, Times and Work* (Aldershot, Brookfield, VT, Singapore and Sydney: Ashgate, 1998), pp. 197–249.

—— 'Birchensha, John', in *The New Grove Dictionary of Music and Musicians*, 2nd edn, ed. Stanley Sadie (29 vols, London: Macmillan, 2001), vol. 3, pp. 603–5.

—— 'Birchensha, John', in *Oxford Dictionary of National Biography*, ed. H.C.G. Matthew and Brian Harrison (60 vols, Oxford: Oxford University Press, 2004), vol. 5, pp. 806–7.

—— 'Birchensha's "Mathematical Way of Composure"', in Barra Boydell and Kerry Houston (eds), *Music, Ireland and the Seventeenth Century* (Irish Musical Studies, 10; Dublin: Four Courts Press, 2009), pp. 108–34.

Flood, W.H. Grattan, *A History of Irish Music*, 3rd edn (Dublin: Brown & Nolan, 1913).

Gaffurius [Gaffurio, Gafori, Gafurio, Gafurius], Franchinus [Franchino], *Theorica musice* (Milan: Filippo Mantegazzi, 1492; facsimile edn, New York: Broude Brothers, 1967; facsimile edn, Bologna: Forni, 1969); trans. Walter Kurt Kreyszig and ed. Claude V. Palisca as *The Theory of Music* (New Haven, CT, and London: Yale University Press, 1993).

—— *Practica musice* (Milan: Giovanni Petro de Lomazio, 1496; facsimile edn, Farnborough: Gregg Press, 1967; facsimile edn, Bologna: Forni, 1972; facsimile edn, New York: Broude Brothers, 1979); trans. with introduction by Clement A. Miller (Musicological Studies and Documents, 20; American Institute of Musicology, 1968); trans. and ed. Irwin Young (Madison, Milwaukee and London: University of Wisconsin Press, 1969).

—— *De harmonia musicorum instrumentorum opus* (Milan: G. Pontanus, 1518; facsimile edn, New York: Broude Brothers, 1979); trans. with introduction by Clement A. Miller (Musicological Studies and Documents, 33; American Institute of Musicology, 1977).

Glarean [Glareanus], Heinrich, *Dodecachordon* (Basle: Heinrich Petri, 1547; facsimile edn, Monuments of Music and Music Literature in Facsimile, 2nd series, 65, New York: Broude Brothers, 1967; facsimile edn, Hildesheim: George Olms, 1969); trans. with commentary by Clement A. Miller (2 vols, Musicological Studies and Documents, 6; American Institute of Musicology, 1965).

Glossographia anglicana nova: Or, A Dictionary, Interpreting Such Hard Words of Whatever Language, as are at present used in the English Tongue (London: for Daniel Brown and others, 1707).

Gouk, Penelope, 'The Role of Acoustics and Music Theory in the Scientific Work of Robert Hooke', *Annals of Science*, 37 (1980): 573–605.

—— 'Music in the Natural Philosophy of the Early Royal Society' (PhD dissertation, University of London, 1982).

—— 'Acoustics in the Early Royal Society, 1660–1680', *Notes and Records of the Royal Society*, 36 (1982): 155–75.

—— *Music, Science and Natural Magic in Seventeenth-Century England* (New Haven, CT, and London: Yale University Press, 1999).

—— 'Wallis, John', in *The New Grove Dictionary of Music and Musicians*, 2nd edn, ed. Stanley Sadie (29 vols, London: Macmillan, 2001), vol. 27, p. 42.

—— 'The Role of Harmonics in the Scientific Revolution', in Thomas Christensen (ed.), *The Cambridge History of Western Music Theory* (Cambridge: Cambridge University Press, 2002), pp. 223–45.

—— 'Music and the Sciences', in Tim Carter and John Butt (eds), *The Cambridge History of Seventeenth-Century Music* (Cambridge and New York: Cambridge University Press, 2005), pp. 132–57.

Grassineau, James, *A Musical Dictionary; Being a Collection of Terms and Characters, as well Ancient as Modern; including the Historical, Theoretical, and Practical Parts of Music* (London: for John Wilcox, 1740; facsimile edn, Monuments of Music and Music Literature in Facsimile, 2nd series, vol. 40, New York: Broude Brothers, 1966).

Griffiths, David, *A Catalogue of the Music Manuscripts in York Minster Library* (York Minster Library Sectional Catalogues, 2; [York], 1981).

Gunther, Robert T., *Early Science in Oxford* (14 vols, Oxford: Oxford University Press, 1923–45).

—— *Early Science in Cambridge* (Oxford: Oxford University Press, 1937).

Hall, Marie Boas, 'Oldenburg, Henry', in *Oxford Dictionary of National Biography*, ed. H.C.G. Matthew and Brian Harrison (60 vols, Oxford: Oxford University Press, 2004), vol. 41, pp. 673–7.

Harley, John, *Music in Purcell's London: The Social Background* (London: Dennis Dobson, 1968).

Hawkins, John, *A General History of the Science and Practice of Music* (5 vols, London: T. Payne, 1776).

Heath, Thomas L., *The Thirteen Books of Euclid's Elements*, 2nd edn (3 vols, Cambridge: Cambridge University Press, 1926; reprinted New York: Dover Publications, 1956).

—— *A History of Greek Mathematics* (2 vols, Oxford: Clarendon Press, 1921; reprinted New York: Dover Publications, 1981).

Heawood, Edward, *Watermarks mainly of the Seventeenth and Eighteenth Centuries* (Monumenta chartae papyraceae, 1; Hilversum: The Paper Publications Society, 1950).

Herissone, Rebecca, *Music Theory in Seventeenth-Century England* (Oxford and New York: Oxford University Press, 2000).

Herlinger, Jan, 'Medieval Canonics'. in Thomas Christensen (ed.), *The Cambridge History of Western Music Theory* (Cambridge: Cambridge University Press, 2002), pp. 168–92.

Highfill, Philip H., Kalman A. Burnim and Edward A. Langhans, *A Biographical Dictionary of Actors, Actresses, Musicians, Dancers, Managers and Other Stage Personnel in London, 1600–1800* (16 vols, Carbondale and Edwardsville, IL: Southern Illinois University Press, 1973–93).

Hill, William Henry, Arthur F. Hill and Alfred Ebsworth Hill, *Antonio Stradivari: His Life and Work (1644–1737)* (London, 1902; reprinted Great Missenden: W.E. Hill & Sons, 1980).

Holder, William, *A Treatise of the Natural Grounds, and Principles of Harmony* (London: J. Heptinstall, 1694; facsimile edn, Monuments of Music and Music Literature in Facsimile, 2nd series, 32; New York, Broude Brothers, 1967).

Holman, Peter, *Four and Twenty Fiddlers: The Violin at the English Court 1540–1690* (Oxford: Clarendon Press, 1993).

—— '"Evenly, Softly, and Sweetly Acchording to All"': The Organ Accompaniment of English Consort Music', in *John Jenkins and his Time: Studies in English Consort Music*, ed. Andrew Ashbee and Peter Holman (Oxford, 1996), pp. 353–82.

—— 'Original Sets of Parts for Restoration Concerted Music at Oxford', in *Performing the Music of Henry Purcell*, ed. Michael Burden (Oxford: Clarendon Press, 1996), pp. 9–19.

Hooke, Robert, *The Diary of Robert Hooke M.A., M.D., F.R.S. 1672–1680*, ed. Henry W. Robinson and Walter Adams (London: Taylor & Francis, 1935).

Hotson, Howard, 'Johann Heinrich Alsted: Encyclopaedism, Millenarianism and the Second Reformation in Germany' (DPhil dissertation, University of Oxford, 1991).

Humphries, Charles and William C. Smith, *Music Publishing in the British Isles*, 2nd edn (Oxford: Basil Blackwell, 1970).

Hunter, Michael, 'The Social Basis and Changing Fortunes of an Early Scientific Institution: An Analysis of the Membership of the Royal Society, 1660–1685', *Notes and Records of the Royal Society of London*, 31/1 (1976): 9–114.

—— 'How to Edit a Seventeenth-Century Manuscript: Principles and Practice', *The Seventeenth Century*, 10 (1995): 277–310.

—— (with contributions by Edward B. Davis, Harriet Knight, Charles Littleton and Lawrence M. Principe), *The Boyle Papers: Understanding the Manuscripts of Robert Boyle* (Aldershot and Burlington, VT: Ashgate, 2007).

Hüschen, Heinrich, 'Puteanus, Erycius', in *The New Grove Dictionary of Music and Musicians*, 2nd edn, ed. Stanley Sadie (29 vols, London: Macmillan, 2001), vol. 20, pp. 634–5.

Huygens, Christiaan, *Œuvres complètes de Christiaan Huygens* (22 vols, The Hague: Société Hollandaise des Sciences, 1888–1950).

Irving, John, 'Consort Playing in Mid-17th-Century Worcester: Thomas Tomkins and the Bodleian Partbooks Mus. Sch. E.415–18', *Early Music*, 12/3 (1984): 337–44.

Jeans, Susi, and Penelope Gouk, 'Brouncker, William', in *The New Grove Dictionary of Music and Musicians*, 2nd edn, ed. Stanley Sadie (29 vols, London: Macmillan, 2001), vol. 4, p. 436.

Kassler, Jamie C., *The Science of Music in Britain, 1714–1830: A Catalogue of Writings, Lectures and Inventions* (2 vols, New York and London: Garland Publishing, 1979).

—— *The Beginnings of the Modern Philosophy of Music in England: Francis North's A Philosophical Essay of Musick (1677) with comments of Isaac*

Newton, Roger North and in the Philosophical Transactions (Aldershot and Burlington, VT: Ashgate, 2004).

—— and D.R. Oldroyd, 'Robert Hooke's Trinity College "Musick Scripts", his Music Theory and the Role of Music in his Cosmology', *Annals of Science*, 40 (1983): 559–95.

Kepler, Johannes, *Gesammelte Werke*, ed. Walther von Dyck, Max Caspar and others (23 vols to date, Munich: C.H. Beck, 1937–2002).

King, A. Hyatt, *Some British Collectors of Music c.1600–1960* (Cambridge: Cambridge University Press, 1963).

Kircher, Athanasius, *Musurgia universalis sive Ars magna consoni et dissoni* (2 vols, Rome: vol. 1, Francesco Corbelletti, 1650; vol. 2, Ludovico Grignani, 1650); facsimile edition in 1 vol., ed. Ulf Scharlau (Hildesheim and New York: Georg Olms, 1970).

—— *Ars magna sciendi sive combinatoria* (Amsterdam: Joannes Janssonius à Waesberge, 1669).

Lindley, Mark, *Lutes, Viols and Temperaments* (Cambridge, New York and Melbourne: Cambridge University Press, 1984).

Lippius, Johannes, *Synopsis musicæ novæ omnino veræ atque methodicæ universæ* (Strasbourg: Carl Kieffer for Paul Ledertz, 1612); ed. and trans. Benito V. Rivera as *Synopsis of New Music* (Colorado College Music Press Translations, 8; Colorado Springs, 1977).

Locke, Matthew, *Observations upon A Late Book, Entituled, An Essay to the Advancement of Musick, &c, Written by Thomas Salmon, M.A. of Trinity Colledge in Oxford* (London: W[illiam] G[odbid], to be sold by John Playford, 1672).

—— *The Present Practice of Musick Vindicated Against the Exceptions and New Way of Attaining Musick Lately Publish'd by Thomas Salmon, M.A. &c.* […] *To which is added Duellum Musicum by John Phillips, Gent. Together with A Letter from John Playford to Mr. T. Salmon by way of Confutation of his Essay* (London: for N. Brooke and J. Playford, 1673); facsimile edn (Monuments of Music and Music Literature in Facsimile, 2nd series, 16; New York: Broude Brothers, 1974).

—— *Melothesia: or, Certain General Rules for Playing upon a Continued-Bass. With a Choice Collection of Lessons for the Harpsicord and Organ of all Sorts* (London: for J. Carr, 1673; facsimile edn, Monuments of Music and Music Literature in Facsimile, 2nd series, 30, New York: Broude Brothers, 1975); ed. Christopher Hogwood (Oxford and New York: Oxford University Press, 1987).

—— *Matthew Locke: Dramatic Music*, ed. Michael Tilmouth (Musica Britannica, 51; London: Stainer & Bell, 1986).

The London Stage 1660–1800. A Calendar of Plays, Entertainments and Afterpieces Together with Casts, Box-Receipts and Contemporary Comment. Part 1: 1660–1700, ed. William Van Lennep (Carbondale, IL: Southern Illinois University Press, 1965).

Mabbett, Margaret, 'Italian Musicians in Restoration England (1660–90)', *Music & Letters*, 67 (1986): 237–47.

Mace, Thomas, *Musick's Monument; or, a Remembrancer of the Best Practical Musick, Both Divine and Civil, that has ever been known, to have been in the World* (London: T. Ratcliffe and N. Thompson for the Author, 1676; facsimile edn, Monuments of Music and Music Literature in Facsimile, 2nd series, 17, New York: Broude Brothers, 1966); facsimile edn, with commentary by Jean Jacquot and musical transcriptions by André Souris (2 vols, Paris: Éditions du Centre National de la Recherche Scientifique, 1966).

McGuinness, Rosamond, 'Writings about Music', in *The Blackwell History of Music in Britain: The Seventeenth Century*, ed. Ian Spink (Oxford: Blackwell, 1992), pp. 406–20.

McIntyre, G.S., 'Brouncker, William, second Viscount Brouncker of Lyons', in *Oxford Dictionary of National Biography*, ed. H.C.G. Matthew and Brian Harrison (60 vols, Oxford: Oxford University Press, 2004), vol. 7, pp. 998–9.

Maddison, R.E.W., *The Life of the Honourable Robert Boyle F.R.S.* (London: Taylor & Francis, 1969).

Mahoney, Michael S., 'Mathematics', in David C. Lindberg (ed.), *Science in the Middle Ages* (Chicago: University of Chicago Press, 1978), pp. 145–78.

Malcolm, Noel, and Jacqueline Stedall, *John Pell (1611–1685) and his Correspondence with Sir Charles Cavendish: The Mental World of an Early Modern Mathematician* (Oxford: Oxford University Press, 2005).

Marshall, P.J., 'Thomas Hyde', in *Oxford Dictionary of National Biography*, ed. H.C.G. Matthew and Brian Harrison (60 vols, Oxford: Oxford University Press, 2004), vol. 29, pp. 156–7.

Mathiesen, Thomas J., 'Greek Music Theory', in Thomas Christensen (ed.), *The Cambridge History of Western Music Theory* (Cambridge: Cambridge University Press, 2002), pp. 109–35.

Matteis, Nicola, *The False Consonances of Musick, Or Instructions for the Playing a true Base upon the Guitarre* ([London: J. Carr, 1682]; facsimile edn with introduction by James Tyler, Monaco: Editions Chanterelle, 1980).

Mersenne, Marin, *Harmonie universelle, contenant la théorie et la pratique de la musique* (Paris: Sébastien Cramoisy, 1636; facsimile edn with introduction by François Lesure, Paris: Centre National de la Recherche Scientifique, 1963).

—— *Harmonicorum libri XII* (Paris: Guillaume Baudry, 1648; facsimile edn, Geneva: Minkoff, 1973).

—— *Correspondance du P. Marin Mersenne, Religieux Minime*, ed. Cornelis de Waard and others (17 vols, Paris: vol. 1, Gabriel Beauchesne & ses fils, 1932; vols 2–4, Presses Universitaires de France, 1945–55; vols 5–17, Centre National de la Recherche Scientifique, 1959–88).

Miller, Leta, and Cohen, Albert, *Music in the Royal Society of London 1660–1806* (Detroit Studies in Music Bibliography, 56; Detroit: Information Coordinators, 1987).

Miller, Leta E., 'John Birchensha and the Early Royal Society: Grand Scales and Scientific Composition', *Journal of the Royal Musical Association*, 115 (1990): 63–79.

Moore, Keith (with additions by Mary Sampson), *A Guide to the Archives and Manuscripts of the Royal Society* (London: The Royal Society, 1995).

Moray, Robert, *Letters of Sir Robert Moray to the Earl of Kincardine, 1657–73*, ed. David Stevenson (Aldershot and Burlington, VT: Ashgate, 2007).

Morley, Thomas, *A Plaine and Easie Introduction to Practicall Musicke* (London: Peter Short, 1597; facsimile edn, Shakespeare Association Facsimiles, 14, Oxford: Humphrey Milford at Oxford University Press, 1937; facsimile edn, The English Experience, 207, Amsterdam: Theatrum Orbis Terrarum, 1969; facsimile edn, Farnborough: Gregg International, 1971); ed. R. Alec Harman as *A Plain and Easy Introduction to Practical Music* (London: J.M. Dent & Sons, 1952).

Newton, Isaac, *The Correspondence of Isaac Newton*, ed. H.W. Turnbull and others (7 vols, Cambridge, London, New York and Melbourne: Cambridge University Press, 1959–77).

Ohlmeyer, Jane, 'Fitzgerald, George, sixteenth Earl of Kildare', in *Oxford Dictionary of National Biography*, ed. H.C.G. Matthew and Brian Harrison (60 vols, Oxford: Oxford University Press, 2004), vol. 19, pp. 793–4.

Oldenburg, Henry, *The Correspondence of Henry Oldenburg*, ed. A. Rupert Hall and Marie Boas Hall (13 vols, 1–9, Madison, Milwaukee and London: University of Wisconsin Press, 1965–73; 10–11, London: Mansell, 1975–77; 12–13, London and Philadelphia: Taylor & Francis, 1986).

[——] '[An Accompt of some Books.] III. An Essay to the Advancement of Musick; by Tho. Salmon, M.A. London, 1672', *Philosophical Transactions*, 6/80 (19 February 1671/2): 3095.

[——] 'An Account of two Books. I. Musica Speculativa del Mengoli [...] in Bologna 1670', *Philosophical Transactions*, 8/100 (9 February 1673/4): 6194–7000 [*recte* 6194–6200].

Ornithoparchus, Andreas, *Musicæ activæ micrologus* (Leipzig: Valentin Schumann, 1517); trans. John Dowland as *Andreas Ornithoparcus his Micrologus or Introduction* (London: for Thomas Adams, 1609; facsimile edn, The English Experience, 160, Amsterdam: Theatrum Orbis Terrarum, 1969); facsimile edn of the 1517 text and 1609 translation as *A Compendium of Musical Practice* (New York: Dover Publications, 1973).

van Otegem, Matthijs, 'Towards a Sound Text of the *Compendium musicæ*, 1618–1683, by René Descartes (1596–1650)', *LIAS: Sources and Documents relating to the Early Modern History of Ideas*, 26 (1999): 187–203.

Owens, Jessie Ann, *Composers at Work: The Craft of Musical Composition 1450–1600* (New York and Oxford: Oxford University Press, 1997).

—— 'Concepts of Pitch in English Music Theory, c.1560–1640', in Cristle Collins Judd (ed.), *Tonal Structures in Early Music* (Criticism and Analysis of Early Music, 1; New York and London: Garland, 1998), pp. 183–246.

Palisca, Claude V., *Humanism in Italian Renaissance Musical Thought* (New Haven, CT, and London: Yale University Press, 1985).

Pepys, Samuel, *The Diary of Samuel Pepys*, ed. Robert Latham and William Matthews (11 vols, London: G. Bell & Sons / Bell & Hyman, 1970–83).

—— *Private Correspondence and Miscellaneous Papers of Samuel Pepys 1679–1703*, ed. J.R. Tanner (2 vols, London: G. Bell & Sons, 1926).

P[hillips], E[dward], *The New World of Words: or a General English Dictionary, Containing the Proper Significations, and Etymologies of all Words Derived from other Languages* [...] *Together with the Definitions of all those Terms that Conduce to the Understanding of any of the Arts or Sciences*, 3rd edn (London: for Nathaniel Brook, 1671).

Pinto, David, 'The Music of the Hattons', *Royal Musical Association Research Chronicle*, 23 (1990): 79–98.

—— 'Placing Hatton's Great Set', *Chelys: The Journal of the Viola da Gamba Society*, 32 (2004): 1–20.

Playford, John, *A Musicall Banquet, Set forth in three choice Varieties of Musick. The first Part presents you with Excellent new Lessons for the Lira Viol, set to severall New Tunings. The second a Collection of New and Choyce Allmans, Corants, and Sarabands for one Treble and Basse Viol, composed by Mr. William Lawes, and other Excellent Authours. The third Part containes New and Choyce Catches or Rounds for three or foure Voyces. To which is added some few Rules and Directions for such as learne to sing, or to play on the Viol* (London: T.H. for John Benson and John Playford, 1651).

—— *A Breefe Introduction to the Skill of Musick for Song & Violl* (London: for John Playford, 1654); as *A Brief Introduction to the Skill of Musick*, 3rd edn (London: W. Godbid for John Playford, 1660); 4th edn (ibid., 1664); as *An Introduction to the Skill of Musick*, 6th edn (ibid., 1672); 7th edn (ibid., 1674; facsimile edn, Ridgewood, NJ: Gregg Press, 1966); 10th edn (London: A.G. and J.P. for John Playford, 1683); 12th edn (London: E. Jones for Henry Playford, 1694; facsimile edn with introduction by Franklin B. Zimmerman, New York: Da Capo Press, 1972); 13th edn (London: E. Jones for Henry Playford, 1697).

—— *Musick's Hand-Maide Presenting New and Pleasant Lessons for the the Virginals or Harpsycon* (London: for John Playford, 1663).

—— *Musick's Recreation on The Viol, Lyra-way: Being a choice Collection of Lessons Lyra-way. To which is added a Preface, Containing some Brief Rules and Instructions for young Practitioners*, enlarged 2nd edn (London: A.G. and J.P. for J. Playford, 1682; facsimile edn with introductions by Gerald Gifford and Nathalie Dolmetsch, Hebden Bridge: Ruxbury Publications, 2002).

—— *The Complete Country Dance Tunes from Playford's Dancing Master (1651–ca.1728)*, ed. Jeremy Barlow (London: Faber Music, 1985).

Plomer, Henry R., *A Dictionary of the Booksellers and Printers who were at work in England, Scotland and Ireland from 1641 to 1667* (London: for the Bibliographical Society by Blades, East & Blades, 1907).

—— *A Dictionary of the Booksellers and Printers who were at work in England, Scotland and Ireland from 1668 to 1725* (Oxford: for the Bibliographical Society by Oxford University Press, 1922).

Poole, H. Edmund, 'The Printing of William Holder's "Principles of Harmony"', *Proceedings of the Royal Musical Association*, 101 (1974–75): 31–43.

Poole, Robert, 'Holder, William', in *Oxford Dictionary of National Biography*, ed. H.C.G. Matthew and Brian Harrison (60 vols, Oxford: Oxford University Press, 2004), vol. 27, pp. 619–20.

Ptolemy [Ptolemæus, Claudius], *Claudii Ptolemæi harmonicorum libri tres, ex codd. MSS. undecim, nunc primum græce editus*, ed. with Latin translation by John Wallis (Oxford: Sheldonian Theatre, 1682).

Rasch, Rudolf, 'Tuning and Temperament', in Thomas Christensen (ed.), *The Cambridge History of Western Music Theory* (Cambridge: Cambridge University Press, 2002), pp. 193–222.

Ravenscroft, Thomas, *A Briefe Discourse of the True (but Neglected) Use of Charact'ring the Degrees by their Perfection, Imperfection, and Diminution* (London: Edward Allde for Thomas Adams, 1614; facsimile edn, The English Experience, 409, Amsterdam: Theatrum Orbis Terrarum, 1971; facsimile edn, Monuments of Music and Music Literature in Facsimile, 2nd series, 22, New York: Broude Brothers, 1976; facsimile edn with introduction by Ian Payne, Kilkenny: Boethius Press, 1984).

Record of The Royal Society, 3rd edn (London: Oxford University Press, 1912).

Rivera, Benito V., *German Music Theory in the Early 17th Century: The Treatises of Johannes Lippius* (Studies in Musicology, 17; Ann Arbor, MI: UMI Research Press, 1980).

Ruff, Lillian M., 'The Social Significance of the Seventeenth-Century English Music Treatises', *The Consort*, 26 (1970): 412–22.

Salmon, Thomas, *An Essay to the Advancement of Musick, by Casting away the Perplexity of Different Cliffs. And Uniting all sorts of Musick {Lute, Viol, Violin, Organ, Harpsecord, Voice, &c.} in one Universal Character* [with preface by John Birchensha] (London: J. Macock, to be sold by John Carr, 1672); facsimile edn (Monuments of Music and Music Literature in Facsimile, 2nd series, 11; New York: Broude Brothers, 1966).

—— *A Vindication of An Essay to the Advancement of Musick, from Mr. Matthew Locke's Observations* (London: A. Maxwell, to be sold by John Carr, 1672).

Sayce, Lynda, 'Continuo Lutes in 17th- and 18th-Century England', *Early Music*, 23/4 (1995): 666–84.

Schultz, Ingo, and Howard Hotson, 'Alsted, Johann Heinrich', in *The New Grove Dictionary of Music and Musicians*, 2nd edn, ed. Stanley Sadie (29 vols, London: Macmillan, 2001), vol. 1, p. 422.

Scriba, Christoph J., 'Mercator, Nicolaus', in *Oxford Dictionary of National Biography*, ed. H.C.G. Matthew and Brian Harrison (60 vols, Oxford: Oxford University Press, 2004), vol. 37, pp. 842–3.

Shadwell, Thomas, *The Complete Works of Thomas Shadwell*, ed. Montague Summers (5 vols, London: The Fortune Press, 1927).

Shaw, H. Watkins, 'Extracts from Anthony à Wood's "Notes on the Lives of Musicians", Hitherto Unpublished', *Music & Letters*, 15 (1934): 157–62.

—— *The Succession of Organists of the Chapel Royal and the Cathedrals of England and Wales from c.1538; Also of … the Cathedrals of Armagh and Dublin* (Oxford: Clarendon Press, 1991).

Simpson, Christopher, *The Division-Violist: or An Introduction to the Playing upon a Ground* (London: William Godbid, 1659; facsimile edn, Performers' Facsimiles, 215; New York, n.d.); 2nd edn as *Chelys minuritionum artificio exornata / The Division-Viol, or, The Art of Playing Ex tempore upon a Ground* (London: William Godbid for Henry Brome, 1665/1667; facsimile edn with introduction by Nathalie Dolmetsch, London: J. Curwen & Sons, 1965).

—— *The Principles of Practical Musick Delivered in a Compendious, Easie, and New Method* (London: William Godbid for Henry Brome, 1665); enlarged 2nd edn as *A Compendium of Practical Musick in Five Parts* (London: William Godbid for Henry Brome, 1667); ed. Phillip J. Lord (Oxford: Basil Blackwell, 1970).

Source Readings in Music History, ed. Oliver Strunk, rev. Leo Treitler (New York and London: W.W. Norton & Co, 1998).

Spink, Ian, *Restoration Cathedral Music 1660–1714* (Oxford Studies in British Church Music; Oxford: Clarendon Press / New York: Oxford University Press, 1995).

Spring, Matthew, *The Lute in Britain: A History of the Instrument and its Music* (Oxford, 2001).

Squire, William Barclay, 'Birchensha, John', in *The Dictionary of National Biography*, ed. Leslie Stephen and Sidney Lee (63 vols, 1885–1900), vol. 5, pp. 70–71.

Strahle, Graham, *An Early Music Dictionary: Musical Terms from British Sources, 1500–1740* (Cambridge, New York and Melbourne: Cambridge University Press, 1995).

Synopsis of Vocal Musick by A.B. Philo-Mus., ed. Rebecca Herissone (Music Theory in Britain, 1500–1700: Critical Editions; Aldershot and Burlington, VT: Ashgate, 2006).

Thompson, Robert, 'The Sources of Locke's Consort "for seaverall freinds"', *Chelys: The Journal of the Viola da Gamba Society*, 19 (1990): 16–43.

—— '"Francis Withie of Oxon" and his Commonplace Book, Christ Church, Oxford, MS 337', *Chelys: The Journal of the Viola da Gamba Society*, 20 (1991): 3–27.

—— 'A Fallacy in Duration? Musical Survival and Revival in Late Seventeenth-Century Oxford', paper read at the Sixth Biennial Conference on Baroque Music, Edinburgh, 10 July 1994.

—— 'Withy [family]', in *The New Grove Dictionary of Music and Musicians*, ed. Stanley Sadie, 2nd edn (29 vols, London: Macmillan, 2001), vol. 27, pp. 451–2.

—— 'Locke, Matthew', in *Oxford Dictionary of National Biography*, ed. H.C.G. Matthew and Brian Harrison (60 vols, Oxford: Oxford University Press, 2004), vol. 34, pp. 231–4.

Tilmouth, Michael, 'A Calendar of References to Music in Newspapers Published in London and the Provinces (1660–1719)', *Royal Musical Association Research Chronicle*, 1 (1961): whole issue.

Tomkins, Thomas, *Thomas Tomkins: Consort Music*, ed. John Irving (Musica Britannica, 59; London: Stainer & Bell, 1991).

A Transcript of the Registers of the Worshipful Company of Stationers; from 1640–1708 A.D., [compiled by G.E. Briscoe Eyre and Charles Robert Rivington] (3 vols, London; privately printed, 1913–14).

The Viola da Gamba Society Index of Manuscripts containing Consort Music, compiled by Andrew Ashbee, Robert Thompson and Jonathan Wainwright (2 vols, Aldershot and Burlington, VT: Ashgate, 2001 and 2008).

Villiers, George, second Duke of Buckingham, *The Rehearsal*, ed. Montague Summers (Stratford-upon-Avon: The Shakespeare Head Press, 1914).

Walker, D.P., 'Seventeenth-Century Scientists' Views on Intonation and the Nature of Consonance', *Archives internationales d'histoire des sciences*, 27 (1977): 263–73; reprinted in his *Studies in Musical Science in the Late Renaissance* (London and Leiden: E.J. Brill, 1978), pp. 111–22.

—— *Studies in Musical Science in the Late Renaissance* (Studies of the Warburg Institute, 37; London: The Warburg Institute / Leiden: E.J. Brill, 1978).

Wallis, John, *Opera mathematica* (3 vols, Oxford: Sheldonian Theatre, 1693–99).

Ward, John M., 'Sprightly and Cheerful Musick: Notes on the Cittern, Gittern and Guitar in Sixteenth- and Seventeenth-Century England', *Lute Society Journal*, 21 (1979–81): whole issue.

Wardhaugh, Benjamin, 'Mathematical and Mechanical Studies of Music in Late-Seventeenth-Century England' (DPhil dissertation, University of Oxford, 2006).

—— 'The Logarithmic Ear: Pietro Mengoli's Mathematics of Music', *Annals of Science*, 64 (2007): 327–48.

—— 'Musical Logarithms in the Seventeenth Century: Descartes, Mercator, Newton', *Historia mathematica*, 35 (2008), 19–36.

—— *Music, Experiment and Mathematics in England, 1653–1705* (Farnham and Burlington, VT: Ashgate, 2008).

—— 'Mathematics, Music, and Experiment', in Jacqueline Stedall, Eleanor Robson and June Barrow-Green (eds), *Handbook of the History of Mathematics* (Oxford: Oxford University Press, 2008), pp. 639–62.

Westrup, J.A., 'Domestic Music under the Stuarts', *Proceedings of the [Royal] Musical Association*, 68 (1941–42): 19–53.

—— and Ian Spink, 'Taylor, Silas', in *The New Grove Dictionary of Music and Musicians*, 2nd edn, ed. Stanley Sadie (29 vols, London: Macmillan, 2001), vol. 25, pp. 141–2.

Whitehead, David, 'Taylor, Silas', in *Oxford Dictionary of National Biography*, ed. H.C.G. Matthew and Brian Harrison (60 vols, Oxford: Oxford University Press, 2004), vol. 53, pp. 982–4.

Wienpahl, Robert W., 'English Theorists and Evolving Tonality', *Music and Letters*, 36/4 (1955): 377–93.

Wing, Donald, *Short-Title Catalogue of Books Printed in England, Scotland, Ireland, Wales, and British America, and of English Books Printed in Other Countries, 1641–1700*, revised 2nd edn, ed. Timothy J. Crist, John J. Morrison and Carolyn W. Nelson (3 vols, New York: The Modern Language Association of America, 1982–94).

—— *A Gallery of Ghosts* (New York: Index Committee of the Modern Language Association of America, 1967).

Wood, Anthony, *Athenæ Oxonienses. An Exact History of all the Writers and Bishops who have had their Education in the most Antient and Famous University of Oxford* [...] *To which are added, The Fasti, or Annals, of the said University, to the Year 1690*, 2nd edn corrected and enlarged (2 vols, London: for R. Knaplock, D. Midwinter & J. Tonson, 1721).

—— *The Life and Times of Anthony Wood, Antiquary, of Oxford, 1632–1695, Described by Himself: Collected from his Diaries and other Papers*, ed. Andrew Clark (5 vols, Oxford Historical Society Publications, 19, 21, 26, 30 and 40; Oxford: Clarendon Press, 1891–1900).

Woodfield, Ian, *English Musicians in the Age of Exploration* (Stuyvesant, NY: Pendragon Press, 1995).

Worthington, John, *The Diary and Correspondence of Dr. John Worthington*, ed. James Crossley (3 vols, Chetham Society, 13, 36 and 114; Manchester, 1847–86).

Zarlino, Gioseffo, *De tutte l'opere* (Venice: Francesco de' Franceschi Senese, 1588–89; facsimile edn, Hildesheim: Georg Olms, 1968).

—— *Le istitutioni harmoniche* (Venice: Francesco de i Franceschi Senese, 1573; facsimile edn, Ridgewood, NJ: Gregg Press, 1966); part 3 as *The Art of Counterpoint*, trans. Guy A. Marco and Claude V. Palisca (New Haven, CT, and London: Yale University Press, 1968).

Index